Militant Aesthetics

Radical Aesthetics – Radical Art

Series editors: Jane Tormey and Gillian Whiteley

(Loughborough University, UK)

Promoting debate, confronting conventions and formulating alternative ways of thinking, Jane Tormey and Gillian Whiteley explore what radical aesthetics might mean in the twenty-first century. This new books series, *Radical Aesthetics – Radical Art* (*RaRa*), reconsiders the relationship between how art is practised and how art is theorized. Striving to liberate theories of aesthetics from visual traditions, this series of single-authored titles expands the parameters of art and aesthetics in a creative and meaningful way. Encompassing the multisensory, collaborative, participatory and transitory practices that have developed over the last twenty years, *Radical Aesthetics – Radical Art* is an innovative and revolutionary take on the intersection between theory and practice.

Published and forthcoming in the series:

Practical Aesthetics: Events, Affects and Art after 9/11, Jill Bennett
Transitional Aesthetics: Contemporary Art at the Edge of Europe, Uros Cvoro
Eco-Aesthetics: Art, Literature and Architecture in a Period of Climate Change, Malcolm Miles
Civic Aesthetics: Militarism in Israeli Art and Visual Culture, Noa Roei
Counter-Memorial Aesthetics: Refugees, Contemporary Art and the Politics of Memory, Veronica Tello
Working Aesthetics: Labour, Art and Capitalism, Danielle Child
Art, Politics and the Pamphleteer, edited by Jane Tormey and Gillian Whiteley
Sociopolitical Aesthetic: Art, Crisis and Neoliberalism, Kim Charnley
Therapeutics Aesthetics: Performative Encounters in Moving Image Artworks, Maria Walsh

For further information or enquiries please contact *RaRa* series editors:

Jane Tormey: j.tormey@lboro.ac.uk
Gillian Whiteley: g.whiteley@lboro.ac.uk

Militant Aesthetics

Art Activism in the Twenty-First Century

Martin Lang

BLOOMSBURY ACADEMIC
LONDON • NEW YORK • OXFORD • NEW DELHI • SYDNEY

BLOOMSBURY ACADEMIC
Bloomsbury Publishing Plc, 50 Bedford Square, London, WC1B 3DP, UK
Bloomsbury Publishing Inc, 1385 Broadway, New York, NY 10018, USA
Bloomsbury Publishing Ireland, 29 Earlsfort Terrace, Dublin 2, D02 AY28, Ireland

BLOOMSBURY, BLOOMSBURY ACADEMIC and the Diana logo
are trademarks of Bloomsbury Publishing Plc

First published in Great Britain 2024
This paperback edition published in 2025

Cover image: Russian artist Pyotr Pavlensky poses after setting fire to the
doors of the headquarters of the FSB security service, November 9, 2015.
(© NIGINA BEROEVA / AFP via Getty Images)

A catalogue record for this book is available from the British Library.

A catalog record for this book is available from the Library of Congress.

ISBN: HB: 978-1-3503-4674-1
PB: 978-1-3503-4678-9
ePDF: 978-1-3503-4675-8
eBook: 978-1-3503-4676-5

Series: Radical Aesthetics – Radical Art

Typeset by Newgen KnowledgeWorks Pvt. Ltd., Chennai, India.

For product safety related questions contact productsafety@bloomsbury.com.

To find out more about our authors and books visit www.bloomsbury.com
and sign up for our newsletters.

For the artists featured in this book. They are the inspiration.

Contents

Figures

Preface

This book is born out of a long-standing fascination with the potential of art to affect meaningful change in society. It is the culmination of an immersive twelve-year odyssey into the intricate interplay between art and activism. My journey began with my doctoral research on 'militant art' from 2011 to 2015 and extended well beyond academia, leading me into the heart of activist collectives across the globe. From 2012 to 2017, I delved into a multitude of diverse art activist circles, conducting comprehensive interviews with twelve such collectives scattered from Europe to the Americas and the Middle East. Unexpectedly, the notorious Russian Voina group, despite being pursued by Interpol at the time, agreed to participate. To my surprise, I was also fortunate enough to receive a Santander Mobility Award, which enabled me to travel to Buenos Aires to engage with Etcétera, a group notorious for targeting banks through their art. Collectively, these twelve interviews significantly shaped the material of this book and underpin the case study analyses. This explains why the book predominantly embraces a transatlantic perspective, although it also ventures into the Middle East with case studies from Israel and an America-based Iraqi artist. While some of the artists I interviewed are not featured in this book, most are. There are also additional case studies from Latin America and Europe that go beyond those I gathered from interviews.

Beyond merely observing and interviewing these artist-activists, I was privileged to participate in some of their activities. I graduated from Thomas Bresolin's *Militant Training Camp*, delved into the mystery of Liberate Tate's *Hidden Figures* and enrolled with the University for Strategic Optimism. Such first-hand experiences enriched the case studies, particularly those presented in Chapters 4 and 6. In all cases, I was a participant in what I was observing and the artists were aware that I was observing them. This methodological approach, known as 'overt participant observation',[1] enabled me to immerse myself in their world and to glean insights into the artists' motivations, understand their methods of employing art as an instrument of change and even join them in the cause. Moving beyond observation to actively aid causes you believe in is an example of 'militant research': a methodology pioneered by the Militant Research Collective at the Steinhardt School of Culture, Education and Human Development (New York University).[2] The combination of overt participant observation fused with militant research has enabled me to provide readers with a first-hand perspective on the artists' motivations, thought processes and an in-depth understanding of the ways in which they employ art as an instrument of change. As such, *Militant Aesthetics* proudly stands in the same lineage as influential works such as *Direct Action: An Ethnography* (2009) by David Graeber, *Dark Matter: Art and Politics in the Age of Enterprise Culture* (2011) by Gregory Sholette and *Strike Art: Contemporary Art and the Post-Occupy Condition* (2017) by Yates McKee. These pivotal books have informed the course of my research, both in their content and their methodological approaches. They have also guided my reflections on the importance of first-hand experience, the relationship between art and politics and the changing landscape of activism in the contemporary world.

Militant Aesthetics will be of interest to artists, activists, scholars and anyone intrigued by the crossroads where art and activism converge. It illuminates how artists wield their craft to voice political messages and instigate social transformation. It delves into the role of militancy within art activism and how aesthetics can be harnessed to create provocative works that challenge societal norms and inspire political action. Readers will be inspired by the creative strategies and methods employed by artist-activists and be encouraged to critically ponder the transformative potential of aesthetics in effecting social change. Welcome to this exploration of the radical fusion of art and activism.

Foreword

Since the close of the twentieth century, there has been a resurgence of interest not only in the complex relationship of art and culture to society and politics, but a *radical* rethinking of the contested term – *aesthetics*. Rather than being condemned as a redundant term, aesthetics has undergone rehabilitation and has re-emerged as a vital issue for critique, exposition and application through practice. Invigorated by this revitalized debate, we initiated the *RadicalAesthetics – RadicalArt (RaRa)* project at Loughborough University in 2009 to explore the meeting of contemporary art practice and different interpretations of radicality through interdisciplinary dialogue. We purposefully set out to consider how art practice engages with different discourses of radicality, its histories and subversions, and to develop the project in a number of directions beyond the confines of the institution.

In 2012, with a series of symposia, events, an ever-expanding network of individuals working at the intersection of art, culture, ideas and activism and various associated curatorial and dialogic initiatives in the planning stages, we launched the *RaRa* book series, initially with I.B. Tauris with Jill Bennett's *Practical Aesthetics: Events, Affects and Art after 9/11*. Subsequently, with Bloomsbury, the series has become well-established, continuing to explore what aesthetics might mean at this critical moment in the twenty-first century. Its fundamental premise is to consider the relationship between practising art and thinking about art, building on the liberation of aesthetics from visual traditions and expanding its parameters in creative and meaningful ways. The series investigates current preoccupations with, for example, sensation, discourse, ethics, politics, activism and community. In short, we hope it continues to provide a forum for an in-depth examination of the intersections between philosophical ideas and practices and between art and aesthetics.

In view of this, we are especially pleased that this current book, Martin Lang's *Militant Aesthetics: Art Activism in the Twenty-First Century*, will be the tenth title in the *RaRa* series. The author draws on extensive research as well as a series of in-depth interviews which Lang carried out with various artist-activists, such as the Russian group Voina and the multidisciplinary Grupo Etcétera based in Buenos Aires. Essentially, the book addresses how art activist practices in the first two decades of this century have come to occupy, hack, antagonize and disrupt the social and political status quo in increasingly militant ways. Besides providing detailed research and analysis of other case studies, including Iraqi artist Wafaa Bilal's controversial performances, a unique aspect of the book is Lang's own direct participation in radical projects such as Thomas Bresolin's *Militant Training Camp.* All this is brought together to provide a wealth of material for reflection on the ethics and politics of activist art operating at the sharpest possible edge of contemporary practice.

Jane Tormey and Gillian Whiteley
RadicalAesthetics – RadicalArt (RaRa) Series Editors

Acknowledgements

This book would not have been possible without the artists whose work I write about. I thank them for their creativity, inspiration and bravery. As well as the art they make, this book is based on conversations and interactions that I have had with these artists. I am extremely grateful to Wafaa Bilal, Thomas Bresolin, Etcétera, Finishing School, The Laboratory of Insurrectionary Imagination, Public Movement, University for Strategic Optimism, Voina and Ztohoven for agreeing to be interviewed: their comments, ideas and descriptions of their art actions have, in many cases, directly informed my writing. Although they can speak English, Voina asked if they could respond to my questions in Russian, for ease and speed. Consequently, this interview was translated into English by Natasha Fedorova, which was only possible thanks to funding from the School of Arts at the University of Kent. I am also indebted to the artists who sent me additional materials and who read drafts of sections of this book, especially John Jordan of the Laboratory of Insurrectionary Imagination, Dana Yahalomi of Public Movement and Heath Bunting, whom I was lucky enough to meet when he spoke as a visiting artist at the University of Lincoln, where I work. I am grateful to Gene Ray for sending me a copy of his essay 'Art Schools Burning'. This text had a big influence on this book.

I participated in actions by Liberate Tate, the University of Strategic Optimism and Thomas Bresolin. These experiences were crucial to my understanding of their practices and were developed into case studies in Chapters 4 and 6. I am especially grateful to Bresolin for living with me for a week as part of his performance camp and for writing and delivering a joint conference paper on the experience at the second Anarchist Studies Network conference (Loughborough, 2012). A version of the paper was later published in *Sanat Dünyamiz*.[1] Thanks to Ozlem Ozarpaci for translating the essay into Turkish. I also previously published an article on *Militant Training Camp* for *Krisis Journal for Contemporary Philosophy* with Tom Grimwood.[2] Although the material has been significantly revised and reframed, these two articles provided a strong basis for my analysis of *Militant Training Camp* (2012) in Chapter 6. Similarly, my work on the neo-avant-garde and Peter Bürger developed from an article I wrote for *Re·bus – a Journal of Art History and Theory*.[3] This article also featured analyses of Black Mask, King Mob, Voina, Grupo Etcétera and The Yes Men (who are all featured in this book). My writing on Women on Waves and Voina developed from an article I wrote for *Art and the Public Sphere*,[4] and the idea of linking Mark Fisher's writing on *Capitalist Realism* to these groups stems from this article.

My analysis of Etcétera's work was made possible by a Santander Mobility Award, which paid for me to travel to Buenos Aires to meet the art collective in 2017. Federico Zukerfeld, Loreto Garín, Augusto Zaquetti, Jacinta Racedo and Jérémy Rubenstein were incredibly hospitable and our conversations were invaluable. My thanks also go to Federico and Loreto for agreeing to speak at the University of Lincoln in 2022, which provided another opportunity to hear about Etcétera and to ask questions that deepened my knowledge of the group.

Research for this book dates back to 2011 when I began my doctoral research. I owe a great deal to my supervisor, Michael Newall, who steered the direction of my research in my second year towards militancy. I am also grateful to Grant Pooke for his supervisory input and for reading draft material and the staff at the Aesthetics Research Centre (University of Kent), whose work has had an unexpected effect on the aesthetic framing of this book. I must also thank Esther Leslie for reading my draft manuscript and critiquing my ideas as part of University of Lincoln's 'research conversation' series. The material on Walter Benjamin was made possible thanks to Professor Leslie pointing me in the direction of his position on 'tendency'. I also thank the College of Arts' research management team at the University of Lincoln for awarding me research leave in 2021. This gave me time to concentrate fully on writing the book.

Lastly, I must thank the *Radical Aesthetics – Radical Art* series editors Jane Tormey and Gillian Whiteley for accepting my book in their series and for their support and patience. Without them, this book would literally not exist.

Introduction

In Argentina, artists hurl human faeces at government buildings and banks (Etcétera, *Mierdazo*, 2002). In America, artists openly defy the Patriot Act by collecting and displaying all the texts it banned (Finishing School, *The Patriot Library*, 2003) and an Iraqi artist is waterboarded as performance art (Wafaa Bilal, *Dog or Iraqi*, 2008). In Copenhagen, swarms of art activists disrupt the United Nations Climate Change Conference using customized bicycles, damaging police cars in the process (The Laboratory of Insurrectionary Imagination, *The Bike Bloc*, 2009). In Russia, artists upturn police cars and even set fire to a prisoner transport wagon declaring it an art action (Voina, *Palace Revolution*, 2010; *Cops Auto-da-fe, or Fucking Prometheus*, 2011). *Militant Aesthetics* is a book about these militant trends in art activism in the twenty-first century. I conceptualize 'militant art' as a discrete type of art activism that is fundamentally opposed to community art and participatory, relational and dialogic practices. Instead, it embraces direct action and leading by example, drawing directly from avant-garde art history.

Militant art is militant because of its radical leftist commitment to avant-garde art and politics. It dares to believe in the possibility of radical political change, going against the prevailing contemporary identity politics that seeks to make minor tweaks to improve specific issues but does not dare to challenge or even imagine an alternative to neoliberalism. Militant art embraces avant-garde notions including shock tactics, disruption, antagonism, confrontation and provocation to expose what must be repressed to sustain the semblance of social harmony. It returns to 'hierarchical' methods of artmaking, such as asserting artistic authorship and leading others, in the vanguard sense, rather than delegating artistic authority to participants, as in many instances of relational, dialogic, participatory and socially engaged art.[1]

Militant Aesthetics is not about social or political movements, such as #MeToo or Black Lives Matter (BLM). These are antithetical to the avant-garde notion of leading by example that underpins militant aesthetics. Militant artists reject horizontalism (leaderless, 'autonomous, directly democratic movement building whose adherents consider it to be non-ideological'[2]) as a valid approach to artmaking as it, ultimately, hinders their militancy. The concept of horizontalism is discussed throughout this book, especially in Chapter 4, where groups like Etcétera and the Laboratory of Insurrectionary Imagination, who are typically understood as horizontalists, are shown to operate in an anarchist tradition of propaganda of the deed – leading by example in an avant-garde manner.

Against the dominant trend for horizontality, *Militant Aesthetics* instead adopts the so-called post-Marxist thought of Alain Badiou and Slavoj Žižek. From Badiou, I take the notion that ethical concerns have grown to dominate politics. He argues that politics cannot be founded on identity, especially not on one's identity as a victim and that ethical principles, based on respect for human rights and reverence for the Other, only serve to reinforce the ideological status quo: 'the ethics of differences, cultural relativism, moral exoticism, and so on [are] at best variations on ancient religious and moral preaching, at worst a threatening mix of conservatism and the death drive'.[3] In place of 'ethical ideology', Badiou's ethics of truths is designed to both sustain and inspire a disciplined, subjective adherence to a militant cause. He concludes that where consensual ethics attempts to avoid divisions, 'the ethic of truths is always more or less militant, combative'.[4]

Žižek is well known for making political observations that appear counter-intuitive, especially to left-liberals, and he positions himself against nearly all contemporary philosophy, except, notably, Badiou.[5] Žižek scholars Sharpe and Boucher note that for him 'identity politics, were unable to provide an effective opposition to the "blackmail" of the reigning liberal ideology, which consists in the idea that a militant defence of democracy or the market is the limit of all possible political action – anything more radical leads directly to totalitarian atrocities'.[6]

Ever since his first book *The Sublime Object of Ideology* (first published in 1989), Žižek has refuted left-liberal notions that we are living in a post-ideological world:

> Today's society must appear post-ideological: the prevailing ideology is that of cynicism; people no longer believe in ideological truth; they do not take ideological propositions seriously. The fundamental level of ideology, however, is not that of an illusion masking the real state of things but that of an (unconscious) fantasy structuring our social reality itself. And at this level, we are of course far from being a post-ideological society.[7]

The very fact that we no longer believe ideologies exist demonstrates the success of liberal democratic capitalist ideology. This ideology is only accepted as the inevitable, natural, order precisely because it is presented as nonideological. This observation underpins the philosophical position of my concept of militant aesthetics. I explore Žižek's notion of how art activists can overidentify with the dominant ideology in Chapter 1 and then apply this to a range of aesthetic tactics emanating from Situationist *détournement* in Chapter 5.

Militant Aesthetics is also aligned with the avant-gardist contemporary art theory of Marc James Léger, McKenzie Wark, Mikkel Bolt Rasmussen, John Roberts and others. Léger, for example, has argued that 'victim politics' is compatible with liberal petty-bourgeois hegemony, which views the revolutionary left as either a matter of nostalgia or a nightmare.[8] Significantly, for militant aesthetics, he worries that politics based on identity can become a means to reject all objective or universal evaluative criteria for works of art,[9] which are deemed disrespectful to otherness. Consequently, identity politics is a weak basis both for militancy and aesthetics and neither identity-based social movements nor art that is based on such movements is the subject of this book. I reject art collectives such as MTL (established 2010) and Decolonize This Place (established 2016) as candidates for militant art on this basis. This might seem counter-intuitive, given their controversial advocacy of violent struggle, but militant art is militant insofar as it retains a belief in what Badiou calls 'strong ideas', Žižek's notion of ideology or what Léger calls 'macro-politics', rather than militant adherence to identity-based 'micro-politics', which is characteristic of the nonideological, horizontalist and participatory nature of protest movements.[10] This subject is given full attention in Chapter 2.

Given the right-wing accusations that BLM has a Marxist agenda, it might seem odd to exclude activist actions to remove 'slaver statues' (for example) from this book, while proclaiming adherence to Marxist (or at least post-Marxist) aesthetics. However, this is entirely consistent with Marx's thought, as evidenced in his writing on literature and art, where he foresaw debates concerning our contemporary statue-toppling situation. Marx declared that the art of the ancient Greeks can continue to have artistic value, even if it is the product of a slave-owning society and a pre-capitalist mode of production. The art of yesteryear cannot be repeated, he claimed, just as an adult cannot become a child again without being childish. Nonetheless, childish innocence can delight adults just as Greek art continues to be the standard for Western art. Marx was unequivocal when he said that the 'charm their art has for us does not stand in contradiction with the undeveloped stage of the social order from which it had sprung'.[11] However, my reason for excluding social movement actions from this book is because of their focus on micro-politics rather than because of an ideological commitment to Marx's assertion that art made in slave societies can be aesthetically valuable. This is not to say that social movements are not important: the Left critically needs to form coalitions against common enemies rather than fight among itself. There is also the reason that this book is about art, not the aesthetic consideration of the actions made by social movements.

Identity politics is not uniquely left-wing. White nationalism is entirely based on identity. *The Turner Diaries* (1978) is a novel that prophesizes the overthrow of the US government and a race war. It inspired Timothy McVeigh (the Oklahoma bomber) and David Copeland (the Brixton nail bomber) to commit militant acts of racial violence. While, in the past, right-wing militants like McVeigh and Copeland tended to operate as 'lone wolves', this is no longer the case. The Alt-right, legitimized by Donald Trump, has become a unified movement and proponents are no longer ashamed or afraid to be identified as such. The Alt-right does not feature in this book for the same reason that left-liberal social movements do not. In fact, the right-wing variants are even poorer examples because they are so reactionary and therefore cannot accommodate the possibility of macro-political change. Or rather, if they caused a revolution it would be regressive and this is a failure of political imagination.

Militant Aesthetics is divided into six chapters. Chapter 1 establishes a scene where militant art arises as a reaction to the persecution of artists after 9/11 and the erosion of civil liberties more generally that accompanied the War on Terror. In this context, I detail how some militant artists were prepared to break the law and risk arrest for their art, on the streets and in public spaces (Finishing School; Heath Bunting; Ztohoven). I describe how others appropriated the visual aesthetics of militancy, utilizing military uniforms, marching, hierarchical structures and so on (Public Movement; Allora and Calzadilla). Others still (Wafaa Bilal; Thomas Bresolin) adopted 'advanced interrogation' techniques in violent and confrontational performances in galleries.

Chapter 2 defines militant art. I establish a definition of, and criteria for, militant art before aligning it with Badiou's four rules for militant art. In the second section of this chapter, I create an ethical scaffolding for militancy by referring to key texts by Christabel Pankhurst, Ulrike Meinhof and Dominic Fox – all of which are shown to be aligned with instances of political upheaval and radical art. In the final section, I develop an aesthetic framework by which to judge militant art as art. To do this, I synthesize three aesthetic theories that all, in their own ways, relate to the intersection of art and politics. This chapter is by far the most theoretical and focuses on the political aesthetic theory of Theodor Adorno (1903–1969), Jean-Paul Sartre (1905–1980) and Jacques Rancière (b. 1940).

Chapter 3 adds an art historical context, situating militant art in the avant-garde tradition. To do this, I analyse the militancy of the so-called historic avant-garde and propose Black Mask and King Mob as more radical examples of the 'neo' avant-garde and examples of proto-militant art. I develop the notion that militant art is based on an avant-garde tradition of hierarchy and leading by example – methodologies that are generally considered objectionable in participatory, dialogic and socially engaged art. Drawing on Rancière and Guy Debord (1931–1994), I argue that militant art is aesthetic because it contains a dialectical tension between art and politics, between ethics and aesthetics.

Chapter 4 addresses militant art after the 2008 banking crisis. It details how artists such as Etcétera, Laboratory of Insurrectionary Imagination, University for Strategic Optimism, Reverend Billy and Pyotr (Petr) Pavlensky have targeted banks. It develops the avant-garde principle of leading by example (established in Chapter 3) by distinguishing the occupations and hit-and-run tactics used by these artists from Nicolas Bourriaud's concept of the 'micro-utopia' – gallery-based consensus groups.[12] Using the anarchist concept of propaganda of the deed and Michel de Certeau's (1925–1986) terms 'the tactical' and 'the strategic',[13] the artists' actions in this chapter are conceptualized as 'mobile hit squads' that lead by example. Paradoxically, their short-term tactical incursions are shown to be more strategic than long-term, community-based art projects, which lose sight of revolutionary change because they are too busy trying to make minor palliative tweaks in the here and now. The final section of this chapter uses flash mob theory to analyse three interconnected 'hit-and-run' mobile hit squad case studies (the Laboratory of Insurrectionary Imagination; Liberate Tate and the Clandestine Insurgent Rebel Clown Army).

Chapter 5 explores militant art's aesthetic potential to reveal absurd and dysfunctional aspects of its target. The first section proposes the Yes Men's 'identity correction' and the Argentine practice of *escraches* as examples of Rancière's notion of 'humorous hijacking'.[14] The second section analyses militant art that uses hacking and doxxing to reveal and denounce in similar ways, as well as to antagonize and disrupt, causing financial or reputational harm in the process. In all these ways (and more), militant art elucidates the workings of contemporary capital to support and ultimately hand over to existing forms of political organization – however weak they may be. The final section considers these actions as an evolved version of the Situationist concept of *détournement*.

Chapter 6 deliberates the double meaning of the word 'demonstration'. It addresses how tactical events of confrontation contain a pedagogic element. The case studies in this chapter demonstrate contingency in the current political order and make the impossible seem attainable. The first part of the chapter sets out the theoretical terrain by drawing on Mark Fisher's ideas about revealing contingency in the apparently inevitable and making the impossible seem attainable. The second section analyses the work of Women on Waves and the Voina group as examples of this theory. The third and final section addresses how artists ensure a long-term effect by training and developing new generations of artists to carry on their work by forming their own art activist collectives. The Laboratory of Insurrectionary Imagination, Thomas Bresolin, Voina and the International Errorist movement provide the final case studies.

1

Art activism after 9/11

To gain a deeper understanding of militant art, it is crucial to examine the political context in which it emerged. This chapter focuses on the impact of anti-terrorism legislation on artists after the tragic events of 9/11. Through three case studies, the first half of the chapter highlights how anti-terror laws were used to target artists, which had significant implications for their freedom of expression. The second part of the chapter explores how artists responded to the curtailment of civil liberties and freedom of speech that followed 9/11. Specifically, it examines two distinct types of art activist responses. The first involves artists who deliberately broke new anti-terrorism laws as a form of protest. The second involves artists who incorporated military aesthetics in their performances as a confrontational and violent response to the political climate. Given the assault on artists' freedom of expression, it is understandable that they would respond militantly. Through this examination of art activism, this chapter sheds light on the complex relationship between politics, artistic expression and activism in the post-9/11 era.

Activists and artists under attack

The green scare

New York-based artist Gregory Sholette describes how after September 11:

> FBI and Secret Service agents actively questioned artists, curators, and directors of art galleries at Columbia College in Chicago, the Baltimore Museum of Art, and the Art Car Museum Houston, Texas over reports of 'anti-American' activity and put direct and indirect pressure on cultural dissidents. Several museum and gallery directors self-censored their own exhibitions by removing socially critical work or adding to shows artworks with a 'conservative' point of view in order to appear more 'balanced'. Exhibitions at Arizona State University, the City Museum of Washington, the Chelsea Market in New York City, and Ohio University removed artwork that was considered critical of the President or his policies.[1]

The Geneva-based American art critic Gene Ray adds how emergency powers were inserted into new legislation such as the Patriot Act (2001), the Military Commissions Act (2006) and the Violent Radicalization and Homegrown Terrorism Prevention Act (2007) and used to reactivate domestic surveillance programmes of anti-war protestors and Quaker peace groups.[2]

The use of 'exceptional powers' designed for combating extremism and terrorism after 9/11 has echoes of McCarthyism and the 'Red Scare', where suspected communists were put under surveillance or otherwise harassed and intimidated. Consider, for example, how, as a suspected communist, American artist Arnold Mesches (1923–2016) was placed under surveillance for twenty-five years by the FBI. His obituary in the *New York Times* recounted how in 1956 his studio was broken into and all his artworks stolen.[3] Mesches always suspected the FBI was the culprit because he had created artworks about the execution of Julius and Ethel Rosenberg, who were convicted of spying for the Soviet Union. By the 1990s, he was creating collages composed of his press clippings and redacted FBI files (which he had obtained under the Freedom of Information Act). Similarly, art historian Grant Pooke's research has revealed that the British Marxist art historian Francis Klingender (1907–1955) was placed under surveillance by MI5.[4]

The East Coast curator Nato Thompson describes how after 9/11 the term 'Green Scare' emerged.[5] You would be forgiven for expecting the 'Green Scare' to be applied to the surveillance of suspected Islamists given that green is the colour of Islam. However, Thompson describes the prosecution of environmental and animal rights activists under anti-terrorism legislation,[6] and how this included the threat of enhanced sentencing provisions usually reserved for terrorists.[7] In the Green Scare, the 'traditional' surveillance of Mesches and Klingender was replaced by an era of 'dataveillance', a term first coined by Roger Clarke in 1988, but which only really began to be fully understood with the arrival of social media. According to Clarke, '*Dataveillance* is the systematic use of personal data systems in the investigation or monitoring of the actions or communications of one or more persons.'[8] Dataveillance can be automated so that machines can scan suspects' emails, or even everybody's emails, to identify potential dissidents.

In 2013, Edward Snowden famously leaked thousands of classified US security documents to the *Guardian*. Anthropologist Gabriella Coleman notes how the 'surveillance apparatus exposed by Snowden is also technologically, and thus historically, distinctive' – a manifestation of dataveillance.[9] She describes the incredible scale of global surveillance orchestrated by America's National Security Agency (NSA) and Britain's Government Communications Headquarters (GCHQ) that Snowden exposed:

> Until 2011, the NSA harvested and stored vast swaths of American emails and metadata under a program called Stellar Wind; the NSA compelled tech giants to hand over data using FISA court warrants – while also covertly tapping into fiber-optic cables, like those owned by Google, to secretly siphon even more data; the NSA hacked into Al Jazeera's internal communications systems; the GCHQ led a DDoS attack against Anonymous and hacked Belgacom, a partly state-owned Belgian telecommunications company; and under a program fittingly called Optic Nerve, the GCHQ intercepted and stored webcam images from millions of

> Yahoo! users. And there was more: a four-month investigation by Barton Gellman and Julie Tate demonstrated that 'ordinary Internet users, American and non-American alike, far outnumber legally targeted foreigners in the communications intercepted by the National Security Agency'.[10]

DDoS attacks (where a user's computer is overwhelmed by malicious incoming traffic) are illegal in America and Britain. GCHQ's attack against Anonymous was the first time that a Western government had used DDoS against its own citizens.

A knock at the door: Hasan Elahi, Paul Chan and the trial of Steve Kurtz

Hasan Elahi is one example of an artist-victim of anti-terror legislation fused with a culture of dataveillance. In 2002, returning from an exhibition in the Netherlands, Elahi was detained at Detroit Airport by the FBI who questioned him regarding the contents of his storage unit in Florida – directly asking him if it contained explosives. Elahi was able to provide detailed answers about his whereabouts at specific times on several dates over a six-month period due to his fastidious use of his online work calendar, which he accessed on his phone during the interrogation. Elahi was released, but the office in Tampa, Florida, where the investigation was initiated, followed up with a phone call, then face-to-face interviews culminating in nine lie-detector tests. Finally satisfied, the FBI decided that he was not a terror threat. However, Elahi was concerned that if one regional office were to miss a memo regarding his innocence, his frequent travel for exhibitions and conferences abroad would result in future airport detentions. The FBI gave him a phone number to call if he encountered any such problems.

To mitigate the risk of future detention, Elahi decided to pre-emptively use the FBI phone number to inform them of every forthcoming trip. Over time, the phone calls turned into emails, which included more and more information, including photographs of his in-flight meals. By 2003, Elahi had built a website (TrackingTransience.net) that traces his whereabouts in real time via a GPS tracker on his phone. He uploads almost hourly photographs (with GPS locations in the metadata) coupled with bank statements to verify that it was really him withdrawing money at that petrol station, paying for coffee at Starbucks or buying food at that airport. Elahi has automated most of these processes so that he can do it all on the move from his iPhone with minimal labour. He notes that by putting his whole life online he is less likely to fall foul of an FBI surveillance error. He boasts that he can monitor himself more accurately and that an FBI bigshot looking for a scoop is unlikely to brag about ascertaining Elahi's whereabouts when it is already published online.

Elahi's excessive compliance can be understood in terms of what Slavoj Žižek calls 'overidentification': where artists excessively adhere to ideologies to expose their inherent excesses or internal contradictions.[11] Žižek conjectures that the greatest threat to totalitarianism is when people take its ideological demands seriously or literally.[12] Elahi overidentifies with surveillance by asking it to go further, advocating full transparency. He asks whether the world might not be better if we demanded that our politicians publish their data in a similar way to how he does. *TrackingTranscience* exposes ethical concerns and hypocrisy: politicians are unlikely to comply, and even citizens who are deeply concerned about terrorism do not take likely to being constantly tracked. In 2003, Elahi was not able to foresee that today his critical project has become the new normal, as people voluntarily upload their locations and activities using social media.

Elahi's concept of 'sousveillance' – or watching the watchers – evokes memories of how East Germany put its citizens under mass surveillance, but also put its spies under surveillance to check whether they were listening and reporting properly. With everybody under surveillance, one wonders if the Stasi had the time to make effective use of the mountain of data they collected. Similarly, Elahi watches who is watching him. TrackingTransience.net's server logs show hits from the FBI, the NSA, the Department of Homeland Security, the Pentagon, the CIA and even the executive office of the president. Elahi's overidentification reveals this internal contradiction with dataveillance. Digital information overload reveals very little about individuals. Photographs might prove Elahi's whereabouts (via their metadata and GPS locations), but they say very little about him or his motives. With so much data available, government agents would have to spend significant time digging around before they found what they were looking for, whereas Elahi feels safe in the knowledge that the evidence he might need to prove his innocence is there, and that he would be able to retrieve it if needed.

The point of dataveillance is not to analyse the data, but to encourage citizens to self-moderate their behaviour. Both the Stasi and modern dataveillance perform the same function as Jeremy Bentham's panopticon, which altered prisoners' behaviour once they accepted that they were always under observation. We might ask how we alter our behaviour now that we know GCHQ (in the UK) or the NSA (in America) are potentially listening to our conversations and tracking our movements via the smartphone in our pocket and that our daily commutes are recorded on CCTV. More recently, we saw concerns about the use of mobile phone apps to track citizens' movements and link them to localized COVID-19 outbreaks.

Artist David Rokeby coined the term 'algorithmic pollution' to describe the way that data collection alters human public behaviour.[13] He outlined his concept during a lecture that was delivered at *Cyber InSecurities* (2013) – an exhibition of artists (including Elahi) who respond to massive data collection. The curator, Lisa Moren, describes how the artists in the show worked with dataveillance and 'societies of control' to create artworks distributed through networks and systems that operated under their own control and rules.[14] The exhibition also highlighted how algorithms can unjustly racially profile people. Moren speculates that Elahi was selected for questioning at Detroit Airport because of 'social sorting': a type of algorithm-based profiling.[15]

In 2004, Hong Kong-born American artist Paul Chan was targeted using anti-terror legislation: not because he was a suspected terrorist (like Elahi) or because of algorithmic racial profiling, but because of his stance on the Iraq War (2003–11). He received an unexpected visit from plain-clothed officers that led to him working in hiding for the next five years and he then took a hiatus from making art at all between 2009 and 2014. Curator Scott Rothkopf described visiting Chan's studio during the period when Chan worked covertly. He had trouble finding it, as it was unlisted in the directory. The elevator attendant was cagey and reticent to give out any details. Instead, he interrogated Rothkopf about his intentions. He would not tell him where the studio was but eventually agreed to accompany him there, down an 'anonymous hall to a door simply marked KNOCK HARD'.[16]

Chan was opposed to military intervention to such a degree that, in 2002, he travelled to Baghdad with the anti-sanctions organization Voices in the Wilderness to protest the imminent invasion. After returning to the United States, his activist practice placed him on the wrong side of the law, but it was hardly an act of domestic terrorism: he plastered Manhattan with posters of the Baghdad citizens that he had photographed during his 'witness-bearing' trip to the Iraqi capital. These photographic portraits were emblazoned with the word 'Baghdad' and the date the images were taken. Chan enlisted the help of about fifty artists and activists to realize this project. Two of these artists, Lytle Shaw and Emilie Clark, were arrested and taken into custody. The police officers explained that this was standard procedure and that it would only take about an hour. Clark and Shaw were separated for processing and fingerprinting, transferred to another precinct two hours later (because of a problem with the fingerprinting machine) and then returned to the first police station. Shaw was cleared to leave after nearly five and a half hours, but Clark (seven months pregnant at the time) was not released until 7 am – seven and a half hours after arrest.

The ordeal revealed how the police viewed, and were preparing for, an anti-war protest the coming weekend. The artists complained that the police tried to dissuade them from attending the protest march throughout the procedure: apparently, 8,000 police officers would be there, mace would be used, they expected violence and it was generally not a good place for a pregnant woman to be.[17] This 'friendly advice' escalated to stark warnings and even a thinly veiled death threat: many of the police would be inexperienced and looking for trouble; they did not want to read their names among the dead in the morning papers. Some might say that the artists deserved to be arrested; after all, they had illegally fly-posted and the delays were regrettable, but unavoidable, due to technical failures. However, the experience – the delays, the friendly advice and warnings – all served to discourage legal protest.

Chan claims that his art and activism are discrete, but it is not so straightforward. When his studio was 'visited' by plain-clothed police officers, Chan was working on *The People's Guide to the Republican National Convention* (2004), a map-cum-handbook for protesters. For Chan, this was not art, but activism, while for Rothkopf the map was 'one of the liveliest and most acute artistic responses to that roiling political season'.[18] Tim Griffin (*Artforum* editor in chief 2003–10) described the map as 'festooned with addresses for delegates' hotels and headquarters of corporations either sponsoring the convention or enmeshed in the military-industrial complex, along with the locations of major media outlets, legal resources, and hospitals – everything, in sum, a good protester would need'.[19] Griffin actively sought ways to circumnavigate legal problems so he could feature the map in *Artforum*, presumably as an artwork. So, why would Chan want to declare that his art and activism are unconnected? Rothkopf speculates it is an attempt to avoid clichéd charges of his art's supposed ineffectiveness.[20] Alternatively, we might consider it an attempt to cleanse his artwork of any politically sensitive aspects that might result in its exclusion from exhibitions or prizes. On the other hand, if he termed his activist map and flyposting 'art', this might afford him some defence against prosecution. Despite Chan's claim to the contrary, it is perfectly reasonable to consider these examples as both art and activism: as art activism.

The most high-profile case of an art activist falling victim to anti-terror legislation, or abuse of legislation, is the trial of Critical Art Ensemble's cofounder Steve Kurtz. In May 2004, Kurtz felt the full weight of the state. He was ruthlessly pursued and prosecuted by the FBI, the Joint Terrorism Task Force and Homeland Security as a suspected bioterrorist. The evidence against him was rather tenuous: he had a home biology laboratory and an exhibition invitation with Arabic text on it. These only came to attention because Kurtz dialled 911 to report that his wife, Hope, had died suddenly in her sleep. Although her death was completely unrelated to the laboratory, Kurtz was subsequently detained and his house completely overturned. He was released after twenty-two hours in custody, but his home and office at the State University of New York at Buffalo, where he was a faculty member, were subjected to a two-day search. Kurtz was hauled before a grand jury. He was acquitted, but that was not the end of the ordeal.

Anti-terror legislation was used to persecute Kurtz for political reasons. Curator Nicola Triscott speculates that the FBI would have quickly realized that there was no bioterrorist case to answer and that they pursued Kurtz for the next four years because of Critical Art Ensemble's criticism of US agricultural, pharmaceutical and biodefence practices.[21] By June, the charges against Kurtz were downgraded from bioterrorism to mail and wire fraud, which thanks to the Patriot Act now carried a custodial sentence of up to twenty years. The FBI alleged that Kurtz had obtained the biological matter under false pretences. The case was unique because no one had complained about being defrauded and no material or money was missing, but the FBI had found an irregularity in the paperwork.

Critical Art Ensemble had been working on an anti-war project with specific attention to the public health impact of germ warfare. Kurtz was working in collaboration with Professor Robert Ferrell, a geneticist at the University of Pittsburgh. Ferrell posted Kurtz some harmless bacteria cultures, something that he and other university scientists do frequently for research purposes. In 2009, when the case came to court, Federal Judge Richard J. Arcara ruled in Kurtz's favour and stated that to use mail fraud legislation in this way was an abuse of the law: 'even had all of the allegations in the indictment been true, no crime would have been committed'.[22] This set a precedent against such prosecutions. However, because Ferrell was undergoing cancer treatment during the trial, he had already pleaded guilty to a misdemeanour. He died shortly after.

There is little evidence that Critical Art Ensemble have self-censored because of Kurtz's ordeal. Much of their work leading up to the trial explored biotechnology, but since 2006 Critical Art Ensemble's practice has moved away from biotech to focus on ecological issues. Kurtz's trial may have influenced this change and in that regard, the US Justice Department may be able to claim a partial victory. However, Critical Art Ensemble's projects are still political and sometimes critique germ warfare and the use of dirty bombs. For example, art critic Colin Perry notes how their 'investigations into legality and biotechnology nearly landed its members with lengthy jail sentences in 2008'.[23] And Critical Art Ensemble gained more press coverage after Kurtz's trial than before. Artist Coco Fusco notes how the trial was covered in *Artforum,* whereas they had received little to no attention in the art press during the twenty years preceding the ordeal.[24] In all three examples, federal interest only enhanced the artists' reputations: TrackingTranscience, the website that mocks FBI surveillance, is Elahi's most well-known work and Chan continued to make political art, albeit with extra security precautions. Nonetheless, it is feasible that other political artists will have been affected by Elahi, Chan and Kurtz's ordeals, either directly or indirectly.

The theme of self-censorship was addressed in *A Knock at the Door* (Cooper Union and Melville Gallery of South Street Seaport Museum, New York, 2005): the first major exhibition of art made specifically in response to anti-terror legislation. There were no images of Abu Ghraib or Guantanamo, but the Visible collective (2004–7) displayed a series of large hanging photographic portraits to draw attention to the US government's detention and deportation of Arabs and Muslims since 9/11 (*GAP, Fresh, Casual Style* 2005). Their director, Naeem Mohaiemen (who is better known for his 2018 Turner Prize nomination) deliberated on artistic self-censorship during a panel discussion that accompanied the exhibition. Cultural theorist András Szántó stressed that America in 2005 was a far call from life in communist Hungary where he grew up and media historian Siva Vaidhyanathan concurred by claiming that in a truly authoritarian surveillance state everybody on the panel would be arrested.[25] This may be true, but it tells us very little about whether curators succumbed to pressure to exclude artworks (as Sholette claims), or whether artists were reticent to make political work or tone down their critique. *A Knock at the Door* featured an artwork by The Yes Men composed of all the rubbish left behind by the FBI during their occupation of Kurtz's house – including many an empty pizza box,[26] but we do not know what art was left out, or what the featured artists did not say or do.

Militant art was born in this environment, despite claims that art activist opposition to the War on Terror was rare and weak. In 2008, renowned art critic Lucy Lippard claimed that 'there is no question that there is less art activism in opposition to the Iraq War than there was during the Vietnam War period' and placed the blame firmly on the 'insidious Patriot Act [that] makes it impossible to support anything but "our troops" or face prosecution'.[27] Writing only three years after the *A Knock at the Door* exhibition, she must have been aware of the significant number of dissenting voices featured in it (sixty individual artists and collectives). Critical Art Ensemble claimed that for the most part, artist opposition to the

War on Terror was 'gentle', taking traditional forms, such as anti-war art and petitions.[28] They speculated that there would not be any significant oppositional practices until there was sustained opposition to the war. I refute these claims.

There was more art activist opposition to the War on Terror than Lippard recognizes and distinctly militant kinds of art activism emerged in the wake of 9/11 and the subsequent erosion of domestic civil liberties. Beyond the work featured in *A Knock at the Door*, there are examples of more overtly militant activist art, starting in the period between 9/11 (in 2001) and the publication of the 2008 *October* issue that featured both Lippard's and Critical Art Ensemble's comments, and proliferating thereafter. The examples that I will give in the rest of this chapter are divided into two kinds. The first kind includes artists who broke new anti-terror laws as part of their practice. The second kind includes artists who appropriate military aesthetics in confrontational and violent performances: from uniforms and marching to 'enhanced interrogation techniques'. Collectively, I conceptualize these new forms of art activism as candidates for a new 'militant art' and these two types frame future instances of militant art throughout the book.

Artistic counteroffensives

Breaking the law: Heath Bunting and Ztohoven

The most unambiguous example of artists breaking anti-terror laws is *The Patriot Library* (2003), a mobile library composed of all the texts banned under the Patriot Act, which Finishing School (established in 2001) subsequently toured across America (see Figure 1.1). The library raised awareness about how the US government was using library records to track potential terrorists and create lists of people who had read 'suspect' books: a twenty-first-century manifestation of dataveillance. For example, during the trial of Steve Kurtz, the FBI even attempted to use the Patriot Act to access records of people who had purchased books by Critical Art Ensemble. Unlike standard US libraries, *The Patriot Library* did not collect any data on the borrowers. In fact, it kept no records at all. This was a key part of the artwork. Finishing School, who I interviewed between February and April 2013, believe that information is not, in and of itself, dangerous and that citizens should be able to inform themselves without government interference. They worked to ensure that *The Patriot Library* conformed to American Library Association's privacy standards by collaborating with librarian Christy Thomas who had 'witnessed the government's violation of library patrons' right to privacy without judicial oversight'.[29] *The Patriot Library* refutes Critical Art Ensemble's claim that 'gentle resistance' to the War on Terror took the traditional forms of anti-war art and petitions: It is a non-traditional form decided by their intent to deliberately break the law.

Anti-terror laws were not exclusive to the United States. In Britain, the controversial Anti-Terrorism, Crime and Security Act,

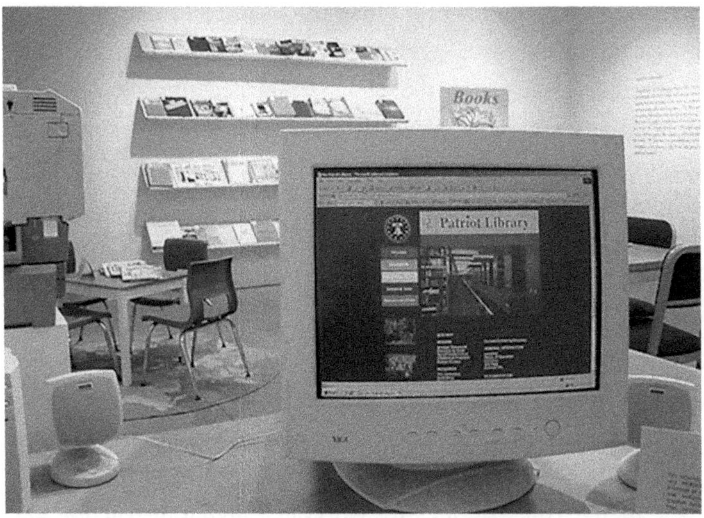

Figure 1.1 Finishing School, *The Patriot Library*, 2003. © Finishing School. Reproduced with the permission of the artist.

2001, which contained many measures not specifically related to terrorism, was introduced just two months after 9/11. After it was used to detain eight foreign nationals without trial (the 'Belmarsh Eight') it was replaced by the equally contentious Prevention of Terrorism Act, 2005, which was itself repealed in 2011. The climate also saw the introduction of legislation that placed restrictions on the right to protest such as the Serious Organized Crime and Police Act (2005), the Serious Crime Act (2007) and the Identity Cards Act (2006), which is somewhat forgotten now, because it was repealed in 2011 by the Conservative/Liberal Democrat coalition government before it came into full effect.

In 2003, BBC journalist Paul Kenyon successfully applied for a provisional driving licence using his own passport photograph and David Blunkett's birth certificate. Blunkett was a high-profile British Member of Parliament at the time – he is also blind: Kenyon acquired an official provisional driving licence for a blind man. The *Guardian* reported that Kenyon only had to make one trip to the Family Records Centre to acquire Blunkett's birth certificate, which, it turned out, is all you needed to apply for a driving licence (a more powerful form of ID than the birth certificate).[30] Kenyon also acquired the birth certificate of Frederick Forsyth (author of *Day of the Jackal*, a book about an assassin stealing a dead person's identity) and subsequently was able to open real bank accounts and acquire credit cards. The point of these hoaxes was to prove how easy identity theft (then a common concern and much-reported issue) was, but it also expressed concerns about the erosion of civil liberties in the form of the impending National Identity Card and National Identity Register database that would store citizens' data. National Identity Cards in Britain never took off, but at the time there was heated debate about their introduction.

British art activist Heath Bunting also demonstrates how one form of ID provides access to other, more powerful, ones. Since 2008, he has run *New Identity Workshops* giving instruction and assistance in constructing new legal identities. The identities are 'legal' in the same way that Blunkett's driving licence was 'legal'. Bunting demonstrates how to obtain an officially issued ID using authentic documents belonging to other people. In doing so, he reveals the power of the humble library card, or supermarket loyalty card, by investigating what other forms of ID can be obtained with them. He goes beyond Kenyon's hoax by building a complex database and identity portrait maps that reveal social patterns relating to identity and class that show how networked our data have become.

Bunting's *Maps of Consequential Paradox* that form part of his *Status Project* (2004–14) are complex. Each node flows to itself (in a loop); to every other node; and to the subject of the map. They are designed to suggest how to reverse power relationships. Maps are, of course, used to navigate and Bunting's maps show routes to homelessness and social exclusion through lack of access to certain forms of ID and therefore access to certain commodities and services. To gain the ID required to access essential goods and services, Bunting's work informs us, you must consent to have your data collected and stored. His work has been described as highlighting 'issues around infringements on privacy or restriction of individual freedom, as well as contexts concerning the mutation of identity; our values and corporate ownership of our cultural/national "ID's", as well as our DNA and investigations into Bio-technologies'.[31] In a climate dominated by debates about COVID-induced domestic passports and the UK government's plan to enable digital identity to be used 'as widely as possible',[32] Bunting's work takes on new meanings.

Czech art activist group Ztohoven (established in 2003) not only obtained official IDs under false pretences; they lived under their bogus identities for a year as a performance. For *Citizen K.* (2009–10), twelve male members of Ztohoven paired up and swapped identities with each other. To do this, they adopted the same haircut for passport-style photographs and then used a computer program to morph these images into composites. They then applied for various new forms of ID using each other's existing (authentic) forms of identification and the new amalgamated images. They lived as each other, under different names, using these official IDs. They were even able to get married, procure a firearms licence and vote in elections. One member of Ztohoven, Roman Týc, remains legally married to somebody whom he never actually married (another member married her, using an ID with his name on it). According to Denisa Tomkova, a dentist was the only person to identify that a Ztohoven ID card photograph did not match its owner.[33] The fact that ID was required to access dentistry illustrates Bunting's point about how ID cards are required to access basic (but vital) everyday services. As Tomkova puts it, 'One cannot decide to choose to live without a national identity card because the system simply does not allow it'.[34]

Citizen K. was a warning about how we are sleepwalking towards a situation where our identity is reduced to data (if we are not there already). As Ztohoven put it, 'We are not numbers, we are not biometric data, so let us not be mere pawns in the hands of the big players on the game board of these times'.[35] ID cards represent both how reliant we are and how much authorities trust and rely on data and official documents. As the group said in the documentary film version of *Citizen K.*, 'I never saw IDs as a form of protection. I've always seen them as a whip, used against the individual. Whenever a police officer asks me to show my ID, I feel … a sense that this card is keeping me in line'.[36]

Citizen K. also warned about the apparent openness of the European Union's internal borders, which can only be fully accessed by exchanging personal data for an official ID card. Ztohoven exhibited the results of the experiment alongside a steel time capsule (with twelve stars on the lid representing the European Union) containing the ID cards. The police attended the opening, closed the exhibition and confiscated all the IDs, which they said were fake. Ztohoven argued that the cards themselves were officially issued and so could not be 'fake'. Roman Týc (real name David Brudnak, or David Hons according to different sources), was arrested, but as all the IDs had been confiscated, he was unable to be identified. The criminal charges had to be dropped, as it was unclear which law had been broken. A civil case was then adopted and Ztohoven members were fined. At this moment, the seemingly liberal European Union was confronted by questions about the role of National Identity Cards and police surveillance: this sort of thing might be expected in communist Czechoslovakia, but in the European Union? Indeed, Tomkova argues that highlighting the 'control and surveillance components of national ID cards that exist in contemporary Europe' was the main aim of this project from the outstart.[37] National Identity Cards never became compulsory in the UK, but today they are issued by all European Union member states, except Denmark and Ireland.

Ztohoven question freedom of movement within the European Union without ID, but Bunting directly exposes its contradictions in this regard by illicitly crossing borders between European Union states without legal documentation. He crossed European Union borders via forests, rivers, mountains and tunnels, painstakingly documenting and recording his movements. In doing so, he revealed restrictions on free movement that governments and bureaucracies put in place. For example, he documents physical barriers between countries (see Figure 1.2), anti-climb fences, barbed wire and so on. I met Bunting in January 2020, shortly before the first COVID lockdown. He talked about crossing the French/Spanish border on foot, explaining that although no border is supposed to exist at the top of the Pyrenees anymore, there is a wire that demarks the frontier. There was also a watchtower from which he was observed and – as if that were not sufficient – a helicopter tracked his movements. This is what the political geographer Alan Ingram calls the 'performative character of frontiers between [European Union] states'.[38] It may seem merely performative, trivial even, until you consider the mass expulsions of Roma people (European Union nationals) from France and Italy (and other European Union member states) to Bulgaria and Romania.[39]

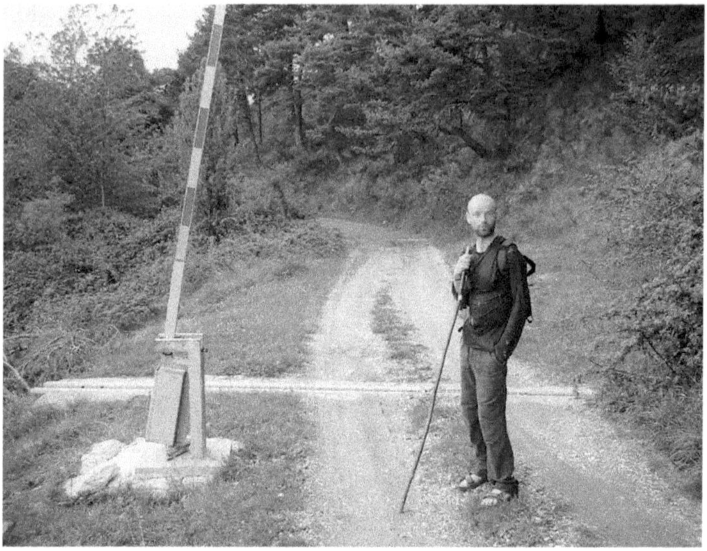

Figure 1.2 Heath Bunting, *BorderXing Guide*, 2002–3. © Heath Bunting. Reproduced with the permission of the artist.

The result of Bunting's expeditions is *BorderXing Guide* (2002–3): a website that displays documentation of his twelve-month border crossing experiences across Europe. Artist Sissu Tarka explains that 'to enter the site one either has to physically travel to one of the locations listed, or apply to become an authorised user'.[40] This comment on the allegedly open-border nature of the internet is a metaphor for the European Union's alleged open borders. In both cases, there is no access for unauthorized guests. Bunting highlights who are monitored or prevented from crossing an internal European Union border.

In crossing the European Union's internal borders, Bunting was supposedly not doing anything wrong, as he was a European Union citizen at the time, and yet Bunting reveals that you are not supposed to cross borders illicitly, you are supposed to cross them by road, rail or other conventional means, which can be tracked and controlled, as art theorist Florian Schneider notes:

> Checks now take place practically everywhere in real time. Chip cards, biometric systems, and electronic collars, regulate access to proprietary, privileged, or otherwise restricted areas, and collate images of human movement in gigantic databases. The surveillance of the electronically equipped border by means of heat, infrared, radar and satellite technology has undergone a dramatic change in significance. Today's borders are not so much about racist permission and refusal of entry as about user profiling.[41]

This is true of the European Union's internal borders, but in 2018 the *Guardian* reported that 34,361 migrants had died crossing the Mediterranean – the EU's natural equivalent to Trump's wall – or in detention blocks, asylum units or town centres, 27,000 drowning at sea since 1993 when the European Union was established.[42]

Appropriating military aesthetics: Public Movement and Allora and Calzadilla

The Israeli art collective Public Movement (established in 2006) appropriate military aesthetics in their performances. This includes the use of flags, carefully choreographed marching and their trademark white uniforms: pristine, starched, reminiscent of military PT, school PE kits from the 1950s or the Israeli Navy. Public Movement's male members wear white trousers; female members wear white skirts – both wear white shirts, socks and plimsolls contrasted with black belts (see Figure 1.3). Initially, they were a self-described hierarchical organization. Founders Dana Yahalomi and Omer Krieger were referred to as the group's 'leaders' until Krieger quit in 2011, leaving Yahalomi as the sole director. When I interviewed Yahalomi in May 2013, she explained that having two leaders at the top, with ten relatively equal members below was part of the Public Movement experiment. The members may be equals, but theatre and performance theorist Daphna Ben-Shaul notes how it was Yahalomi who 'initiates, conducts research and organizes major [Public Movement] projects'.[43] Other members contributed,

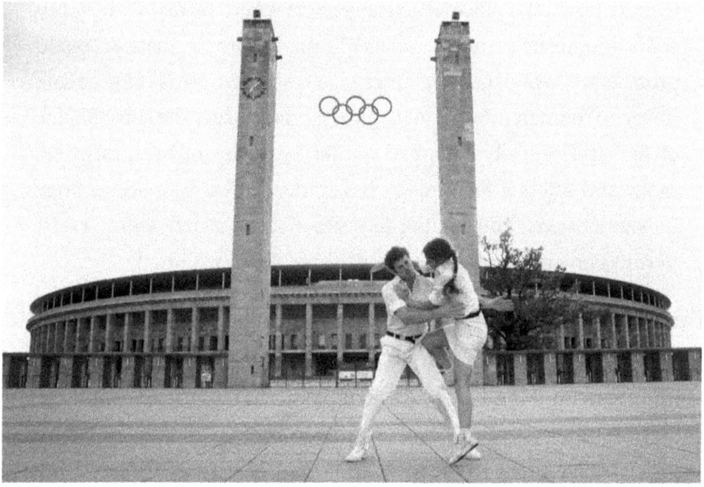

Figure 1.3 Public Movement, *Also Thus*, 2009. © Public Movement. Photograph by David Schmidt. Reproduced with the permission of the artist.

but in a subordinate manner: either under the direction of the leaders or acting independently, as 'authorized operators' who had the leaders' permission.[44]

Public Movement are a product of the specific geopolitical situation in Israel. In Israel, conscription is universal for both men and women. Although there are members of Public Movement who have not served in the military, most have been soldiers, trained to march and salute and they have experienced the hierarchy of the military system. They all live extremely close to war, the threats and causes of war and the constant War on Terror. This informs the formal, as well as geopolitical aspects of Public Movement's performances, which can be divided into four categories: the re-enactment of rescue routines performed by emergency services; the aestheticization of ceremonial codes; simulation of military ceremonies and site-specific civic acts.

Public Movement's militaristic aesthetics also emanate from a post-9/11 context. They were formed after 9/11, during both the Iraq and Afghan wars and during a period when the War on Terror was still escalating and domestic civil liberties were still being eroded. This context of vulnerability to Islamic insurgency, coupled with Public Movement's penchant for the re-enactment of rescue routines in a state of emergency, conceptually connects their actions to the post-9/11 narrative that I am proposing. Several of their early performances support such a reading. *Emergency* (2008) is one such example. Public Movement dressed in the uniforms of civilian rescue services, recovered bodies from the rubble, fastened some onto stretchers and simulated CPR, while others were merely placed into body bags and unceremoniously dragged away like garbage. Later, some members throw rocks from behind larger boulders. This artwork speaks to the Arab-Israeli conflict, but, in a post-9/11 context, we realize that such events are now also applicable to Western nations. Public Movement are often antagonistic and controversial. For example, *Rebranding European Muslims* (Berlin Biennale, 2012) played with PR and advertising languages to reveal underlying prejudices in political campaigns and remind us of the media struggle to control the image of European Muslims, which is treated as a brand and political football to justify domestic anti-terror legislation and aggressive foreign policy.

Positions (2009–13) exemplifies the atmosphere created by George W. Bush's aphorism 'Either you are with us, or you are with the terrorists!'[45] Public Movement asked different publics to physically take positions on politically sensitive issues. The action begins with a 'call' made by two Public Movement agents using megaphones. Each agent is positioned on opposite sides of the space. The call is always presented as a binary decision: Socialism/Capitalism, Men/Women, Gay/Straight and so on. This forces participants to take sides. The calls in *Positions*, as with Bush's declaration, make it impossible to be neutral. Individuals spontaneously form two rival groups that embody the demands, preferences and aspirations put forward by Public Movement. *Positions* reveals geopolitical variations, as the same calls garner different results depending on when and where they are pronounced. For example, the call 'Israel/ Palestine' has different results in different countries. The same can be said of other calls that manifest political positions, world views or moral claims. The result is a choreography for a demonstration that, through the physical positions taken, reveals public opinions. In their interview with me, Public Movement talked about how they want to awaken the politics that exists in every person's body. They refuse to acknowledge the left–right dichotomy and have even, controversially, worked with right-wing organizations, in Germany for example. The mere act of Jews working with right-wing Germans raises an obvious history and warnings about far-right politics.

Public Movement's appropriation of military aesthetics and nationalistic ceremonies questions, challenges and even ridicules nationalism to expose the excess of power required to support a national ideology. Take *Also Thus*, an action that was first performed at the Al Amal Israeli-Arab school in Acre, Israel (2007). Acre is known for its mixed population of Arabs and Jews, so the choice of the location shows that Public Movement were not afraid to acknowledge tensions and confrontations. *Also Thus* was later recreated in Berlin (2009). Since 'also' means 'thus' in German, one wonders if the action was always planned for a German context. In the second iteration, they perform a series of choreographed marches in the large Plaza in front of the Berlin Olympic Stadium (built by the Nazis in 1936). At one point, Public Movement line up and the agent in the second position (a male member) violently pushes the person in front of him (a female member) to the floor. He then proceeds to run towards her and simulates kicking her prone body before sprinting to the back of the queue as if to await his next turn (see Figure 1.3). This moment points to the dangers of power surpluses, suggesting they can result in aggression and violence directed towards your own society as well as against others. But the next person does not run and kick the prone woman. Instead, three members rush to her aid and carry her away, horizontally, raised above their heads. The rest of the troops accompany them in a manner that resembles the emergency services rescuing an injured person, perhaps on the streets of Tel Aviv following a suicide bombing. There are fascistic overtones to this performance. Not only in the second location, but also in the use of flags, the fetishization of uniforms, the violence and at one point a female running with a flaming torch to light the word *Jetzt* (now).

Like Public Movement, Allora and Calzadilla appropriate military aesthetics, such as uniforms and marching, but they also appropriate military songs. Art historian Hannah Feldman describes how their sound and performance-based sculptural works trace the relationship between 'sonic militarism' and 'contemporary culture and political ideology' explaining that these works were commissioned by 'North American art institutions during the US-led invasions of Afghanistan and Iraq'.[46] This demonstrates that Sholette's narrative about artistic censorship after 9/11 was not universal. For *Clamor* (2006) – part of their 'war song series' – Allora and Calzadilla made a military-style concrete bunker with brass instruments protruding from 'arrow slits' normally reserved for guns. Inside, a band plays military music from around the world: from military marches of the Ottoman Empire to ballads from the October Revolution, but also protest songs such as 'Bruce Springsteen's "Born in the USA", [and] Twisted Sister's "We're Not Gonna Take It"'.[47] Twisted Sister's heavy metal anthem was used during the US invasion of Panama (1989) where PSYOP loudspeaker teams blasted Manuel Noriega (military dictator of Panama, 1983–9) 24–7 … until he couldn't take it anymore and surrendered. Echoes of this can be heard in the use of 'loudspeaker assaults' in Iraq, where heavy metal music (which is considered culturally offensive) was similarly used to prevent insurgents from sleeping and to irritate and frustrate them – impairing their ability to fight and increasing the chances of surrender.[48] 'Born in the USA' was allegedly used during the torture of inmates at Guantanamo.[49]

Allora and Calzadilla also use artistic techniques to analyse militarism, linking conflict with sensory values and taste. *Balance of Power* (2007, performed at Tate Modern, London, in 2019), for example, is not what it seems. Performers wear military uniforms, but also adopt yoga poses. Allora and Calzadilla question how these two seemingly unrelated aspects (yoga and the military) might not be so unconnected after all. For example, they delve into the origins of the 'warrior pose', explore the discipline in both yoga and the military and anticipate that armed forces will adopt yoga and mindfulness in combat training. In doing so, they compare the body in yoga with the body of the military. This draws attention to the individual behind the homogenizing uniform.

Allora and Calzadilla straddle two categories of militant art: we have seen how they appropriate military aesthetics, but they are also prepared to break the law. For example, for *Land Mark (Footprints)* (2001–2), they manufactured rubber shoe soles embossed with personalized protest messages for wearers to imprint in the sand as they walked illegally across a US naval bombing range in Puerto Rico (where the artists are based). The protest-action worked: the US naval occupation, which started during the Second World War, ended the following year, in 2003. Art historian Yates McKee terms this kind of action 'tactical cartography'.[50]

Enhanced interrogations: Wafaa Bilal and Thomas Bresolin

Other artists responded to 9/11 by creating violent performances that appropriated the forms of 'enhanced interrogations'. Between 2007 and 2010, US-based Iraqi artist Wafaa Bilal made a series of violent performances about the Iraq War. The timing of Bilal's performances coincided with the so-called American 'troop surge' of 2007: the war was still raging, even after the execution of Saddam Hussain in 2006. By 2007, Bilal had become increasingly frustrated with how remote the war appeared to Americans. For example, the military was able to attack Iraqi targets from the safety of New Mexico or Colorado, from where they pilot mobile drone attacks. Since most of Bilal's family was still living in Kufa, a holy city near Najaf, the war was much closer to him. In 2004, an unmanned drone scoped out an area of Kufa, before a helicopter was sent in to bomb a checkpoint, killing Bilal's brother Haji.

Domestic Tension (or Shoot an Iraqi) (2007) is probably Bilal's best-known work. The title points to living under the constant threat of a bomb landing on your house (or killing a relative at a checkpoint, or a car bomb blowing you up at the market). At the same time, we could read into it a connection with US domestic policy. For this art performance, Bilal lived in a gallery space for thirty days subjecting himself to constant surveillance, just as Americans were giving up civil liberties in the fight for freedom (the invasion of Afghanistan was codenamed 'Operation Enduring Freedom' and the invasion of Iraq 'Operation Iraqi Freedom': President Bush famously claimed of US enemies that 'They hate our freedoms'). While living in the gallery, Bilal was exposed to a paintball gun twenty-four hours a day for thirty days. Audiences could control the gun via the web and choose to 'shoot an Iraqi' if they so wished. Some did; others chose to move the paintball gun away from Bilal to give him a rest.[51] An accompanying online message forum drew out anger and racism. Many of the comments were from relatives of service personnel who had died in Iraq. They blamed Iraqis for this and relished the chance to see one punished – oblivious to the irony that Bilal was a refugee who had fled Iraq during the first Gulf War (when he was a conscientious objector) to escape Saddam Hussein's brutal dictatorship, which also limited freedom of expression for artists.

Bilal explores the democratic potential of the internet, as well as revealing its potential to descend into mob rule evident in Twitter pile-ons and call-out culture today. His violent performances connect with public anger and prejudices. In *Dog or Iraqi* (see Figure 1.4), Bilal asked a virtual audience to vote on who should be waterboarded: a dog (a pug called Buddy) or the artist. Of course, the dog was never going to be tortured: Bilal wanted to experience waterboarding. However, the project's now-defunct website (dogoriraqi.com) elicited outraged complaints from animal rights activists that perfectly illustrated the point of the artwork: the rights of an Iraqi are seen as less than those of a dog. The complainants rightly pointed out that while Bilal was entering into this arrangement of his own free will, aware that he might be tortured, the dog was unaware and had not agreed to any terms. Bilal replied by saying that 'the dog might have valuable information' and that waterboarding is not torture, at least not according to the US government.[52] In any case, Bilal lost the vote (by fewer than ten votes) and was waterboarded.

Protests against Bilal's exhibition at Rensselaer Polytechnic Institute (2008, Troy, New York), based on the mistaken assumption that the show featured an Iraqi terrorist, meant he had to look for a new location to stage the waterboarding. These protests forced *Dog or Iraqi* underground, which in a way was much more appropriate. It took place in Troy, in a dank dusty basement with cables hanging from the ceiling. The project's website described the action as an experiment where a company called TortureChoice recruited Bilal to experiment with new forms of torture. It was a sombre affair with only a very select audience that included a couple of RPI students, both of whom, according to Bilal, were planning careers in the military.[53] A video (still available on YouTube) shows Bilal blindfolded and tied to what looks like a makeshift stretcher. Lit from a single naked light bulb, the performance certainly looks like a torture scene. A man disturbingly dressed in a Santa beard and hat (to disguise his identity) stuffs what looks like a rag (but is, in fact, a skullcap) into Bilal's mouth before pouring a jug of water over it. The skullcap prevented Bilal from closing his throat, so iced water poured down both his throat and, he claims, his trachea, into his lungs. Bilal gags almost instantly: he is not enjoying the procedure, which is stopped almost immediately. With the blindfold removed, he sits up coughing. The whole thing lasted about one minute. He

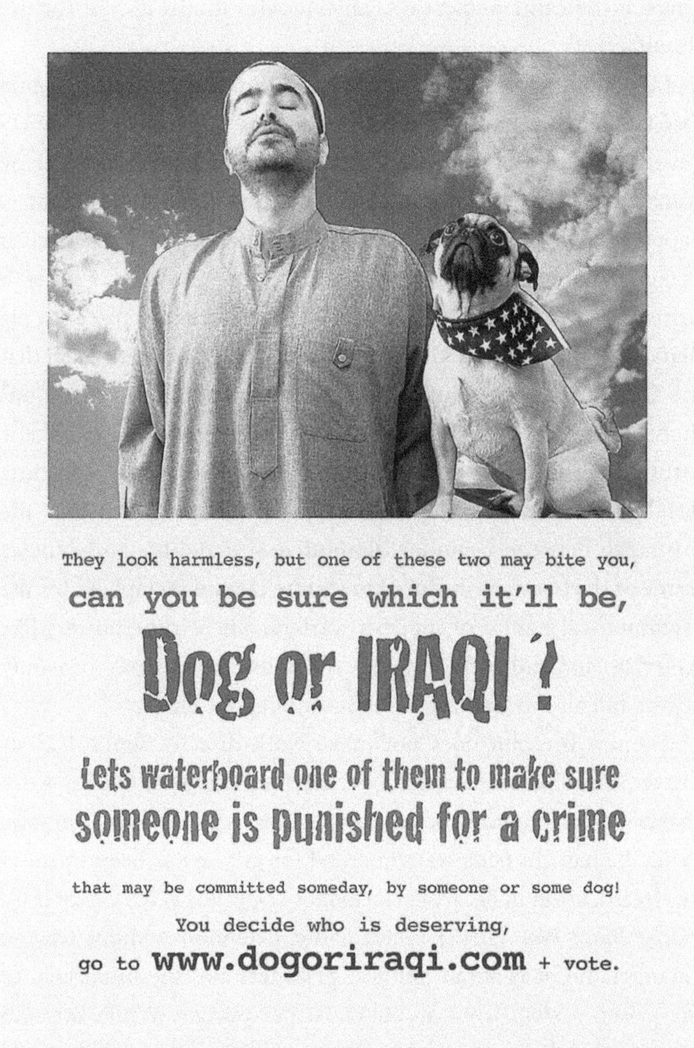

Figure 1.4 Wafaa Bilal, *Dog or Iraqi*, 2008. © Wafaa Bilal. Reproduced with the permission of the artist.

looks at the camera and says, 'anyone who thinks it's not torture should try it'.

Like Bilal (and the year before him), Guatemalan artist Regina José Galindo re-enacted a waterboarding as a comment on the US government's use of 'enhanced interrogation techniques' on 'enemy combatants' (see Figure 1.5). Waterboarding could not, of course, happen on US or British soil. So, instead, it happened in places such as Guantanamo Bay (a US naval base in Cuba) and Diego Garcia (a British overseas territory). Galindo's performance took place at Caja Blanca, on the island of Mallorca, 'because it had been revealed that the CIA used it as a transit point for its "extraordinary rendition" flights of men they had kidnapped to countries where they could be tortured'.[54] This draws our attention to the globalization of torture. Art historian and curator Julian Stallabrass speculates that the mismatch between Galindo's diminutive size and the bodybuilder frame of the bouncer she hired to torture her are metaphors for the asymmetrical nature of modern warfare, where superpowers like America can manhandle less powerful countries like Iraq – not only in war, but also in trade agreements and regime changes.[55]

Thomas Bresolin does not make work directly about 9/11 or the erosion of domestic civil liberties that followed, but his work shares methodological and conceptual links with Bilal and Galindo. While he has not been waterboarded for art, he has been tortured by electrocution in an art performance (*Dog*, 2012, see Chapter 6). While *Bitch War* (2012) is not about detention without trial in Guantanamo, it is about political prisoners and the unfairness of the prison system from an anarchist perspective. While Bresolin does not break the law in his art practice, he draws much of his inspiration from the Anarchist Black Cross (ABC), a prisoner support organization that openly supports those who commit crimes to further revolutionary aims. Although the ABC was specifically established to support anarchist political prisoners, it believes that 'prisons serve no useful purpose (except for the benefit of the ruling classes) and should be abolished along with the State'.[56]

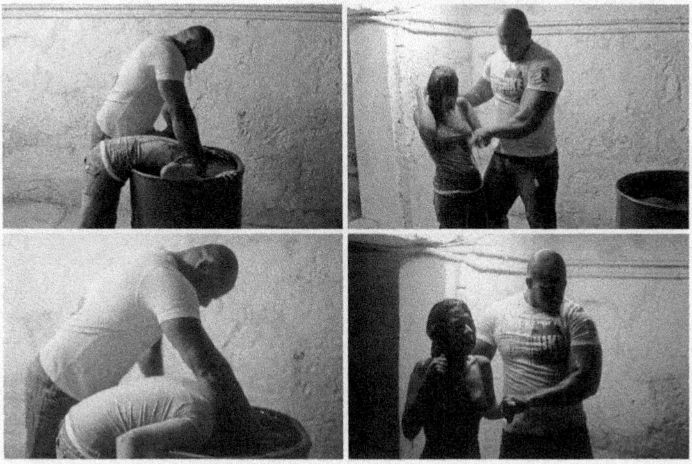

Figure 1.5 Regina José Galindo, *Confesión*, 2007. © Regina José Galindo. Photograph by Julian Stallabrass. Reproduced with the permission of the artist and Julian Stallabrass.

It defines itself in opposition to Amnesty International, who it claims 'balk at supporting anyone accused of so-called violent acts, thus insinuating that anyone who resists oppression and takes up arms in self-defence, or during a revolutionary insurrection, is not worthy of support'.[57]

Like *Domestic Tension*, *Bitch War* was an act of endurance and solidarity. Where Bilal's thoughts were with his family and other Iraqis who were being terrorized in their homes, *Bitch War* included a week-long hunger strike in solidarity with political prisoners. Bresolin blogged from his studio throughout the exhibition, releasing daily hunger strike statements that pronounced his political motives. He explained that, day one of the hunger strike was in solidarity for 'my imprisoned comrades in Belarus'; day two for the Cleveland Four; day three for comrades prosecuted for the Conspiracy of Fire Cells case (an anarchist firebombing campaign in Greece); day four was dedicated to Noureddin Mohamed who died in the centre of Calais in the early hours of Saturday 7 July 2012 'murdered by security forces'; day five for the Syrian anarchists

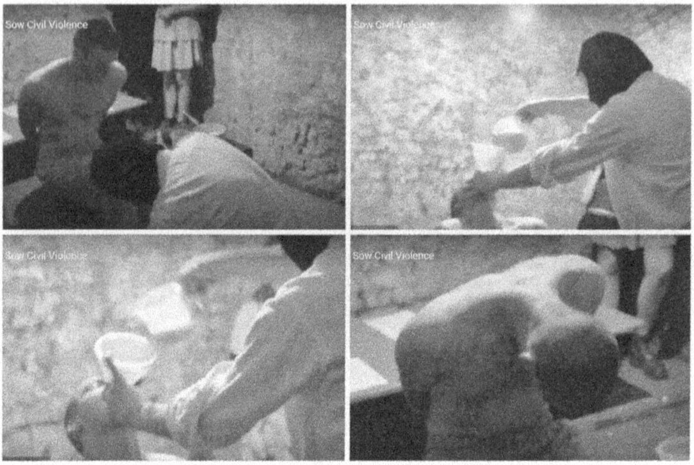

Figure 1.6 Thomas Bresolin, *Sow Civil Violence*, 2012. © Thomas Bresolin. Reproduced with the permission of the artist.

(accompanied by a long text); day six for Pussy Riot; day seven dedicated to the 2011 firebomb attack on Canning Circus police station (Nottingham).[58] On the eighth day, *Bitch War* culminated with a performance titled *Sow Civil Violence* (10 August 2012) where Bresolin was force-fed (see Figure 1.6).

The *Bitch War* exhibition took place at The Victorian Vaults (London, 2012), a dimly lit crypt that bore more than a little resemblance to a dungeon, or the basement where Bilal was waterboarded. It consisted of three main pieces, each in its own alcove. The first artwork was a projection of a text written specifically for the exhibition by long-term prisoner John Bowden, who was released in 2020, after forty years of incarceration. The use of a slide projector worked to set your imagination in motion as you slowly began to piece together the story from whatever slide you happened to see first. I entered the show at the slide where Bowden invites you to imagine an authoritarian, totalitarian world. When I realized that Bowden was describing life in prison, I still did not know that he was the prisoner, describing his life, until I reached the corresponding slide that reveals such information. Bowden was emblematic of resistance to the prison system. While incarcerated, he organized various uprisings and once took a governor hostage, invoking the harshest of responses.

In the second alcove, correspondence between Bresolin and Bowden was displayed on benches for audiences to read amid some gruel-like substance in a saucepan with a hosepipe and a funnel nearby that were later used in the aforementioned force-feeding. Visitors were confronted with a human element through Bowden's neat, open-minded (and articulate) handwritten letters in contrast with Bresolin's word-processed printouts. This provided an outlet for Bowden to tell his story and reach new audiences. The force-feeding performance, *Sow Civil Violence*, took place in this alcove, on International Prisoners Day.

In the final alcove, there was a video projection of Bresolin being repeatedly whipped – leaving significant marks on his naked body. All this was realized in a framework that aimed to raise public awareness regarding some of the dehumanizing aspects of prison life. *Bitch War* was an exploration of the body as a visceral object: a site for potential violence and a tool for protest when the right to express yourself has been taken away. Violent performances, such as those outlined in this chapter, raise ethical questions. Is it justifiable for artists to enact violence on themselves, but not on others? If so, why is it more acceptable to inflict violence on yourself? Once a concrete cause is attached to a performance, how can it be viewed as art? There are aesthetic questions that must be answered as well as political and ethical ones. These questions and more will be answered in the next chapter.

2

Refuse/resist

This chapter examines the ethics and aesthetics of 'militant art', a concept introduced in Chapter 1. The first part of this chapter presents a definition of militant art, which is compared to Alain Badiou's rules for militant art and contrasted with his idea of official art. The concept of NGO art, as proposed by BAVO, is examined as a contemporary example of official art, and both are presented as opposing forces to militant aesthetics. In the second part, an ethical defence for militancy is established, drawing on the history of avant-garde art to argue that the connection between art and militancy is not coincidental, but inherent. The chapter contends that militancy can create aesthetic possibilities and that art can help us understand political problems and envision political alternatives. In the third and final section, the chapter synthesizes three different aesthetic frameworks to construct an aesthetic scaffolding that is suitable for evaluating militant art. The chapter concludes by arguing that militant art contains a dialectical tension between ethics and aesthetics and that this tension is integral to its assessment.

Militant art defined

Militant art is a kind of art activism. The Tate Gallery defines activist art as art that 'addresses political or social issues' and which 'is about empowering individuals and communities and is generally situated in the public arena with artists working closely with a community to generate the art'.[1] This definition makes it clear that there are social elements to art activism – that art activism is a kind of socially engaged art. Not all art activism is militant, just as not all socially engaged art is activist. Militant art should be understood as being nested within art activism, which is itself nested within socially engaged art. Accordingly, I apply the term 'militant art' to art that is (1) a subset of art activism that is (2) in itself militant (it does not seek to merely represent militancy in the way paintings or films about militancy do), (3) operates in the political sphere, retaining a belief that fundamental political change is possible, (4) contains an event of tactical confrontation that includes being prepared to break the law, (5) contains a dialectical tension between its aesthetic autonomy and political commitment and which is (6) either situated in the 'real' world, or uses galleries as sites to plan militant actions, display and disseminate the results of militant actions, or to perform violent and confrontational acts.

Attributes 1–5 are not individually sufficient to qualify as militant art – not all art activism is militant, not all militant or political acts are art and not all acts of confrontation or lawbreaking are art or militant (getting a parking ticket is not militant, for example). Attributes 1–5 are, however, all necessary conditions for militant art. Attribute 6 identifies two distinct kinds of militant art – one gallery based, the other not. It is a necessary condition only in an either–or sense.

Alain Badiou's rules for militant art

In 2010, at a gallery in New York, Alain Badiou defined 'militant art'.[2] In this unpublished speech, he contrasts 'militant art' with 'official art'. Official art is the art of kings, the church, or the state that glorifies what has already happened. Consequently, it is always conservative. Militant art, according to Badiou, is official art's opposite. It is that which is yet to be decided; it is of conflicting ideas. This position is consistent with the Cuban artist Tania Bruguera's declaration that 'political art has doubts, not certainties',[3] and her proclamation that 'you can be a civic artist or an independent artist'.[4] Although opposites, militant art and official art are both ideological and they sometimes even share the same ideology. In his talk, Badiou established four rules for militant art that are broadly compatible with my definition, but with one key exception. I will introduce the four rules first, before explaining the exception.

Firstly, Badiou tells us that militant art must be linked to local political activities. This is necessary, he says, because today there is no 'strong ideology' capable of creating the global idea of another possibility. Where before the West had political differences (communism and capitalism), now we have (almost) universal democratic consensus and there is no battle of ideas. Struggles and resistance exist, for sure, but affirming the possibility of a true political alternative has not been possible. The militant artist, according to Badiou, must therefore temporarily substitute an ideological position for a real, concrete, proximity. This, we are told, will lead to new formal means, which will be found in the process. Secondly, militant art must recognize contemporary attempts to break free of post-politics and return to strong ideologies. To achieve this, one must acknowledge the current position of weakness but also, crucially, the possibility to go beyond it: 'to return to a strong idea concerning the global destiny of human beings'.[5] Thirdly, the militant artist must participate in the formal shift away from representation and towards presentation. Badiou does not give examples, but this assertion recalls statements by various contemporary artists from Bruguera's demand that 'I don't want an art that points at a thing, I want an art that *is* the thing',[6] to Jeremy Deller's declaration that he 'went from being an artist who made things, to being an artist who made things happen'.[7] Lastly, militant art must create a synthesis of the first three rules.

I contend that where art is rooted in local political movements, social causes or community groups, this constitutes today's 'official', rather than militant, art and this is where my concept of militant aesthetics differs from that of Badiou. Such official art is not commissioned by monarchs or the church, as official artists were in the past, but it is supported by the state. Sometimes this comes in the form of bursaries for the arts. For example, Project Art Works (established in 1996) is an Arts Council England National Portfolio Organisation. This means they receive regular state funding (via the Arts Council) for which they are accountable. Similarly, artists who do not qualify as a National Portfolio Organisation can apply for a National Lottery Projects Grant, so long as their 'project' will benefit the community. Other times, state funding for education, social regeneration or crime reduction is used. However, the distinction between arts funding and social funding is not always clear.

In Britain, the merging of the two funding streams is a legacy of Tony Blair's New Labour policies that increased arts funding using education and social care budgets with the expectation that artists would make educational and social projects.[8] Such funding initiatives coerce indebted and underemployed artists to step in to plug gaps where state capital used to be before austerity-induced cuts and privatizations. In this context, it is unsurprising that Project Art Works deliver educational workshops that fulfil care and support roles and their website declares that the collective includes 'paid and unpaid caregivers who help each other to navigate through the complexities of health and social care systems'.[9]

The situation in the United States is comparable. Marc James Léger draws our attention to a New York State proposal to provide '$10,000 of student loan forgiveness to cultural workers who provide services to children, adolescents and seniors'.[10] It is revealing that the term 'artist' has been replaced here by 'cultural worker' (in the UK, the term 'creative practitioner' is preferred). In Léger's example, 'artworks' are replaced by 'services', this is also true in Britain, although my Arts Council examples here refer to 'projects'. Rather than working directly for the state (as artists, or as social workers), today's official artists assume the role of private contractors (unpaid or on precarious contracts, of course) replacing the carers, community workers, social workers and educators the state has recently made redundant.

Even when no funding is available to remunerate community artists, they are still official because they fulfil an official role: plugging gaps left by cuts. When artists make ethically commendable work for altruistic reasons, they gain moral kudos and with this comes official recognition in the form of art prizes and residencies. All the artists nominated for the Turner Prize 2021 were socially engaged art collectives that work closely and continuously with communities across the breadth of the UK to inspire social change: Gentle/Radical's members include conflict resolution trainers, equalities practitioners and youth workers based in Cardiff; the Array collective produce collaborative actions about language, gender and reproductive rights in Belfast; Black Obsidian Sound System (BOSS) was formed to create a community of queer, trans and non-binary Black people and people of colour; Cooking Sections' work addresses climate change; and Project Art Works collaborate with neurodivergent artists to make work at the intersection of art and care. The Turner Prize provided official recognition for the ethically commendable social work that these collectives have done (funded or otherwise) in a manner that recalls how MBEs are awarded to community workers.

The 2021 Turner Prize also conferred official status on the nominated artists through the way it advertised and defined their work. From the descriptions on the websites of the Tate Gallery (that runs the prize) and the Herbert Gallery (that hosted it), you would think that there is nothing more to their work than their identities, politically correct compositions and actions. This attitude was echoed across events comprising the Coventry UK City of Culture 2021 festival (of which the Turner Prize was a part). For example, wall texts dedicated more words to describe the identities or ethically commendable acts of the artists than the artworks on display. This seemed like a defensive action to protect the artist from criticism. It might as well have read: 'before you judge this artwork, I just want you to know that it is beyond reproach because the artist is a saint or a victim of oppression (and didn't they do well considering?)'. Being politically correct is now as much the official role of the socially engaged artist as making actual social change.

BAVO's NGO art

The Dutch research collective BAVO share my apprehensions that the pressure on artists to be politically committed and make a quantifiable difference in the real world neutralizes their ability to be militant. In their concern for helping victims of neoliberal policies, well-meaning socially engaged artists end up merely making minor palliative tweaks to the system that caused the problems in the first place. BAVO would term my examples 'NGO art': art characterized by 'interventions that help disadvantaged populations and communities to deal with the problems they are facing'.[11] NGO artists are highly suspicious of organized politics, which they associate with totalitarianism. Instead, they embrace community projects and identity politics: a move that Léger worries 'threatens to supplement rather than challenge neoliberal governance'.[12] BAVO argue that the philosophy of helping victims first and worrying about politics later in practice becomes 'no politics, victims only' and consequently NGO art leads to a 'diarrhoea of unconnected, highly specific, ad hoc interventions that, although offering instant relief, extinguishes any possibility of a long-term solution'.[13] They assert that NGO art is inherently unpolitical because 'the question of what can be done here and now, and how this can be achieved most efficiently is more important than exposing and combating more underlying structures – which should be the essence of politics'.[14]

Militant art is macro-political while NGO art is micro-political. The task of the militant artist is to expose the demand for practical, micro-political, solutions as symptomatic of the system that caused the problems in the first place. Macro-politics is characterized by big ideological struggles. It is essentially the same as Badiou's notion of strong ideology. NGO artists give up on the possibility of radical political change and try to make the best out of the current situation instead. BAVO calls for artists to do the opposite: 'make the worst of it, to turn it into the worst possible version of itself would thus entail a refusal of the current blackmail in which artists are offered all kinds of opportunities to make a difference, on the condition that they give up on their desire for radical change'.[15] In other words, BAVO call for artists to choose between micro-political tweaks that ultimately support neoliberalism or adopt a strategy of overidentification, such as the example of Hassan Elahi given in Chapter 1, to awaken viewers to the fact that other political orders are possible.

As we have seen, Badiou reasons that today, in the absence of strong ideologies, it is necessary for militant art to tactically embrace micro-politics in the short term. By contrast, official art is aligned with already-decided, macro-political, strong ideologies. Historically, these were religion, monarchy and totalitarian political ideologies. However, today's NGO-style official art has already decided that there can be no alternative to neoliberalism and that we might as well try to make the best of it. This is the genius of capitalist ideology. It masquerades as the nonideological, as that which is natural and inevitable, as Žižek has argued (see introduction to this book). For Badiou, militant art is weakened by the lack of strong official art and therefore the possibility of a dialectical relationship between the two. Without such a dialectical relationship, he tells us, militant art cannot be distinguished from purely experimental art. However, militant art does enter into a dialectical relationship: one with NGO-style socially engaged art. It enters into an ideological battle with the seemingly natural and inevitable order of things and to do this it must retain the possibility of macro-political change.

In contradistinction to Badiou's claim that militant art is necessarily embedded in local politics, I maintain that it should be wary of getting embroiled with micro-political causes. BAVO are correct to say that political artists have plenty of scope to 'develop their own specific tactics and practices of resistance or even to criticize and distance themselves from radical social movements'.[16] NGO-style socially engaged art conforms with Badiou's first rule (to be rooted in local politics) and his third rule (it does not represent but presents micro-politics). However, it does not adhere to his second rule: to retain the possibility of a return to strong ideology (or Léger's macro-politics). Militant art must retain the possibility of macro-political chance, and this key aspect differentiates it from other kinds of art activism and socially engaged practices.

An ethical scaffolding for militancy

In this section, I will develop an ethical apology for militancy, referring to the philosophy of three writers, namely: Christabel Pankhurst (1880–1958), Ulrike Meinhof (1934–1974) and the contemporary British author and blogger Dominic Fox. Respectively, each writer is contemporaneous to a period of what Claire Bishop calls 'political upheaval and movements for social change', namely 'the triumph, heroic last stand and collapse of a collectivist vision of society'.[17] Bishop connects these three moments with 'social turns' in art. The ethical justifications for militancy that follow therefore correspond with the evolution of socially engaged and, as I shall argue in Chapter 3, avant-garde art.

Christabel Pankhurst's ethical justification for militancy

The suffragette movement's actions were truly militant and yet they are generally considered to have been ethical. They famously smashed windows and went on hunger strike when arrested, but between 1909 and 1914 the suffragettes also launched a nationwide campaign of bombing and arson and they even attacked Members of Parliament (including Churchill and Asquith), slashed Velazquez's

Rokeby Venus (1647–51, National Gallery, London) and smashed the mummy cases at the British Museum. Cultural historian Fern Riddell gives a comprehensive account of the most militant acts during this period, likening the suffragettes to a 'regulated army with professional soldiers, seeing the Edwardian period as a civil war between the sexes'.[18] Nonetheless, official approval of their acts dates back at least as far as 1930, when Prime Minister Stanley Baldwin (1867–1947) unveiled a statue of the movement's founder, Emmeline Pankhurst (1858–1928), next to the Houses of Parliament. In 2018, the centenary of women over thirty gaining the vote in the UK, another statue was unveiled in Manchester, where Pankhurst was born. In 2006, a blue plaque was placed on the house in Notting Hill where she and her daughter Christabel (1880–1958) lived. Although Christabel was arrested and imprisoned several times,[19] by 1936 she was appointed a Dame Commander of the Order of the British Empire.

Christabel Pankhurst's text 'What Militancy Means' (1913) is an explicit, manifesto-style, apology for militancy that can be summarized in three points. Firstly, that 'British constitutional freedom has been won by militancy. Some freedom – the freedom of women – still remains to win. That is why militancy is still needed'.[20] Secondly, she explains that laws may be broken to 'vindicate a higher law' and 'violence may be done to prevent greater violence'.[21] By way of example, Pankhurst quotes the home secretary, Reginald McKenna (1863–1942). McKenna responded to a charge that he had broken the law by releasing a suffragette hunger striker by making an analogy with rescuing a person from a burning building. He explained that if the door is locked and the windows closed you would have to break the law to enter the house and rescue the occupant. Nevertheless, this would be justified – your duty even. Thirdly, Pankhurst asserts that a militant cannot justify going to prison for her own sake and that no militant can tolerate torture to redress a personal grievance. However, a militant is justified in making sacrifices, such as being arrested or going on hunger strike, so long as this helps achieve a cause or greater good (for others) and a militant is permitted to break the law and commit acts of violence to achieve this cause.

The language in Pankhurst's text is very much of its time and can be likened to Filippo Tommaso Marinetti's 'The Futurist Manifesto' (first published in 1909). In it, Marinetti declared, 'We intend to glorify war – the only hygiene of the world – militarism, patriotism, the destructive gesture of anarchists, beautiful ideas worth dying for, and contempt for woman'.[22] While the attitude towards women's rights could not be more different, both texts compare militant acts to 'hygiene' and 'cleansing'. Pankhurst states that just as the violent act of childbirth is necessary for a new life, great storms create new and fresh worlds, great wars cleanse human society and 'cut out cancerous wrongs' and that the 'militancy of women is doing the work of purification'.[23] Both the Futurists and the Suffragettes were pro-war. The Futurists' call for violence in 1909 and the suffragettes' militant turn (1909–14) came just a few years before Bishop's first 'social turn' in art: the historical avant-garde of 'circa 1917' and the birth of communism in Russia.[24]

Ulrike Meinhof: From protest to resistance

Ulrike Meinhof outlined her apology for militancy in a 1968 essay called 'From Protest to Resistance', which fits perfectly with Bishop's second social turn: the neo-avant-garde and communism's apex with the revolutionary events of 1968.[25] Unlike the suffragettes, the Baader-Meinhof Gang (properly known as the Red Army Faction) are still controversial. There has been a renewed interest in their actions following the release of Uli Edel's film *The Baader-Meinhof Complex* in 2008,[26] the same year that Seven Stories Press published an anthology of Meinhof's twenty-eight articles for *Konkret* journal in English for the first time.[27] The fascination with Meinhof, more than with her partner in crime Andreas Baader (1943–1977), is that she was a reputable journalist and a married mother of two who gave it all up to become a committed communist revolutionary.[28]

Meinhof's distinction between protest and resistance is useful to help distinguish between an activist and a militant. She wrote, 'Protest is when I say I don't like this. Resistance is when I put an end to what I don't like. Protest is when I say I refuse to go along with this any more [*sic*]. Resistance is when I make sure everybody else stops going along too.'[29] The activist *protests* but need not necessarily *resist*. A militant does more than merely protest: A militant acts; a militant refuses and resists. Strikers are activists, as they 'say that they do not like something and will not go along with it'. A clear case of activism turning militant (or protest becoming resistance) would be when strikers seize their factory or dockyard to take control of the means of production. If strikers form a picket line, they attempt to 'make sure that everybody else stops going along too', but a picket line is still a form of protest because it appeals to a higher authority to make a judgement. It is a form of lobbying rather than direct action and it is not necessarily violent. The picket line may serve to dissuade workers from going to work, it may use persuasive skills that border on emotional blackmail, but it is only when the strikers become prepared to physically stop workers from crossing the picket line that they become militant: that they 'put an end to what they do not like'.

Dominic Fox's militant dysphoria

Dominic Fox's characterization of a world of passive dejection describes the conditions during Bishop's third social turn: the 'resurgence of participatory art in the 1990s' and the demise of communism, as evidenced in the fall of the Berlin Wall in 1989 and subsequent collapse of the Soviet Union in 1991.[30] The end of the Cold War and the apparent victory of liberal, democratic capitalist democracy ushered in a period of post-political end of History narratives, where communism not only ceased to be an actually existing alternative, but where it became virtually impossible to even imagine that alternatives were possible. Fox reasserts the possibility of revolutionary politics in such a culture, also claiming that new aesthetic possibilities can arise from militancy.[31] For Fox, people become militant when they are separated from and turned against the world. They are not just angry, bitter or outraged; the militant has 'decisively rejected every source of consolation'.[32] He coins the term 'militant dysphoria' to describe political displeasure concentrated and directed against its source.[33] It is in this state of dejection that, for Fox, new aesthetic possibilities arise, because once militants are separated from the world they begin to see it in new ways.

Fox substantiates this claim through analyses of various artistic outputs ranging from Black Metal music to Coleridge's poem 'Dejection: An Ode' (1802), in which the narrator longs for a storm to erupt (just as the Futurists and Pankhurst did) so that the violence might 'startle this dull pain, and make it move and live!' to end the 'void, dark, and drear, A stifled, drowsy, unimpassioned grief, Which finds no natural outlet, no relief'.[34] The narrator in Coleridge's poem describes a numbness, a deadening of all his feelings: he is anaesthetized. To break free from this condition requires militancy: to become aestheticized once more (the etymology of 'aesthetics', when traced back to its Greek root *aisthetikos,* means to sense or to feel). Here is the link between militancy and aesthetics. After a state of dejection, the subject begins to see the world in a new light. Following the realization that there is nothing left to lose, a militant reawakening becomes possible wherein the subject can deeply feel the world again. Artists can use militancy to aestheticize people by challenging post-political and end of History narratives, facilitating a return to macro-politics.

An aesthetic framework for militant art

I have argued that militant art is a subset of socially engaged art, but that certain kinds of socially engaged art are prone to falling into militant art's opposite: institutionalized 'official' art that is judged only by its social effects and ethical intentions. Since, by implication, militant art should not be judged by these criteria, we must ask how it should be assessed aesthetically. The most high-profile debate in recent times about the role of aesthetic quality versus art's social function took place between Claire Bishop and Grant Kester – initially on the pages of *Artforum* (2006) and subsequently in their books *Artificial Hells* (2012) and *The One and the Many* (2011). Bishop provides a succinct summary of the debate:

> The social discourse accuses the artistic discourse of amorality and inefficacy, because it is insufficient merely to reveal, reduplicate, or reflect upon the world; what matters is social change. The artistic discourse accuses the social discourse of remaining stubbornly attached to existing categories, and focusing on micropolitical gestures at the expense of sensuous immediacy as a potential locus of disalienation.[35]

Bishop criticizes theorists who promote art that privileges social conscience over and above (or even to the exclusion of) aesthetic values: those critics who promote art as being good because it realizes some other, social or ethical, end. She singles out Kester for being 'perfectly content to allow that a socially collaborative art project could be deemed a success if it works on the level of social intervention even though it founders on the level of art'.[36] Kester's counterargument accuses Bishop of rejecting art activism for being 'politically correct' and 'consigned to decorating floats for the annual May Day parade'.[37] This impasse is unresolved in art discourse and many scholars bemoan the fact that others still bring it up. However, it is of fundamental importance to how we should judge militant art aesthetically. If we adopt the social discourse, there is no way to judge militant art *as art* and it potentially becomes indistinguishable from political or social activism. If militant artists adopt the artistic discourse, the militancy of militant art becomes merely symbolic, rendering it indistinguishable from other kinds of political art. To address these unresolved problems, I will draw on three philosophies of art: the ethical criticism of art, the political criticism of art and Jacques Rancière's regimes of art. Individually, each one is insufficient to complete my theory of militant aesthetics. However, with some adaption, they can be mapped onto one another and synthesized to provide an aesthetic framework appropriate for judging militant art.

The ethical criticism of art: Autonomism, moralism and ethicism

'The ethical criticism of art' exists in parallel to the Bishop–Kester debate. It is little known in fine art circles, yet it has developed into a field of aesthetics in its own right.[38] It aims to determine whether moral factors can or should count towards an artwork's aesthetic assessment, usually by referring to narrative-based artworks and literature. It seems somewhat outdated and unsuitable for newer forms of art, such as socially engaged art or art activism, which necessarily contain political and ethical dimensions that *must* count towards their aesthetic judgement. Nonetheless, it provides a useful aesthetic framework for militant art that will determine how militant artists can avoid the impasse that Bishop describes. It also provides the key to synthesizing the other frameworks.

There are two extremes in the ethical criticism of art. On the one hand, there is aesthetic moralism: 'the view that the aesthetic value of an artwork is determined by its moral value.'[39] Radical moralists hold the view that morality is the 'only criterion of aesthetic value,'[40] reducing 'all aesthetic value to moral value.'[41] For radical moralists like Leo Tolstoy (1828–1910), aesthetics is only of value if it serves a moral or social function: in Tolstoy's case, this meant a Christian cause.[42] On the other hand, there is aesthetic autonomism: the view that 'it is inappropriate to apply moral categories to art; they should be evaluated by "aesthetic" standards alone.'[43] For radical autonomists like Oscar Wilde (1854–1900), 'There is no such thing as a moral or an immoral book. Books are well written, or badly written. That is all.'[44] This position is synonymous with the nineteenth-century concept of *l'art pour l'art* (art for art's sake).

The extremes of the ethical criticism of art are comparable to the Bishop–Kester debate. The 'social discourse,' where social change is considered more important than a work's aesthetics, is like aesthetic moralism. Kester is an aesthetic moralist. The title of his book, *The One and the Many*, comes from Spinoza's (1632–1677) moralist warning against aesthetic autonomy and his reconciliation of the individual with the collective. Kester problematizes artistic autonomy by championing works that blur the boundaries between art and life and he sees traditional aesthetics as a barrier to new forms of art, such as art activism. Bishop explains that the social discourse holds the view that aesthetics is implicated with bourgeois connotations of connoisseurship and hierarchy and it attempts to demonstrate how 'aesthetics masks inequalities, oppressions and exclusions (of race, gender, class, and so on).'[45] Because aesthetics is associated with whiteness, patriarchy and heteronormativity, it is considered immoral and in need of updating, if not abolishing.

Immediately before their Turner Prize nomination, Project Art Works were artists in residence at Hastings Contemporary (22 March to 2 May 2021) where they made window displays so that the public could see art while the gallery was closed because of the COVID lockdown. This ethically commendable work, and the identity of their neurodivergent collaborators, are the reasons why they were shortlisted for the prize – why the work was judged to be *artistically* significant. In this discourse, the aesthetics of the work is irrelevant. To criticize the artistic merit of the project would be seen as an assault on neurodivergent minorities. Furthermore, it would be seen as missing the point, which is that the ethically commendable work they do has aesthetic value *in and of itself* – a clear moralist position. Seen in this way, Project Art Works not only make ethically laudable work, they also challenge an exclusionary art world (one that also happens to fund their projects and select their work for prestigious prizes for these very reasons).

Aesthetic autonomism can be compared to Bishop's artistic discourse, where artistic freedom to challenge moral conventions is considered more important than a work's ethics, or ability to enact social change. In other words, the artistic discourse is autonomous from moral or political concerns. In this way of thinking, a painting glorifying Hitler might be morally reprehensible, but it could be well painted and therefore good (or even great) aesthetically. Bishop's artistic discourse relies less on traditional aesthetics, but still asserts aesthetic quality and artistic freedom to question morality and social structures. For example, when Santiago Sierra pays drug-addicted prostitutes to have a line tattooed on their back (*160 cm Line Tattooed on 4 People*, 2000) or pays homeless women to stand facing a wall (*Group of People Facing a Wall*, 2002), he is not performing ethical acts or improving these people's lives: the prostitutes are only paid enough for their next hit and the homeless women are only paid enough for one night in a hostel. Nonetheless, Bishop defends the work's right to raise difficult questions about the society that ignores (or even tolerates) such a dark underbelly. Bishop believes that it is 'crucial to discuss, analyse, and compare [participatory and socially engaged art] critically *as art*,'[46] but she falls short of declaring moral or political dimensions completely irrelevant. For these reasons, I argue she should be considered an 'ethicist,' rather than an autonomist.

Ethicism is an aesthetic concept coined by aesthetician Berys Gaut that provides a way out of the moralist–autonomist bind. Gaut reasons that moral aspects are also aesthetic because they elicit emotional responses and

> If these responses are unmerited, because unethical, we have reason not to respond in the way prescribed. Our having reason not to respond in the way prescribed is a failure of the work. What responses the work prescribes is of aesthetic relevance. So the fact that we have reason not to respond in the way prescribed

> is an *aesthetic* failure of the work, that is to say, is an aesthetic defect.[47]

This means that if an artwork is ethically reprehensible, it is *to that degree* an aesthetic failure – but it might still be successful according to other aesthetic criteria. The degree to which the ethical flaw impinges on other aesthetic criteria depends on the severity of the transgression and the work's other aesthetic qualities. Equally, if a work of art is ethically commendable, it is *to that degree* an aesthetic success – but this success could be undermined by other aesthetic factors (such as poor technical or conceptual qualities, or intellectual inconsistencies). Ethical messages or qualities are not necessary for an artwork to be aesthetically successful, but these factors do count towards (or against) its aesthetic assessment.

The political criticism of art: Adorno's autonomy and Sartre's commitment

With some adaption, the ethical criticism of art can be mapped onto Theodor Adorno's political criticism of art, as outlined in his essay titled 'Commitment' (see Table 1). The synthesis of these two aesthetic frameworks will facilitate the development of a distinct concept of militant aesthetics that is both autonomous as art and politically militant. To do this, it is first necessary to discern three categories of art in Adorno's text to match the three categories in the ethical criticism of art: aesthetic moralism, autonomism and ethicism. This is not so straightforward. At first, it appears to be a twofold system differentiating only between aesthetically 'autonomous' art and politically 'committed' art. However, there is a third, often overlooked, concept which he terms 'tendency.' The first two terms are fairly straightforward to explain, but the third will take some unpacking, especially as Adorno elides it with commitment on occasion.

Adorno's autonomous art is broadly comparable with aesthetic autonomism. It is an end in and of itself and serves no other

Table 1

Ethical criticism of art	Moralism	Ethicism	Autonomism
Political criticism of art	Tendency (*Tendenzkunst*)	Commitment	Autonomy

purpose, be it economic, religious, political or educational. As Adorno explains, 'the principle that governs autonomous works of art is not the totality of their effects, but their own inherent structure.'[48] The autonomous work of art supposedly acts as a form of resistance to society in and of itself. However, Adorno somewhat paradoxically argues that art, 'even in its opposition to society remains a part of it [because it] must close its eyes and ears against it.'[49] He concludes that 'an emphasis on autonomous works is itself socio-political in nature.'[50] We might say that all art is political, but autonomous art exists independently from overt political messages or social commentary.

Committed art (art that takes directly political positions, contains political messages or makes social commentaries) is subordinated to politics in a similar way to how moralist works are subordinated to their ethical messages or traits. Indeed, Adorno likens politically committed art to moral art on several occasions. For example, he says that 'Committed works all too readily credit themselves with every noble value, and then manipulate them at their ease.'[51] He criticizes Bertolt Brecht's plays for being 'infected by the deceptions of his commitment,'[52] noting that audiences 'cannot help hearing that they are [being] talked into something.'[53] This sounds a lot like propaganda and, for Adorno, when politically committed messages become didactic and coercive this undermines the work as art. Hence there is a link between propaganda art (which subordinates art to politics) and aesthetic moralism (which subordinates art to ethics). However, politically committed art is not the same as propaganda art. Adorno argues that 'In aesthetic theory, "commitment" should be distinguished from "tendency".

Committed art in the proper sense is not intended to generate ameliorative measures, legislative acts or practical institutions – like earlier propagandist (tendency) plays.'[54] As he does not elaborate on the nature of tendency art in 'Commitment', it is necessary to turn to the original German-language version to understand the term.

Adorno uses the word *Tendenzstücke* only once in *Engagement oder künstlerische Autonomie?* (Commitment or Artistic Autonomy?).[55] Literally, it means 'tendentious play' but it is translated into English as both 'propagandist' and '(tendency) plays' in the quotation cited earlier in the text. György (Georg) Lukács (1885–1971) wrote *Tendenz oder Parteilichkeit?*, which was translated by Leonard F. Mins in 1934 as 'Propaganda or Partisanship?'[56] but as 'Tendency or Partisanship?' by David Fernback.[57] In their introduction to the latter version of this essay, reprinted in *Art & Theory*, Harrison and Wood explain that this essay was 'an intervention in the dispute between "tendentious", self-professed "proletarian" art … and a more sober art with its heritage in bourgeois tradition'.[58] Adorno refers to this debate when he contrasts commitment with tendency. The British Marxist art historian Andrew Hemingway explains how, although Marx and Engels 'were interested in the propagandist uses of Tendenzkunst or Tendenzliteratur in spreading revolutionary ideas – that is, in didactic forms of art and literature that pointed to a desired historical outcome – [they] distinguished such work from true realist art'.[59] *Kunst* means 'art', so *Tendenzkunst* and *Tendenzliteratur* can be, crudely, translated as tendency art and tendency literature respectively. However, *Tendenz* has several meanings depending on the context. We have already seen that it can mean 'tendency' or 'propaganda', but it can also mean 'tendentious' or, 'trend'. Due to this ambiguity, from here on I will use the word *Tendenzkunst* to refer to Adorno's concept of tendency art.

Tendenzkunst should be understood in terms of aesthetic moralism. Where aesthetic value is subordinated to 'ameliorative measures, legislative acts or practical institutions', this is equivalent to the moralist belief that ethical traits are what give artworks aesthetical value. The Dutch artist Theo Van Doesburg (1883–1931) set out a treatise against *Tendenzkunst* arguing that if 'art strengthens tendentious proletarian instincts, it uses the same means as ecclesiastical and nationalist art … it is essentially the same whether one paints a Red Guard with Trotsky at the head or an Imperial Guard with Napoleon at the head'.[60] In Badiou's terms, in both these examples art becomes 'official' and therefore conservative. As Van Doesburg notes, *Tendenzkunst* effectively 'fights neither for art nor for a new order of life – but – unwillingly or knowingly – for the bourgeoisie'.[61] When Léger likens *Tendenzkunst* to politically correct art that 'takes a progressive stance but lacks aesthetic interest',[62] he could be describing Project Art Works. I considered their work earlier in terms of aesthetic moralism because its ethically commendable nature, its inherently politically correct inclusivity and progressive stances are the only criteria by which it is judged aesthetically. Both *Tendenzkunst* and NGO-style socially engaged art fail to imagine macro-political change and instead support the status quo. In doing so, they both subordinate art to politically ideological positions.

Although I emphasize similarities between politics and ethics, to infer that politically correct attitudes are inherently moral would be reductive. Adorno demonstrates that even supposedly ethical acts can be morally questionable. For example, he states that even under fascism, 'no atrocity was perpetrated without a moral veneer', warning that 'Those who trumpet their ethics and humanity … are merely waiting for a chance to persecute those whom their rules condemn, and to exercise the same inhumanity in practice of which they accuse modern art in theory.'[63] This eerily predicts the excesses of 'call out' and 'cancel culture' today. This is why Bishop was right to declare that 'Either social conscience dominates, or the rights of the individual to question social conscience. Art's relationship to the social is either underpinned by morality or it is underpinned by freedom.'[64]

Just as it was necessary to go back to Marx's concept of *Tendenzkunst* to understand Adorno's 'tendency' in terms of aesthetic moralism, it is necessary to turn to Jean-Paul Sartre to understand Adorno's 'commitment' in ethicist terms. Adorno's essay is largely based in opposition to Sartre's notion of politically committed literature. In *What Is Literature?* (first published in 1948), Sartre argued that all literature is inherently political, even the outwardly apolitical kinds. Fictional escapism, for example, implies there is something to escape from and thereby makes a political statement. This position is comparable to Adorno's assertion that autonomous art is socio-political in nature. However, while Adorno sides with aesthetic autonomy, Sartre sides with political commitment. He reasons that since all literature is intrinsically political, authors should recognize this and take responsibility by asserting their political commitments. He likens writing to a loaded pistol where the author can either wave the gun around and wait for it to go off, or point it at something.[65] Either way, the text is 'loaded', so authors should choose the latter option. This point about the loaded gun initially sounds as though commitment subordinates art to politics in a similar way to how moralism subordinates art to ethics – and indeed this is Adorno's concern. However, I contend that political commitment is not the sole criterion by which to judge the work, but rather that it can count towards (or against) the work's aesthetic appreciation and therefore commitment is comparable to ethicism (see Table 1).

Commitment can be further aligned with ethicism if we compare Sartre's notion of an ethical appeal to Gaut's merited response argument. Sartre sees literature as an ethical appeal to the reader's freedom to collaborate in the production of the work. It is an appeal to freedom because you are 'perfectly free to leave that book on the table. But if you open it, you assume responsibility for it'.[66] This means that once readers are aware of the message, they cannot claim ignorance of it. It is an invitation to collaborate because, without the reader, literature is just marks on a page and, more than just deciphering these words to understand their message, the reader must engage their imagination and apply what they read to their own experience. Sartre declared that 'nobody can suppose for a moment that it is possible to write a good novel in praise of anti-Semitism'.[67] This sounds like aesthetic moralism. However, such a novel is not bad because anti-Semitism is bad. Rather, Sartre reasons that the ethical appeal to the reader's freedom to be anti-Semitic conflicts with the fact that freedom is a universal right and that to approve of the enslavement of others is unmerited.[68] To paraphrase Gaut: as the demand is unmerited, because unethical, we have reason not to respond in the way prescribed and, as prescribed responses are of aesthetic relevance, it is to this degree an *aesthetic* failure. It is not the immoral message per se, but the unmerited response that is the *aesthetic* defect.

To clarify the distinction between commitment and tendency, I will turn to Walter Benjamin. Like Sartre, he believed that all literature is inherently political and that the writer has a responsibility to choose whether to directly engage with the political issues of their time or not. For example, in 'The Author as Producer' (1934), he explains that the 'bourgeois writer of entertainment literature [who] does not acknowledge this choice [to embrace their political commitment, or not]', knowingly or not, works 'in the service of certain class interests'.[69] Conversely, writers who recognize that they must make a political choice and, for example, side with the proletariat, render their aesthetic autonomy subordinate to 'what is useful to the proletariat in the class struggle'.[70] Benjamin terms such writing 'tendentious', which is in keeping with the description of *Tendenzliteratur/Tendenzkunst* that I have given so far. However, he complicates the notion of tendency when he says, 'You can declare: a work that shows the correct political tendency need show no other quality. You can also declare: a work that exhibits the correct tendency must of necessity have every other quality'.[71] According to Benjamin, politically engaged literature can be aesthetically innovative and engaging while remaining true to its political message. He suggests that writers should strive to integrate their political message into the *form* of their work, rather than simply stating their beliefs in a didactic manner. Benjamin argues that such literature can be both politically engaged and aesthetically powerful, and that this concept of literary tendency (*Tendenzliteratur*) provides a way for writers to use their work to effect social change without sacrificing artistic quality. When Benjamin says that 'the tendency of a literary work can be politically correct only if it is also literarily correct',[72] he is not using the term 'politically correct' in the sense it is commonly used today. Instead, we might infer the idea of a work's political message being effectively conveyed in unison with a literary aspect. For simplicity, we might substitute 'politically correct' for 'politically coherent'. Benjamin is suggesting that a work with a strong political message but poor literary quality is unlikely to be effective in conveying its message, which will be recognized as a didactic attempt at propaganda. He goes on to argue that a political tendency (message) in a literary work must also include a 'literary tendency', by which he means style: that the politically engaged work must also be innovative and well crafted in terms of its literary style, structure and form. Benjamin further adds that 'this literary tendency, which is implicitly or explicitly contained in every *correct* political tendency of a work, alone constitutes the quality of that work'.[73] In other words, the literary quality of a work of literature is inseparable from its political message. Therefore, the political tendency of a work includes its literary quality *because it includes its literary tendency*.

In essence, Benjamin is arguing that a politically engaged work must be both artistically sound and politically coherent to be effective. This position is entirely compatible with my concept of dialectical ethicism (as outlined in the next section). Indeed, Benjamin acknowledges the necessity of a dialectical approach to surpass debates around form and content and to provide an 'indication of the correct determination of the relation between tendency and quality'.[74] He starts his essay by declaring that authors who acknowledge their political commitments subordinate their art to political ends, and he terms this 'tendentious'. Later in the essay, however, he clarifies that a 'political tendency is a necessary but never sufficient condition for the organizing function of a work'.[75] If it were sufficient, it would be aligned with aesthetic moralism and the conceptualization of *Tendenzkunst* presented so far. However, because Benjamin's concept of politically engaged art necessarily contains a dialectical tension between form and content, it is better aligned with ethicism and Sartrean commitment. Therefore, even though he uses the term 'tendency' in his defence of politically engaged literature (and by implication politically engaged art), his position is better aligned with the Sartrean concept of commitment, while *Tendenzkunst* remains aligned with aesthetic moralism.

Militant aesthetics holds that all art is political (siding with Adorno and Benjamin against Sartre). Sartre believed that art was different from literature, reasoning that prose is always political because it must say something, while poetry could be purely formal. For him, poetry is not really about what the words mean, so much as how they sound. Consequently, poetry could be marvelled in the same way that a statue can: formally. For example, the Dadaists made nonsense poem recitals, such as Hugo Ball's *Karawane* (1916). This is true, but it does not mean that poetry is not inherently political. I contend that artists, like writers, can either embrace their political commitments, or they can make work without direct political commentary. Following Sartre's logic, the first option is like aiming at a target, while the latter is like waving a loaded gun around and waiting for it to go off, because all art imparts some kind of meaning or feeling. The abstract art of the time Sartre was writing falls into the latter camp: it does not contain direct political messages. Sartre tells us that 'if a writer has chosen to remain silent on any aspect whatever of the world … one has the right to ask … "Why have you spoken of this rather than that."'[76] In Benjamin's terms, remaining silent serves certain class interests and the status quo. We similarly might ask abstract artists or practitioners of nonsense poetry why they make art about form, but not politics. In this sense, poetry and abstract art are not so different from Sartre's escapist fiction example.

While militant aesthetics is aligned with Adorno's claim that all art is political, it sides with Sartre against him in that militant artists must embrace their political commitments and take aim. Let us consider an example from contemporary art. Swiss artist Thomas Hirschhorn's 'monuments series' (1999–2013) is the visual art equivalent to Sartre's ethical appeal to the reader's freedom to engage with and complete works of literature (or to reject this appeal). These installations express Hirschhorn's love for four major writers and thinkers and provide possibilities for audiences to learn about them. However, the success of the work lies in the possibility, not whether the possibility becomes manifested as action. It is possible to observe one of his artworks, decline the invitation to read about Spinoza, Deleuze, Bataille or Gramsci and still contemplate the possibility of doing so. This is what he means when he says that the work 'only provides the possibility of activation. It wasn't necessary that it should be activated – neither for the work nor for the spectator'.[77]

Hirschhorn is useful to illustrate autonomous art that is also politically committed. Hirschhorn repeatedly proclaims: 'I am an artist and not a social worker. My project is an art project that aims to assert its autonomy as an art project!'[78] Yet, at the same time, it is politically committed. Not in the sense that it carries overt, didactic, political messages (this would become moralist *Tendenzkunst*), but in the sense that he takes complete responsibility for what he does. For Hirschhorn, what artists do, where they stand, what positions they take and how this relates to others is intrinsically political. Hirschhorn takes absolute responsibility for the artwork—from its materials and formal properties to its ethical ramifications and, for him, this is 'doing art politically'.[79] This is equivalent to Sartre's assertion that writers must take responsibility for their political commitments, which are evident in the work, even in what they leave out. Sartre's notion of commitment carries direct political messages, which count towards (or against) the work's aesthetic estimation, but when these messages become propagandistic, coercive or fundamentally untrue they fatally undermine the work aesthetically and become *Tendenzkunst*. Likewise, Hirschhorn must assert his artistic autonomy to avoid descending into moralist *Tendenzkunst*. Militant art is committed in more confrontational and provocative ways than Hirschhorn, but both make ethical appeals to the viewer's freedom to engage with the work.

As an autonomist, Adorno is critical of art with overtly political messages or social commentary – yet, at the same time, he criticizes Sartrean commitment for only highlighting choices and not taking sides. He admits that commitment has an aesthetic advantage over *Tendenzkunst*, but he argues that the very fact it is not didactic 'renders the content to which the artist commits himself inherently ambiguous … it is itself nothing other than a declaration by a subject of his own choice or failure to choose'.[80] It seems that Adorno simultaneously wants art to remain autonomous from political commitments, while also being more politically effective. I will now take this position seriously by likening it to Rancière's regimes of art.

Dialectical ethicism and Rancière's regimes of art

Like Adorno, Rancière is sceptical about art with overtly political messages and, for some, this makes his concept of art inherently unpolitical. Political theorist Oliver Marchart, for example, has argued that declaring all art to be already political negates the need for overtly political art, let alone art activism.[81] He considers the emergence of new art activist practices since 2011 to invalidate Rancière's claims about art's autonomy from direct political messages. Indeed, he accuses him of propagating an antipolitical ideology that defangs truly radical art, which must necessarily get its hand dirty through its association with grassroots social movements. If Rancière's concept of art collapses into aesthetic autonomism, as Marchart suggests, then it is a flawed theory for assessing militant art. If Marchart's concept of 'conflictual aesthetics' relies on art activism's allegiance to 'propaganda practices, that is, of emerging oneself in the muddy waters of social struggle',[82] as he argues, then it collapses into moralist *Tendenzkunst*. This is equally defective as an aesthetic framework to appreciate militant art. A middle ground between these two positions is needed. With some adaption, Rancière's concept of political art allows for this.

Rancière divides art history into three 'artistic regimes' that can be understood in terms of the ethical criticism of art (see Table 2). Under the 'ethical regime,' art was judged according to how useful it is to society. This is evident in ancient Greece where there was no word for art because art was not seen as distinct from craft. Instead, the Greeks applied the word 'techne' to both arts and crafts. Art was judged by its moral message or educational benefit, which is akin to moralism. In Rancière's 'representative regime,' art became autonomous from, and superior to, craft. It became free from, and elevated above, common labour, but at a cost. Under this regime art became elitist, detached from everyday life and associated with the nobility or bourgeoisie. This is akin to aesthetic autonomism. The 'aesthetic regime' of art breaks down the various hierarchies of the other regimes: art above craft and art above life. Art can still be free from the restrictions of common craft (be autonomous), but it doesn't have to be shackled to any particular noble content that distinguishes it from everyday life. I contend that this is compatible with ethicism.

How, exactly, can art cease to be detached from everyday life, while maintaining its autonomy? Rancière's solution is to separate art and activism into two distinct practices of aesthetics and politics: 'Art's singularity stems from an identification of its own autonomous forms both with forms of life *and* with political possibilities. These possibilities can never be integrally implemented except at the price of abolishing the singularity of art, that of

Table 2

Ethical criticism of art	Moralism	Ethicism	Autonomism
Political criticism of art	Tendency (Tendenzkunst)	Commitment	Autonomy
Rancière's regimes of art	Ethical regime of images	Aesthetic regime	Poetic/ representative regime

politics, or both together.'[83] Although art and politics are related, they must be kept separate. This leads some to classify Rancière as an autonomist. For example, in a footnote, Marchart claims that, although Rancière's philosophical position is based on a tension between art's autonomy and heteronomy, he is 'clearly biased' towards autonomy and delegitimates heteronomy.[84] I contend that even though Rancière calls for art to maintain its autonomy from politics, this does not make him an aesthetic autonomist. Rather, his assertion should be understood as a call for art to remain autonomous from ethical and political ends, while still permitting political elements of an artwork to count towards its aesthetic assessment, which ethicism allows. We might summarize that all art is political, but only moralist *Tendenzkunst* is subordinated to a political purpose.

The complexity of Rancière's position becomes apparent when he states that it is incumbent upon artists to repair a broken social bond:[85] how is it possible for the artist to repair the broken social bond (be politically effective) and yet maintain art's singularity (autonomy)? Rancière offers the following advice:

> Suitable political art would ensure, at one and the same time, the production of a double effect: the readability of a political signification and a sensible or perceptual shock caused, conversely, by the uncanny, by that which resists signification. In fact, this ideal effect is always the object of a negotiation between opposites,

> between the readability of the message that threatens to destroy the sensible form of art and the radical uncanniness that threatens to destroy all political meaning.[86]

Rancière's 'double effect', which contains the paradoxical 'belief in art's autonomy *and* in it being inextricably bound to the promise of a better world to come',[87] is predicated on this dialectical tension between the 'message' (the political content of art activism) and the 'sensible form of art' (its aesthetic or formal qualities), the combination of which can itself constitute a new aesthetic. I term this new aesthetic 'dialectical ethicism' because, like ethicism, both aspects count towards art's aesthetic estimation. While Gaut is not especially interested in a dialectical tension between art's formal properties and its moral attributes (he just holds the opinion that both can count towards an artwork's aesthetic appreciation) only ethicism can accommodate Rancière's double effect. Both moralism and autonomism attempt to collapse this tension into a consensual order. Moralism does this by collapsing aesthetics into ethics, or art into everyday life; autonomism does this by subordinating ethics to aesthetics.

Dialectical ethicism is not the same as Rancière's double effect. For Rancière, suitable political art must disrupt 'the relationship between the visible, the sayable, and the thinkable without having to use the terms of a message as a vehicle'.[88] For him, political artworks must embody their politics within their form, rather than represent them in an overt message. Overt political messages are possible in dialectical ethicism, so long as they do not dominate the work and subordinate it to this message. That is, so long as the work does not lose the dialectical tension and become *Tendenzkunst*. Dialectical ethicism is not explicitly required in Badiou's rules, but it is an essential aspect of militant aesthetics. Militant art is necessarily both autonomous and must contain an event of confrontation of some kind. Sometimes this is manifested in Sartrean commitment, where the artists recognize that their work is inherently political and take aim. Confronted by the committed, militant, artwork, the viewer becomes aware of their free choice to engage with the political proposition, or not. This is not the same as propaganda art.

Neither Badiou nor Adorno nor Sartre explicitly address the question of the use of militancy as an aesthetic strategy. The theorist who comes closest is Bishop. We have already seen that she locates socially engaged art within an avant-garde art history (something which Kester contests). In the chapter that follows, I will argue that this avant-garde history is precisely what distinguishes militant art from its participatory and socially engaged cousins. While Bishop does not directly refer to militancy, she does consider the role of antagonism and conflict in participatory and relational art. I address this concept of 'relational antagonism' in the final section of Chapter 3.

3

Avant-garde militancy

This chapter provides an art historical context for the concepts outlined in Chapter 2, demonstrating that Marc James Léger's concept of *Vanguardia* is compatible with Badiou's notion of militant art. Léger argues that 'Vanguardism is work in leftist militancy',[1] and art 'that is in a concrete relationship with local political experiences and that creates a common space based on the existence of a strong ideology and strong organizations'.[2] This perspective is not only compatible with that of Badiou, it also aligns with militant art's affinity with the avant-garde. This connection with the avant-garde is further explored through Jacques Rancière's concept of the double effect (as outlined in Chapter 2) in relation to the writing of Guy Debord and the work of the Situationist International (1957–72). The chapter argues that militant art is part of an art history that stretches back to the provocative and antagonistic actions of the historical avant-garde, but that its identity really begins to develop in Situationism, particularly in the more radical splinter groups, Black Mask and King Mob. Finally, the chapter distinguishes militant art from relational, dialogic art and participatory art, which are positioned as today's official art. In opposition to Grant Kester's concept of art activism, militant art is demonstrated to embrace its hierarchical and autonomous avant-garde qualities.

Rancière's double effect and Debord's double movement

My concept of dialectical ethicism is predicated on Rancière's notion of the 'double effect' (see Chapter 2), but it also has an art historical predecessor in Debord's concept of the 'double movement'. The term 'double-movement' belongs to Gene Ray, who uses it to describe Debord's Situationist concept of revolutionary art that combines Dada negation with Surrealist realization. In *Society of the Spectacle*, Debord argued that where 'Dadaism sought to *abolish art without realizing it;* surrealism sought to *realize art without abolishing it*' and claimed that the Situationists had developed a 'single *transcendence of art*' that dialectically combined Dada negation and Surrealist realization.[3]

Debord's terms 'negation' and 'realization' merit unpacking. Ray provides a concise clarification:

> To transform art into a revolutionary weapon, it would first be necessary to 'abolish' – that is, negate, decompose, dissolve, liquidate – the bourgeois paradigm of art. This negative movement would disentangle the truth of art – its promise of happiness and utopian force – from the untruth of the commodity form. Set free, this truth would then be carried on in a positive and creative movement that goes beyond – transcends or 'realizes' – the bourgeois paradigm in the construction of new practices.[4]

Ray explains that for art to realize its revolutionary potential it would need 'in a simultaneous *double-movement*, to liquidate itself as a separate and separating sphere of activity and, linking up to a systemic critique of the social given, apply itself directly to the experimental decolonization of everyday life and the destruction of domination'.[5] This is different, but analogous, to Rancière's double effect, which is a tension between art's political message and its autonomous aesthetic form.

Boris Groys gives some illuminating art historical context that complicates the dialectical tension between art's negation and realization. He explains that the 'historical avant-garde was based on the equation – "negation is creation" – already formulated by Bakunin, Stirner, and Nietzsche. Iconoclastic images of destruction and reduction were destined to serve as the icons of the future'.[6] The term 'negation is creation' comes from Mikhail Bakunin (1814–1876) who asserted that the 'passion for destruction is a creative passion too'.[7] There is a tension already present in Dada's attempts to abolish art, because this can be seen as an inherently creative act. As Groys clarifies, the avant-garde artist 'was supposed to effectuate a radical break with the past, to erase, to destroy the past, to achieve a zero point of artistic tradition'.[8] At the same time, however, the iconoclastic gesture 'had the positive goal of revealing the materiality of the artwork, its pure presence',[9] and its place in art history. On the one hand, the Dadaists both abolished and realized art (because negation is creation), but, on the other, they failed to abolish art, because the 'iconoclastic and the new can only be recognized by the art historically informed, museum-trained gaze. This is why, paradoxically, the more you want to free yourself from the art tradition, the more you become subjected to the logic of the art historical narrative and to museum collecting'.[10] Both these positions complicate Debord's assertion that Dada abolished art without realizing it.

Negating (or abolishing) art can be understood as a form of 'active nihilism'. The term comes from Friedrich Nietzsche (1844–1900) who distinguished it from its passive counterpart.[11] The passive nihilist sees the realization of life's meaninglessness as an endpoint and either gives up or ascribes to religion or other mass movements to find meaning. The active nihilist has the same experience of despair, but, instead of succumbing, destroys all the false beliefs that purport to give meaning to life. This is compatible with Fox's militant dysphoria and Meinhof's concept of resistance, or putting an end to that which displeases her (see Chapter 2). The Dadaists exemplified active nihilism. They were negative and iconoclastic – ripping up old art to make the world reassess its values. This sense of negation can be understood as an active cleansing after a period of madness and destruction – sweeping away the mess that Western culture had produced. However, they were yet to formulate a (positive) political ideology. Referring to Sartre's notion of commitment (see Chapter 2), we might say that they waved loaded guns around, but did not point them at specific targets. For this reason, I consider Dada to be pre-political art that is yet to be committed to a cause.

The Dadaists also embodied Nietzsche's concept of 'ressentiment', where individuals 'develop a reactive and negative sentiment against the oppressive masters'.[12] For Nietzsche, this is an important stage for slaves in their political awakening through which they recognize their masters as 'evil'.[13] The Dadaists recognized the cultural values (including art) that delivered the mechanized slaughter and rampant nationalism of the First World War as absurd, if not evil. This is widely acknowledged in art history. For example, art historian David Hopkins explains how the Dadaists 'equated the war which was raging elsewhere with a conviction that the values attaching to pre-war art were largely decadent ones. If oil painting and bronze-cast sculpture had become synonymous with the interiors of high-class boudoirs, the Dadaists would assemble new structures from bits of paper or from pre-existing objects'.[14] Helena Lewis, the author of *Dada Turns Red: The Politics of Surrealism*, notes that Dada opposed such decadence in a negative sense 'with the intent of destroying [those bourgeois] aesthetic values'.[15]

Hopkins's and Lewis's accounts appear to corroborate Debord's assertion that Dada abolished bourgeois art, but failed to realize new forms, but Ray feels this assessment is harsh and that 'members of Berlin dada did make strong collective moves in this direction'.[16] Indeed, the Dadaists did turn away from traditional media such as painting and sculpture to pioneer photomontage, the readymade, improvised dance, cardboard costumes and performance art. Dada cabarets included nonsense poetry (see Chapter 2) and Marcel

Jancko, Tristan Tzara and Richard Huelsenbeck performed poetry simultaneously in English, French and German as a comment on the absurdity of the First World War.

After the war, the Dadaists, who had congregated in neutral Switzerland, went back to their home countries – creating Dada cells in Paris, New York, Cologne and Berlin, among other places. In Berlin, they created a march as an artwork. The procession followed the funeral root of Rosa Luxemburg (1871–1919) and Karl Liebknecht (also 1871–1919), who had been recently murdered following the Spartacist Uprising (5–12 January 1919). Gavin Grindon notes that the march 'combined religious, military, and political forms of public performance'.[17] For example, they played the old Prussian national anthem (a funeral lament) to parody *Friekorps* funeral marches. The march was a success. They had already sold all 7,600 copies of their satirical pamphlet-cum-newspaper *Jedermann sein eigner Fussball* (*Every Man His Own Football*) by the time they encountered the arresting officers on Alexanderplatz.[18] They also made an infamous exhibition called the *First International Dada Exchange* (1920). While the exhibition contained paintings, it was more of an installation, complete with a pig dressed in a Prussian military uniform hanging from the ceiling (John Heartfield and Rudolf Schlichter, *Prussian Archangel*, 1920).

Dada's pacifism (the movement was founded in neutral Switzerland by draft dodgers during the First World War) makes it an unlikely place to find the roots of militant art. However, a compelling case can also be made that it was militant. The aforementioned *Jedermann sein eigner Fussball* newspaper was 'confiscated immediately on publication for urging renewed revolutionary activities'.[19] The march demonstrates that the Berlin Dadaists were prepared to confront authority, break the law and even go to prison for their cause. The German satirical author Walter Mehring (1896–1981), who participated in the action, stated: 'We carried a supply of stickers saying "Hurrah Dada!" for sticking on the walls of police cells.'[20] Indeed, the Dadaist participants were all arrested, tried and sentenced to eight months in prison. All except for John Heartfield (born Helmut Herzfeld) escaped custodial sentences at appeal. Militant artists today draw upon Dada's revolutionary anti-authoritarianism. Despite being anti-war, anti-authoritarian and anti-nationalist, Dada was not opposed to violence. For example, Tate curator Matthew Gale recognizes that there was an ideological divide that 'was confirmed in Dada's … appearance at Socialist and Anarchist venues' where on occasion fighting broke out between the two groups.[21]

The reason the Surrealists failed to abolish bourgeois art is not that they 'wanted to hang on to their identities and prestige as (bourgeois) artists',[22] as Ray argues, but because of their lack of political commitment. This claim might seem counter-intuitive because, unlike the anarchic Dadaists, the Surrealists had well-known communist sympathies. John Heartfield and George Grosz were 'card-carrying members of the German Communist Party (KPD)',[23] and André Breton (once associated with Dada, but better known as the leader of the Surrealists) joined the French Communist Party in 1927. In 1929, he purged the Surrealist movement and issued the *Second Manifesto of Surrealism*, which affiliated them more explicitly with Marxism and in particular Trotskyist resistance to Stalinism. However, he had an uneasy relationship with communism and was careful to keep the group (if not its members) independent of the Communist Party. Consequently, Surrealist art was never politically committed in the sense that Sartre meant. The Surrealists found it easier to realize new forms of art than abolish bourgeois art precisely because their art was autonomous from politics.

The Situationists might have successfully combined Dada negation and Surrealist realization, as they claimed, but they appear not to have successfully combined art's political message and its autonomous aesthetic form in a dialectical tension (Rancière's double effect) – at least not for long. Their so-called artistic period only lasted from 1957 to 1961 and even then, their politics dominated. The Danish art historian Mikkel Bolt Rasmussen claims the Situationists 'sought to dominate the artistic media and use art as a propaganda tool'.[24] This is true, at least during their first phase. According to my schema set out in Chapter 2, propaganda ceases to be militant art and descends into moralist *Tendenzkunst* because it loses the aesthetic arm of dialectical ethicism. Rasmussen explains that in 1966 there was a 'split in the group resulting in the creation of a rival Situationist group led by Jørgen Nash who wanted to continue using art in the battle against a boring and repressive society'.[25] This wing of the Situationist International is less well known than the one run by Debord in France and Belgium, which from 1962 to 1968 entered its political period. They famously played a key role in the events leading up to May 1968.[26] Their artistic output during this time was limited to graffiti and posters printed from the occupied lithography studios of the École des Beaux-Arts.[27] This period also saw the publication of their two key texts, Debord's *Society of the Spectacle* and Vaneigem's *Revolution of Everyday Life* (both 1967). By 1972, they had disbanded.

Proto militant art: Black Mask and King Mob

Militant art is part of an art history reaching back to the provocative and antagonistic actions of the historical and neo-avant-gardes. Rasmussen notes that although the Situationist International 'was without doubt the organisation or group that not only most clearly addressed the activities of Dada and Surrealism after 1945 but developed a coherent theory of the avant-garde as well, they have not been part of the reception and discussion of the avant-garde and the neo-avant-garde'.[28] This is concerning for my narrative, which places the Situationists – and in particular their lesser-known, more militant, fringe groups – as the true successors to the historical avant-garde.

Even if radical groups like the Situationist International are accepted as neo-avant-garde, this does not solve my art historical narrative of militant art. Peter Bürger (1936–2017), one of the leading avant-garde theorists, famously dismissed the neo-avant-gardes of the 1950s and 1960s as inherently compromised. He condemned the neo-avant-garde as merely institutionalizing 'the *avant-garde as art* and thus negat[ing] genuinely avant-gardiste intentions', arguing that this is true:

> independently of the consciousness artists have of their activity, a consciousness that may perfectly well be avant-gardiste. It is the status of their products, not the consciousness artists have of their activity, that defines the social effects of works. Neo-avant-gardiste art is autonomous art in the full sense of the term, which means that it negates the avant-gardiste intention of returning art to the praxis of life.[29]

If Situationist art, as part of the neo-avant-garde, is 'autonomous art in the full sense of the term' then it cannot contain the dialectical tension between negation and realization or between art's message and its aesthetic form. If Bürger is right, then there is no hope for revolutionary Situationist art, or indeed for my claim that militant art has its roots in avant-garde art history. Consequently, it will be necessary to revise Bürger's narrative.

Hopkins correctly identifies that Bürger's book, which has so heavily defined the term neo-avant-garde, tends to focus on 'French Nouveau Réalistes and Andy Warhol'.[30] For example, Bürger questions the political efficacy of Warhol's screen prints, arguing that his 'painting of 100 Campbell soup cans contains resistance to the commodity society only for the person who wants to see it there. The Neo-avant-garde, which stages for a second time the avant-gardiste break with tradition, becomes a manifestation that is void of sense and that permits the positioning of any meaning whatever'.[31] Bürger is right to criticize such movements for being weaker and institutionalized manifestations of the historical avant-garde, but if he is looking for radically political art that seeks to fuse art and life, he is simply looking in the wrong place.

Alongside Nouveau Réalisme and Pop, other post-war movements that have been termed 'neo-avant-garde', such as Neo-Dada, Minimalism and Conceptual Art, are also poor successors to the radical political project of the historical avant-garde. Despite the name, even Neo-Dada fails to follow the historical avant-garde spirit, as Debord notes: Neo-Dadaists 'make careers out of repeating the style invented before 1920, exploiting each pumped-up detail and using it to develop an acceptable "style" for decorating the present world'.[32] Benjamin Buchloh and Hal Foster posit Daniel Buren and Marcel Broodthaers as examples of artists who potentially exemplify a return to praxis by critiquing art's institutional conditions.[33] Hopkins sets out a convincing argument that Bürger, Buchloh and Foster all have it wrong, arguing that they have neglected the more radical forms of art practice in the 1950s, 1960s and 1970s. However, Hopkins also neglects the more militant examples of the neo-avant-garde.

The true, militant, radical and political neo-avant-garde can be found in what Gavin Grindon terms the 'other neo-Dada'. He describes how art collectives emerged 'from European and American social movements, through groups such as the Provos, Kommune 1, Diggers, Yippies, Black Mask, and Chicago Surrealists'.[34] Elsewhere, he lists the following groups: 'In New York, the Yippies and Black Mask, in California the Diggers, in Chicago the Rebel Worker Group, in the UK King Mob.'[35] These groups were far from toothless and, according to Grindon, they inspired contemporary art activists such as The Yes Men, Reverend Billy and the Church of Stop Shopping, Etcétera, the Laboratory of Insurrectionary Imagination and the Centre for Tactical Magic, whom he collectively terms 'second-wave Situationism'.[36] Reverend Billy and the Church of Stop Shopping, Etcétera and the Laboratory of Insurrectionary Imagination all provide case studies that I analyse in Chapter 4.

Here, I will investigate Grindon's claim (that the true neo-avant-garde lies in this 'other neo-Dada') through an analysis of two of his interconnected and Situationist-related examples from the 1960s and 1970s: the New York-based anarchist art collective Black Mask (1965–8); and the radical English group King Mob, who were based in London in the late 1960s and early 1970s. Both examples were completely overlooked by Bürger, Foster, Buchloh and Hopkins, suggesting that Rasmussen was right: the Situationist International (and its more militant splinter groups) was overlooked in the classification of the neo-avant-garde.

Black Mask were primarily influenced by Futurism. The founding members (Ben Morea, Dan Georgakas, Ron Hahne) were inspired by its apparent science, elegance and violence and stories such as Marinetti beating up Wyndham Lewis in a toilet before hanging him by his coat collar on some spiked railings. The front cover of the first issue of their eponymous publication *Black Mask* expresses clear Futurist sympathies and tone:

> DESTROY THE MUSEUMS – our struggle cannot be hung on walls. Let the past fall under the blows of revolt … Goddamn your culture, your science, your art. What purpose do they serve? Your mass-murder cannot be concealed. The industrialist, the banker, the bourgeoisie, with their unlimited pretence and vulgarity, continue to stockpile art while they slaughter humanity … The machine, the rocket, the conquering of space and time, these are the seeds of the future, which freed from your barbarism, will carry us forward. We are ready … Let the struggle begin.[37]

The Futurists were arguably the most militant of all the historical avant-gardes. Futurist *serate* (soirees) resembled Dada cabarets, only they were more violent and more obviously politically charged. Hopkins acknowledges that the provocative elements of Dada cabaret owed much to these Futurist performances of 1909–13, although he claims their knowledge of Futurism was only limited.[38] Futurists shouted political slogans in the hope that they would provoke their audience, or even incite a riot. Bishop describes how they often ended with the audience throwing projectiles onto the stage,[39] and how Marinetti recognized the need to 'launch assaults from theatres and to introduce the fisticuff into the artistic battle'.[40]

The Futurists left the confines of the theatre and took to the streets to antagonize. They plastered walls with political posters and made leaflet drops from aeroplanes into Italian Piazzas.[41] They held Venice in particularly low regard, calling it a putrid city and a 'magnificent sore from the past' that needed curing.[42] They proposed to heal Venice by industrializing and militarizing it, filling in the canals and burning the gondolas so that it could dominate the Adriatic.[43] In 1910, they launched a three-year attack on the city and on one occasion, they hurled 80,000 copies of their leaflet 'Against Passé Venice' from the bell tower of Saint Mark's Square and gave a speech that resulted in a brawl.[44]

Bürger would admit that Black Mask possessed 'a consciousness that may perfectly well be avant-gardiste' but he would tell us to examine 'the status of their products' which, according to him, as part of the institutionalized neo-avant-garde, would be found wanting. Let us examine some of their actions and determine whether he was right. Black Mask's first act was to call for the closure of the Museum of Modern Art (MoMA). An account of this action, along with correspondence with MoMA, is published in *Black Mask* issue 1 (1966). The following exchange with Louise Crowley of MoMA gives an insight into their motivations:

> [From the Press Release sent to MoMA]
>
> On Monday, October 10 at 12.30 pm we will close the Museum of Modem Art. This symbolic action is taken at a time when America is on a path of total destruction, and signals the opening of another front in the world-wide struggle against suppression. We seek a total revolution, cultural, as well as social and political – LET THE STRUGGLE BEGIN.
>
> [Response from Louise Crowley at MoMA]
>
> Dear Friends ... why start with the museums??? ... if you want to end the slaughter, attack the war machine; if you oppose oppression, attack the state. Or is it really only the pretence and vulgarity – not the power – of the bourgeoisie that bugs you? If so, it's not enough to build a revolution on. The man-power it takes to

> overthrow a system won't come from the small minority of us that are concerned with culture; it'll come from the mass oppressed by power. And most of them don't give a damn whether the Museum of Modem Art is open or closed, or whether it exists at all; their problems are much more vital, like whether they're going to die in Vietnam or from a cop's bullet in the back.[45]

The exchange continued with Black Mask demonstrating their adherence to macro-political struggle. They declared Crowley's concerns about the workforce needing to overthrow the system to be misguided, seeing Black Mask not as part of a small minority, but rather a broader worldwide struggle. Rather than calling on others to 'start with museums', or join them in their attack on galleries, their proposed action against MoMA was intended to open another front in support of a greater struggle. They rejected Crowley's claim that only a small minority is concerned with culture on the grounds that she only considered Western, bourgeois culture. The Vietnamese, they argued, were fighting against the destruction of their culture as well as their land and 'African revolutionaries have always been concerned with the preservation of their culture in the face of colonialism'.[46] Domestically, in America, they saw the same kind of struggle within indigenous, Black and Hispanic communities.

Black Mask were temporarily successful: MoMA closed through fear of what they might do. Afterwards, they disrupted and sabotaged dozens of art lectures, exhibitions and Happenings.[47] In one action, they shot the poet Kenneth Koch (with blanks) as a symbolic assassination of the bourgeoisie.[48] They worked outside and in opposition to the gallery system. Such actions are hardly the typical behaviour of a group co-opted into the art world. They also embraced a dematerialized art practice that fused art (performance art) with life (protest). This is an excellent counterexample to Bürger's criticism of the neo-avant-garde as the negation of the historical avant-garde 'intention of returning art to the praxis of life'. Black Mask's militant institutional critique was about as far from being institutionalized as an art movement can be.

Black Mask not only attacked art institutions, they also attacked symbols of capitalism. One of their most infamous stunts, *The Mill-in at Macy's* (1967), involved organizing large numbers of people to enter the famous New York store in small groups posing as regular shoppers or staff. They aimed to cause maximum disruption during the store's peak business hours in the build-up to Christmas. They systematically moved stock around, stole and broke items, gave things away and released animals, such as dogs and cats, into the food department. Decoy activists identified themselves with flags and banners but made sure to stand alongside regular shoppers, who were subsequently roughed up and chucked out by security. In the last statement of the last issue of *Black Mask*, the group proclaimed 'We are thru being assimilated: we will no longer make objects/our Art is Life/our medium revolution/& in a world based on repression our only message is Liberation. Our function is to make the Left hip & to make the "Hippies" left/to bring the body & mind back together/the unification of social consciousness & body consciousness/the creation of the Total Man.'[49] This statement announces an intention that embodies everything that Bürger claims cannot exist in the neo-avant-garde, but once more we must analyse their actions, not their intentions.

Like the Situationists, Black Mask became increasingly political to avoid being co-opted by the art world. In late 1968, they went underground and reformed as Up Against the Wall Motherfucker (henceforth UAW/MF). Early UAW/MF members included those from Black Mask plus John Sundstrom, Alan Hoffman, Alan Phillips and Herbert Marcuse's stepson, Tom Newmann. UAW/MF's first action was to attack a major arts institution: they dumped garbage on the Lincoln Center of Performing Arts (New York, 1968). New York was in the middle of a garbage collection strike and, although the richer areas were able to hire private contractors to clear up the mess, the poorer neighbourhoods were in an increasingly desperate state. UAW/MF saw cultural production as somehow masking uncivilized practices present in American foreign and domestic policy. In their words, 'America turns the world into garbage, it turns its ghettos into garbage, it turns Vietnam into garbage.'[50] Therefore, they proposed a 'cultural exchange' of garbage for garbage. In doing so, they aimed to put an end to a situation where the garbage strike mess was excluded from sterile palaces of culture that distract from America's cultural attacks in Vietnam and on its own Black and indigenous peoples.

UAW/MF were even more militant than Black Mask. It was not long before MoMA became their target again. They objected to an exhibition called *Dada, Surrealism and Their Heritage* (1968). The inclusion of artists like Robert Rauschenberg offended UAW/MF enough to inspire them to organize 400 down-and-outs to storm the exhibition on the night of the private view, screaming obscenities, hurling paint, flour and smoke bombs.[51] For UAW/MF, the artists in the show lacked the revolutionary and militant credentials to demonstrate an avant-garde heritage. Their chief goal was the integration of art into the political programme of anarchist revolution.[52] From a certain perspective, we might consider that UAW/MF achieved this goal. They dispersed after many of their members were arrested and imprisoned for terms ranging from ten days to ten years. Fleeing New York City, UAW/MF spread across America attempting to form individual, independent cells. Running from the law might have been the catalyst, but the result was the propagation of their members and, consequently, their ideas, across the United States.

King Mob was a similar radical art collective that sought to emphasize the cultural anarchy and disorder that they saw as being ignored in Britain at the time. Like Black Mask, they were aware of, and inspired by, the historical avant-garde, but they were not simply institutionalized repetitions of it. Their most dominant members, the Wise brothers, studied art in Newcastle where they developed a combination of hard-edged politics derived from Russian nihilism with the disruptive anti-art potential of Dada and Surrealism. As the British-Indian novelist Hari Kunzru puts it, 'they found fundamental questions being asked about value, politics and the (lack of) social function of art' in texts such as Dmitry Pisarev's 'The Destruction of Aesthetics' (1865).[53] After they moved to London's Notting Hill district, the brothers met the English Situationists, two of whom (Chris Gray and Donald Nicholson-Smith) later became King Mob members. They also met, and worked with, John Barker who would subsequently serve seven years of a ten-year prison sentence for his role in the Angry Brigade – a far-left militant group described in the *Observer* as the 'British Baader-Meinhof' gang,[54] and by the *New Statesman* as having roots in French Situationism and 'London's anarchist King Mob group'.[55] These accounts link the ethical case for militancy predicated on the example of the Baader-Meinhof Gang (that I set out in Chapter 2) and the militancy of the Situationist International that I am arguing in this chapter.

Black Mask and King Mob embodied dialectical ethicism: there is a tension between the autonomy of their actions as art and their political commitment. They cannot be termed aesthetic autonomists, because of their avowed radical intentions to merge art and life to aid an anarchist insurrection. They completely negated traditional art media, turning political actions into artworks instead. Their militant acts distinguished King Mob and Black Mask from the Situationists. The Situationist International even expelled the English Situationists (the Wise Brothers plus Donald Nicholson Smith, Charles Radcliffe and art historian T. J. Clark) because they supported Black Mask.[56] King Mob had hung out with Morea in the 1960s and co-signed at least one statement by UAW/MF.[57] The accounts I have given so far make it difficult to accuse Black Mask and King Mob of being autonomists, less still toothless or co-opted.

Black Mask and King Mob cannot be termed moralist *Tendenzkunst*, because their actions contained poetic and humorous qualities not found in activism proper. Despite their anti-art rhetoric and aggressive behaviour, their actions were distinctly art, rather than purely political, actions. For example, inspired by Black Mask's *Mill-in at Macy's*, twenty-five members of King Mob stormed London's Selfridges, with one member (Ben Trueman) dressed as Santa Claus to distribute the store's toys to children. The police were called and forced the children to return their 'presents'. This action influenced Malcolm McLaren, who claimed to have been at the Selfridges event and who adopted and adapted their Situationist methods in the promotion of the Sex Pistols. In another action, the group stormed a private West London park dressed as gorillas and pantomime horses. They tore down its gating to open the park up as a children's playground in a critique of the ownership of public and private spaces. Although these examples are distinctly performative, they are also inherently political (in the manner that Sartre and Hirschhorn mean).

The examples of Black Mask and King Mob demonstrate how militant and politically radical the Situationists' trajectory could become, while still retaining its autonomy as art. Bürger's assertion that historical avant-garde protest became accepted as art does not necessarily mean that neo-avant-garde protest is inauthentic. It does not matter if Black Mask and King Mob are accepted as art. They were authentic in their politics as in their aesthetics. They used protest as part of their performance practices, causing mayhem in shops and invading private spaces to fill them with rubbish or convert them into public spaces. The fact that they attacked art galleries and art schools and that they were shunned by, and even expelled from, the Situationist International is evidence that these groups were no tame variety of protest co-opted by the art world: they constituted an authentic neo-avant-garde practice.

Relational antagonism and horizontalist community art

If the avant-garde is not unrepeatable, but was continued in a neo-avant-garde that included the Situationist International (as I argue), then could contemporary art activism be seen as a third-wave avant-garde? Grant Kester thinks not. In a letter to *Artforum*, he expressed surprise at Bishop's assertion 'that "politically engaged" collaborative art practice constitutes today's avant-garde'.[58] In the text that so angered Kester, Bishop had made the modest claim that art that uses 'social situations to produce dematerialized, antimarket, politically engaged projects that carry on the modernist call to blur art and life … arguably forms what avant-garde we have today'.[59] Instead, Kester feels that contemporary art activism is a continuation of 'traditions of performance art and socially engaged collaborative practice that extend back to the 1960s', working 'in collaboration with environmentalists, AIDs activists, trade unions, anti-globalization protestors, and many others'.[60] Black Mask and King Mob are not what Kester has in mind. They are part of a 1960s performance tradition that worked collaboratively, but with militant anarchist groups (like the Angry Brigade) and radical feminists (like Valerie Solanas, who shot Andy Warhol in 1968). Kester's 'surprise' seems a little strong and when he restated this case in *The One and the Many* (2011); he did so with toned-down language compared to that in his letter to *Artforum* in 2006. However, his underlying claim remains important for understanding militant aesthetics.

Kester must assert that art activism is not part of an avant-garde tradition, because avant-gardism is incompatible with his concept of 'dialogic aesthetics'. For him, key avant-garde features include 'a particular model of reception (based on shock or disruption), the a priori assumption of the viewer's perceptual or cognitive naïveté, and a belief in the intrinsically transgressive or liberatory power of desire or a-rational somatic experience'.[61] Traits such as these are too hierarchical and autonomous for his moralist stance (even though avant-garde calls to collapse art and life are the very opposite of protecting art's autonomy). Instead, Kester's dialogic aesthetics privileges the egalitarian relationship between artist and non-artist collaborator. To complicate things further, some of the collaborative art collectives that Kester promotes see non-hierarchical modes of collaboration (i.e. non-autonomist, participatory art) as a new kind of avant-garde. Kester is aware of the contradiction, as he quotes Park Fiction saying just this.[62] Kester is right to assert that this kind of art is not avant-garde (or militant), because it is moralist *Tendenzkunst*.

Just as Kester must deny that art activism is part of an avant-garde art history, I must affirm that it is. This is not to say that Kester's lineage of activism, performance art and social engagement in art does not also apply. It is an accurate description of the socially engaged, dialogic, art that he promotes. However, the model of reception based on shock or disruption that Kester identifies in avant-garde art, an approach that he deems outmoded and undesirable, plays a key role in the development of militant aesthetics. In fact, it is an essential element. Bishop's concept of 'relational antagonism' helps to explain how.

In contrast to Kester's dialogic variants of socially engaged art, with their penchant for making ameliorative or palliative measures in the here and now, relational antagonism is 'predicated not on social harmony, but on exposing that which is repressed in sustaining the semblance of this harmony'.[63] Bishop argues that 'a democratic society is one in which relations of conflict are sustained, not erased. Without antagonism, there is only the imposed consensus of authoritarian order – a total suppression of debate and discussion, which is inimical to democracy.'[64] Accordingly, relational antagonism tends towards a 'more complicated imbrication of the social and the aesthetic' that necessarily requires situations that involve conflict, where audiences are confronted with projects that they may not necessarily agree with.[65] For Bishop, antagonism, confrontation, shock, distress, frustration and absurdity can contribute to a work's aesthetic impact, just as moral traits count towards an artwork's aesthetic assessment in ethicism (see Chapter 2). Audiences can be antagonized, but antagonism can also be inherent within the work (as dialectical ethicism). In militant art, relations of conflict, provocation and imagination are sustained in dialectical tension with aesthetics.

Kester is right to assert that the avant-garde was hierarchical. Its groups had strict memberships and we have already seen there were purges and expulsions from the Surrealist and Situationist movements. Philosopher and cultural theorist Sadie Plant even describes the Situationists as bearing 'the illegitimate arrogance of political totalitarianism'.[66] Fluxus, another group I consider to be part of the neo-avant-garde, was equally hierarchical. Its founder, the Lithuanian-American artist George Maciunas (1931–1978), ran the movement in a totalitarian fashion. Any dissent from within the group was met with 'excommunication followed by public denunciation'.[67]

Militant aesthetics unashamedly embraces hierarchy against the mainstream preference for horizontalism (as defined in the introduction). Understandably, the predominant trend in post-war art has been anti-hierarchical. Art practices with rigid leadership structures (such as the avant-garde) or those that discriminate between artists (as authors of their artworks) and non-artists (who participate in the artwork under the artist's direction) were viewed with suspicion and began to fall out of favour. My example of the Turner Prize 2021 in Chapter 2 provides a contemporary example of this inclination. Public Movement's hierarchical leadership structure (described in Chapter 1) bucks this trend, although they are reticent to be described as such and have taken steps to become more egalitarian. Nonetheless, they are part of a wider move towards militancy after 9/11.

Militant aesthetics does not stand alone against horizontalist egalitarianism. Žižek calls for us to 'fearlessly follow Badiou's suggestion: in order to effectively awaken individuals from their dogmatic "democratic slumber", from their blind reliance on institutionalized forms of representative democracy, appeals to direct self-organization are not enough: a new figure of the Master is needed'.[68] He calls on us to reject 'anarchic horizontalism' and instead 'shamelessly reassert the idea of "vanguard", when one part of a progressive movement assumes leadership and mobilizes other parts.'[69] This is a recurring position in Žižek's thought. We can see this distinction between effective vanguards and impotent horizontalism throughout his work. For example, on the *Gilets Jaunes* (yellow vest) movement he writes that their 'fatal limitation resides precisely in their much-praised "leaderless" character, their chaotic self-organization.'[70] Elsewhere he notes that 'all the imagined democratic-multitude-grassroots changes "from below" are ultimately doomed to fail, so the only way to effectively break the vicious cycle of global capitalism is some kind of "militarization".'[71] These are political reasons, but a similar case can be made for aesthetics.

Hierarchically leading by example provides a better model for militant art than anarchic, horizontalist, participatory art. An analysis of two seemingly similar neo-avant-garde practices reveals why. For militant aesthetics, the most important distinction between Fluxus Happenings and Situationist 'constructed situations' is that the former was concerned with activating audiences, while all Situationist forms of constructed situations (unitary urbanism, psychogeography, the *dérive*) involved leading by example. Happenings can therefore be seen as an early form of participatory art, while the Situationists embraced vanguardism, aiming to invoke a revolution 'from capitalist spectacle to non-authoritarian communism.'[72] In this sense, they were hierarchical: elevating themselves above their participants. Although art historian Frances Stracey (1963–2009) declared that constructed situations were anti-hierarchical, all she meant was that they were collectively planned and developed by members of the Situationist International, as equals.

There are similarities between these two neo-avant-garde practices. Jon Erickson notes that Happenings 'were also the creation of "situations" by artists and their friends', and that both Happenings and constructed situations were 'concerned with either evading or confronting a commercialized art establishment coupled with an administered culture' and both were inspired by

Dada and Surrealism 'insofar as they attempted to eliminate the distinction between art and life'.[73] Both Happenings and constructed situations adhere to Badiou's rule to move from representation to presentation, in the sense that they do not make things, but make things happen; both encourage participants to be mindful of their surroundings and pay attention to everyday activities, *as aesthetic experiences*.

Despite their similarities, only the constructed situation retains the possibility of macro-political change. Constructed situations were developed along a Marxist vanguard model of resistance to the spectacle. As Stracey explains, the Situationists demanded an art with 'an equal commitment to a revolutionary politics aimed at overturning capitalism'.[74] They were committed to a total transformation of life and constructed situations were precursory events that enabled the 'ground clearing required for the revolutionary reconstruction of a non-spectacular society'.[75] She also declares that the Situationists were inspired by Marx's idea that 'history is made, albeit under conditions that are not chosen. In other words, history is constructed from its situatedness'.[76] By contrast, Happenings were more often organized along anarcho-horizontalist lines. Indeed, Erickson notes that in Happenings, 'anarchy appears to be the guiding principle. Kaprow says as much in a 1958 manifesto'.[77] Although, it should be recognized that Kaprow's Happenings were 'scored', so he maintained a semblance of authority and control over his participants. Erickson acknowledges this when he notes that in some Happenings 'audiences were seduced or coerced into active participation'.[78] In these cases, they transgressed from Sartre's ethical appeal into didacticism.

The Situationist critique of Happenings is useful to demonstrate why participatory art is not militant. They opposed Fluxus Happenings, despite their foundational idea of 'constructing situations' being strikingly similar. Debord compared Happenings to team projects reminiscent of the capitalist co-option of the worker.[79] Similarly, Vaneigem warned that in this kind of participation 'the ultimate logic of the happening and its derivatives is to supply the society of masterless slaves … with the spectatorless spectacle it will require'.[80] Whether or not Debord and Vaneigem treated Happenings fairly (it is unclear whether they ever visited a Happening in France, let alone in America), their concerns help to conceptualize two kinds of event: one that is vanguard and retains a macro-political belief in changing society; the other participatory and micro-political.

Debord's and Vaneigem's criticisms are evocative of critiques about participatory art. The argument usually goes that artists emancipate audiences by encouraging them to participate and, therefore, all participation is political, since if you are participating you are producing rather than passively consuming. Bishop's argument – that although participatory artists oppose capitalism in principle,[81] in practice, they adopt many of its facets and forms, such as 'networks, mobility, project work, affective labour',[82] – recalls Debord's and Vaneigem's accounts of Happenings as just rehashing the tropes of capitalism. Bishop reminds us that in reality television shows 'ordinary people can participate both as would-be celebrities and as the voters who decide their fate'.[83] The same is true for social networking sites or any other platform that relies on user-generated content. Far from activating the masses, such participation merely delivers 'an endless stream of egos levelled to banality'.[84] Bishop also reminds us that corporate awaydays often include team building exercises where employees are encouraged to participate in games and activities.[85] She posits that the end goal is not to create emancipated teams, but to improve worker efficiency or morale.[86] These examples, she explains, make us question whether participatory art is formally any more political or oppositional than any other kind of art.[87] The proponents of Happenings (Allan Kaprow, Jean-Jacques Lebel, Claus Oldenburg and Yayoi Kusama) began this trend of abdicating responsibility to participants through the well-meaning, but ultimately patronizing, intention of 'empowering' them.

Thomas Hirschhorn works in the avant-garde tradition of constructed situations rather than the participatory tradition of Happenings. He confronts his audience with a possibility, stating that rather than 'triggering the participation of the audience, I want to implicate them. I want to force the audience to be confronted with my work. This is the exchange I propose.'[88] Hirschhorn's art avoids becoming didactic *Tendenzkunst* by appealing to his audience's freedom to participate in the artwork. For him, confrontation is key but it is up to the viewer how they respond. To take one example, for *Bataille Monument* (2002) he employed immigrant taxi drivers to shuttle art lovers between Documenta 11, in the German city of Kassel, and a nearby social housing estate where he employed twenty to thirty residents to work in the library, snack bar, television studio and public sculpture that comprised his monument to Georges Bataille (1897–1962). Initially, the work appears to rely on the public visiting the library, reading books on Bataille or eating in the snack bar. However, Hirschhorn is adamant that the artwork still exists even if nobody participated, or even looked at it. For him, artists cannot rely on somebody else to complete the work, they must 'take the responsibility for the artwork, including responsibility for its failure'.[89] While this work superficially resembles relational and participatory art, upon closer inspection it is politically committed: Hirschhorn hierarchically leads by example, taking responsibility for the work and making Sartrean ethical appeals (as described in Chapter 2).

Hirschhorn is not a militant artist (at least, not according to the definition I set out in Chapter 2). I include his example in this chapter to illustrate militant art's opposition to participatory art and to demonstrate how this is compatible with Sartre's notion of commitment (see Chapter 2). Hirschhorn even declares that to judge an artwork's success or failure by its level of participation is 'totally delusional'.[90] Militant art is not participatory: it hierarchically leads by example. Hirschhorn exemplifies how militant artists can adopt vanguard leadership roles in relation to their audiences, without falling into the moralist *Tendenzkunst* trap. I shall develop this concept in the following chapter when I consider provocations as 'propaganda of the deed'.

4

Tactical confrontations

This chapter explores instances of militant art that emerged after the global financial crisis of 2008 and interprets them as contemporary manifestations of leading by example, as previously discussed in Chapter 3. These instances are approached as indicative of a renewed interest in macro-politics by employing Michel de Certeau's terminology, 'the strategic' and 'the tactical'. By examining various militant art actions, the argument put forward is that short-term tactical interventions are militant, whereas long-term 'strategic' interventions risk falling into Badiou's notion of 'official art' (as discussed in Chapter 2). Counter-intuitively, it will be demonstrated that tactical interventions are in fact more strategic because they preserve macro-political possibilities, whereas strategic interventions become mere ameliorative official art. Subsequently, later examples of militant art are evaluated through the lens of flash mob theory, which emphasizes the potency of short-term actions in revealing and disrupting power structures. Prior to delving into the Global Financial Crisis of 2008, a case study from Argentina, where the financial collapse reached its peak six years prior to the United States and Europe, is analysed to contextualize the following discussion.

Rage against the bank

Art activism after the Argentine Great Depression (1998–2002)

In 2002, the Argentine collective Etcétera (established in 1998) made an infamous action on the coat-tails of the Argentine Great Depression (1998–2002) and the insurrection against the International Monetary Fund's imposition of austerity measures on Argentina. The rebellion held true to its slogan *¡Que se Vayan Todos!* (Out with Them All!), toppling four different governments in a fortnight. Etcétera's response, the *Mierdazo*, or 'shit storm',[1] was an unusual performance that began by installing a red carpet and a toilet outside the Congress building in Buenos Aires while the Argentine government debated austerity measures inside. A bizarre ceremony followed where Etcétera member Antonio 'Checha' O'Higgins, dressed wearing a suit and a sheep mask, sat on the toilet and excreted while wearing a sign that read *Me Cago en el Sistema* (I Shit on the System) (see Figure 4.1).

The *Mierdazo* was participatory. Etcétera invited the public to defecate in the toilet, bag their excrement and deliver it to the gates of the Argentine National Congress. Curiously, there was no shortage of takers and the action was widely reported on Argentine television. When a journalist asked a middle-aged woman why she was participating, she responded that the government 'treats us like shit, but we're not shit. We're people' (my translation). The event culminated in the public angrily hurling their faeces at the Congress building and later, as Brian Holmes testifies, there was 'a similar assault on transnational banks like HSBC'.[2] Fatefully, it was a transnational bank that funded me to travel to Buenos Aires to interview the group in 2017.[3]

The seemingly spontaneous uptake during the *Mierdazo* was actually the result of a pre-planned performance that a neighbourhood action group voted for, as Etcétera founding member Federico Zukerfeld explains:

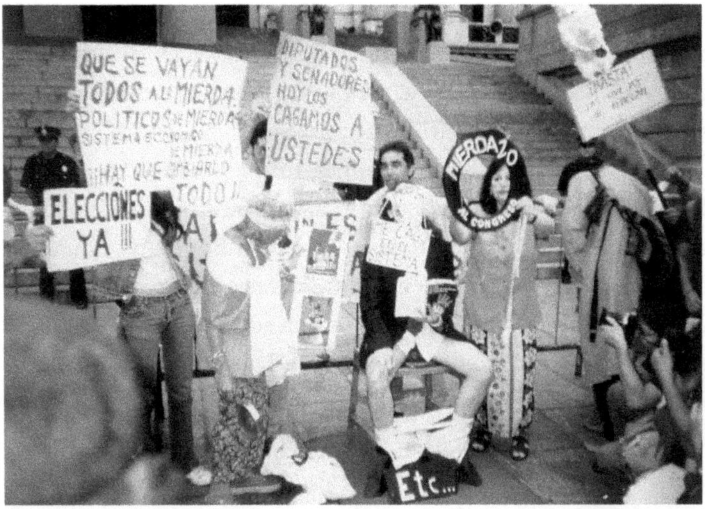

Figure 4.1 Etcétera, *El Mierdazo*, 2002. © Etcétera. Reproduced with the permission of the artist.

> After the uprising [against austerity], people had created popular assemblies in each neighborhood, and these all met up together every Sunday. These assemblies were huge gatherings where everybody voted – voted not to pay the external debt, for example. So [Etcétera member Polo Tisieira] went to this interneighborhood assembly and made the proposal for *El Mierdazo*: now that we had nothing, we should give back to the politicians the only thing we had left, our shit.[4]

This origin story leads interdisciplinary scholar Jennifer Ponce de Léon (formerly Jennifer Flores Sternad) to consider the social relations in the *Mierdazo* as emblematic of the 'horizontalist politics operative in the sociopolitical conjuncture of which it formed a part'.[5] Writer, activist and former member of the Occupy Wall Street legal team Marina Sitrin explains that the origin of the term 'horizontalism' comes from Argentina during the Great Depression.[6] In her book *Horizontalism: Voices of Popular Power in Argentina*, she describes how the Spanish word *horizontalidad* came to 'embody the new social arrangements and principles of organization of these movements in Argentina'.[7] The movements Sitrin refers to include occupations of factories by workers who then ran them collectively, as well as the kinds of neighbourhood action groups that Zukerfeld describes earlier in the text.

These are typical, but misleading, readings of Etcétera's work. I contend that Etcétera operate in a vanguard, not horizontalist, manner. Take these statements from the group's founding members: 'We always defend the existence of political parties. The fact that there are many tells us that society is alive, that there exists [*sic*] different points of view',[8] and 'The strategy that has to be followed, we said, is to not abandon the flags, the pamphlets, the megaphone, the figure of the leader, but we are going to question them'.[9] This vision hardly reflects the leaderless, autonomous, directly democratic movement-building that characterizes horizontalism.[10]

Etcétera's vanguardism stems from their Surrealism. Ana Longoni (Director of Public Activities at the Museo Reina Sofía, Madrid) explains that Etcétera even 'define themselves as Surrealists'.[11] When I invited them to speak as visiting artists at the University of Lincoln in 2022, they recounted Surrealism's role in their foundation. The group was formed while squatting a house that belonged to the Surrealist artist Juan Andralis (1924–1994), who was part of the Paris group led by André Breton during the 1950s. Breton sent him back to Argentina to establish Surrealism there and he promptly set up a print shop and publishing house in his home. Initially unaware of the house's connection with Surrealism, Etcétera discovered letter presses and print facilities alongside Surrealist texts and memorabilia. In their artist talk, Etcétera explained how Surrealism, and the historical avant-garde more generally, was out of fashion in the 1990s under the dominant 'end of History' viewpoint. Against this trend, they deliberately rekindled the Surrealist tradition, which goes some way to contextualize the formal aspects of the *Mierdazo*.

The *Mierdazo* was an avant-garde instance of leading by example. Zukerfeld explained how Etcétera had to convince others to go along with the action. He described how Etcétera initially struggled to gain support from local art groups and had to convince them by contextualizing the act, citing Piero Manzoni's use of excrement as an art historical precedent.[12] A closer art historical precedent can be found in an action by UAW/MF, who dragged a toilet to St Marks Place (New York City) and 'held a community "shit-in" which proved highly popular until a squad of infuriated; blushing, highly Protestant fuzz arrived and, perfect symbolical [*sic*] end of a perfect symbolical [*sic*] evening, literally beat it to pieces with their nightsticks'.[13] Like UAW/MF, Etcétera designed a highly unusual spectacle; unlike UAW/MF, they convinced their public to participate in the action. Despite their aforementioned democratic efforts, Etcétera still proposed and planned the action, which was performed by a relatively small, vanguard, group led by O'Higgins.

The *Mierdazo* was macro-political. Zukerfeld proclaims, 'The militant subject is basic for us. The basis of a militant attitude is: first, the commitment to the cause; second, solidarity; third, to value your colleague as yourself, because you're struggling for a collective way out; fourth, coherence; fifth, to fight for a large scale change, not only small scale.'[14] Their chosen medium (shit) is something we all have in common, but at the same time defecation is usually a private act. By bringing it out into the open, Etcétera socialized the issue of how elites shit on the people, cutting across identity politics to create a unified subjectivity – or as Ponce de León says, the *Mierdazo* allegorizes 'a move from individualized subjective feelings and the atomized confines of private spaces and private property (e.g. individuals' feelings about their own diminished savings) toward collective action that creates a common space for refusal, based in similar experiences of exploitation and in a shared and unmediated political agency'.[15] This would not have been possible if the event had been planned in a truly horizontalist, micro-political, manner.

The *Mierdazo* was performed in the hope of inspiring a popular uprising. Etcétera considered the action as a kind of catalyst for protest and an 'outlet for a drive that was already present in the people'.[16] They tapped into the insurrectionary spirit of 2001 in a manner comparable to Che Guevara's *foco* theory of revolution through guerrilla warfare, most famously put into action during the Cuban Revolution (1953–9). Guevara conceptualizes *foco* theory as where a vanguard leads by the example of acts of terrorism to inspire a popular uprising.[17] Both *focos* and the *Mierdazo* were vanguard militant actions that encouraged citizens to take arms (guns in the case of the former; bags of poo in the latter) and take aim at the government to remove the administration from power.

None of the artists I interviewed for this book cited *foco* theory as an influence on their practice. In line with the tenets of the Global Justice Movement and Occupy, many of them are sceptical about Marxism and identify with anarchism and horizontalism instead. Anarchism and horizontalism have significant crossovers. For example, the anarchist historian Mark Bray describes how 'horizontalism and anarchism overlap in their advocacy of federal, directly democratic, direct action-oriented, autonomous organizing' and he notes how unsurprising it is 'that many anarchists have thrown their lot in with the horizontalist mass movements of the past decades in order to safeguard and promote their anti-authoritarian tendencies'.[18]

Nonetheless, recognizing that anarchism and horizontalism are not the same is key to understanding militant aesthetics. While Argentine protesters forced out four successive governments, their horizontalism lacked a unified vision, a method for insurrection and a shared understanding of the history of class struggle. The same could be said of later horizontalist movements such as Occupy or the Egyptian Revolution of 2011. Andrew Flood, of the Irish Workers Solidarity Movement, argues that horizontalism 'lacks power except the power of the individual bodies putting themselves in harm's way … In Argentina the power of the unemployed assemblies rested only in the power derived from blocking motorways and bringing the flow of commerce to a halt.'[19] He concludes that these manoeuvres are 'tactics of protest and not of transformation',[20] or as Meinhof would put it, protest not resistance (see Chapter 2).

Horizontalism's powerlessness stems from its belief that any kind of pre-planned vision is authoritarian and will therefore lead to tyranny. With no sense of shared vision, strict adherence to consensus decision-making and the veneration of all minority voices, horizontalist movements grind to a halt. Bray correctly identifies that consensus decision-making 'works best when all members of a group have a shared sense of purpose'.[21] Even when Occupy Wall Street modified consensus to require only 90 per cent, rather than 100 per cent agreement, 'when members of a body are working at cross purposes it only takes 11% to shut down the objectives of the other 89%'.[22] Bray points out that 'consensus has become so ubiquitous in certain horizontalist/anarchist circles that some don't realize that the majority of anarchists throughout history have implemented majoritarian voting'.[23] Flood concurs, adding that horizontalism 'includes aspects of what are sometimes incorrectly described as anarchist methods, in particular consensus decision-making, which actually entered radical politics via Quaker influence on the peace movement of the 60's'.[24]

While both anarchism and horizontalism are opposed to political parties and sceptical about creating detailed political programmes, anarchists generally have a shared vision of a cooperative society and expect to achieve this through insurrectionary means. A shared vision and methodology (insurrection) enable anarchists to lead by their example (towards the vision) in the manner described in Chapter 3 and this accounts for the anarchist practice of propaganda of the deed. The concept of propaganda of the deed is similar to Guevara's *focos,* in that both lead by example. It was first theorized by Carlo Pisacane (1818–1857) in his 'Political Testament' (1857). The Anarchist Library defines propaganda of the deed as a 'specific political action meant to be exemplary to others and serve as a catalyst for revolution … including bombings and assassinations aimed at the ruling class, but [it] also had non-violent applications'.[25]

In 2008, the UK government published a report that sought to provide 'a new definition of Propaganda of the Deed relevant to today's fast-changing political landscape where social and political agendas are interpreted and shaped by global media'.[26] The authors defined propaganda of the deed as 'an act of violence whose signal and/or extreme nature is intended to create an ideological impact disproportionate to the act itself'.[27] The report concluded that propaganda of the deed was 'more than an operational technique intended to produce "shock and awe"' and that it is not a single event, but 'part of a process of narrative construction, reinforcement and confirmation through deeds'.[28]

Propaganda of the deed is a form of leading by example and, as such, it is necessarily undemocratic. Contrary to her statements about the *Mierdazo*'s radically democratic mode of organization,[29] and her previous assertion that it was emblematic of the horizontalist politics of its time, Ponce de Léon also likens the *Mierdazo* to a formal rejection of representational democracy and the adoption of direct action.[30] This is more compatible with propaganda of the deed and, I think, a description that Etcétera would recognize. They lead by example in the manner of propaganda of the deed, rejecting representational democracy in favour of direct action.

Art activism after the global financial crisis (2007–8)

Etcétera's literal move, from targeting the government with bags of shit to targeting banks, prefigured a conceptual shift in art and activism after the financial crisis of 2008. It was not for nothing that Occupy took place on Wall Street in New York City, rather than Pennsylvania Avenue in Washington, DC, and in Britain, Occupy's original target was the London Stock Exchange in Paternoster Square, rather than Parliament Square in Westminster (as it transpired, Paternoster Square is private property, so the camp had to relocate to nearby St Paul's Cathedral). At the same time, art activists followed Etcétera's lead and began to target banks. The

Laboratory of Insurrectionary Imagination (henceforth LabofII) was one of the first, and their actions had avant-garde traits. For example, *The People vs The Banksters* (2009) was a snowball fight targeting bankers at the Royal Bank of Scotland in the City of London. It evoked Futurist provocations such as their *serate*, or when they instigated a brawl in Venice (see Chapter 3), only the LabofII action was more humorous. Most bankers watched from behind large glass windows and doors, while some accepted the challenge from the forty-strong mob of artists. City police looked on: at times amused, at times indifferent. On the one hand, this was just a game but on the other it was also a metaphor for how bankers had been recklessly playing with people's money, destroying the economy and the climate in the process.

In that same year, LabofII launched *C.R.A.S.H. – A Postcapitalist A to Z* at the G20 summit protests (London, March 2009) where they distributed 'postcapitalist' badges. Later, they launched a two-week, free 'crash course' linking art, activism and permaculture and a series of street interventions. *C.R.A.S.H. Culture* was composed of eight postcapitalist interventions. These actions included displaying effigies (in the Dada vein of *The Trail of Maurice Barrès*, 1921) of bankers' decapitated heads made from clay, wax, hair and severed sheep necks impaled on pikes (see Figure 4.2). In keeping with English custom, the heads were covered with tar to preserve them and displayed on London Bridge, the traditional place for traitors' heads. Other actions included building temporary living spaces in London's financial district; a bicycle-powered kitchen for cooking foraged city plants; a workshop making radios out of junk and thirteen ironic bench plaques with messages such as 'In loving memory of easy credit' or 'this bench can be used as a barricade'.

The University for Strategic Optimism (henceforth UfSO) was another British group that made militant actions in response to the financial crisis. Although their work was expressly about cuts to education, they directly blamed the banking bailout for the threefold increase in tuition fees and the end of the Educational

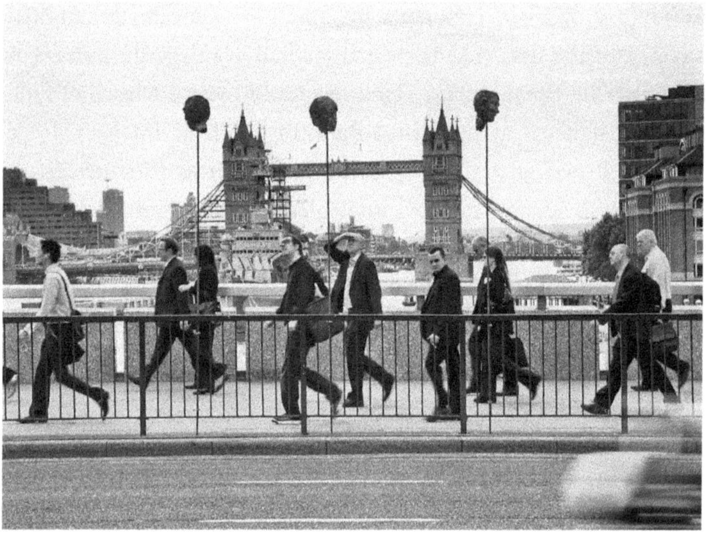

Figure 4.2 Laboratory of Insurrectionary Imagination, David Fryer's 'Severed Heads' as part of *C.R.A.S.H. Culture*, 2009. © Laboratory of Insurrectionary Imagination. Photograph by Immo Klink. Reproduced with the permission of the artist.

Maintenance Allowance. They reasoned that state-owned banks were an appropriate site for defunded higher education: if university departments would have to shut down or raise fees to the point of putting off poorer students, then the UfSO would have to occupy banks to give their 'lectures'. The inaugural lecture was held at the Borough High Street branch of Lloyds TBS (London, 24 November 2010). A large group descended on the bank, like a flash mob, and unveiled a banner bearing the university's name in front of 'Dr Etienne Lantier' who read a statement reassuring the public that 'nobody will be harmed during this lecture'. A security guard immediately approached him and told him to stop or he would call the police. A meek 'boo' broke the silence before the crowd erupted into chatter and the guard lost his air of authority. After some kerfuffle, the lecture went ahead. At times the crowd applauded, at times they shouted out answers to Lantier's questions and the lecture turned into a sort of rally. A policeman arrived before the lecture finished, but struggled to enter the building as it was so crowded. A 'course syllabus' was distributed with details of lectures 'to be delivered at places yet to be disclosed' and Dr Lantier invited everybody to join the university.

While the *Mierdazo* was inspired by the Surrealists and LabofII's actions had Futurist and Dadaist influences, the UfSO had strong Situationist sympathies. When I interviewed 'Professor Effra', he was keen to clarify that their actions were not performance art, but political actions – akin to strikes. Indeed, the UfSO are considerably removed from gallery-based work and they do not even consider themselves to be artists. They do, however, work in the avant-garde anti-art tradition and they draw on Situationist techniques, such as the constructed situation described in Chapter 3, and they even cited the movement as an inspiration in my interview with them. They raised questions about public and corporate space that would come to dominate protest discourse during the Occupy movement, especially when its London iteration was unable to occupy the land outside the London Stock Exchange because it is privately owned.

The UfSO demand (that the banks end their bonuses and repay the public what they received in the bailout) was a symbolic attack on the economic structures and systems that caused the crash and the subsequent cuts in education funding. This sentiment is echoed in the art criticism of Sebastian Loewe who condemns so-called Occupy art for focusing on the actions of individuals (the 1 per cent) who, in most cases acted perfectly legally. Loewe identifies a moralistic element in Occupy's central claim 'we are the 99%' that conceptualizes the so-called 1 per cent as 'the other' (greedy bankers, for example).[31] Their behaviour might well have been immoral, but the system encouraged and rewarded risky investments with large bonuses. Therefore, he contends that blaming individuals only moralizes a debate where critiquing the system is required. This necessitates retaining the notion that a return to macro-politics is possible. If the political system cannot be changed, then critiquing it merely becomes a symbolic rant that descends into moralistic attacks on individuals (who may well be culpable but whose prosecution, or persecution, will not prevent future transgressions).

Beyond Argentina in 2001 and Britain around 2009–10, artists were also prepared to break the law in performative actions against multinational banks in America and France. In 2012 and 2013, Reverend Billy and the Church of Stop Shopping accused banks of putting profit ahead of environmental concerns. Wearing yellow masks depicting the golden toad, a species that they say has become extinct because of major banks' investment in fossil fuels, they targeted JP Morgan Chase – according to Reverend Billy, the bank with the highest greenhouse gas emissions in the world. At Chase, Reverend Billy's followers paraded around, stopping to bow and shout 'earthallujah' while the reverend gave a sermon, from inside a small tent they had erected, to educate Chase customers about their bank's investments and to urge them to withdraw their funds. The congregation placed pot plants around a tent from which the reverend emerged, megaphone in hand, and announced he was leaving them as a gift. The *Guardian* reported that Reverend Billy and choir director Nehemiah Luckett were arrested and charged with riot, trespass, unlawful assembly and disorderly conduct, for which they faced up to a year in prison.[32]

In 2017, the controversial Russian performance artist Pyotr (Petr) Pavlensky set fire to the Banque de France in Place de la Bastille, Paris (*Lighting*, 2017) declaring, 'The Banque de France has taken the place of the Bastille, and bankers have taken the place of monarchs'.[33] He was arrested, tried and sentenced to three years in prison. Pavlensky had previously set fire to the FSB (formerly KGB) headquarters in Moscow (*Threat*, 2015). Incredibly, he took time to pose for artistically composed photographs in front of the flames on both occasions. In 2016, Pavlensky was awarded the Václav Havel

International Prize for Creative Dissent (Czech Republic) and Russia's Innovation Art Prize, but both were withdrawn following his endorsement of lawbreaking and violence as valid tactics to combat oppression. By then, Pavlensky had already donated his prizemoney (around £10,000) to the Primorye Guerrillas, who were held in a Russian jail for murder at the time, meaning he effectively funded armed resistance against the state.

Pavlensky selects targets in areas with heavy police surveillance to force an event of confrontation and the subsequent arrests become part of the artwork. Like Hirschhorn, he declares himself to be an artist, not an activist.[34] Both Hirschhorn and Pavlensky assert their artistic autonomy, both take full responsibility for their actions and both make ethical invitations to third parties' freedom to complete the work. In Pavlensky's case, the ethical appeal is confrontational. As Anastasia Chaguidouline, curator of public programmes at Casino Luxembourg, notes, Pavlensky 'does not see himself as an idealist, nor an activist. As an artist, he is doing political art that functions within the apparatus of power, forcing the power to reveal itself.'[35]

I conceptualize these actions against banks as the first great withdrawals of rage against the rule of money and a return to macro-politics. I take the term 'withdrawal of rage' from the German philosopher Peter Sloterdijk, who posited that rage should be understood as a form of capital – something that could be spent or invested.[36] He describes how rage for justice and recognition is historically 'invested' in 'rage banks', to be 'withdrawn' at a later date. With the collapse of the great central rage banks of old – ideologies such as Christianity and communism that offered the promise of eternity in paradise or a utopian society on earth – there was only one place left to invest rage: in the neoliberal promise of material rewards through deregulation.

I use the term 'rule of money' to refer to the creeping marketization of everything from British universities (through tuition fees) to the NHS (through private finance initiatives or PFIs) – both New

Labour Policies that indicate how even the Left failed to imagine structural alternatives to neoliberalism. We could privatize those things, it seemed, while effectively nationalizing banks. Between the end of History (following the fall of the Berlin Wall in 1989 and the disintegration of the Soviet Union in 1991) and the global financial crisis of 2008, free market capitalism dominated and appeared untouchable. However, there was a growing sense of dissatisfaction building up and bubbling away under the surface. The Marxist sociologist John Holloway claims that the object of this rage was the rule of money increasingly controlling everything from health and education to housing and the environment.[37] Following Holloway, the object of rage for the art activists I have been analysing was the rule of money; following Sloterdijk, their actions are evidence that they had nowhere to invest it.

As the banking system collapsed, so too did the last great ideological rage bank. As political and cultural theorist Mark Fisher (1968–2017) argued, what happened in 2008 'was the collapse of the framework which has provided ideological cover for capitalism since the 1970s. After the bank bailouts, neoliberalism has, in every sense, been discredited.'[38] Sloterdijk predicted that without the 'central rage banks' to connect different people across continents there would be a retreat into 'subcultural narratives' such as ethnicity.[39] With the current dominance of identity politics (what Léger calls 'micro-politics' or 'victim politics'), it appears he has a point. After the banking crisis, micro-politics ruled in the Occupy camps. With nowhere to invest their rage, activists began to turn on one another and fragment into evermore numerous splinter groups or else they attempted to pick up the pieces and make the best out of a bad situation – either way, a return to macro-politics seemed impossible. At the same time, the banking crash opened up conceptual space for militant art and a move away from micro and towards macro-politics. This is evident in the kinds of art that moved away from an Occupy ethos towards one of tactical trespass; from building micro-utopias to creating mobile hit squads.

From micro-utopias to mobile hit squads

Militant aesthetics asserts a more direct, militant, art that, following Badiou, must be rooted in local politics without becoming 'official' or losing sight of what he terms the possibility of 'strong ideas' (see Chapter 2). To determine how it might achieve this, the analysis that follows contextualizes militant art within de Certeau's terms 'the tactical' and 'the strategic'. Nato Thompson utilizes these terms to distance socially engaged art from relational art.[40] He interprets the 'tactical' as temporary interventionist forms of trespass and the 'strategic' as a long-term investment in space. Thompson singles out art biennales for being 'tactical', accusing them of trading in the symbolic culture of activism without engaging with it in a long-term and meaningful way. He makes a convincing case. At times the international art world does seem to parachute into cities to replicate the biennial format, which is practically the same whether in Venice, Sao Paulo, Taipei, Gwangju, Sharjah or Sydney. For Thompson, the rise in long-term community-based projects (that is, art that is strategic rather than tactical), such as Rick Lowe's *Project Row Houses* (1993–Present), might counter issues with relational art that, being short-lived, tend to be easily consumed.[41] This complies with Badiou's first rule, to be rooted in local politics.

Socially engaged art is strategic but micro-political. Following Thompson, it is strategic because it is long-term and community-based. However, because of the emphasis on community work, it is vulnerable to becoming official art, or moralist *Tendenzkunst*. We might turn Thompson's assessment on its head and declare that when socially engaged art becomes embroiled in community work, providing palliative solutions in the here and now, it loses its strategic sense of macro-political change, what Badiou calls the possibility of a return to strong politics. This is why long-term community projects do not characterize militant art.

Relational art is tactical *and* micro-political. Where socially engaged art is moralist, relational art is autonomist: neither has the potential for dialectical ethicism. Relational art also completely lacks a militant adherence to the possibility of macro-political change. It is purely tactical and purely autonomous art. Instead of working with community groups, or political activists, Nicholas Bourriaud's solution is for artists to form what he terms 'micro-utopias'. Micro-utopias are small-scale convivial acts that bring like-minded people together in galleries and project spaces. They provide opportunities for meetings and discussions that might be symbolically non-compliant, but that do not challenge the political order or attempt to change people's opinions. Micro-utopias are open to at least two criticisms: the first is that they are critically ineffective – that they lack imagination; the second is that they are politically ineffective – that they lack commitment.

Micro-utopias are critically ineffective because Bourriaud is guilty of post-political 'end of History thought'. When he wrote that it is 'more pressing to invent possible relations with our neighbours in the present than to bet on happier tomorrows',[42] he was urging us to simply get on and make the most of it, because, as Margaret Thatcher famously said, 'there is no alternative'. He asserts that 'any stance that is "directly" critical of society is futile' and he dismisses critical theory, and Frankfurt School thought in particular, as 'a magnificent but ineffectual toy'.[43] For him, utopian projects are over. His line of thinking considers Badiou's call for an art that retains the possibility of renewed macro-politics to be well-intentioned but unrealistic dreaming. Bourriaud's rejection of utopian thinking is defeatist as from the outset it accepts the political order as unshakeable: it fails to imagine that political alternatives are even possible. The lack of criticality and imagination make micro-utopias a fundamentally ineffective model for politically committed art.

Micro-utopias lack commitment because, for Bourriaud, art can have no real social impact, or even serve as a model to imagine concrete structural alternatives. Although his call for relational art to no longer form imaginary and utopian realities, but 'actually be ways of living and models of action within the existing real'[44] appears to conform to Badiou's third rule (to shift away from representation and towards presentation), his 'models of action' are phoney. They do not authentically present alternatives. As these occur within the gallery system (including the biennial circuit) they tend to attract like-minded people who, if the work is successful, interact and form affinity groups that do not challenge the political order, or even attempt to change people's opinions. *New York Times* art critic Roberta Smith describes how, at best, relational aesthetics' aim is remedial:

> The goal of 'relational aesthetics' is less to overthrow the museum than to turn it upside down, wreaking temporary havoc with its conventions and the visitor's expectations of awe-inspiring objects by revered masters. The larger point is to resensitize people to their everyday surroundings and, moreover, to one another in a time when so much – technology, stress, shopping – conspires against human connection.[45]

Militant art is a combination of the tactical (in that it embraces the short-term 'hit-and-run', the ephemeral and the opportunistic) and the strategic (in that it is idealistic and believes in long-term goals or visions). The actions against banks (described earlier in the text) share methodological similarities. They are all short-lived hit-and-run actions that retain their autonomy as art, but they are also politically committed. The actions against banks are tactical, but they are also strategic because they retain belief in the possibility of radical political change: the short-term tactical intervention becomes part of a larger political plan.

When militant artists form affinity groups, they do so as mobile hit squads making tactical interventions to antagonize, confront and lead by example in the Situationist vein described in the last chapter. This is not at all like Bourriaud's micro-utopias, which (although also small-scale and short-lived) hold that structural alternatives are unimaginable. Relational art is vulnerable to institutionalization, but socially engaged art is equally prone to co-option, although more often by social, rather than art, institutions. Militant art avoids this kind of recuperation by being tactical. It is tactical insofar as it adheres to the vanguard principle of leading by example. It avoids being co-opted by neoliberalism by being short-lived, autonomous, critical and confrontational. At the same time, militant art is strategic, insofar as its tactical confrontations retain the *possibility* of systemic change, of organizing and building towards a new politics, even if they do not achieve this as art.

From occupy to trespass

The Global Justice Movement protests of the first decade of the twenty-first century targeted temporary events, from the WTO Ministerial Conference of 1999 (known as the 'Battle in Seattle') to the G8 Summits (Genoa, 2001, was one of the bloodiest protests in Western history). As these events were brief and transitory, trespass became a pragmatic tactic and long-term occupation was an impossibility. For this reason, although the artists in the first part of this chapter purportedly 'occupied' banks, their actions are more analogous to trespass than occupation. However, unlike the Global Justice Movement, which was a horizontalist coalition without a shared vision, their short-term trespasses were strategic. Leading by example enabled them to posit a macro-political vision. Militant art operates in this vein, tackling global, systemic, issues, through tactical, hit-and-run, actions aimed at short-term events, rather than moralistic, micro-political occupations.

Methodologically, militant mobile hit squads resemble flash mobs.[46] For example, the UfSO descended, uninvited, to occupy spaces. As well as banks, they occupied shopping malls and supermarkets. In November 2010, they gave their second lecture *Market Education, Instant-Mix Degrees and the Commodification of Everything* at the Tesco Superstore on the Old Kent Road (South London). In March 2011, the UfSO created a 'Free Education Market' outside the Institute of Contemporary Arts (London), overidentifying with the logic of cuts, arguing that 'everything must go'. The UfSO's actions broke the norms of acceptable behaviour to reveal their limits. They refer to these actions as 'flash-lectures'. During this time the UfSO was also heavily involved in the university occupations and 'teach-ins', creating a link between occupations (trespasses) and flash mobs.

Theorizing the tactical confrontations that I have described in this chapter, as well as those that are to follow, in terms of the flash mob is useful because flash mobs are fundamentally militant. They are, first and foremost, hierarchical. According to flash mob theorist Rebecca Walker, they typically begin with a person acting as an organizer who sends emails or text messages to people, 'inviting them to arrive at a specific place at a certain time and to wait for further instructions'.[47] In early flash mobs, leaders were anonymized to protect their identities. Although not in complete control, as anybody could turn up and potentially subvert the flash mob (they are mobs after all), the organizer still took a lead. The hierarchical nature of the flash mob is essential. As Walker notes 'it is the very ability to follow orders and take instruction that flash mob participants use to disrupt the order of everyday society'.[48] Participants in flash mobs follow a chain of command and operate more like soldiers than collaborators in relational, participatory or socially engaged art.

Later flash mobs became more choreographed, rehearsed and otherwise prearranged. Walker argues that flash mobs are 'essentially choreographed group tricks … played out within the quasi-public realm of the capitalist City, exposing its heretofore unrealized methods of operation'.[49] This has Situationist overtones, evoking their concepts of unitary urbanism ('the combined use of arts and techniques as means contributing to the construction of a unified milieu in dynamic relation with experiments in behavior') and psychogeography (the study of the effects the geographical environment has on emotions and behaviour).[50] While the choreography of a flash mob could be organized non-hierarchically, as with the *Mierdazo*, the flash mob is still a vanguard that leads by their hit-and-run example.

As a rule, flash mobs are apolitical, but Walker refers to the UfSO as an example of new hybridized flash mobs that promote particular political or social agendas.[51] The aim of the flash mob, she explains, is to 'upset and unmask the power structures that operate in our daily lives'.[52] The UfSO unmasked the contradiction in neoliberal logic that dictates banks should be bailed out, while universities should be defunded. They did this by overidentifying with the neoliberal logic of entrepreneurialism: attempting to make the best of it because, 'there is no alternative'. This is consistent with Walker's declaration that flash mob 'participants break the norms of acceptable behaviour and by doing so perform the dual function of (1) waking up their own participant bodies to the idea that other options for behavior exist and (2) reminding the audience of the absurd and arbitrary nature of so-called normal behavior'.[53] According to Walker, flash mobs highlight how institutions influence 'normal' behaviour, by creating what she calls 'docile bodies'. This could be as simple as a queuing system in a bank, or something much more complex and sinister. The following three case studies are read as forms of tactical trespass through Walker's flash mob theory.

LabofII: Blocking the COPs

LabofII made a tactical incursion into the 2009 United Nations Climate Change Conference, commonly known as the COP15. Their action *Put the Fun between Your Legs: Become the Bike Bloc* began life at the Arnolfini Gallery in Bristol as part of PLATFORM's *C-Words* exhibition (October 2009), before moving to the Nikolaj – Copenhagen Contemporary Art Center. At both venues, LabofII trained volunteers to repair and transform bicycles into tools for civil disobedience to be used during the COP15 that was to take place in Copenhagen the following December. Anybody who has visited Copenhagen will know that its streets are full of cyclists and will not be surprised to hear that there are plenty of abandoned broken bicycles in the city. The *Bike Bloc* descended on the streets of Copenhagen like a swarm of guerrilla cyclists. Some of these machines of creative resistance contained loudspeakers that broadcast pirate radio or sounds composed by artists using MP3 players and car stereo amps. Some bikes were welded together to make two-person, four-wheeled, machines that elevated their riders well above the normal height (see Figure 4.3). Some used sirens to lure police away from other sites of action. Others just repaired bikes to be used in disruptive ways. They brought major roads to a standstill, even blocking two lanes of a motorway at one point. They distracted the police and interrupted their operations by acting as barriers and roadblocks. They also protected activists trying to breach the UN security perimeter. Grindon reports that

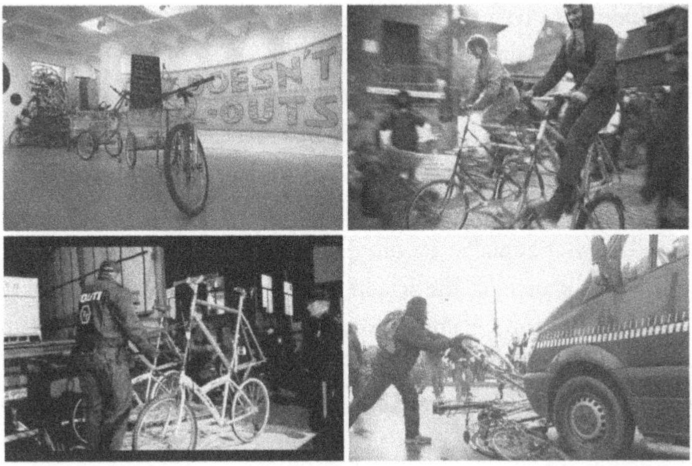

Figure 4.3 Laboratory of Insurrectionary Imagination, *Bike Bloc*, 2009. © Laboratory of Insurrectionary Imagination. Clockwise from top right: Photograph © John Jordan; Kristian Buus; Laboratory of Insurrectionary Imagination; Emily James (from the film *Just Do It*). Reproduced with the permission of the artist.

> Overall, *Bike Bloc* assisted the aim of the day of action: to enter the grounds of the Bella Centre and set up an alternative, critical, people's summit in co-operation with the 200 delegates who left the centre to join the activists outside. Though its methods were more militant, the aim was once again the constitution of a counter public sphere of genuine democracy.[54]

Riders supposedly acted autonomously, but the *Bike Bloc* only functioned so well because its participants were trained to create a swarm. Although this may have been leaderless on the day of action, various planning and training sessions across Copenhagen built on the initial training and launch of the idea at the Arnolfini and the Nikolaj: demonstrating that LabofII took overall responsibility for the action and played a leadership role. Training sessions included how to make 'hive manoeuvres' and 'sound swarms', so it would be misleading to characterize the action as a participatory artwork where everybody made their own bike and then just did whatever they wanted. Even though the first part of the workshop at the Arnolfini was given over to teaching consensus decision-making and the participants were encouraged to co-design the project, it was LabofII who initiated it and created the framework for people to get involved and become part of the *Bike Bloc*. When I interviewed LabofII founding member John (Jay) Jordan, he even went as far as to say, 'the main aim is direct action, not debate', so it was not a completely horizontalist action.

LabofII's stance on the relationship between artistic autonomy and delegating responsibility to participants can be compared to Suzanne Lacy's five different levels of audience participation. Lacy outlined this concept in her book *Mapping the Terrain: New Genre Public Art* (1995), likening it to concentric ripples in a pond after a pebble has been thrown in. The first level, the centre or the first ripple, represents the people who directly participate. For the *Bike Bloc*, this was the people who designed, made and took part in the project: they made the initial splash. The second ripple includes the people who see or who are directly targeted by the event. In the case of the *Bike Bloc*, the second-level audience included the police, journalists who were at the UN conference and photographers who documented the events. The third level of audience includes people who are not directly targeted by the project, but see it anyway – live and in reality. Third-level audiences for the *Bike Bloc* included passers-by, for example. The fourth level would be people who see a representation of the event: people who read about it or see photographs of it, but who never saw the live event. Finally, the fifth level is where the myth of the event occurs. This is the kind of wild narrative where people recall the day that groups of militant artists built war machines out of bikes in Copenhagen to disrupt the police and the COP15. For the *Bike Bloc* (and other LabofII works), the relationship between the artist's intention and audience interpretation depends on these levels of audience, with the level of control over the message decreasing the further you move from the 'inner circle'.

The *Bike Bloc* is militant and hierarchical for the same reasons I characterized the *Mierdazo* in these terms: because it leads by example. This interpretation runs contrary to how these groups are usually understood, but it is not a slight on their work. The hierarchical leadership elements that I discern undermine horizontalist participation, but not Jordan's self-professed anarchism. The 'bike bloc' part of the title refers to the anarchist tactic known as 'black bloc', where protestors collectively dress in black clothing, including hoodies and bandanas with sunglasses or ski masks to conceal their faces, to make it difficult for authorities to distinguish between protestors and thereby hindering criminal prosecutions. The work is still anarchist because the Bike Bloc operates in the rich anarchist traditions of propaganda of the deed and direct action.

LabofII were prepared to break the law to disrupt the COP15. The initial proposal that they pitched to the Nikolaj repeatedly explained that they were planning an act of civil disobedience. Despite this, the gallery staff seemed somewhat surprised that they were actually going to follow through with their proposed intentions and they eventually dropped the project.[55] Not only did the *Bike Bloc* refuse to do what it was told, but bikes were also thrown under police cars, damaging them so that they could not continue working: they moved from protest to resistance.

Bike Bloc retained its aesthetic autonomy. Jordan told me about minor tensions working with activists who just wanted to bolt together the bikes quickly and efficiently and then get going because being effective was their only concern. He recounted another story about an engineer who wanted to wrap a bike, which they had spent ten days making, in plastic, because it was raining. Jordan complained that it looked ugly, but the engineer said that he didn't care, he just wanted it to work. For LabofII it has to both work and be beautiful: it must contain dialectical ethicism. Its aesthetics are important to create a legacy in people's minds through strong images (Lacy's last circle). The engineer was thinking tactically, while LabofII were playing a longer, strategic game.

At the same time, *Bike Bloc* was politically committed in the Sartrean sense, embracing its green politics and taking aim at the COP15. LabofII led by example to spread their message dialectically, as propaganda of the deed and as an ethical invitation to the viewers' freedom to engage with the work and to imagine new political orders by acknowledging contradictions in current politics. Audiences, on any of Lacy's levels, were free to reject, mock or take up the proposals inherent in the *Bike Bloc* – either as participants or observers – and LabofII took full responsibility for this, rather than leaving the work open to any interpretation.

Tactically, the *Bike Bloc* was a success. It set out to create new forms of civil disobedience using bicycles to syphon the police away from a zone where activists were going to try to break into the UN conference centre and it achieved this: each group of bikes took the attention of dozens of police. However, we might ask if it worked strategically. It certainly did not end climate change. The negotiations failed, but they also failed to completely corporatize the climate, which was a concern. The strategic success lies in the potential to spark people's imaginations, to inspire them to dare to imagine the possibility of macro-political change. It achieved this on several of Lacy's different levels. *Bike Bloc* affected Lacy's fifth level through the stories participants tell others and the media representation of the actions. Many new art activist groups have come out of LabofII experiments, each making new tactical confrontations. It created an affinity between new groups of people, bringing them together to work in authentic moments of rebellion: Lacy's first level.

Liberate Tate: Occupying museums and galleries

Like Black Mask and King Mob (see Chapter 3), since 2008 several contemporary art activist groups have made actions against galleries and museums. Unlike their neo-avant-garde predecessors, they did so in the context of the austerity and the Occupy movement. For example, in the United States, Occupy Museums were established during the first month of Occupy Wall Street (September 2011) with the expressed goal 'to reclaim space for meaningful culture by and for the 99%', because 'art and culture are the soul of the commons. Art is not a luxury!'[56] In their various actions, they reignite a rich tradition of institutional critique that includes analysing museum finances and funding, making a connection 'between the corruption of high finance and the corruption of "high culture" '.[57]

In Britain, a year before Occupy Wall Street, Arts against Cuts (established in 2010) occupied Tate Britain to disrupt the Turner Prize ceremony (December 2010). They staged a sit-in and chanted their demands while some wore dunce's hats.[58] Like UfSO, they were incensed by the austerity measures ushered in by the Conservative–Liberal Democrat coalition government – especially the cuts to arts education. I mention these examples as a corrective to the impression that the occupations of museums and galleries followed Occupy Wall Street. To my mind, it is the other way round: there were various occupations of art schools and museums in London and elsewhere (including America) before Occupy Wall Street began in September 2011. Liberate Tate (established in 2010) was founded with a mission to rid Tate of oil money and to make sponsorship from oil companies in the arts as unacceptable as tobacco sponsorship in sport. Liberate Tate made several high-profile actions inside the Tate galleries. Five of these actions occurred before Occupy Wall Street, namely: *License to Spill* (June 2010); *Collapse* (July 2010); *Sunflower* (September 2010); *Human Cost* (April 2011); *The Exorcism of BP* (July 2011).

Liberate Tate's action *Hidden Figures* (6 September 2014) had much in common with Walker's description of a flash mob. It began with a call for participants via social media. I responded and was given instructions by email to go to the first level bridge over the Turbine Hall at Tate Modern at a specific time and date, dressed in black, and to wait there for further instructions. I arrived at the Tate to find increased security, including bag checks. Since I had no bags, I walked in without stopping. *Hidden Figures*, like other Liberate Tate actions, was pre-planned and organized by a core group. The details of the plan were kept secret from volunteers like me, so it was a clear example where artists led volunteers, rather than a horizontalist action based on consensus decision-making. Like Walker's notion of a flash mob, Liberate Tate had choreographed a group trick, factoring in how to lead volunteers like me and Gavin Grindon, who I somehow recognized.

Hidden Figures was a creative act of civil disobedience. Like a flash mob, the group had descended, uninvited, to produce a pre-planned spectacle. Liberate Tate trespassed into the Tate Gallery and would not have left if asked to do so. In this respect, they were prepared to be arrested, although they knew this was unlikely. Tate had tolerated the group's previous actions, which placed the gallery in a similar position to the targets of the Yes Men's identity correction. If they came down heavy-handedly and had the protestors arrested, it would lose face. This would reveal the hypocrisy of promoting art activism in general, while stopping an art activist action against the Tate – the duplicity of declaring a progressive stance on climate change, while accepting money from one of the four corporations responsible for 10 per cent of the entire world's carbon emissions since 1965.[59]

Hidden Figures was full of metaphors. Once on the bridge, I realized we were only a decoy for the artists on the ground floor. A couple pushing a buggy came into view, but rather than a baby, it contained a package. I heard someone laugh 'how did they get that through security', as they began to unwrap the bundle. We were invited to go downstairs to help. By the time we reached the lower level, Liberate Tate had unveiled a 64 m^2 fabric black square. This referenced the exhibition of Malevich's *Black Square* at Tate Modern at that time. It also referred to a series of black squares redacting information regarding BP's sponsorship deal with Tate in the minutes of their Ethics Committee and Board of Trustees.

Hidden Figures was politically committed while retaining its aesthetic autonomy. The fabric square was raised to waist height by about a dozen people (myself included) holding onto each side. Some of the group ran under the cloth. Now hidden from view, the apprehension was visible on security guards' faces and the atmosphere was palpable: only Liberate Tate knew what was going to occur underneath. By now large crowds had gathered on the lower level, the bridge and balcony levels and people were also viewing from behind the glass on other levels. In the end, there was nothing to worry about: no oil spills and no objects deposited, as in their previous actions against Tate. The black square now evoked the Deepwater Horizon oil spill of 2010 (the largest marine oil spill in history). It was, at times, pulled tight over the participants' bodies, suggesting flora and fauna covered in oil. At other times the cloth was flapped loosely, conjuring oil on water.

Following Walker's characterization of a politically committed flash mob, *Hidden Figures* aimed to unmask a power structure – on this occasion the power of corporate sponsorship. By becoming literal 'hidden figures', Liberate Tate alluded to the 'hidden figures' in Tate's accounts. Tate had refused to reveal how much money BP donate, and Liberate Tate speculated that it might not be as much as you would think, given the amount of publicity they afforded the oil company. Not only were BP logos splattered across the website and the gallery walls, leaflets and banners, but Tate also hosted displays such as the 'BP Spotlight', 'BP British Art Displays' and the 'BP Walk through British Art'.

In March 2016, it was widely reported in the art press that Tate was ending its twenty-six-year sponsorship deal with BP, although this did not come into effect until 2017.[60] Coupled with Liberate Tate's successful freedom of information request, *Hidden Figures* forced Tate to reveal how much money it received from BP. In January 2015, it disclosed that between 1990 and 2006, BP sponsorship money amounted to '£224,000 per year on average: less than 0.3 per cent of Tate's current annual operating income'.[61] This raised questions about why Tate was so keen to keep these figures hidden while simultaneously giving BP such high levels of exposure.

C.I.R.C.A.: Trespassing over the summit

The foundation of the Clandestine Insurgent Rebel Clown Army (henceforth C.I.R.C.A.) in 2003 by John Jordan, L. M. Bogad, Jen Verson and Matt Trevelyan as another one of LabofII's 'experiments' was a strategic move. C.I.R.C.A. is an example of LabofII's attempt to create a doorway through which people can enter and engage with social movements. By creating a clown army, they aimed to create something that was accessible and fun but also brought people into radical politics. For most people, radical politics is dangerous, boring, tedious and sacrificial; not something fun, pleasurable or fulfilling. C.I.R.C.A. hoped to seduce regular people with clowning to make them (eventually) feel comfortable enough to make the leap into activism.

C.I.R.C.A. heeded Badiou's call to participate in a formal move away from representation and towards presentation. They ran

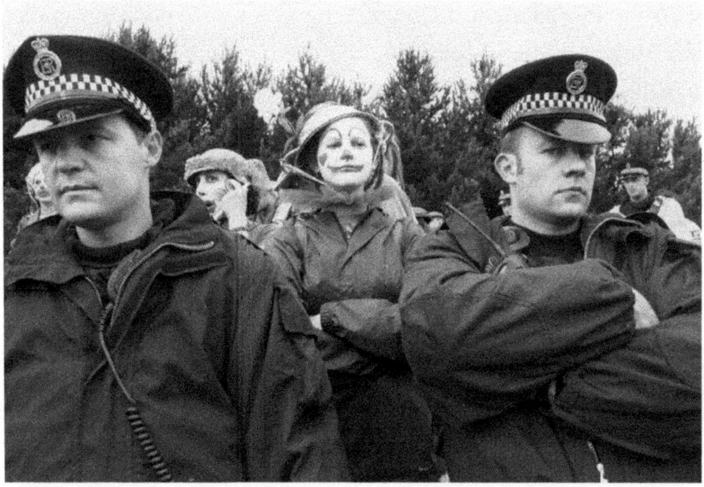

Figure 4.4 Clandestine Insurgent Rebel Clown Army (C.I.R.C.A.), Some of the 200 Clown Army recruits mock power through imitation, during direct action against the G8, Gleneagles, 2005. © Laboratory of Insurrectionary Imagination. Photograph by Ian Teh. Reproduced with the permission of the artist.

'intense' clown training camps, with the intention that participants would not pretend to be clowns (represent clowns) but actually to be clowns.[62] Their recruits were unleashed in 2005 at the G8 Summit at Gleneagles, Scotland (see Figure 4.4). Social and political theorist Christian Scholl describes how the Scottish police were unprepared for a marching clown army:

> When, on their way to blockade one of these roads, the Clown Army met the first police line, they were able to just cross this line by continuing to march along past the rather astounded police officers … the application of the military marching tactic meant that the clown army could pass the police line as a compact and determent group.[63]

The clown army successfully combined aesthetic confusion with politically committed subversion: a dialectical double movement where, 'Confusion is not an end in itself, but becomes a means to confront an opponent'.[64] One of C.I.R.C.A.'s core premises is that 'mocking and utterly confusing the enemy can be more powerful than direct confrontation'.[65] Another key principle is to use absurdity to undermine the aura of authority, as they explain:

> To be effective, authority has to be perceived as such, otherwise people would never obey its commands. On the other hand, who ever takes a clown seriously? Rebel clowning used this slippery dichotomy to great effect, turning the tables on authority in the street by posing in mock-serious fashion next to lines of cops, as well as at the highest levels of power, by pointing out the clownish behavior of George W. Bush and other authority figures.[66]

C.I.R.C.A. display many of the characteristics of militant art: they are prepared to break the law, they appropriate military tropes and they retain a belief in macro-politics – as evidenced through their strategic goal to radicalize their recruits. Like the Berlin Dadaists, C.I.R.C.A. were not only prepared to break the law, they actively intended to get arrested: like Pavlensky, this was part of the performance. C.I.R.C.A. members stay in character while being arrested to create a spectacle and encourage onlookers to wonder what the clowns have done, like King Mob's Ben Trueman being accosted while dressed as Santa Claus (see Chapter 3). They adopt other militaristic tropes, such as marching and ranks (Kolonel Klepto (John Jordan), Major Up Evil (Isabelle Fremeaux) and Corporal Punishment (LM Bogad)), and they even entered army recruitment offices and attempted to join up – causing some offices to close.

Tactical hit squads risk collapsing into an aesthetic autonomist gesture that can easily become merely symbolic and politically ineffective when they lose sight of their long-term strategic goals, while strategic confrontations become moralist *Tendenzkunst* when they lose their identity as art and become co-opted for political ends. Ultimately, mobile hit squads are redeemable if they contain what Scholl calls 'pedagogic dialectics'. He argues that through an event of confrontation it is possible to learn how the ruling regime is organized, therefore 'an antagonistic approach to activist art interventions makes it necessary to "know your enemy" '.[67] The knowledge gained from confrontations can inform future actions. Scholl concludes that any such art must be able to communicate what has been learned without any external referent and that the 'immediacy of a confrontational moment leads to an abstraction about the social organization of the world'.[68] In other words, it must be autonomous while confrontational – another iteration of dialectical ethicism.

5

The absurd and the dysfunctional

This chapter focuses on how tactical confrontations, introduced in Chapter 4, can be utilized to expose the dysfunction or absurdity of a given target. The argument put forth is that, within dialectical ethicism, it is the aesthetic aspect, rather than the politically committed aspect, which accomplishes this goal, as it has the potential to render the target powerless. This highlights that aesthetics is not an isolated element from art's political effectiveness, but can serve as a more potent means for achieving long-term change. The case studies presented in this chapter draw upon aspects of Situationist *détournement*. It is argued that, over the past five decades, this technique has evolved into a suitable methodology for militant art that accommodates dialectical ethicism, tactical confrontations and macro-politics. The case studies show how different forms of militant neo-*détournement* are fused with overidentification, humour and other direct confrontational practices, exemplified in methodologies including hacking, doxxing and the Argentine practice of *escraches*. This is contextualized by a time when newspapers became hackers, and hackers and activists took on the mantle of investigative journalism.

Compromised

The Yes Men's 'identity correction'

The Yes Men's practice of 'identity correction' exposes immoral, dishonest or corrupt people and institutions in humorous ways. The Yes Men (Mike Bonanno (real name Igor Vamos) and Andy Bichlbaum (real name Jacques Servin)) describe identity correction as the opposite of identity theft.[1] With identity theft, innocent people are victims of scoundrels who steal their personal details to impersonate and (often) defraud them. Identity correction, however, targets unethical and criminal individuals and corporations and assumes their identity to 'offer correctives'.[2]

Early instances of identity correction were humorous, critical and mischievous. For example, in 1993, Bonanno switched the voice boxes in G. I. Joes and Barbie dolls so that the G. I.s would say 'math is too hard' and the Barbies would say 'dead men tell no lies'.[3] Bonanno returned the dolls to the shop, but with a fake helpline sticker attached for those having trouble with their dolls. The phoneline led to a news desk, ensuring media coverage. They also sent reporters videos 'featuring an inside look at the "gender transformation laboratories" of the Barbie Liberation Organization'.[4]

As identity correction developed, the Yes Men recognized a more militant potential to damage corporations by exposing ethical sore points. In 1997, Mike Bonanno and Ray Thomas founded RTMark (pronounced 'arty mark', sometimes stylized as '®™ark'). RTMark started as an activist website that evolved into a collective in its own right that sought to subvert the corporate shield of registered trademarks. RTMark retroactively claimed the Barbie Liberation Organization stunt as their first action. They also fabricated the story that RTMark had funded the prank to the tune of $5,000. In 1999, they released Reamweaver, a software that allowed users to clone websites. In the same year, RTMark (or The Yes Men, according to some sources) purchased the GWBush.com domain and cloned

Bush's real election campaign site, GeorgeWBush.com. Then, they set about correcting his identity, highlighting how Texas had become the most polluted state in America under his governorship, Bush's track record of failure in business, his refusal to deny that he had taken cocaine and his grandfather's ties to the Nazi Party. Bush responded by claiming that 'there ought to be limits to freedom' – thus revealing his true character.

On the back of this success, The Yes Men were emboldened to imitate several corporate websites to similar ends. For example, Bichlbaum explains that in 1999, inspired by the Global Justice Movement, they made a fake website (www.gatt.org). GATT (the General Agreement on Tariffs and Trade) was the predecessor of the World Trade Organization (WTO). Gatt.org soon came up near the top of Google searches about the WTO. Eventually, The Yes Men started receiving correspondence intended for the WTO, including invitations to speak at conferences and events – which they accepted with mischievous results.[5]

The Yes Men's use of humour could be mistaken for mere MTV-style pranks, but, upon closer inspection, it operates in the same mould as Dada's absurdist performance tactics. They presented bizarre ideas, products and services in the various interviews and presentations that resulted from their faked websites. These performances, presented to academic or corporate groups in deadpan and slick presentations, assume a surreal yet serious political edge.

One example is *Vivoleum* (2006). Bonanno, pretending to be Exxon representative Florian Osenberg, and Bichlbaum, under the guise of National Petroleum Council spokesman Shepard Wolff, gave a keynote address at the GO-EXPO (Canada's largest oil conference, Calgary, 2006). Bonanno explained that, while climate change would result in human deaths, the resulting corpses could be turned into Exxon Mobile's new, renewable, biofuel: *Vivoleum*. As Bichlbaum spoke over a 3D animation that explained the process, candles made from wax mixed with human hair were distributed to the audience.

When lit, the candles smelled like burning human flesh. They then presented a tribute video to Reggie Watts, a comedian playing the role of a terminally ill Exxon janitor who had volunteered to be turned into biofuel, into a candle. As the Yes Men were ejected from the stage, they protested that they were not allowed to hold a vigil for an employee who had died. While speaking to the press backstage, the police arrived and arrested them.

The Yes Men correct identities in one of two ways. Both involve assuming the identity of their victim. In the first way, they apologize and offer to make good (in the knowledge that their target is unable, or unwilling to make amends). Once the hoax is revealed, the target is forced into the surreal situation where they must deny ethical practices promised by their impersonators. In the second way, they overidentify with the target, promising to do more, even worse, things in the name of profit. In this approach, they openly discuss ethical limits and profit margins. *Dow Does the Right Thing* (2004) best illustrates the former approach, while *Dow's Golden Skelton* (2005) exemplifies the latter.

In *Dow Does the Right Thing*, The Yes Men impersonated the Dow Chemical Company by setting up another fake website: DowEthics.com. The BBC contacted them, asking for a representative to comment on the twentieth anniversary of the world's worst industrial accident: the Bhopal disaster (1984). Over half a million workers were exposed to dangerous gases and chemicals in Bhopal (India) with thousands of deaths and long-term injuries. Even worse, the ground and water supplies were contaminated – reportedly causing a further one death per day since the accident.[6] The corporation that owned the plant, Union Carbide (which Dow purchased in 2001), refused to accept responsibility. Instead, they settled out of court for $470 million. This equated to only $500, or one year's medical care per surviving victim. A Dow spokesperson subsequently called the amount of compensation 'plenty good for an Indian'.[7] Bichlbaum, under the pseudonym 'Jude Finnistera' (see Figure 5.1), announced live on BBC News 24 that:

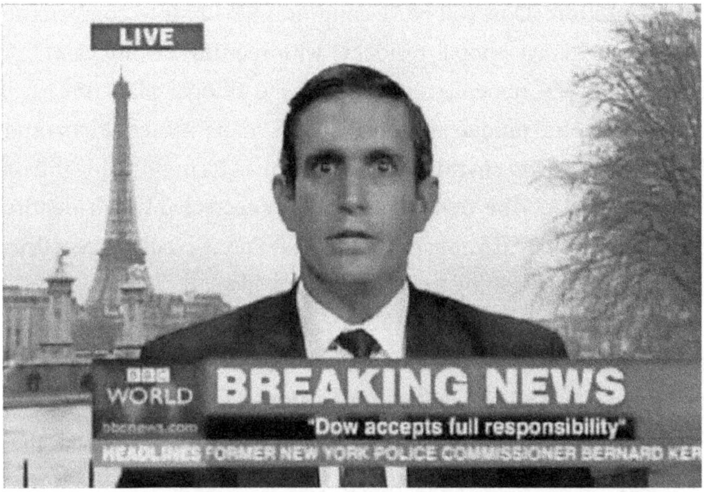

Figure 5.1 The Yes Men, *Dow Does the Right Thing: Live on BBC*, 2004 (Television Still). © The Yes Men. Reproduced with the permission of the artist.

> Dow will accept full responsibility for the Bhopal disaster, and has a $12 billion dollar plan to compensate the victims and remediate the site. (Dow will raise the $12 billion by liquidating Union Carbide, which cost them that much to acquire.) Also, to provide a sense of closure to the victims, Dow will push for the extradition of Warren Anderson, former Union Carbide CEO, to India, which he fled following his arrest 20 years ago on multiple homicide charges.[8]

Dow Does the Right Thing is militant because it forced Dow into an impossible situation whereby they either had to honour the faked commitments (at a cost of $12 billion) or publicly deny that they will 'do the right thing'. As Dow took two hours to respond, the interview was aired twice and the news spread. Dow stock subsequently plummeted by $2 million. A prank that can affect share value differs little from violence against property. The company was forced to announce that it would not be paying any compensation. The Yes Men issued a fake press release 'clarifying'

Dow's position: 'Dow will NOT commit ANY funds to compensate and treat 120,000 Bhopal residents who require lifelong care … . Dow will NOT remediate (clean up) the Bhopal plant site … . Dow's sole and unique responsibility is to its shareholders, and Dow CANNOT do anything that goes against its bottom line unless forced to by law.'[9] The Yes Men successfully corrected Dow's identity by simultaneously demonstrating their dubious business practices and what the right thing to do would look like.

The following year, The Yes Men were erroneously invited to represent Dow at a London banking conference, where they presented the 'Acceptable Risk Calculator' (*Dow's Golden Skeleton*, 2005) as a new 'industry standard for determining how many deaths are acceptable when achieving large profits'.[10] Hosted on dowethics.com, this online tool enables subscribers to weigh profits against costs in human life or health, suggesting that Dow used such a process when considering the ethical implications of their business practices, including manufacturing Agent Orange, which was used with devastating effects during the Vietnam War. This action nodded towards real-life historical examples where corporations have attempted to place a dollar sign on the value of human life: a contentious result of utilitarian logic where the 'greatest good for the greatest number of people' becomes 'cost–benefit analysis'.

One of the most famous examples of a cost–benefit analysis gone wrong was revealed by the *Grimshaw v. Ford Motor Company* lawsuit (1978). In May 1972, a Ford Pinto car stalled on a freeway and was hit in the rear by another car in San Bernardino, California. The Pintos' fuel tank burst into flames killing the driver and severely burning, and permanently disfiguring, a thirteen-year-old passenger (Richard Grimshaw). In the following lawsuit, it was revealed that Ford knew about the fault and had made a cost–benefit analysis (in 1973) to determine whether it was financially worth installing a protective shield that would prevent the fuel tank from exploding. The *Washington Post* reported that 'Ford's own records, obtained by the plaintiffs' attorneys in discovery proceedings, indicated that the company could have given the gas tank extra protection with metal and plastic for about $10 to $15 a car, but declined to do so for cost and weight-saving reasons.'[11] Ford calculated that across their 12.5 million cars this would cost Ford $137 million. They projected the cost of an estimated 180 deaths, assigning a value of $200,000 per death, 180 injuries at $67,000 and 2,000 vehicle repair bills at $700 per car. This totalled only $49.5 million, so they decided not to recall the cars to make the repairs. There were more deaths and injuries and Ford lost several lawsuits relating to the Pinto scandal, but *Grimshaw v. Ford Motor Company* case of 1978, in which Ford was fined $128.5 million (about one month's profit), was the largest.

In 2000, Philip Morris ČR (the Czech subsidiary of the major American tobacco company) made a cost–benefit analysis to argue against increased tobacco duty in the Czech Republic. Although they acknowledged there were increased healthcare costs for smoking-related diseases, they argued that smoking had a net benefit for the country due to tax revenue and healthcare, pensions and housing savings from premature death.[12] I cite these two real-life examples of cost–benefit analysis to emphasize how The Yes Men's bizarre and ethically reprehensible 'Acceptable Risk Calculator' was taken seriously by big business.

Etcétera's *escraches*

The Yes Men's humiliation of their targets is comparable to the Argentine practice of *escraches*. Latin American cultural theorist Brian Whitener describes *escraches* as 'something between a march, an action or happening, and a public shaming' of former members of the Argentine military junta (1976–83) who escaped justice when Carlos Menem (President of Argentina 1989–99) pardoned them.[13] Jennifer Flores Sternad (now Jennifer Ponce de León) describes them as 'the social condemnation of a selected individual by publicly exposing and denouncing his or her past crimes. They can be understood as a symbolic expulsion of an individual from an ethical community. An *escrache* usually instigates the actual social alienation of the individual who has been "outed" (many have lost their jobs and/or they have been forced to move).'[14]

Escraches are the analogue antecedents of doxxing: the online shaming of individuals by publicly revealing private information, such as their address, phone number or membership of a proscribed political organization. Doxxing smacks of moralizing – in the vein that Loewe describes when referring to targeting the 1 per cent or greedy bankers instead of systemic problems (see Chapter 4). Doxxers act as if the best way to enact political change is to be as judgemental as possible about others. After calling out their target and casting a few stones, they go about their business with a sense of smug satisfaction and moral superiority. *Escraches* target individuals, at their homes or places of work, but they also aim to influence the government policies that make them immune to prosecution. Additionally, at least one *escrache* has targeted a corporation, the Ledesma Group, for being complicit in the dictatorship and its state violence.

Initially, *escraches* were purely political. They were first developed by the H.I.J.O.S. collective (established in 1995) in 1996.[15] H.I.J.O.S. worked with the communities where their targets lived to make 'flyers, posters, and graffiti to disseminate information about the person being denounced, including his or her full name, address, and telephone number; a description of his or her crimes and condition of impunity; and a recent photograph of his or her face'.[16] This was just preparation for the *escrache*, which involved organizing a march to the target's front door to publicly denounce them. Once at the home of the *genocido* (literally 'genocider' or one who commits genocide) speeches were made. The stakes here are higher than when doxxing somebody for making a perceived moral transgression.

By 1998, *escraches* had evolved to incorporate artistic elements. This shift happened when H.I.J.O.S. began working in collaboration with artist groups like Etcétera and Grupo de Arte Callejero (established in 1997). Grupo de Arte Callejero contributed to the *escraches* by generating graphics, including manufacturing street signs that read 'genocider lives here' or 'mass murderer, 200 metres'. In her comprehensive account of *escraches*, Longoni characterizes the newer, aesthetically infused, kind 'as a specific kind of militancy … Neither politics as subject, content, or external reference, as in so-called "political art", nor the aestheticization of politics, their work seeks to create "a space where art and politics can be part of a single mechanism of production" '.[17]

Etcétera introduced theatrical elements to these gatherings. Longoni describes how they 'gave a defined visual and performative identity to the *escraches*'.[18] For example, they used props such as 'large dummies, masks, and costumes for performances given at the end of each *escrache*'.[19] Ponce de Léon terms the results 'Situated Materialist Theatre',[20] while Mexican-Canadian artist Rodrigo Martí describes some of these actions as 'denunciatory plays'.[21] These theatrical performances served to distract the police and security services, allowing activists to gain access to their targets' often heavily guarded properties.[22] They also added a sense of Surrealist humour.

Take, for example, *Argentina vs Argentina: Escrache a Leopoldo Fortunato Galtieri* (1998), a football match organized by Etcétera outside General Galtieri's home. Both sides wore the Argentina national kit, which made for a bizarre enough spectacle, but they also wore masks which gave the performance a sinister cartoony aspect – like when the bank robbers wear caricature masks of US presidents in *Point Break* (1991). Federico Langer, dressed in military uniform and wearing a Groucho Marx-style nose and glasses, played a recurring character called 'El Militar' to mock Galtieri. The action allegorically pointed to how Galtieri had used both the 1978 FIFA World Cup (which was held in Argentina) and the 1982 Falklands War to cement a sense of national unity, while simultaneously persecuting and 'disappearing' the Argentine Left. Hence *Argentina vs Argentina* was a metaphor for the hidden internal strife under the military dictatorship. It also distracted the police for long enough to allow activists to fire red paintballs at Galtieri's house.

Rancière's humorous hijacking

I propose The Yes Men's 'identity correction' and Etcétera's *escraches* as examples of Rancière's concept of humorous hijacking. Rancière writes that humour 'is the virtue to which artists nowadays most readily ascribe,' humour that hijacks or deflects 'the ways of presenting a sign sequence or arrangement of objects'.[23] Hijacking has obvious militant connotations, while humour does not. However, it is the combination of humour and hijacking that allows for dialectical ethicism – the tension between art's aesthetics (in this case represented by humour) and political commitment (the hijacking).

Identity correction is a clear example of humorous hijacking. The Yes Men hijack websites and corporate identities with mischievous and hilarious results. This has one of two effects on its live audience. The first effect is that audiences accept the identity correction and agree with their unethical propositions without realizing that The Yes Men are imposters. In this case, there is no humour at the time of delivery. Only when viewing the filmed live audience's reaction do we encounter humour, while the fooled corporations will experience embarrassment or anger instead.[24] The second effect is to anger the live audience, who, enraged, turn on The Yes Men. This category can be further divided into two kinds. In the first kind, the audience attacks The Yes Men as if they were corporate officials: that is, they still believe in The Yes Men's faked corporate identity, but they see past the absurdity of the product or service they are offering and attack the phoney corporation on ethical grounds. In this case, the live audience's incredulity is the vehicle for the secondary audience's humour. In the second kind, corporate audiences realize that they are being mocked by imposters. Once more, at the live event, there is no humour, only discomfort. The live audience may experience humour, discomfort, or a combination of both. The secondary audience finds humour in the audacity of the action and pleasure, or *Schadenfreude*, in seeing corporations and security services realize that they have been fooled and mocked by The Yes Men.

Escraches are also humorous, but theirs is a dark, surrealist humour. For example, in the *Escrache a Raúl Sánchez Ruiz* (1998), 'El Militar' returns to declare that he wants a baby, specifically, a redhead. This pronouncement seems absurd because of how it is delivered and because of the Groucho Marx-style nose and glasses he is wearing. A midwife positions herself beside a 'pregnant' woman. A 'doctor' appears and violently punches the woman in the stomach to make a baby pop out. It is pure Punch and Judy. El Militar then declares that the baby has memories of his mother's 'red womb.' This was a performance about Doctor Raúl Sanchez Ruiz, who worked in the ESMA: officially the Navy Petty-Officers School, but, during the dictatorship, it was the largest concentration camp in Argentina. Doctor Sanchez Ruiz was employed to keep the 'disappeared' alive during torture sessions. He also attended to the pregnant women who gave birth at the concentration camp. The babies were taken from their mothers to be adopted by right-wing families and friends of the military junta. It is alleged that Doctor Sanchez Ruiz knows the whereabouts of their children, who in many cases have still not been reunited with their mothers.

While identity correction always retains its autonomy as art, *escraches* are an example of political action fused with cultural production. The earlier instances of *escraches* were committed, but it is not clear that they retained their artistic autonomy or a dialectical tension between art and life. In Rancière's terms, they hijack, but not necessarily with humour. Etcétera added an aesthetic element that was humorous but also clearly emanated from avant-garde art history. The Yes Men's identity correction also contains elements of

Dada puppetry and Surrealist twists, but to a lesser extent, and this is somewhat subordinated to their humour.

Etcétera added to *escraches*, but they also gained from them. As founding member Loreto Garín reflects, 'We realized that associating ourselves with social organizations, in artistic militancy terms, resulted in moderating certain aspects of our development in order to respect the logic of an organization.'[25] This also demonstrates an affinity with Badiou's mandate to be rooted in local politics. Garín describes Etcétera's participation in *escraches* as the first militant moment in their oeuvre. It is through their participation in *escraches* that Etcétera developed a rich, politically informed art practice – including the *Mierdazo* that I described in Chapter 4.

Hacktivism and doxxing

The first two decades of the twenty-first century can be characterized as an age where newspapers became hackers, and hackers and activists took on the mantle of investigative journalism. For example, the UK phone hacking scandal (2011) exposed how British journalists from the Murdoch press had been hacking the voicemails of celebrities, politicians and the families of deceased soldiers, victims of the London Bombings (2005) and even murdered schoolgirl Milly Dowler (1988–2002). While the Leveson Inquiry exposed these actions in 2011, they happened during the preceding decade and possibly for as long as voicemail has existed. At the same time, we saw the emergence of Anonymous (established in 2003) and WikiLeaks (established in 2006) who, alongside the so-called Twitter Revolutions (Moldova, 2009; Iran 2009–10; Tunisia, 2010–11; Egypt, 2011), demonstrate that it is not the case that 'real' activism takes part on the street, while its online variant is entirely toothless. The Franco-German curator Alain Bieber argues that the media 'lost credibility and power because severe pressure to save money has led to severe drops in quality. Investigative journalism is no longer conducted by the media, but by hackers like Julian Assange – or artists'.[26] He was right: art activists adopted hacking, leaking and doxxing as methodologies, as the following examples evidence.

Ztohoven: Phone hacking as identity correction

We saw elements of hacktivism in identity correction, but Ztohoven provide a more concrete example of this methodology as militant art practice. *Moral Reform* (2012) occurred during a debate about whether the Czech politician David Rath should be immune from prosecution for accepting bribes because of the Czech equivalent to parliamentary privilege. The debate was broadcast live on television. According to hacker Juraj Bednar, Rath looked straight down the lens of the camera to address the nation, rather than towards the politicians who would vote on his fate and he was unrepentant.[27] Ztohoven describe how Minister of Foreign Affairs Karel Schwarzenberg responded as any sane person would: by falling asleep.[28] The deputy prime minister, Karolína Peake, was caught on camera doing something on her iPad rather than paying attention to Rath's testimony. Whatever she was doing was interrupted when she received a text from Schwarzenberg, who somehow sent it while asleep. Viewers watched more and more disinterested politicians fiddling with their phones and looking bemused. They had received SMS messages that appeared to have legitimately come from other politicians' phones. Each one encouraged another politician to do the right thing and enact cross-party moral reform. The key to who was behind this stunt lay in one message that read *Morální reforma je jediná možnost jak z toho ven* (Moral reform is the only way out of it). In Czech, 'the way out' (*z toho ven*) and 'one hundred shits' (*Sto Hoven*) sound the same. *Moral Reform* evokes memories of the UK parliamentary expenses scandal of 2009 when British politicians similarly appealed to the supreme court that their financial wrongdoings were protected by parliamentary privilege.

Moral Reform was both a kind of identity correction and a virtual *escrache*. It performed the same function as The Yes Men's *Dow Does the Right Thing* because, like The Yes Men, Ztohoven placed their targets in a position where they had to declare that they would not, in fact, 'do the right thing'. Once the politicians realized it was a hoax, they had to renege on the messages and promises that they had purportedly sent by SMS: they had to refuse to commit to moral reform. In reality, it was Ztohoven who had hacked their mobile phones and sent more than five hundred text messages from politician to politician, each one urging the other to do the right thing. The hacking of mobile phones was very much in the public consciousness following the aforementioned UK phone hacking scandal, which was widely reported internationally. *Moral Reform* was a kind of *escrache*, or contemporary doxxing, because Ztohoven published the Czech politicians' mobile phone numbers in an installation titled *Morální reforma* (Moral Reform) as part of the *Cartographies of Hope: Change Narratives* exhibition (22 November 2012–21 February 2013) at the appropriately named DOX Centre for Contemporary Art in Prague.

Ztohoven's actions are art, rather than pure activism or trivial media pranks, because of their dialectical ethicism. When I interviewed them, they proclaimed that activism always has a specific political goal, but that they do not know what the outcome of their actions will be. The fact that their work is undecided puts it firmly in Badiou's militant, rather than official, camp. At the same time, Ztohoven led by example: their work always has a basic message, which provides the basis for discussion. While they aim to generate debate, they told me that they retain responsibility for the work and try to avoid misinterpretations by publishing manifestos as well as poetic texts.

Ztohoven are prepared to break the law as part of their art practice. They 'hacked' all 750 subway posters in the Prague metro, replacing them with a question mark (*Subconsciousness Raped*, 2003). This was the first action for which they were prosecuted. The title refers to how advertising invades homes through television and radio, but also floods the streets, on the sides of buses, taxis and billboards: it is inescapable. They argue that, through such means, advertising gradually and unobtrusively rapes the subconscious of each and every one of us. There is a geopolitical element to this observation. Growing up in communist Czechoslovakia advertising was rare, but following the fall of the Berlin Wall and the formation of the Czech Republic, it flooded in. It was no worse than in any other Western country, where it is seen as normal, but it was noticeable in former Eastern Bloc countries because of the rapid change.

In *Media Reality* (2007), Ztohoven hacked a weather channel 'to draw attention to the distorted view of reality in the media'.[29] A live weather broadcast showed a mushroom cloud appearing in the background. They were threatened with three years in prison, but instead, they won the Prague National Gallery newcomers' prize. In the same year, they hacked forty-eight Prague traffic lights, replacing the red and green filters so that the figures on pedestrian crossings appeared as people drinking beer, urinating, defecating, or performing other incongruous acts (*Semafory*, 2007). Roman Týc was arrested for this action. He paid for repairs but was imprisoned for thirty days when he refused to pay his fine.

Paolo Cirio: Doxxing Cayman Island corporations

Paolo Cirio's *Loophole for All* (2013) is simultaneously an act of subversive affirmation and a kind of *escrache*. It is like an *escrache* insofar as Cirio hacked the Cayman Islands government registry to leak the names of over 200,000 firms registered there. Like Etcétera and Ztohoven, Cirio named and shamed practices that are immoral and corrupt, although sadly in this case they are legal. Cirio displays the names of corporations in floor-to-ceiling wall texts: a necessary display method, given the sheer number of companies registered in the Cayman Islands (see Figure 5.2). The names are supplemented with an infographic explaining how the tax system works. *Loophole*

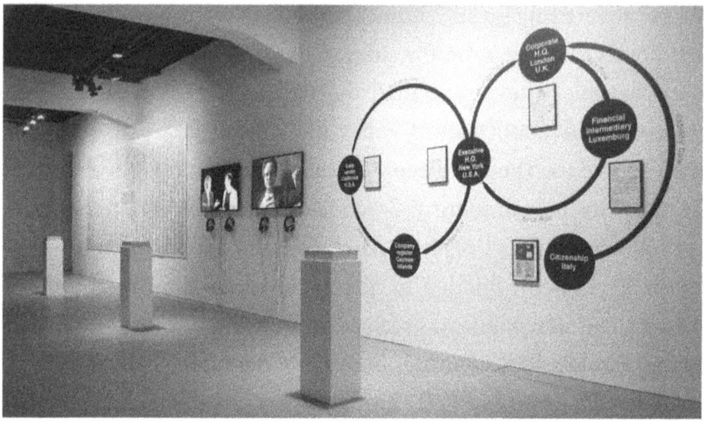

Figure 5.2 Paolo Cirio, *Loophole for All*, 2013. © Paolo Cirio. Reproduced with the permission of the artist.

for All is subversive affirmation because it exposes the obvious truth that the system will not work if we all take advantage of its loopholes – yet this is exactly what Cirio proposes. The work explains how offshore tax avoidance works and encourages private individuals to take advantage of such tax loopholes. Cirio offers private individuals the ability to avoid paying tax in the same way that global corporations do by forging and selling 'certificates of incorporation', issued with the artist's real name and signature. These certificates supposedly allow individuals to issue invoices from the Cayman Islands, thus avoiding paying tax in the country where they trade. In doing so, he overidentifies with the system, revealing how absurd and dysfunctional it would be if we all stopped paying tax or, as Cirio puts it, 'The absurdity of the unsolved legality of offshore business helps to expose to everyone the disorder of our times and the need for radical change.'[30]

Cirio is prepared to break the law to expose such absurdity, even if he did not hack the Cayman Islands' government servers. A senior registrar from the Cayman Islands Online Registry Information Service (CORIS) issued a statement claiming that all the information Cirio supposedly leaked was available for a nominal fee. Art historian Monica Steinberg recounts how the same registrar then accused Cirio of scamming the public by selling counterfeit certificates of incorporation.[31] Cirio retorted that CORIS was the real scammer, declaring that 'the Caymans government sell incorporation to fake shell companies, whose main purpose is to defraud the rest of the world'.[32] In other words, where the Cayman Islands sell real certificates for fake shell companies, Cirio sells fake certificates for real individuals, proposing 'a system in which anyone could steal the identity of a real, anonymous company in the Cayman Islands, and in doing so democratized tax evasion'.[33] Evidently, if Cirio did not hack the servers then this artwork does not belong in a section on Hacktivism, but if he did not, one wonders why he was subjected to 'ten legal threats and two cease-and-desist letters from Chinese firms'.[34]

There is growing awareness and indignation of tax avoidance practices, infused with a 'WikiLeaks culture' of hacking, leaking and exposing wrongdoing. Cirio's action prefigured the Panama Papers (2016) and Paradise Papers (2017): leaks that exposed the tax avoidance of major corporations including Apple and Nike, for example. In 2021, five years after the Panama Papers scandal, 130 countries agreed to a new framework for international tax reform, proposing a 15 per cent global minimum rate for corporation tax.

Loophole for All is militant for at least four reasons. Firstly, Cirio sees his work as operating in the avant-garde tradition. He describes how before the internet he was 'building pirate radio transmitters, while reading about [Bertolt] Brecht, Situationism, the historic European avant-garde … combined with theories and practices of semiotic guerrilla movements that were very fertile in Italy'.[35] Secondly, *Loophole for All* is militant because Cirio was prepared to break the law (if not by hacking, then by counterfeiting certificates) to realize a greater cause (awareness of tax avoidance) and because he unilaterally took action that could cause harm to corporations (through doxxing). Thirdly, Cirio focuses on systemic inequality (tax avoidance, but also money laundering) rather than micro-political issues. He explains how he starts by 'analyzing a specific problematic financial vehicle, such as a law, a market, or a scheme, then I find flaws in it ... this process requires the involvement of artists, because they are able to circumnavigate conventions and take on challenges that even the professionals in finance do not know how to approach creatively, and make comprehensible to everyone.'[36] A fourth reason that *Loophole for All* is militant is that Cirio leads by example. Steinberg puts forward a case for such direct action, arguing that he 'performatively produced a kind of authority' and that 'maybe one needs to engage in a bit of small stakes criminality in order to reveal the more insidious high stakes crimes.'[37] Or as Cirio puts it himself, 'If we can't stop corporations from hiding in the Cayman Islands to avoid taxes, we all need to become pirates.'[38]

Loophole for All builds on Cirio's *Hacking Monopolism Trilogy* (2005–11): three artworks targeting three major internet companies, made in collaboration with artist Alessandro Ludovico (see Figure 5.3). Each constituent artwork has its own title: *Face to Facebook*, *Amazon Noir* and *Google Will Eat Itself*. Each part of

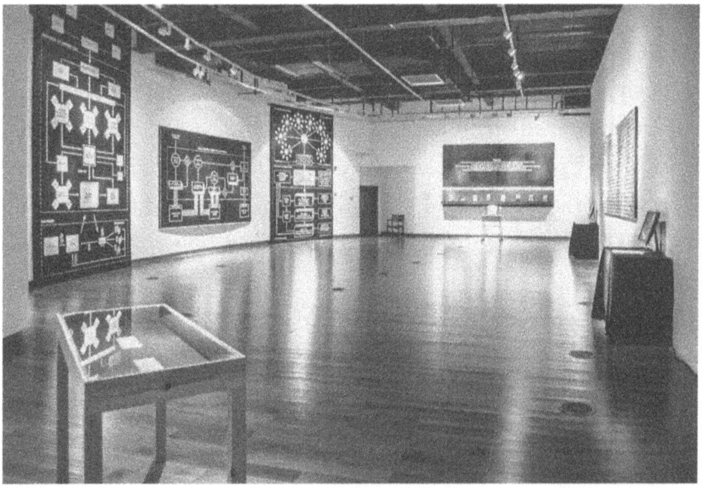

Figure 5.3 Paolo Cirio and Alessandro Ludovico, *Hacking Monopolism Trilogy*, 2005–11. © Paolo Cirio. Reproduced with the permission of the artist.

the project involved hacking a major internet company (Facebook, Amazon, Google) and then exhibiting how this was done through Cirio's trademark flowcharts that explain the algorithms and processes used in the artwork. The actions garnered legal threats, which are displayed as part of the installation. This series of works prefigured the Facebook-Cambridge Analytica scandal that came to light in 2016. Like Cambridge Analytica, Cirio harvested and used user data.

For *Face to Facebook* (2011), Cirio appropriated 1 million Facebook profiles and posted 250,000 of them on a custom-made dating website (Lovely-Faces.com). These new profiles were sorted by social temperament using artificial intelligence that analysed the facial expressions in their profile pictures. The project garnered 'eleven legal threats, five death threats, and several letters from the lawyers of Facebook, which had to confront this artistic intervention made with its appropriated material and as a result of its security flaws'.[39] This project reminds us of Elahi's work on surveillance (see Chapter 1) and the related issues of privacy and the power and responsibilities that social media monopolies have.

For *Amazon Noir* (2006), Cirio hacked Amazon's 'search inside' feature to harvest entire books, convert them into PDFs and distribute them for free. Cirio sees this work as a comment on the 'criminalization' of internet piracy.[40] He returns the digitized books to an analogue format by reprinting them for his installation, which also features analogue (and antiquated) overhead projectors as well as his flowcharts. A printed book, displayed inside a human incubator, is conceived as the physical manifestation of the hacking action. The incubator points to the premature relationship between a global super-corporation like Amazon and international copyright law. *Amazon Noir* won the 2007 IBM Expanded Media Award.

Google Will Eat Itself (2005) was made in collaboration with Alessandro Ludovico and the Ubermorgen artist duo (established in 1999). Together, they hacked Google's 'AdSense' initiative to generate income. Artist and curator Liz Flyntz describes how they 'purchased Google text ads, placed them on hidden websites, and used bots to click the ads, which created revenue that was then used to purchase Google shares'.[41] These shares were then 'distributed back to random visitors to the website for GTTP Ltd (Google to the People Public Company)',[42] in an attempt to turn Google into a public company. Google's legal team sent a cease-and-desist letter to the artists threatening legal action and requesting reimbursements for the money earned from the fraudulent scheme created for the project.

Like Ztohoven's *Moral Reform*, *The Hacking Monopolism Trilogy* is a kind of militant identity correction. These artworks respectively expose corporate wrongdoing (Facebook, Amazon and Google) and political corruption (of Czech politicians). *The Hacking Monopolism Trilogy* reveals how internet companies monetize and misuse their users' data. They operate in the mould of the mobile hit squad, prepared to break the law to cause direct economic damage, either to share prices (clients were concerned about their data security) or, in the case of *Amazon Noir*, through theft. *Moral Reform* is aligned with identity correction, as it forced politicians to take a position: do the right thing and keep a moral commitment, or publicly announce that they will not keep it because the promise was made under false pretences (hoax text messages). *The Hacking Monopolism Trilogy* corrects identities in a manner more akin to *escraches*. Cirio leaks hacked information, which garners legal threats. This reveals the hypocrisy of the tech giants who make money from selling their users' data, most notoriously in the Facebook-Cambridge Analytica scandal.

The artists featured in this chapter should be understood as belonging to a 'hacker class'. Some of them hack in 'traditional' ways – using computers to gain unauthorized access to data. Some, like Cirio, use these data to expose wrongdoing and distribute digital information for free. Ztohoven have used hacking to disrupt television broadcasts and parliamentary debates. However, other artists in this chapter use analogue means that are not usually thought of as hacking at all. I take the term 'hacker class' from media theorist McKenzie Wark, which she contrasts with what she calls the 'vectoralist class': 'the emergent ruling class of our time'.[43] The three tech giants that Cirio targets epitomize this vectoralist class which, according to Wark, control and monopolize various vectors (or pathways and networks) to information, which they commodify.

Wark's account of hacker and vectoralist classes is macro-political. She conceptualizes it as a new class warfare. The hacker class is composed not only of computer hackers but also programmers, artists, writers, scientists and musicians who produce new information by hacking various codes including 'programming language, poetic language, math or music'.[44] The vectoralists then dispossess the hackers of their intellectual property and commercialize it. Not only does Wark's *A Hacker Manifesto* analyse hacking in terms of class warfare, but it is also structured into short, numbered paragraphs – a clear nod to Debord's *Society of the Spectacle*. This, combined with the fact that it is a manifesto, demonstrates that Wark's interpretation of hacktivism is compatible with a return to vanguardism and macro-politics. Hacktivism infused with identity correction can be understood as a form of advanced Situationist *détournement*.

An evolved *détournement*

Détournement is methodologically compatible with the flash mob theory that I described in Chapter 4: both reveal the inherent contradictions or deficiencies of their target. For example, the Situationists *détourned* paintings to reveal how they had become commodity-spectacles. Founding member Giuseppe Pinot-Gallizio (1902–1964) pioneered what he called 'Industrial Painting': abstract paintings on rolls to be bought by the metre like wallpaper. Gallizio's 'Manifesto of Industrial Painting' was published in

Internationale Situationniste (Issue 3, 1959). Asger Jorn (1914–1973) defaced paintings by painting over them in what is known as his Defigurations Paintings series. These graffiti-like abstract marks, text and grotesque imagery seem to mock traditional notions of aesthetic beauty and call into question the values of Western art. Karen Kuczynski describes them as 'expression as vandalism'.[45] The legacy of Jorn's defigurations paintings can be seen in the Chapman Brothers' defacement of Goya's Disasters of War series of etchings. Sadie Plant reasons that 'Set free by their détournement, commodified meanings reveal a totality of possible social and discursive relations which exceeds the spectacle's constraints.'[46]

Apart from *détourning* art, the Situationists also promoted the *détournement* of advertising, the media and political messages – perhaps most famously in their use of posters and graffiti during the May 1968 Paris uprising. They defined *détournement* as 'Short for "détournement of preexisting aesthetic elements" [not just art] … a method of propaganda … which reveals the wearing out and loss of importance of those [pre-existing aesthetic elements]'.[47] Today, activists *détourne* billboard advertisements with graffiti or subvert corporate logos in memes. Liberate Tate *détourned* the BP logo (a yellow and green flower that espouses their supposed green credentials) by putting it on a tube of black oil paint. Political messages are *détourned* through graffiti, in memes and through audio and video parodies such as Cassetteboy's video 'cut ups' and early mix tapes.

If *détournement* is to be a suitable tactic for militant art, it must contain dialectical ethicism. Rancière recognizes the legacy of Situationist *détournement* in the work of contemporary artists when he says that where 'the critical artist depicted the lurid icons of commercial domination or imperialist war, the video artist slightly deflects [*détournes*] video-clips'.[48] Not only does he use the word *détournes*, but also his use of the term 'hijack' (outlined previously) is a clear nod to *détournement*, which can be literally translated as 'diversion' (*détournement d'un cours d'eau*), 'misappropriation' (*détournement d'actif, de fonds*), or 'hijacking' (*détournement d'avion*).

Debord, however, distanced *détournement* from humour, stating that 'the accumulation of detourned elements, far from aiming to arouse indignation or laughter by alluding to some original work, will express our indifference toward a meaningless and forgotten original, and concern itself with rendering a certain sublimity'.[49] Instead, he asserts that the 'literary and artistic heritage of humanity should be used for partisan propaganda purposes',[50] potentially rendering *détournement* a kind of *Tendenzkunst*. However, Rancière speaks of *détournement*'s legacy, which has evolved significantly over the past half century since the Situationists defined the term.

Umberto Eco's semiological guerrilla warfare

Umberto Eco's (1932–2016) contribution to the evolution of *détournement* is to ground it in semiotics – that is, to remind artists that to *détourne* a message they must be aware of how it operates as a sign. Eco explains that communication functions because the people involved use pre-established rules, but in 'extreme cases', such as art, the message can be 'deliberately ambiguous precisely to foster the use of different codes'.[51] This ambiguity adds aesthetic strength to the work of art, allowing it to exist outside the specific reference to a particular political point in space and time. In other words, it can still resonate in thirty years, even though the social, political and technological circumstances have changed. This is entirely compatible with *détournement*, where the original message's meaning becomes *détourned* because the rules (or code, or terms of reference) for how it is supposed to be interpreted are subverted.

Eco demonstrates why *détournement* is such a powerful political tool. In 1967, nearly a decade after the Situationists published their definition of *détournement*, he declared, 'Today a country belongs to the person who controls the communications', and that military takeovers are now redundant in industrialized countries.[52] This seems to predict our contemporary condition. As I write, Russia has invaded and occupied Ukraine, but there is also a lot of talk about 'hybrid warfare': a term coined by Lieutenant Colonel Frank Hoffman (a Research Fellow in the Center for Emerging Threats and Opportunities at the Marine Corps Combat Development Command) in 2007. The term describes a fusion of conventional warfare with unconventional methods including cyberwarfare incorporating fake news. Hybrid warfare's sister concept, 'disinformation', can be seen in elections influenced by the spreading of fake news through social media: from Cambridge Analytica's role in the Brexit referendum to allegations that Russia directly intervened in the 2016 US presidential election, ostensibly to elect a candidate whom they could influence or blackmail. Disinformation is commonly applied to Vladimir Putin's tactics, but the concept was developed by Debord in his *Comments on the Society of the Spectacle* (first published in 1988).[53]

Returning to de Certeau's concepts that I applied to art in Chapter 4, *détournement* should be seen as tactical. This is evident in Eco's 'Towards a Semiological Guerrilla Warfare', where he writes, 'I believe it is wrong to consider the battle of man against the technological universe of communication as a strategic affair. It is a matter of tactics.'[54] For Eco, the strategic 'is summed up in the sentence "We must occupy the chair of the Minister of Information" or even "We must occupy the chair of the publisher of the *New York Times*"'.[55] He acknowledges that while the strategic option, seizing control of the *New York Times*, for example, can be politically effective, he fears that it will do little to challenge the power and effects of communication itself. Consequently, Eco concludes that 'for the strategic solution it will be necessary, tomorrow, to employ a guerrilla solution'.[56]

Conversely, Plant argues that *détournement* depends 'on the possibility of some strategic sense of its purpose and an analysis of the nature of the social relations it contests',[57] concluding that 'détournements of existing values are tactics in a larger strategy.'[58]

This is exactly what I argued in Chapter 4: short-term, tactical confrontations that retain a belief in macro-political change are paradoxically more strategic than long-term, apparently strategic, occupations or community work. While at first, occupying the headquarters of the Ministry of Communications appears to be strategic (and indeed Eco terms it as such), it is only a short-term intervention unless it is part of a longer plan (a strategy). This is why artists do not need to take over News Corp to be militant: they need to *détourne* their messages. Indeed, Eco almost acknowledges this when he reasons that we must occupy every armchair in front of a television screen.[59]

Eco's concept of semiological guerrilla warfare demonstrates that *détournement* does not simply change the message, or the medium (both could remain unchanged): it interferes with the signal, or how the message is received. Proponents of Marshall McLuhan's theorem 'the medium is the message' are like aesthetic autonomists, as they privilege the form of the message, while those who foreground the content of the message are like aesthetic moralists. For Eco, however, there is a third element. After the medium and the message comes the code: pre-agreed rules or social conditions that influence how the message is to be interpreted (irrespective of its medium or message). Eco is at pains to clarify that he is not advocating new measures of control over public opinion, as with propagandistic *Tendenzkunst*. Instead, he proposes giving back control to interpret the message in other ways.[60] This complements my concept of dialectical ethicism because it does not fully adhere to form or content, politics or aesthetics and it fits with Badiou's assertion that militant art is that which is yet to be decided.

Culture jamming and tactical media

Détournement has also developed through the related concepts of 'culture jamming' and 'tactical media'. Culture jamming was first outlined by cultural critic Mark Dery in a 1990 article for the

New York Times, titled 'The Merry Pranksters and the Art of the Hoax'.[61] He later developed the term in his seminal text 'Culture Jamming: Hacking, Slashing and Sniping in the Empire of Signs' (first published in 1993). This text has since been published online and in Marilyn DeLaure and Moritz Fink's anthology, *Culture Jamming: Activism and the Art of Cultural Resistance*.[62] In his foreword to the anthology, Dery gives a succinct definition of 'culture jamming' (in the most militant of terms) as 'media hacking, information warfare, terror art, and guerrilla semiotics'.[63] He describes culture jammers as 'part artistic terrorists, part vernacular critics' and likens them to Eco's 'communications guerrillas', who disrupt communications and encourage 'idiosyncratic, unintended interpretations'.[64]

DeLaure and Fink give a more in-depth explanation in the anthology's introduction, asserting that it refers to:

> a range of tactics used to critique, subvert, and otherwise 'jam' the working of consumer culture. These tactics include media pranks, advertising parodies, textual poaching, billboard appropriation, street performance, and reclamation of urban spaces for non-commercial use. Using various forms of semiotic defamiliarization, culture jamming seeks to interrupt the flow of mainstream, market-driven communications – scrambling the signal, injecting the unexpected, jarring audiences, provoking critical thinking, inviting play and public participation.[65]

The phrases 'jamming the working of consumer culture' and 'scrambling the signal' (rather than the medium or the message) are nods to Eco's influence, while their examples mirror *détournement*, whose development into culture jamming, via punk, has been noted by Simon Ford of the National Art Library.[66] DeLaure and Fink also link culture jamming with the avant-garde, claiming it is part of a tradition of artistic resistance that reaches back to Dada and Surrealism, 'Situationist *détournement*, alternative media practices, Yippie antics and graffiti art'.[67]

The distinction between culture jamming and the related term 'tactical media' is not straightforward. While *détournement* and culture jamming use graffiti to target street advertisements and reclaim urban spaces, tactical media is usually associated with new media. However, culture jamming also uses new media, and Ray and Sholette liken examples of Lebanese graffiti to its Situationist antecedents during the May 1968 uprisings as a reminder that 'tactical practices are not exclusively electronic, and that physical spaces can still be a sustained site of social and political contestation, even if "public space" erases its own record of these discourses'.[68] While the 'media' part of tactical media is negotiable, the question remains whether it is necessarily opposed to strategic thinking and macro-politics or whether this is only by convention.

By 2003, tactical media artists themselves were seriously reconsidering tactics and at the *Next 5 Minutes International Festival of Tactical Media 4*, they discussed a return to strategy.[69] However, since the tactical is a defining feature of tactical media, Critical Art Ensemble reason that if it were to abandon the tactical in favour of strategy it would cease to exist as a distinct category.[70] This is a convincing point given the similarities between culture jamming and tactical media. However, it need not be problematic for artists, as these are merely labels that can be applied to activist actions.

While tactical media can be confrontational, Critical Art Ensemble note that 'traditional practitioners of anti-authoritarian resistance tend to dwell on the micro phenomena of tactics'.[71] Ray and Sholette assert that, while they understand the reasons behind the shift from macro to micro, from party to identity politics, 'a strategic deficit is one of its consequences'.[72] They describe how tactical media was a product of post-political thinking, stating that because it arose in 'a world without heroic visions or alternatives, the art of everyday resistance seemed preferable to the methodical work of building sustained opposition only to wind up with a new boss, the same as the old boss', but assert that 'the need now is for a return to strategic thinking about structures and forms of struggle'.[73]

They conclude that tactical media is not 'without militant potential', but that it 'generally lacks the unequivocal commitment to anti-capitalist struggles and utopian anticipations', and the ad hoc nature of tactical media actions prevents them 'from transforming and solidifying into a structure of authority'.[74]

Critical Art Ensemble offer a solution to this problem that reiterates my argument that tactical mobile hit squads can be strategic if they retain the possibility for macro-political change. While Critical Art Ensemble feel that strategy is out of reach for tactical media practitioners, they propose 'a new coalition is possible that has a common strategic enemy (corporate capitalism) and hence, as long as tactical action is tied to this aggregate strategic initiative, it can have strategic effect'.[75] This is like the difference between horizontalism and anarchism that I outlined in Chapter 4. Tactical media practitioners have never been inclined towards coalitions or compromise. Instead, they rely on affinity groups. This characterization could describe Bourriaud's micro-utopias, but it might also describe mobile hit squads who, having formed an 'affinity group', decide to lead by example in the strategic hope of inspiring systemic change – and this can be done through tactical interventions. This stems not from a lack of belief that systemic change is possible, but from a militant lack of interest in compromising on a vision for change. This is why democratic models such as consensus decision-making are not possible for militant art, which must lead by example instead.

Boris Groys's total aestheticization

Groys and Sholette both hold that we are living in the society of the spectacle where everything, including politics, has already been aestheticized, but they differ in their interpretation of the potential for this aestheticization. Groys embraces what he terms 'total aestheticization' as a weapon to render ideological and cultural power into functionless objects of pure contemplation. He gives two historical examples. The first is how the French *Ancien Régime* became aestheticized once its art and palaces were opened to the public for aesthetic contemplation – as was the case with the Louvre.[76] His second example is Lenin's Mausoleum, which rendered the great man into an object of contemplation – proving to the public that he was really dead.[77]

Conversely, Sholette notes that the art world aestheticizes social struggles and community activism.[78] When I visited the Turner Prize 2021 exhibition (September 2021 to 12 January 2022, Herbert Gallery, Coventry), I could not help but feel a sense of social tourism: as if the pub, nightclub and community groups were on display for people who never engage with such things. All five of the shortlisted collectives operate in the community, so it seemed strange to convert their practices into gallery spectacles. Not only were the Turner Prize artists instrumentalized as NGO-style official art (as I argued in Chapter 2), but their commonplace, real-life, sites and activities were also aestheticized in the manner that Sholette describes.

Sholette is critical of Groys's positive interpretation of total aestheticization. He asks where social movement culture (the range of social movements and their related cultural and aesthetic outputs, from the Global Justice Movement to BLM) fits into newly emerging definitions of art activism. He notes that its practitioners shun the label 'artist', which they associate with class division, where art lies in the domain of 'expert elites' who do not fit with their horizontalist politics.[79] This is incompatible with militant art, which must take total responsibility for its actions and be able to (hierarchically) lead by example. Militant art must target the root of the cause, whether the state, the corporation or others, to reveal how it is absurd or dysfunctional, so that it loses all credibility and (in the long term) its power. Social movement art is simultaneously prone to becoming NGO-style official art (losing its identity as art) or institutionalized (losing its identity as activism), as evidenced by the Turner Prize 2021.

Sholette criticizes Groys's 'total aestheticization' for allowing 'the seemingly assimilated practice of institutional critique [critique of the *Ancien Régime* or Leninism] to be reborn as activist art' and he quips that it would presumably 'also be far more politically and critically effective than all that messy well-intentioned social movement culture and Occupy DIY art combined'.[80] Militant aesthetics holds that it would. When Sholette says that (for Groys) 'Yes Men Survivaball antics' could never 'truly compete with the democratizing effect brought about by death from total aestheticization',[81] he does not recognize their institutional critique as art activism. I hold the opposite: identity correction (and militant art more generally) is autonomous from 'social movement culture' and it aestheticizes its targets (which could include social movements), *détourning* their messages (corporate, political or otherwise).

The Yes Men operate in an avant-garde art tradition of *détournement*, which is compatible with Groys's notion of total aestheticization. Their identity correction, a combination of *détournement* and overidentification, works because it reveals the absurd and dysfunctional elements in corporate and governmental practice. It also potentially causes real fiscal damage (to share prices for example) and brand damage. This has more agency and strategic fallout than purely tactical actions that attempt to destroy a given target without retaining faith in macro-political change. For example, tearing down statues of a dictator might well signal the end of an era, but it does nothing to strike at the dictatorship itself, whereas displaying a dictator's corpse in a mausoleum dispels myths about his superhuman status. This is the same argument that Eco made about how occupying the means of communication does little to challenge the power and effects of communication itself. For Groys, the point is not to destroy statues of dictators after their regimes have fallen, but to put them in museums, aestheticize them and render them totally useless – to turn them into art. This strips them of their power so they can never return.

6

Demonstration

This chapter explores the transformative power of tactical interventions. At the core of this discussion lies the concept of demonstrations, which can be understood in both political and pedagogic senses: one connoting protests, the other showing how something is done. Through these demonstrations, militant artists will be shown to critique the status quo and mobilize the masses: the essential function of political art, according to Boris Groys.[1] However, the chapter will also argue that militant aesthetics does not rely on mobilization for its effectiveness, following Sartre's and Hirschhorn's examples from earlier in the book. Drawing from Mark Fisher's insights, the importance of revealing the contingency of the present order and making the impossible seem achievable will be highlighted as a catalyst for political change. The chapter will demonstrate how militant art does this, and why it is important. Tactical interventions in militant art will be explored as powerful tools for unveiling political alternatives and inspiring transformative change by fostering spaces for imagining new futures. By demonstrating, in both senses of the word, militant artists are shown to create a space for imagining new futures and effecting transformative change.

Militant pre-enactments and horizontalist prefigurations

A sixty-page pamphlet titled 'A User's Guide to (Demanding) the Impossible', produced by LabofII in 2010, contains similar ideas about 'demonstration'. The authors, Gavin Grindon and John Jordan, argue that art activists can 're-produce the feelings and excite the senses which used to bear the name "art" ' and yet they build different desires and worlds, perhaps even ones that some people once dared to call impossible. This is the art that does not show the world to us, but changes it'.[2] The pamphlet makes multiple references to the avant-garde, including quotations from Bertolt Brecht, Joseph Beuys and Sylvia Pankhurst. It expresses a commitment to direct action that pertains to the anarchist tradition of propaganda of the deed and it functions in the avant-garde tradition of leading by example. The title points to the Situationist slogan 'Be Realistic, Demand the Impossible!' which appeared as graffiti on the streets of Paris during the May 1968 uprisings. This recalls Fisher's debunking of the end of History narratives. He reminds us that what was once deemed impossible (mass privatization including utilities and railways, obedient and weak unions and so on) is currently commonplace, while what was once deemed obvious is now considered impossible (real, macro-political change).[3] Counter-intuitively, this seemingly hopeless situation gives rise to hope, as the impossible has become possible (albeit in a negative sense) and the apparently obvious state of affairs is shown to be contingent, and therefore change is possible. Indeed, Rebecca Solnit reminds us that just before the fall of the Berlin Wall, nobody predicted the collapse of the Soviet Union. Similarly, the Arab Spring and Occupy movements emerged seemingly out of nowhere. Therefore, she reasons, there is always hope in the dark.[4] The artist examples that follow in this chapter heed the Situationist call to demand the impossible and Fisher's call to reveal the contingency of the present order and make the impossible seem achievable.

Militant artists must demonstrate alternatives and reveal contingencies, but there are pitfalls to avoid. Christian Scholl outlines some concerns:

> Activist art interventions become an end in themselves, because they create, at least for a moment and in a nutshell, the world in which activists want to live … This means that activist art has to be based on ethical considerations, which focus on attuning the means to the desired ends, instead of being based on instrumental considerations, where reaching an end becomes an instrumental consideration. David Graeber has brilliantly captured this tendency toward ethics as a neglect of strategy when he states: '[t]he motto might be, "If you are willing to act like an anarchist now, your longterm vision is pretty much your own business." '[5]

Graeber was correct to note that this ethical turn neglects strategic vision. Recall that Badiou holds similar concerns about ethics (see introduction). Under Badiou's schema, militant art must retain the possibility of a return to macro-politics when demonstrating alternatives, rather than get bound up in ethical concerns about how to initiate projects in inclusive, democratic and participatory ways. I argued in Chapter 4 that it can do this through mobile hit squads that lead by their example with exemplary gestures. However, Scholl writes that the 'pretension of providing an exemplary gesture relies clearly on the logic of representation. The immediate act *represents* the possible better world of the future.'[6] If this is true, then such art is representational and, following Badiou's rules, cannot be militant.

Scholl's concerns can be allayed if we reconfigure 'exemplary gestures' – not as representations – but as what Oliver Marchart (referring to Public Movement actions) terms 'pre-enactments': 'the *pre*-formance of a future political event'.[7] Pre-enactments should not be confused with 'prefigurations'. The term 'prefiguration' dates to the 1960s, but it has more recently been applied to the Occupy Movement's general assemblies. The general assemblies 'prefigured' a world organized along horizontalist politics. That is, from the very start Occupy was conceptualized as an exemplary leaderless, inclusive and egalitarian model. These are admirable goals, but Scholl rightly warns against adopting 'the anti-strategic defeatism of prefigurative politics that ultimately contradicts the will to be participatory by its exclusive elitism. The exclusive elitism lies precisely in the orientation towards an alternative for a small group ("some of us"), which implies the abandonment of the idea of egalitarianism.'[8]

By contrast, pre-enactments are 'the artistic anticipation of a political event to come'.[9] Anticipation of a future politics necessitates the retention of the possibility of a return to strong ideology. Pre-enactments can lead by example and retain the possibility of imagining macro-political alternatives, while prefigurations cannot. Militant art's tactical confrontations are pre-enactments in the sense that they do not represent, but rather, through their demonstration, rehearse what was previously deemed impossible. Since future politics are still to be decided, this is not a rehearsal in the strict sense – hence why the term pre-enactment is preferable.

Scholl tells us that art activists often create 'small cracks': disruptive moments in the reality of global capitalism that must be extended to achieve systemic change.[10] This is entirely consistent with Fisher's philosophy, where the 'tiniest event can tear a hole in the grey curtain of reaction which has marked the horizons of possibility under capitalist realism. From a situation in which nothing can happen, suddenly anything is possible again.'[11] This is the political purpose of militant art, but it is important to note that the success of the artwork is not dependent on whether others enact this pre-enactment. The artwork is successful so long as it makes such a Sartrean ethical appeal, which exists in dialectical tension with the work's aesthetic autonomy. This futureproofs the artwork, as beholders can contemplate the possibility of enacting upon the appeal in the exemplary gesture at the time that it is made, or 100 years later when the socio-political conditions have changed.

Demonstrate contingency

Women on Waves: Revealing how abortion law is contingent

Women on Waves reveal how abortion law is historically and geographically contingent. Established in 1999 by Rebecca Gomperts, a trained artist and abortion doctor, this Dutch feminist art activist collective is an example of a group that demonstrates alternatives and reveals contingency. They do this through a combination of the pedagogic and political meanings of the term 'demonstration'. Women on Waves converted a shipping container into a mobile abortion clinic designed by the renowned art activist Joop 'Atelier' Van Lieshout, who also named it *A-Portable* (see Figure 6.1). The container is installed on ships that Women on Waves charter and sail to countries where abortion is illegal. They moor the ship in international waters – twelve miles offshore – where they are subject to Dutch law and can legally offer sonographs and non-surgical abortions, regardless of the law just twelve miles away. Women on Waves come ashore to offer medical advice and

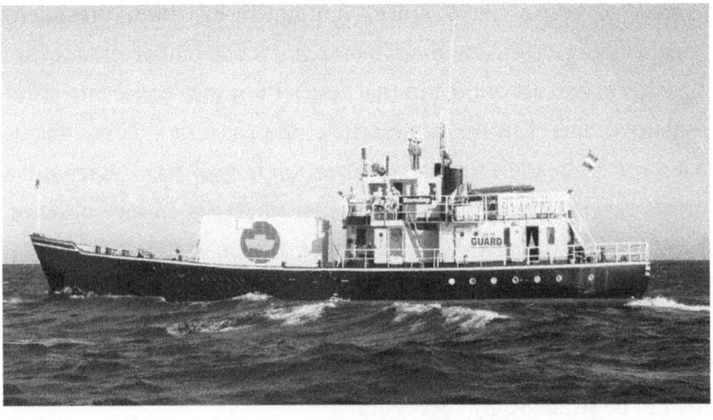

Figure 6.1 Women on Waves, *A-Portable aboard the Borndiep*, 2004. © Women on Waves Foundation. Reproduced with the permission of the artist.

sex education: the pedagogic sense of the word 'demonstration'. Their actions beg the question: what if all women had access to free and safe birth control?

Women on Waves are tactically successful: they provide women with access to free, legal and safe abortions, but the long-term (strategic) effects of their actions are debatable. The first country they targeted (Ireland 2001) has since legalized abortion, but the second (Poland 2003) has become more reactionary since their intervention. Poland continues to criminalize abortion except for medical reasons (such as a threat to the life of the mother-to-be), or when the pregnancy results from rape or incest. In 2015, a measure to implement a complete abortion ban, even in these cases, was only narrowly defeated in Parliament. In 2018, an amendment was proposed to ban abortion in all cases except where there is a threat to the woman's life. The proposed measure was withdrawn when tens of thousands of protestors took to the streets in the so-called Black Friday Protest.

Poland is not the only country to have tightened up its anti-abortion laws in recent times. In 2022, the American Supreme Court reversed the federal right to abortion that followed the Roe versus Wade case (1973). This landmark ruling was made possible because of conservative judges appointed by (then president) Donald Trump. The *New York Times* reports that half of all states are expected to ban abortion and that restrictions may come into effect in many others.[12] In the same article, the *New York Times* details that there is already a full ban on abortion in twelve US states and a further two have banned abortions after six weeks. In several states, abortion is now illegal even in the case of rape or incest, including Texas, where abortion is now a federal offence punishable by life in prison.[13] Critics might argue that this is evidence that Women on Waves have negligent to no effect on abortion law, but I consider them to be strategically successful.

It is not Women on Waves' burden to change abortion law, just as it is not the militant artist's burden more generally to be the agent of political change. This would be to instrumentalize art, rendering it moralist, *Tendenzkunst*. To have a strategic effect, Women on Waves must reveal to citizens the contingent nature of their current abortion laws and enable them to imagine a society where it is legal. They do this by demonstrating another way of living (one where women are in control of their bodies) and they reveal contingency (the ship is only twelve miles offshore). They create Scholl's 'small cracks' that ignite political imaginations. These can then be extended by other parties. It is up to them whether they accept Women on Waves' ethical appeal to their freedom to engage with the work but if they do, they cannot claim ignorance of the issues and must take responsibility for their actions, or inaction. Militant artists must do this at some point if social change is to be achieved. Bishop notes that the 'historic avant-garde was always positioned in relation to an existent party politics (primarily communist) which removed the pressure of art ever being required to effectuate change in and of itself'.[14] This most definitely does not mean that militant artists must subscribe to a totalizing ideology or social movement. There is no need to follow the party line: after all, militant art is that which is yet to be decided. Nor does it mean that militant art cannot be tactically effective in the political sphere. It is up to citizens of countries where abortion is illegal to decide whether they want to press for legalization.

Women on Waves neither create micro-utopias nor do they produce NGO art. This claim will take some substantiation because they do produce short-term solutions for a select few and they are a registered non-governmental agency. As a single-issue group, they do not directly conform to the rule to retain belief in macro-political change. However, I contend that their challenge to authoritarian regimes (principally the church and religious lobby groups), their clever use of international law (and international waters) and their extra-governmental direct action also ignite other kinds of macro-political imagination. The nomadic nature of the onboard clinic is key here. This is not the same as creating a clandestine (and illegal) abortion clinic in Texas, for example. This would only serve those in the know and would be a sort of micro-utopian reaction to Texan abortion laws. The same would be true if they only performed their action once. By sailing from country to country the message is clear: global change is possible and you are only twelve miles away from your country's laws. They do not, however, seek to establish permanent offshore clinics. This would decline into NGO art. Having planted the seed of change, Women on Waves can leave, handing over the baton to others. Without doing so, artists risk becoming entangled in activist work, trying to see the cause through to its conclusion. When this happens, exhaustion becomes a real threat and there is also a danger of losing an aesthetic sense: losing the art and being overtaken by activism, thus becoming militant art's opposite: official art. It also risks losing its strategic potential by becoming rooted in the here and now of a specific geopolitical issue. The mobile clinic functions like the mobile hit squad I described in Chapter 4. It is a symbolic gesture that functions as propaganda of the deed.

Women on Waves are militant. Although their actions are technically legal, encouraging women to have abortions is comparable to inciting people to break the law or commit a violent act – at least in the eyes of the pro-life lobby. Women on Waves risk assault or possible arrest while onshore, as presumably some reactionary countries will not take likely to foreigners encouraging their citizens to engage in activity that is outlawed within their borders. By exploiting a legal loophole, Women on Waves can legally publicize their actions – albeit at some personal risk – and name and shame the country in question in a manner that recalls the Argentine *escraches*, but which also offers a concrete solution. They lead by the example of their actions, as a vanguard. I shall return to why Women on Waves' actions contain the dialectical tension between being militant and being aesthetic after the next, related, case study.

Voina: Making the impossible seem attainable

The Russian Voina Group's actions ask what would happen if we stood up to authoritarian states in the face of human rights abuses. One of the main goals of their protest Actionism is to awaken young people: this is a pedagogic aim. They set an example by showing that they can stand up to authority and teach others, through demonstration, how to create active, brave and resolute protests. Or as they put it, Russia 'has lived in fear for so many decades, we are trying to wake it by kicking it'.[15] Such disdain for authority recalls Jordan's statement about C.I.R.C.A.: that 'authority has to be perceived as such' to function (see Chapter 4).[16] Militant artists can remove this perception by revealing absurd and dysfunctional traits.

Like Pyotr Pavlensky and C.I.R.C.A., Voina 'break the law in a calculated fashion, as part of their artistic strategy, but they feel forced to do so by a society in which the majority of the population mistrust authorities'.[17] I began this book with a description of how American artists were harassed following the Patriot Act (2001). The situation in Russia since 2001 is immeasurably worse and this accounts for the extreme actions taken by Russian artists such as Voina and Pavlensky (see Chapter 4). I interviewed Voina in 2012, the same year that they co-curated the seventh Berlin Biennale. This was some achievement, as they were in hiding at the time following the issue of an international arrest warrant. I made contact with the group who, to my surprise, agreed to do the interview via email. The following analysis of Voina's actions demonstrates why they were wanted by Interpol.

For *A Dick Captured by the FSB* (2010) Voina members drew a 65-metre-high cock and balls on the tarmac of the famous Saint Petersburg Liteyny Bridge. The bridge is a bascule bridge, like London's Tower Bridge, meaning the drawbridge opened so that the giant phallus was erected opposite the FSB (former KGB) headquarters. A video, shot from multiple angles, of Voina making the action shows their members mixing white paint in large bottles in the back of a van while traffic crosses the bridge and other members line up along its side rail.[18] There are no automatic barriers on this bridge and the video shows an attendant pulling railings across by hand while a bell rings. He then has to prevent a cyclist from attempting to pass through and is seen shouting at a car while pushing it back from the barrier. It seems like a very inefficient and stressful way of closing a major bridge in a busy city. There are still pedestrians on the bridge when Voina members creep out of the van with their bottles and buckets of white paint, which they pour as they run along the bridge to make the drawing. Officials manage to tackle and apprehend at least one Voina member and the video clearly shows them punching him in the head while he is restrained, face down, on the floor. While this is going on, the drawbridge is raising to reveal the drawing, like a slowly extending middle finger. As the bridge was now up for the night, the paint had plenty of time to dry.

A Dick Captured by the FSB demonstrates a certain lack of fear and lack of respect, but it also demonstrates the consequences of not conforming and is therefore a kind of identity correction. The Russian Ministry of the Interior initiated more than ten criminal cases against Voina for this action. At the same time, Voina was awarded one of Russia's most prestigious art prizes: the Ministry of Culture and the National Center for Contemporary Art's 'Innovation award' (2011). The two opposite interpretations demonstrate the complete schizophrenia of the Russian authorities (the same schizophrenic reaction that Ztohoven received for *Media Reality*, as described in Chapter 5). Voina did not attend their award ceremony and they later issued the following statement: 'We want to make a type of art that no longer inspires anyone to the idea of awarding us an art prize. But if the museums and institutions can't let go and continue to suggest us for their idiotic competitions, they are going to regret it.'[19]

Voina's reception of the award was featured in *Flash Art,* which reported criticisms of the Voina action from both the Left and the

Right.[20] Those on the Left accused Voina of taking a politically ambiguous stance and those on the Right disapproved on the basis that the selection committee was a bunch of left-wing intellectuals who wanted to promote dangerous and provocative ideas. However, curator Yulia Tikhonova asserts that people on the street identified with the action, claiming that after the image went viral 'it became a symbol of speaking truth to power in a country where few manage to do so'.[21] By acting without fear, Voina demonstrated what it might be like to live in a less authoritarian country.

The Liteyny Bridge action makes an ethical appeal to the viewer's freedom to engage with the work: to be involved in the process of meaning. Some view the 65-metre cock as a symbol of national pride in the face of authoritarianism, while others see it as an insult to the Russian nation. Either way, this divisive art action obliges audiences to engage politically and to take sides. Voina's actions are art (not merely activism) precisely because they contain this dialectical tension. Voina declare that artists should walk on the razor's edge between art and non-art. Describing their action *Cops Auto-da-fe, or Fucking Prometheus* (2011), when they burned a police prisoner transport vehicle as a work of art, they clarify this position:

> If an activist secretly burns a cop truck at night, it won't be art. It will be the revenge of an activist … But to burn it openly and proclaim to the entire country: 'I am an artist. I burned down your prison, symbol of totalitarianism. This autodafe [*sic*] is our art action,' then it becomes a piece of art. We made people discuss it as an artistic action.[22]

Palace Revolution (15 September 2010) involved turning seven police cars onto their roofs. A video of the action on their blog shows a boy playing with a football. The video cuts to night-time and we see the ball running underneath a police car. The camera cuts to a sign for the State Russian Museum (Saint Petersburg) and then back to Voina members looking for the ball under the car. We go back to see a guard closing the museum's gates, then we are shown several members of Voina crossing the road in single file before marching, military-style, towards the car. They line up with their backs to one of its sides, crouch and lift the car. The alarm immediately goes off while they continue to lift it, turn it onto its roof and then scarper. In an interview with *Bomb* magazine, Alexei Plutser-Sarno (Voina's media strategist) claimed that the action was intended to 'tell the world that it had gone mad and topsy-turvy' and, with an allusion to Jean-Jacques Rousseau, that 'it's urgent to "set it on its feet"' again.[23]

A Dick Captured by the FSB, *Palace Revolution* (and many other actions) evidence how Voina are prepared to risk arrest for their art. In November 2010, three Voina members, Leonid Nikolayev, Oleg Vorotnikov and Natalya Kozlenok were detained for their role in *Palace Revolution*. Vorotnikov's wife, Natalya Sokol and son Kasper were not held, but Sokol's ID card and passport were confiscated, preventing them from travelling or accessing healthcare: a menacing reminder that the more hypothetical concerns raised by Bunting and Ztohoven about ID and surveillance in Chapter 1 were not unfounded. Vorotnikov and Nikolaev were only released, after four months in prison awaiting trial, when Banksy raised their bail money from an online auction of his work. The *Guardian* reported that Banksy paid £80,000 towards their legal fees,[24] while the BBC reported that this figure included 300,000 roubles (£6,500) each for bail.[25] Vorotnikov subsequently skipped bail and managed to avoid further imprisonment despite being arrested again when he assaulted a police officer at a political rally.

In July 2011, international arrest warrants were issued for Vorotnikov and Sokol. Despite the outstanding arrest warrants, Voina co-curated the seventh Berlin Biennale (2012). Chief curator Artur Żmijewski, who organized political actions as part of the biennial to support causes including freeing Belarus's political prisoners and the Occupy Movement, invited Voina to co-curate. Voina, alert to being recuperated by the art world, issued a statement clarifying that they would play no part in exhibition management, as they consider exhibitions to be detrimental to contemporary art. They also stated that they would not leave Russia during the biennial, as that is where their 'front line' was. However, Plutser-Sarno had already fled to Estonia, where he had previously studied philosophy at Tartu University.

After the Berlin Biennale, Vorotnikov, Sokol and their son Kasper escaped Russia and absconded to Venice where, in July 2014, Vorotnikov was arrested. He was bailed with the condition that he report to the Venice police twice a week. In September 2016, *Artforum* reported that he had been arrested in Prague and that Czech authorities had 'initiated extradition proceedings for him and his wife, Natalya Sokol' to Russia where they faced up to ten years in prison.[26] They sought asylum in the Czech Republic, but on 20 May 2019, Vorotnikov was arrested in Germany. It is difficult to ascertain the exact movements of the Voina members who are on the run and in hiding. The art press has only made sporadic and cursory coverage of this group, and mainstream newspapers and media outlets have been only slightly better. The website free-voina.org (and its English language counterpart free-voina-en.tumblr.com) has the best information, but at the time of writing, Vorotnikov and Sokol's exact whereabouts are unclear.

Both Voina and Women on Waves create events of confrontation outside the gallery system, in the real world, but their actions are already conceived and composed for their later media distribution. They are planned to be documented so that they become future media icons. Oliver Johnson argues that they rely on the 'response of the authorities, the media and the mass audience' to complete the work.[27] He notes that 'Voina's physical actions are the starting point for a networked performance that emerges from and depends on the mass participation of its online audience'.[28] This is at odds with my declaration that participation is not necessary for militant art (see Chapter 3). Instead, I consider militant art actions as an ethical appeal to their audiences – whether they see the work in person or later, via media representations – to contemplate the possibilities and ramifications demonstrated by the actions. The art actions are complete regardless of whether these audiences interact with them or enact their proposals (have an abortion, campaign for abortion rights, stand up to the government and so on).

In Chapter 2, I argued that militant artists are prepared to break the law and risk arrest, but being arrested is not a requirement for the work to qualify as militant. Following Sartre's and Hirschhorn's thoughts, it is sufficient for audiences to contemplate the possibility (of arrest, or of avoiding arrest). However, to qualify as militant, the artwork must contain a dialectical tension between art and life and in this regard, when an action is banned (by art institutions or the government), or when artists are arrested, this evidences half of the dialectical tension. Referring back to Suzanne Lacy's different levels of audience participation (see Chapter 4), we can see that a reaction from the second-level audience, the people directly targeted by the event, can function to confirm that, far from being recuperated, institutionalized or toothless, militant art actions have political potency. This is not the same as requiring audience participation to complete the work. When a mobile hit squad strikes, second-level audiences are forced to react – whether they are the police, corporations (in the case of The Yes Men, for example), national governments (Women on Waves) or others. Even if they choose not to react, they are forced into choosing this nonreaction. This is not the same as an art which requires participation to complete it.

Like Johnson's assessment of Voina, Harvard art historian Carrie Lambert-Beatty theorizes that Women on Waves' mobile clinic is a kind of red herring, or type of disinformation, that distracts from their real goal – that of 'media politics'.[29] She highlights how the inclusion of *A-Portable* in the forty-ninth Venice Biennale was not accessible to the general public: its exhibition only represented the real version, which was in Ireland.[30] However, this symbolic version started rumours that the clinic could be visited, but only by women seeking antenatal care. This helped to give the artwork a mythical status – the final level of audience in Lacy's theory. When seen in this way, Women on Waves contain the dialectical tension between being activism and being media art. This would not be possible if they created and maintained long-term, community-based, abortion clinics. While the act of actually performing abortions is crucial (and saving lives from botched illegal abortions is laudable), the symbolic potential of the imagination should not be overlooked and could have a greater strategic effect on the political imagination in the long term, regardless of its effect on abortion law.

Both Voina and Women on Waves construct stories that ignite the imagination. What if we stood up to the authoritarian state in the face of human rights abuses? What if all women had access to free and safe birth control? Their actions demonstrate such possibilities (in short-term tactical interventions) and their media representations create slow-burning ideas. It is not that Russians were previously unaware of liberal democracy, nor is it the case that people in Ireland, Poland and other countries where abortion is illegal were unaware of this possibility. However, sometimes it takes a symbolic gesture to remind people that these alternatives are real and achievable – if they want them. This ethical appeal to the viewer's freedom to engage with the work (or not), is achieved through short-term hit-and-run tactics that ignite long-term strategic imaginations, creating a dialectical tension between art and life, politics and aesthetics.

Militant art education

Militant artists often shun art school education. Only 50 per cent of the artists I interviewed had studied at art school, compared with 98 per cent of contemporary artists more generally.[31] Why, when you are supposed to be able to do practically whatever you want at allegedly radical art schools, do art activists choose to train elsewhere? Art schools have radical histories but, in the UK, they have mostly been incorporated into university art departments. Under the rubric of academia, they have become academicized and employability has been embedded into the art degree curriculum. Classes on how to write a CV or develop a personal statement seem somewhat extraneous to the committed militant artist. This professionalization of the arts might be one reason that militant artists are put off.

Another reason is that art schools have historically underplayed the role of the avant-garde. After the Second World War, the radical avant-garde was co-opted and misunderstood, or wilfully misrepresented, by overemphasizing individual artists and underplaying the role of art collectives. This led to a diminished understanding of the importance of the group ethos: that the artists of the historical avant-garde were both members of art collectives and members of political avant-gardes. Academics ignored the militant commitment and causes behind the artistic avant-gardes, reducing them to a mere political supplement to the 'real' artwork. Writing in 2006, Ray noted that, despite access to more information through the internet and a plethora of archives that we now have, the more militant histories of the avant-garde were still not taught in art schools to any great extent. Why else would there be a need for a master's degree called 'Art: Politics: Transgression: 20th Century Avant-Gardes' (University of Glasgow) if this was sufficiently taught at art school?

Art courses not only neutralize the revolutionary history of the avant-garde but, according to Ray, they also prevent students from being exposed to 'anti-capitalist adventure' and from becoming 'autonomous and ungovernable'.[32] Such curricula inevitably reduce the appeal of the courses to collectives. Students have rebelled against the academic focus on the individual (the Leeds 13 are a case in point), but these were exceptions. If art schools neglect the militant histories of the avant-garde, and if they insist on individual submissions of work for assessment, they atomize potential art collectives and retreat into old notions of individual artistic genius. The fact that most of the militant artists I interviewed were collectives might account for why half of them chose not to study at art school.

The plethora of new courses dedicated to art and politics demonstrates an attempt to rectify this historical oversight, but it also co-opts and institutionalizes radical art activism. For example, an online short course titled 'Art, Ethics and Social Change' (University of the Arts London (UAL), Central Saint Martins) charges £95 per ninety-minute class and states that it provides a certificate of attendance, boasting that 'Certificates are a great addition to your CV'.[33] We have also seen the rise of new full-time educational programmes dedicated to art and social change in the UK and the United States.[34] The Maryland Institute College of Art (MICA) offers a suite of 'Art of Activism Graduate Programs' that aim to prepare artists 'who are committed to social change through real world application'.[35] Whether these courses will cater for and attract militant artists remains to be seen. If UAL is representative of these other courses, then there remains a danger that they will only produce NGO-style official artists: MICA's suite of 'art activist' courses includes an MFA in Community Art, for example. Even if other new programmes are more radical, it is unclear how they can accommodate militant art practices. It is surely impossible to condone lawbreaking, even on a course dedicated to creating social change. Perhaps this is why the following case studies take it upon themselves to train militant art activists.

The Laboratory of Insurrectionary Imagination's experiments and Voina's art school for activists

Some militant art groups utilize the pedagogic sense of 'demonstration' to train art activists. The Laboratory of Insurrectionary Imagination (LabofII), for example, train activists methodologically (in 'hive manoeuvres' and consensus decision-making, which they teach at the beginning of every workshop) and practically (in bicycle repair, for example, that was put to activist use in the *Bike Bloc*, as described in Chapter 4). They have also spawned other successful art activist groups. The Clandestine Insurgent Rebel

Clown Army (C.I.R.C.A.) that I featured in Chapter 4 began as one of LabofII's 'experiments', before growing into a collective of its own. Recall that this started with an 'intense training camp for clowns'. LabofII intended to use clowning and fun as a way to engage with first-time activists who may otherwise be put off by political action. Subsequently, C.I.R.C.A. also ran formal training events, meaning their recruits do not pretend to be clowns but become real, trained, clowns. This complies with the anti-representational requirement of militant art. Both LabofII and C.I.R.C.A. can be viewed as teachers who train art activists. As LabofII also trained C.I.R.C.A. to do this, they can also be considered teacher-trainers.

Liberate Tate were also born out of a LabofII training session. In 2010, Tate Modern commissioned LabofII to run a two-day workshop on art activism called 'Disobedience Makes History' that would explore the most appropriate ways to approach political issues within a publicly funded institution. It was promoted on the homepage of the Tate website and it soon sold out. The night before the workshop, which took place in January 2010, Tate sent an email announcing that any action against the Tate Gallery or its sponsors would not be allowed. LabofII used the email as a pedagogic aid, projecting it onto the wall of the workshop and asking the participants whether they thought the decree should be obeyed. Jordan told me that they did not name and shame the curators who wrote the email, which was probably for the best as they were in the room when it was projected. Two-thirds of the group decided not to obey the order, but to make an intervention targeting Tate's relationship with oil company sponsors instead. Writing for *Art Monthly*, Jordan describes what happened next:

> The following Friday, I was summoned to Tate to discuss the planned intervention. I was met by four people, including head of visitor services and the head of safety and security. They asked me what was going to happen and I told them that I knew as much as they did: that, following the Lab of ii's methodology, the workshop was now entirely self-managed by the participants and

> that the intervention would be designed by them during the final workshop.[36]

This sounds like abdicating responsibility to the participants, rather than leading by example, until you consider that 'Disobedience Makes History' was both tactical (a short-term workshop led by LabofII) and strategic. LabofII knew what might happen and they were in control of the bigger picture. In the short term, they led by example by training the participants. In the longer term, they set in motion a group of nascent art activists who went on to become Liberate Tate. The disobedient participants simply placed the words 'Art Not Oil' in the top floor windows of Tate Modern as a symbolic act of defiance. By the end of the workshop, all the participants (even the obedient ones) had witnessed Tate's various attempts to influence, control and censor them. Following the meeting that Jordan describes earlier in the text, additional staff were placed in the workshop under instruction to halt any action not 'commensurate with Tate's mission',[37] including embarrassing Tate's sponsors.

Like LabofII, Voina also train others to take up the mantle and continue the fight in their own ways. Plutser-Sarno told me that no Voina members had trained at art school, declaring instead that the Voina group is the best art school for the activists who have participated in their actions. They see art schools in the European tradition as conservative environments that teach how to be a good functionary in arts. Voina make tactical interventions but they also strategically influence new generations of members across Russia. They have attracted hundreds of young people who come and work with the group and claim that they are bringing up a new generation of activists. They are said to have had up to two hundred members at one point.[38] Voina also encourage artists to propose actions to be carried out under the Voina 'brand name'. Any art activist can write to them to propose an action to be created independently, but under the Voina moniker (like a franchise). For example, Igor Tchepkasov, an activist from Saint Petersburg declared himself the anarcho-syndicalist wing of the Voina group. He now independently creates actions under their name, with their blessing.

Voina heed my call for artists to take responsibility for their actions by leading by example. Even though they identify as anarchists, Voina have a hierarchical structure with defined roles. Founding member Oleg Vorotnikov is the group's leader. Natalya Sokol is the group's chief coordinator and together they have participated in every Voina action. They were shortly joined by Alexei Plutser-Sarno (the group's media officer and author of their texts), Leonid Nikolaev (the group's president and 'face' of the group)[39] and Yana Sarna, the group's photographer. Together these core members form a leadership team. They declare their actions to be art, and they require others to request permission to work under their name. In 2009, they expelled husband and wife Pyotr Verzilov and Nadezhda Tolokonnikova (who had participated in high-profile Voina actions including *A Dick Captured by the FSB*) reproaching them for being traitors and informers. They accused Verzilov of touring European galleries claiming Voina actions as his own original works, selling and commercializing the 'brand'. Nonetheless, they were unable to prevent Verzilov, Tolokonnikova and Yekaterina Samutsevich from forming the Moscow faction of Voina.

Pussy Riot (established in 2011) is the most famous group to graduate from the Voina art school for militants. The feminist punk band developed from Voina's Moscow faction when Tolokonnikova and Samutsevich were joined by Maria Alyokhina, who was also previously a member of Voina (between 2007 and 2009). The band grew and soon had a fluid membership of between ten and twenty. Pussy Riot gained widespread international sympathy when Tolokonnikova, Samutsevich and Alyokhina performed *Punk Prayer: Mother of God, Chase Putin Away!* at Moscow's Cathedral of Christ the Saviour (2012) – a protest against the Orthodox Church's support for Putin during his election campaign. Five Pussy Riot members entered the cathedral dressed in bright colours and wearing their trademark coloured balaclavas. They crossed themselves and bowed down as if praying before performing the punk song in front of some fans, photographers, bemused churchgoers and staff before they were stopped by security officials.

Punk Prayer bore a striking resemblance to an earlier Voina action. After Russian curator Andrei Yerofeyev was arrested for inciting religious hatred in his exhibition *Forbidden Art* (Sakharov Museum, Moscow 2009) Voina stormed the courtroom under the persona of a punk band called Cock in the Ass. They had smuggled in guitars and, unbelievably, were able to plug in amplifiers before performing a raucous punk song titled 'All Cops Are Bastards' in the courtroom as a theatrical gesture of solidarity with Yerofeyev and his co-defendant. The action, also called *Cock in Ass* (2009), was another demonstration of how citizens can disrupt and stand up to authoritarian regimes.

Three members of Pussy Riot (Tolokonnikova, Samutsevich and Alyokhina) were arrested for performing *Punk Prayer*. They were charged with hooliganism motivated by religious hatred and sentenced to two years in a penal colony (after more than five months remanded in custody). Expelled from Voina, and having lost the founding members of the new Moscow faction, Verzilov became Pussy Riot's unofficial spokesman during their trial. Just before the Winter Olympics in Sochi (2014), all three were released in a cynical act to whitewash Russian authoritarianism. If the Putin administration thought they would remain silent during the Olympics, it was mistaken. The group protested at the Olympics by performing a song titled 'Putin Will Teach You to Love the Motherland'. A video of the performance was widely circulated online. It shows Cossacks, who had been drafted in as additional security for the games (and as a sign of Russian masculinity), beating the girls with whips and pepper spray.

After the Olympics, Tolokonnikova and Alyokhina began to make money from tours and they even made a cameo appearance in the Netflix series *House of Cards* (season three, episode three,

2014), for which they were commissioned to record a song that was used over the end credits. Unhappy with Tolokonnikova's and Alyokhina's commercial enterprises, the group fractured before disbanding in 2015, only to reform for the 2018 FIFA World Cup final, when they invaded the pitch dressed as police officers to protest political arrests.

Thomas Bresolin's *Militant Training Camp*

Thomas Bresolin appropriated the form of the militant training camp as an artwork. An advertisement issued a call for participants, explaining that it would involve physical and mental training in preparation for the inevitable apocalypse and collapse of capitalism. I responded to the advertisement and subsequently attended a recruitment meeting in January 2012 at Arcadia Missa Gallery (South London), where the camp was to be hosted between 8 and 11 March 2012 as part of their *Survival Series*. I met Bresolin, the gallery staff and other potential recruits, all of whom were artists. Bresolin explained that to engage fully on a psychological level, and so that the experience was as intense as possible, the camp needed to be residential: all the recruits would sleep in the gallery. No one would be allowed to go home to their consumerist luxuries: once you were in, you were in for the duration. Bresolin explained some of the particulars of the camp itinerary and what we would be expected to do – at one point intimating that he would train us to make letter bombs. Unsure whether this was a joke, I signed up to become a participant in *Militant Training Camp* anyway. What could go wrong?

The camp began in a manner reminiscent of the scene in *Fight Club* where would-be recruits are denied entry and repeatedly told to go away: only those who refuse to leave and wait outside, enduring verbal and physical abuse with no sustenance, exposed to the elements, for days on end, are allowed to join.[40] On arrival at the gallery, on a cold night in March 2012, the volunteers were kept waiting outside in the rain while, one by one, we were issued uniforms and had our personal belongings, including clothes and mobile phones, confiscated. Once changed into the grey, prison-like, tracksuits, we were subjected to a compulsory exercise regime consisting of press-ups, sit-ups, sprints and squat thrusts, in puddles, on the concrete. This set the acetic tone for the camp and, like the recruits to *Fight Club's* 'project mayhem', we were eventually allowed to enter the gallery.

The camp mimicked aspects of fundamentalist military training camps and prison culture, and Bresolin always kept some information back so we were never quite sure what was going to happen next. From the outset, contact with the outside world was strictly regulated. Our daily routine was rigidly controlled, both to avoid boredom and to maximize the effects of the camp through a militarized regime. We ate a basic diet of simple rations (mainly consisting of rice) and we divided our time between rigorous physical exercise and mental indoctrination through watching at least two daily propaganda films or documentaries about resistance, militancy, anarchism and revolution.

There were regular group marches across London to sites of protest. The first was a march to the recently vacated Occupy camp at Saint Paul's, where the group discussed the limitations of the movement before visiting the relocated protesters at the new Finsbury Square site. Under strict orders not to talk to the public during any of the visits, the militants assumed a subservient relationship to Bresolin, who did all the communicating. On another occasion, Bresolin took his recruits to Colorama in the Elephant and Castle area of South London. Colorama is a long-term anarchist squat, bicycle repair shop and cinema famous for its series known as 'full unemployment cinema' (free film screenings against work). After a screening, Bresolin surprised the squatters with a passionate call to arms and he invited them to the Heygate Estate, where he would unveil his plan for an insurrection in South London. Once there, Bresolin produced a scarily detailed plan drawn onto a large map of

London. He explained that this was part of an Arts Council funding bid to initiate an insurrection. The briefing lasted quite some time. The next excursion was to Freedom Press (Britain's largest anarchist bookshop and oldest anarchist publishing house) in Whitechapel, East London. Bresolin had hired a meeting room and booked a guest speaker – his father Ian, a Canadian who gave a PowerPoint presentation entitled 'No Banks' and called on us to consider Native American social systems as alternatives to capitalism. The trainee militants participated in all these events, but as student recruits rather than horizontalist collaborators.

All this training was an experiment on Bresolin's part to see if he could instil in his participants the militant mindset needed to participate in acts of violence and he would not allow us to participate in the performances until we had completed our training, which lasted several days. The first performance, *Propaganda of the Deed* (8 March 2012), was well attended, shockingly simple and effective. On International Women's Day, Bresolin repeatedly punched Rozsa Farkas (the gallery director) in the face for a full five minutes, while she was seated on a chair (see Figure 6.2). The audience looked on in silence. The performance, which was lit by a single spotlight, featured the camp's banner as a backdrop and another 'militant' standing calmly to attention with a stopwatch: allusions to 'enhanced interrogation' techniques were unavoidable. The punches were 'pulled', but occasionally caused a loud enough crack to make the audience wince: it was uncomfortable to watch. The event left enough bruising for Farkas to struggle to conceal with make-up twenty-four hours later. Her partner was present at the performance, which added to the tension, but she seemed more concerned about an impromptu visit from her father that week.

The performance, as with the entire training camp, was based on permission and compliance. Farkas had volunteered to participate in this performance, which was a recreation of an earlier version where it was Bresolin who was punched in the face. She was fully aware of what the performance would entail, having already seen

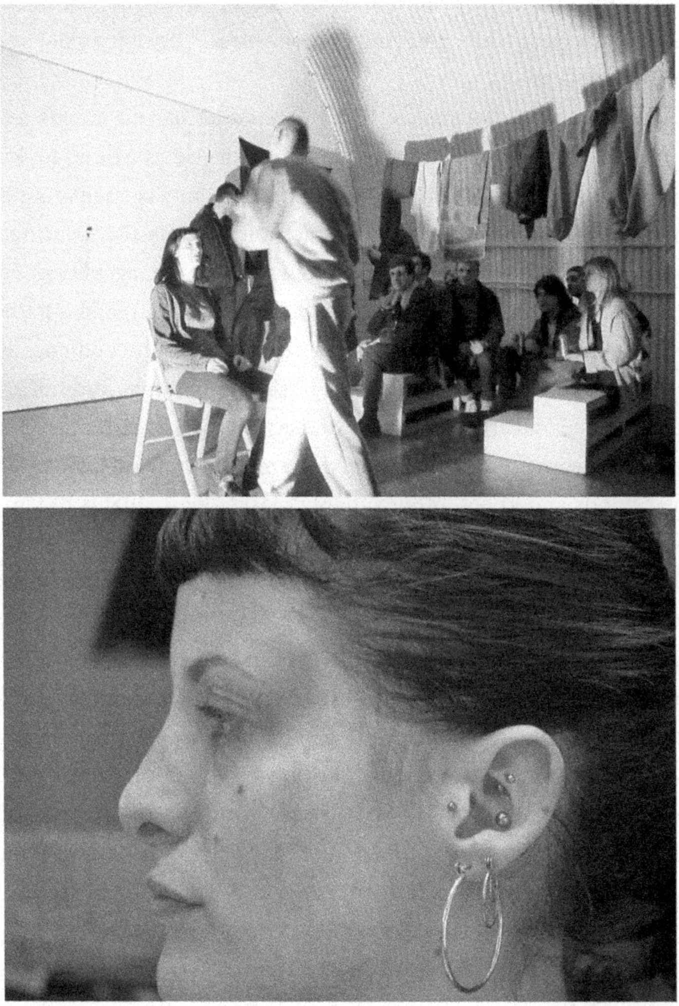

Figure 6.2 Thomas Bresolin, *Propaganda of the Deed*, 2012. © Thomas Bresolin. Reproduced with the permission of the artist.

a video of the earlier version. This tinged the performance with a kind of melancholy. Just as people endure abusive relationships, we too allow ourselves to be implicated in the systemic violence of neoliberalism. After the performance, the audience would probably return to their lives unable to resist the luxuries that consumer capitalism offers while ignoring homelessness, unemployment and in-work poverty.

The second performance, *There Is a Kettle in Our Heads and It Must Be Destroyed*, led by militant recruit Alexis Milne, took a more comic approach. Milne, like all the militants participating in this project, was wearing his grey tracksuit. He was also wearing a badly fitting homemade balaclava and holding a megaphone. He attempted to chart a history of dissent from the 1960s linked to the length of male haircuts. Then he invited some of the audience to wear high-viz vests and don masks of riot police, dogs and horses. Some 'police officers' rode on the 'horses' piggyback-style, carrying vacuum cleaner pipes that served as makeshift truncheons. On their hands and knees, other suitably masked participants became 'police dogs'. The rest of the audience was supplied with masks of famous revolutionaries and revolutionary writers. Milne had been telling us for some time about how we had an inner policeman in our heads and how the police had 'become a kettle'. Encouraging the audience to become one with the kettle, Milne commanded a police charge on the unsuspecting masked audience before, much to everyone's surprise, the police broke down into a dance-cum-mosh pit while punk rock blared out of a stereo. I had the impression that something important had just occurred, but through the chaos, comedy and bewilderment some of it was inevitably lost, or confused. This reminds us that witness testimonies (including those of the police) in the middle of protests and riots cannot be 100 per cent reliable.

Propaganda of the Deed (see Chapter 1) had aesthetic similarities with Wafaa Bilal's *Dog or Iraqi* (see Figure 1.4) and Regina José Galindo's *Confesión* (see Figure 1.5) and this reminds us of the far-reaching aesthetic consequences of the War on Terror. Another of Bresolin's performances *Dog* (2012) also appropriates the aesthetics of 'enhanced interrogations'. American artist Charles Stanton-Jones seated Bresolin in a chair, while prison blues music wailed woefully on a stereo. He stripped Bresolin to the waist and cable-tied him to the same chair where Farkas had been punched, before shaving two patches, one on either side of Bresolin's head. The audience watched in silent anticipation as Stanton-Jones, wearing his militant uniform and a balaclava, attached electrodes to Bresolin's head, chest and arms. I started a PowerPoint presentation that Bresolin had provided, projecting a strange mix of images, consisting of news footage and movie clips, over Bresolin's body while Stanton-Jones, facing straight forward and not even looking at Bresolin, electrocuted him for thirty minutes (see Figure 6.3).

The shock of this performance began to wear off and even get boring the longer it went on. The problem was that some of the video clips and news footage were quite interesting and, as you could not see the electricity, viewers were drawn into watching television and ended up ignoring the torture going on right in front of them: and that was the genius of the performance. Bresolin managed to bring home just how quickly the media can aestheticize violence and how easily we can choose to ignore suffering in favour of banal

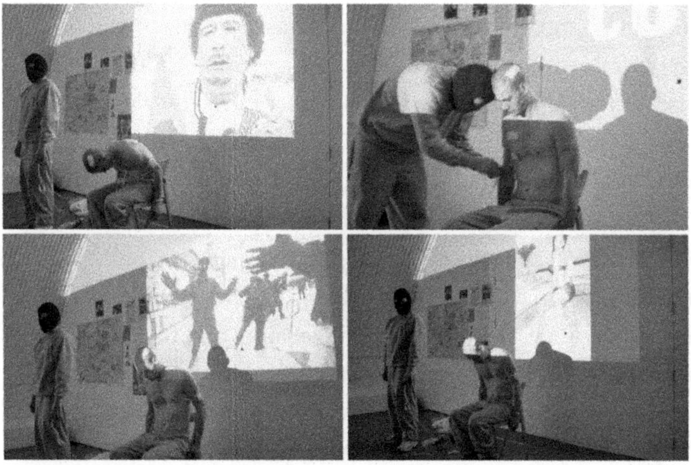

Figure 6.3 Thomas Bresolin, *Dog*, 2012. © Thomas Bresolin. © Thomas Bresolin. Reproduced with the permission of the artist.

television. Bresolin did wake up his viewers at various points: when the movie clips stopped and we were faced with graphic images of violence and consumerism or when he fiercely convulsed or foamed at the mouth, drawing attention to the fact that he was clearly in some pain. This was brought home even more forcefully when the performance finally ended and Stanton-Jones leapt into action quickly cutting the cable ties and electrodes before dragging Bresolin out of the gallery with a sense of urgency, to safety.

The performance of *Militant Training Camp* was not a re-enactment of a 'real' training camp for militants, but authentic training – a pre-enactment. The fact that the participants lived and trained in the gallery space for a week complicates labelling the camp a mere performance, or recreation of militancy. The rehearsals of militant activity (marching, fasting, exercising and so on) blur the line between performing and being. Do we not constantly perform ourselves in different settings? We behave differently when at work than with our family, for example. How does the way we 'perform ourselves' when we attend a political rally or protest differ from the way Bresolin's recruits 'performed' being trainee militants? The participants were beginning to live the life of trainee militants and this exemplary gesture can be read as a pre-enactment. It was a pre-enactment of a mode of resistance against neoliberalism rather than a prefiguration, which would have formed a micro-utopian model of how it believed the world should be while precluding the possibility of strategically changing the world in the long term.

Militant Training Camp blurred the boundaries between representation and presentation. The public performances morphed into the space that the artists were living in. The detritus of the camp, the washing line, the coffee-making facilities and the sleeping bags all remained in the space, infiltrating the performances. Audiences came to experience a performance, but they were confronted with the possibility that they were also tourists, participating in a kind of *Big Brother*-style voyeurism as they viewed the living space and daily actions of the militants. This was not merely part of a performance of living in a gallery space: it was part of the formal shift away from representation and towards presentation that Badiou calls for.

The final exhibition of the camp (Sunday 11 March 2012) was both documentation of something performative, but also something more. It featured Bresolin's South London insurrection map and Arts Council application, his militant's flag, all the debris from the last week and a documentary film of the project as a whole. These objects and the documentation of the camp were never intended to be the artwork, but they did add something to the live performances. They morphed the real (the flag, the map and the detritus) with the performed (evident in the documentaries of visceral performances of genuinely violent acts). This combination realized the dialectical tension between activism (pre-enactment training) and art (installation and video).

Although *Militant Training Camp* was hierarchical, it was also an ethical appeal to the participants' and audiences' freedom to engage with the work and take on Bresolin's propositions. The final performance, *Community Support*, which took place on Saturday 10 March, the day before the exhibition, was intended to signal a kind of graduation from *Militant Training Camp*. During the public opening, a sixth militant suddenly reversed a van into the gallery. The militants, who were all wearing uniforms and balaclavas, jumped out, under instruction to beat up Bresolin for two minutes, then throw him into the back of the van and drive away. This was supposed to signal a rejection of his leadership so that the group could become one of equals, in the vein of an anarcho-syndicalist autonomous commune. The beating was real and performed with gusto but did not last the full two minutes, perhaps signalling sympathy and camaraderie. In any case, the speed with which the performance was executed only added to the shock factor as the audience was left baffled by what they had just witnessed. *Militant Training Camp* created a paradox. It simultaneously used violence and propaganda to convince people of its political aims and, at the same time, used these tools to encourage free thought and debate.

Bresolin's project was certainly committed, but it never felt didactic. Through the artwork, audiences were made aware of political alternatives and that their doing nothing, going along with life as it is presented to them, is also a political choice: one in support of neoliberalism.

Bresolin's tactic of hierarchically leading by example, but intending to evoke the subject's free will, is emblematic of the concept of militant art that I have been trying to evoke throughout this book. He was probably not aware of Sartre's notion of commitment or his 'ethical appeal' (see Chapter 2). Nonetheless, he wears his political commitments on his sleeve, takes aim at his enemies but then steps back. He refuses to be a long-term leader, or be responsible for macro-political change himself, and hands over the baton to others. This pattern is discernible in LabofII and Voina: the former training others to form their own art activist collectives; the latter encouraging the formation of new cells under their name. It is also evident in Etcétera's work: the final example (and a particularly apt one that exemplifies militant art in so many ways) that will conclude this book.

International errorism

Since 2005, Etcétera have become synonymous with a movement called the *Internacional Errorista* (Errorist International), which was born out of a response to post-9/11 anti-terror legislation, taking us back to the start of this book and the claim I made in Chapter 1. In 2005, new anti-terror legislation was passed in Argentina, under pressure from the United States. This was met with scepticism on the Left, some of whom saw its potential to be used to curb political movements and protests. Ponce de León details how some even went as far as to term it 'state terrorism'.[41] In the exhibition guide to *La Normalidad* (Normality) (Palais De Glace, Buenos Aires, 14 February–19 March 2006), Etcétera described how these new laws 'establish sanctions on images or words that can be interpreted as symbolic weapons' and are thus a direct threat to artists and artistic freedom of expression.

The Errorist movement was born during the fourth Summit of the Americas (Mar del Plata, Argentina, 2005), which George W. Bush attended in person. Unsurprisingly, the event had maximum security. The Argentine Navy was stationed offshore and the air force imposed a strict 100-mile no-fly zone over the city, under orders to shoot down any unauthorized planes or helicopters. Three concentric rings of chain-linked fences were erected and more than twenty streets were closed. About 10,000 local security forces were deployed (including the Argentine National Gendarmerie) and, of course, American security forces were on the ground. This is how free trade deals were now made. The Errorist's founding action, *Operación BANG!*, was an example of tactical trespass, in the context of international summits that I detailed in Chapter 4.

The Errorists had hijacked the summit with humour. They emerged from the sea at San Sebastian Beach near the city centre, seemingly bearing arms, and took the beachhead (see Figure 6.4). It was as if a commando unit had just crossed the Atlantic but then unfurled a banner that read *Erroristas*. The police quickly confronted them, but were somewhat embarrassed when they realized that their guns and bazookas were only photocopies mounted on cardboard and some had red pennants protruding from the barrels that, in cartoon-style, said 'BANG!' They told the police that they were making a film about how the media overreact to perceived terrorist threats. The forces demanded to see their filming permit, which to their surprise was duly produced (artists can be skilled forgers). Around that point, Airforce One flew overhead and the Errorists took aim with their cardboard weapons. The use of humour distinguishes this militant art action from political activism and, in this case, the use of cardboard guns separates Errorism from terrorism. The Errorists retain a strong aesthetic element, which is held in tension with the real-life antagonistic situation they find

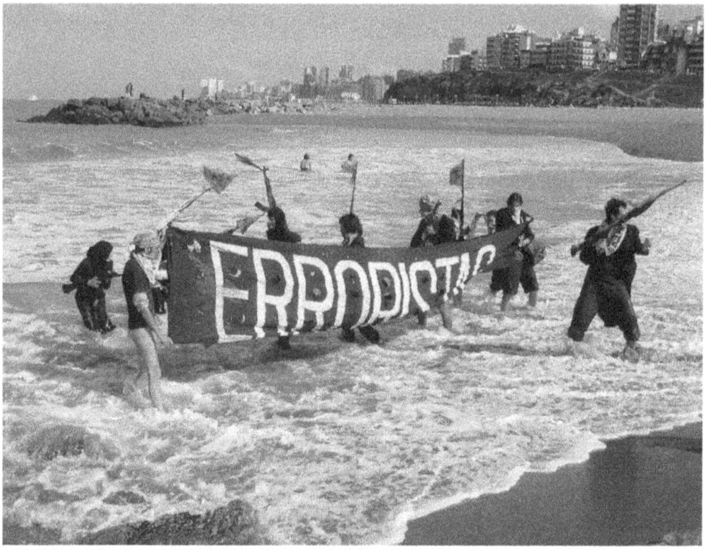

Figure 6.4 Etcétera, *Operación BANG!* 2005. © Etcétera. Reproduced with the permission of the artist.

themselves in (confronted by the police, but also the situation more generally in Mar del Plata).

The Errorists appropriated military aesthetics: they wore all black (like the anarchist Black Blocs – see Chapter 4), keffiyehs that partially covered their faces and they carried cardboard Kalashnikovs. The composite image of the militant – part anarchist, part Islamist – echoes Wafaa Bilal's *The Night of Bush Capturing: A Virtual Jihadi* (2008), where the artist hacked the Quest for Saddam video game and inserted himself as a suicide bomber. He imagined that after learning of his brother Haji's death (see Chapter 1), he was recruited by al-Qaeda and set off on a quest to find George W. Bush. The hacked game features images of crusader knights wearing explosive belts and carrying Uzis.

Operación BANG! was both tactical (in its temporary incursion) *and* strategic (in the way it was composed for its later media distribution). Ponce de León describes how the Errorists 'composed two series of photos, titled and captioned them in ways that mimic conventions of journalistic reportage on breaking news, and disseminated them on *Indymedia Argentina*.[42] 'Headlines' included 'Errorists Take a Beach in Mar del Plata' and 'Errorists Continue Advance across Mar del Plata's Coast'. The Errorists risked arrest by exposing how the United States could dictate security operations abroad to obscure trade deals made across the Americas and prevent protests. *Operación BANG!* revealed how the media reports such international summits and how they report terrorism.

Returning to Lacy's five levels of audience (see Chapter 4), we can see that Etcétera engaged: (1) the people who directly participated; (2) the people who saw or who were directly targeted by the event (the police, for example); (3) the people who were not directly targeted by the action, but who saw it anyway – live and in reality (passers-by); (4) people who saw a representation of the event, who read about it or saw photographs of it (in the media or future exhibitions), but who never saw the live event and (5) the people who would one day recall the day when Errorists stormed a beach during the Summit of the Americas – the myth of the event, the wild narrative.

The Errorists led by the example of their action, what Ponce de León describes as 'a kind of surrealist guerrilla force',[43] but also through issuing statements. They issued a *Primera Declaración* (First Declaration) in 2005 that read:

1. 'Errorism': Concept and action are based on the idea that 'error' is reality's principle of order.
2. 'Errorism' is a philosophically erroneous position, a ritual of negation, a disorganised organisation: failure as perfection, error as appropriate move.
3. The field of action of 'Errorism' contains all those practices that aim at the LIBERATION of the human being and language.
4. Confusion and surprise – black humour and absurdity are the favourite tools of the 'Errorists'.
5. 'Lapses' and failed acts are an 'Errorist' delight.[44]

This was followed by the *Internacional Errorista Manifiesto* (Manifesto of the Errorist International), which is sometimes numbered 1, 2, 3, 5, 6, other times 1, 2, 3, 5, 5, 1 (with one being repeated verbatim), but which I have numbered here chronologically (my translation).

1. We are all Errorists.
2. Errorism bases its actions on error.
3. Errorism is a mistaken philosophical position, a denial ritual and a disorganized organization.
4. Errorism exists and does not exist.
5. Failure as perfection. Error as success.

Etcétera did not want to fully define Errorism: they wanted to kick-start a movement where others would establish cells in different cities across the world. They wanted new Errorists to contribute to the movement, rather than blindly follow Etcétera's guidance, which is why the statements are more enigmatic than dogmatic. When I asked Etcétera about Errorism, they seemed evasive for the same reason: they did not want to explain it to me, they wanted me to become my own kind of Errorist. Indeed, before we met, I had sent them a video declaring the founding of the UK Errorist cell.

This cellular approach that Etcétera proposed was already evident in al-Qaeda and Anonymous and would become a key part of the Occupy movement. While Occupy was famously a leaderless, horizontalist movement, al-Qaeda was different. Ostensibly it was hierarchical, with Osama bin Laden at its head. In reality, cells operated independently, following the actions performed by other terrorists, 9/11 being the main example to follow. This was not copied literally but rather interpreted into equivalent acts such as the 2004 Madrid train bombings or the '7/7 attacks' (London, 2005) where three underground trains and a bus were bombed; 9/11 was a propaganda of the deed act of leading by example, which independent cells followed, and this is the model that Etcétera was appropriating in their formation of the *Internacional Errorista*.

This book has argued that militant artists must lead the way in demonstrating contingency and making the impossible seem achievable, but that they must do so without falling into the traps of didactic or purely propagandistic or aesthetically autonomist art. The examples of the Errorists and other artists showcased in this book managed to strike this delicate balance in their unique and innovative ways and illustrate the successful navigation of this tricky territory. Whether readers find them unusual, humorous or even shocking, their shock tactics, disruption, antagonism, confrontation and provocation have been demonstrated to belong in an avant-garde tradition that exposes what must be repressed to sustain the semblance of social harmony. I trust that this book will inspire future generations of art activists to push the boundaries and create new and exciting ways of engaging with the world around us.

Notes

Preface

1 See Barbara B. Kawulich, 'Participant Observation as a Data Collection Method', *Forum Qualitative Sozialforschung/ Forum: Qualitative Social Research*, qualitative-research.net, 6, no. 2 (May 2005), https://doi.org/10.17169/fqs-6.2.466.

2 For more information on militant research, see Stevphen Shukaitis, David Graeber and Erika Biddle, eds, *Constituent Imagination: Militant Investigations/Collective Theorization* (Edinburgh: AK Press, 2007); Natalie Bookchin, Pamela Brown, Suzahn Ebrahimia, Colectivo Enmedio and Alexandra Juhasz, *Militant Research Handbook* (New York: New York University, 2013), http://www.visualculturenow.org/wp-content/uploads/2013/09/MRH_Web.pdf; Sam Halvorsen, 'Militant Research against-and-beyond Itself: Critical Perspectives from the University and Occupy London', *Area* 47, no. 4 (2015): 466–72, https://doi.org/10.1111/area.12221; Tania Herrera, 'Militant Research', *Krisis Journal for Contemporary Philosophy*, no. 2 (2018): 10–11; 113–14, https://krisis.eu/wp-content/uploads/2018/07/Krisis-2018-2-Tania-Herrera-Militant-research.pdf?.

Acknowledgements

1 Martin Lang and Thomas Bresolin, 'Militant Training Camp: The Debriefing', *Sanat Dünyamiz*, no. 131 (2012): 30–41.

2 Martin Lang and Tom Grimwood, 'Militant Training Camp and the Aesthetics of Civil Disobedience', *Krisis Journal for Contemporary Philosophy*, no. 3 (2012): 37–51.

3 Martin Lang, 'Counter Cultural Production: A Militant Reconfiguration of Peter Bürger's "Neo-Avant-Garde"', *Re·bus – a Journal of Art History and Theory*, no. 8 (2017): 24–49, https://www1.

essex.ac.uk/arthistory/research/pdfs/rebus/rebus_issue_8_vol_1.pdf#page=27.

4 Martin Lang, 'Spectacular Malaise: Art and the End of History', *Art & the Public Sphere* 8, no. 1 (1 July 2019): 63–82, https://doi.org/10.1386/aps_00006_1.

Introduction

1 For an in-depth critique of art that delegates authorship to non-artist participants, see my article 'Hazlitt on Aesthetic Democracy and Artistic Genius', *Hazlitt Review* 14 (2021): 25–36.

2 Mark Bray, 'Horizontalism', in *Anarchism: A Conceptual Approach*, ed. Benjamin Franks, Nathan Jun and Leonard Williams, eBook (New York: Routledge, 2018), 138.

3 Alain Badiou, *Ethics: An Essay on the Understanding of Evil*, trans. Peter Hallward, Radical Thinkers (London: Verso, [1998] 2001), 90.

4 Badiou, *Ethics*, 75.

5 See Ken Jackson, 'The Great Temptation of "Religion": Why Badiou Has Been So Important to Žižek', *International Journal of Zizek Studies* 1, no. 2 (2007), https://zizekstudies.org/index.php/IJZS/article/view/32/29; Matthew Sharpe and Geoff M. Boucher, *Zizek and Politics: A Critical Introduction*, 1st edition (Edinburgh: Edinburgh University Press, 2010), 5; 84; 222.

6 Sharpe and Boucher, *Zizek and Politics.*

7 Slavoj Žižek, *The Sublime Object of Ideology*, Paperback edition, Essential Žižek (London: Verso, [1989] 2008), 30.

8 Marc James Léger, *Vanguardia: Socially Engaged Art and Theory*, Illustrated edition (Manchester: Manchester University Press, 2019), 6.

9 Léger, *Vanguardia*, 201.

10 Léger, *Vanguardia*, 1–2.

11 Karl Marx and Friedrich Engels, *Marx and Engels on Literature and Art: A Selection of Writings*, ed. Lee Baxandall and Stefan Morawski (St Louis, MO: Telos Press, 1973), 135.

12 Nicolas Bourriaud, *Relational Aesthetics*, trans. Simon Pleasance, Collection Documents sur l'art (Dijon: Presse du réel, 2002), 30–2.
13 Michel de Certeau, *The Practice of Everyday Life*, trans. Steven Rendall (Berkeley: University of California Press, 1988).
14 Jacques Rancière, *Aesthetics and Its Discontents*, trans. Steven Corcoran (Cambridge: Polity Press, 2009), 54.

1 Art activism after 9/11

1 Gregory Sholette, *Dark Matter: Art and Politics in the Age of Enterprise Culture*, Marxism & Culture (London: Pluto Press, 2011), 136.
2 Gene Ray, 'History, Sublime, Terror: Notes on the Politics of Fear', in *The Sublime Now*, ed. Luke White and Claire Pajaczkowska (Newcastle Upon Tyne: Cambridge Scholars Publishing, 2009), 141.
3 William Grimes, 'Arnold Mesches, Artist Who Was Recorded by the F.B.I., Dies at 93', *New York Times*, 9 November 2016, sec. Arts, https://www.nytimes.com/2016/11/10/arts/design/arnold-mesches-artist-who-was-recorded-by-the-fbi-dies-at-93.html.
4 Grant Pooke, *Francis Klingender 1907–1955: A Marxist Art Historian out of Time* (London: Gill Vista Marx Press, 2007).
5 Nato Thompson in Benjamin H. D. Buchloh, Rachel Churner, Zainab Bahrani, Judith Barry, Christopher Bedford, Claire Bishop, Susan Buck-Morss, Critical Art Ensemble, T. J. Demos, Rosalyn Deutsche, Okwui Enwezor, Hannah Feldman, Harrell Fletcher, Coco Fusco, Liam Gillick, Mark Godfrey, Tim Griffin, Hans Haacke, Rachel Haidu, David Joselit, Silvia Kolbowski, Carin Kuoni, Carrie Lambert-Beatty, Pamela M. Lee, Simon Leung, Lucy R. Lippard and Nato Thompson, 'Questionnaire: In What Ways Have Artists, Academics, and Cultural Institutions Responded to the U.S.-Led Invasion and Occupation of Iraq?' *October*, no. 123 (Winter 2008): 167.
6 Thompson in Buchloh et al., 'Questionnaire', 167.
7 Ray, 'History, Sublime, Terror', 141.
8 Roger A. Clarke, 'Information Technology and Dataveillance', *Communications of the ACM* 31, no. 5 (1988): 499, https://doi.org/10.1145/42411.42413 (italics in original).

9 Gabriella Coleman, *Hacker, Hoaxer, Whistleblower, Spy: The Many Faces of Anonymous*, eBook edition (London: Verso, 2014), 317.
10 Coleman, *Hacker*, 316.
11 Slavoj Žižek first outlined this concept in his 1993 essay, 'Why Are Laibach and the Neue Slowenische Kunst Not Fascists?' in *The Universal Exception*, ed. Rex Butler and Scott Stephens, Expanded edition (repr., London: Continuum, [1993] 2007), 63–6.
12 Slavoj Žižek, *The Sublime Object of Ideology*, Paperback edition, Essential Žižek (repr., London: Verso, [1989] 2008), 24.
13 David Rokeby, 'Algorithmic Pollution' (Lecture, Cyber Insecurities Panel, Pepco Edison Place Gallery [Washington, DC], September 2013).
14 Lisa Moren, 'Algorithmic Pollution: Artists Working with Dataveillance and Societies of Control', *Media–N: Journal of the New Media Caucus* 13, no. 1 (20 August 2017): 58–85, http://median.newmediacaucus.org/uncovering-news-reporting-and-forms-of-new-media-art/algorithmic-pollution-artists-working-with-dataveillance-and-societies-of-control/.
15 Moren, 'Algorithmic Pollution', 71.
16 Scott Rothkopf, 'Embedded in the Culture: The Art of Paul Chan', *Artforum* 44, no. 10 (Summer 2006): 305.
17 Lytle Shaw and Emilie Clark, 'LISTSERV 16.5 – POETICS Archives', University at Buffalo: State University of New York, 20 February 2003, https://listserv.buffalo.edu/cgi-bin/wa?A2=ind0302&L=poetics&D=1&P=555973.
18 Rothkopf, 'Embedded in the Culture', 305.
19 Tim Griffin in Buchloh et al., 'Questionnaire', 71.
20 Rothkopf, 'Embedded in the Culture', 305.
21 Nicola Triscott, 'Performative Science in an Age of Specialization: The Case of Critical Art Ensemble', in *Interfaces of Performance*, ed. Maria Chatzichristodoulou and Janis Jefferies (Farnham: Ashgate, 2009), 165.
22 Gregory Sholette, 'Critical Art Ensemble', in *Oxford Art Online* (Oxford University Press, 16 September 2010), https://doi.org/10.1093/gao/9781884446054.article.T2088814.
23 Colin Perry, 'Heath Bunting', *Art Monthly*, no. 334 (March 2010): 30.
24 Fusco in Buchloh et al., 'Questionnaire', 54.

25 Nancy Princenthal, 'Taking Liberties', *Art in America* 93, no. 11 (December 2005): 70.

26 This material would later be included in Critical Art Ensemble's artwork *Seized* (2008), which also features all the documents and objects confiscated by the FBI.

27 Lucy Lippard in Buchloh et al., 'Questionnaire', 105.

28 Critical Art Ensemble in Buchloh et al., 'Questionnaire', 31.

29 Nato Thompson, 'Living as Form', in *Living as Form: Socially Engaged Art from 1991–2011*, ed. Nato Thompson, Illustrated edition (New York: Creative Time Books, 2012), 154.

30 Stuart Millar, 'Easy to Commit, Hard to Detect: Identity Scam Is Growing Threat', *The Guardian*, 27 February 2003, Online edition, sec. UK news, https://www.theguardian.com/uk/2003/feb/27/ukcrime.stuartmillar.

31 Marc Garrett, 'Heath Bunting, The Status Project & The Netopticon', in *Heath Bunting: How to Build a New Legal Identity*, ed. Katerina Gkoutziouli, Marianna Christofi and Maria Varela (Athens: Frown Tails, 2014), no pagination.

32 Department for Digital, Culture, Media & Sport and Matt Warman, 'Next Steps Outlined for UK's Use of Digital Identity', GOV.UK, 1 September 2022, https://www.gov.uk/government/news/next-steps-outlined-for-uks-use-of-digital-identity.

33 Denisa Tomkova, 'From Dialogical Aesthetics in Eastern European Art to "Falling in Love" with the Other(s): Discourses on Hospitality in Contemporary Europe', *Third Text* 34, nos 4–5 (2 September 2020): 491, https://doi.org/10.1080/09528822.2020.1836814.

34 Tomkova, 'From Dialogical Aesthetics', 490–1.

35 Ztohoven, 'Citizen K.', Ztohoven.cz, accessed 18 October 2021, https://www.ztohoven.cz/?page_id=87.

36 *Občan K. (Citizen K.)*, directed by Michal Dvořák, produced by Ztohoven (Czech Republic: ROMEOFILMS, 2012).

37 Tomkova, 'From Dialogical Aesthetics', 488.

38 Alan R. Ingram, 'Making Geopolitics Otherwise: Artistic Interventions in Global Political Space: Making Geopolitics Otherwise', *The Geographical Journal* 177, no. 3 (September 2011): 220, https://doi.org/10.1111/j.1475-4959.2011.00415.x.

39 See, Robert Gould, 'Roma Rights and Roma Expulsions in France: Official Discourse and EU Responses', *Critical Social Policy* 35, no. 1 (2015): 24–44, https://doi.org/10.1177/0261018314545595; European Greens, 'Freedom of Movement and Roma Expulsions', European Greens, accessed 20 October 2021, https://europeangreens.eu/content/freedom-movement-and-roma-expulsions.
40 Sissu Tarka, 'BorderXing: Heath Bunting', *Afterall: A Journal of Art, Context and Enquiry*, 19 March 2009, https://www.afterall.org/article/borderxing.heath.bunting.sissu.tarka.
41 Florian Schneider, 'Intermedia Art: Reverse Authentification', Tate, June 2002, https://www.tate.org.uk/intermediaart/entry15468.shtm.
42 Niamh McIntyre and Mark Rice-Oxley, 'It's 34,361 and Rising: How the List Tallies Europe's Migrant Bodycount', *The Guardian*, 20 June 2018, sec. World News, 361, https://www.theguardian.com/world/2018/jun/20/the-list-europe-migrant-bodycount.
43 Daphna Ben-Shaul, 'Critically Civic: Public Movement's Performance Activism', in *Performance Studies in Motion: International Perspectives in the Twenty-First Century*, ed. Atay Citron, Sharon Aronson-Lehavi and David Zerbib (London: Bloomsbury Methuen Drama, 2014), 119.
44 This hierarchical, militaristic, structure characterizes the group's earlier years, but it is less representative of their activity since 2011, which is conceived and led by various in-group collaborations, which they see as key to their sustainability and ongoing development.
45 George Bush W., 'President Bush's Speech in Full', *The Telegraph*, 21 September 2001, sec. World News, https://www.telegraph.co.uk/news/worldnews/northamerica/usa/1341316/President-Bushs-speech-in-full.html.
46 Hannah Feldman, 'Orchestral Maneuvers in the Light', in *Allora & Calzadilla*, ed. Beatrix Ruf (Zurich: JRP|Ringier, 2009), 29.
47 Hannah Feldman, 'Sound Tracks: The Art of Jennifer Allora and Guillermo Calzadilla', *Artforum* 45, no. 9 (May 2007): 338.
48 Beatrix Ruf, ed., *Allora & Calzadilla* (Zurich: JRP|Ringier, 2009), 126.
49 Feldman, 'Sound Tracks', 338.
50 Yates McKee, 'Wake, Vestige, Survival: Sustainability and the Politics of the Trace in Allora and Calzadilla's Land Mark', *October*, no. 133 (2010): 20–48.

51 Bilal kept a video diary (accessible on his website) documenting his deteriorating mental and physical condition over the duration of the performance. By the end of the exhibition, Bilal is suffering from exhaustion. This echoes tensions that exist in communities vulnerable to military attacks, where a bomb could explode on a house at any moment and where a car bomb could explode in any market on any given day. In addition to vitriolic comments and actions, some of the web-based public acted to protect Bilal by moving the gun so that it pointed away from him.

52 Wafaa Bilal and Kari Lydersen, *Shoot an Iraqi: Art, Life and Resistance under the Gun*, eBook edition (San Francisco: City Lights Publishers, 2008), 174.

53 Bilal and Lydersen, *Shoot an Iraqi*, 138.

54 Dora Apel, 'The Body as Political Corpus', in *War Culture and the Contest of Images*, eBook (New Brunswick, NJ: Rutgers University Press, 2012), 112.

55 Julian Stallabrass quoted in Apel, 'The Body as Political Corpus', 113.

56 'What Is the Anarchist Black Cross?' Anarchist Black Cross Network: Resistance Is Global, 17 October 2008, https://web.archive.org/web/20081017144747/http://www.anarchistblackcross.org/abc/why.html.

57 'What Is the Anarchist Black Cross?'

58 Thomas Bresolin, 'Daily Hunger Strike Statements', Blind Tom Bresolin, Blog, 2012, http://blindtombresolin.blogspot.co.uk/2012_08_01_archive.html.

2 Refuse/resist

1 Tate, 'Activist Art – Art Term', Tate, accessed 9 October 2018, https://www.tate.org.uk/art/art-terms/a/activist-art.

2 Alain Badiou, 'Does the Notion of Activist Art Still Have Meaning?' (Keynote, Miguel Abreu Gallery [New York], 13 October 2010), https://vimeo.com/16453571.

3 Tania Bruguera cited in Alain Bieber, 'I Revolt, Therefore I Am', in *Art & Agenda: Political Art and Activism*, ed. Robert Klanten, Mattias

Hübner, Alain Bieber, Pedro Alonzo, Gregor Jansen and Silke Krohn (Berlin: Gestalten, 2011), 53.

4 Tania Bruguera, 'Political Art Statement', taniabruguera.com, 2010, http://www.taniabruguera.com/cms/388-0-Political+Art+Statement.htm.

5 Badiou, 'Does the Notion of Activist Art Still Have Meaning?'

6 Tania Bruguera cited in Nato Thompson, ed., *Living as Form: Socially Engaged Art from 1991–2011*, Illustrated edition (New York: Creative Time Books, 2012), 21 (italics in original).

7 Jeremy Deller cited in Nato Thompson, ed., *Living as Form: Socially Engaged Art from 1991–2011*, Illustrated edition (New York: Creative Time Books, 2012), 17.

8 Lang and Reeve give a thorough account of how New Labour required galleries and museums to provide educational and social services. Caroline Lang and John Reeve, *The Responsive Museum: Working with Audiences in the Twenty-First Century* (London: Routledge, 2016).

9 Project Art Works, 'About Us', Project Art Works, accessed 13 June 2022, https://projectartworks.org/the-organisation/.

10 Marc James Léger, *Vanguardia: Socially Engaged Art and Theory*, Illustrated edition (Manchester: Manchester University Press, 2019), 1.

11 BAVO, ed., *Cultural Activism Today: The Art of Over-Identification*, 1st edition (Rotterdam: Episode Publishers, 2007), 23.

12 Léger, *Vanguardia*, 2.

13 BAVO, *Cultural Activism Today*, 27.

14 BAVO, *Cultural Activism Today*, 291.

15 BAVO, *Cultural Activism Today*, 28.

16 BAVO, 'Artists, One More Effort to Be Really Political', in *Art and Activism in the Age of Globalization*, ed. Lieven De Cauter, Runem De Roo and Karl Vanhaesebrouck, Illustrated edition, vol. 8, Reflect (Rotterdam: NAi Publishers, 2011), 295.

17 Claire Bishop, *Artificial Hells: Participatory Art and the Politics of Spectatorship* (London: Verso, 2012), 3.

18 Fern Riddell, 'Suffragettes, Violence and Militancy', British Library, 6 February 2018, https://www.bl.uk/votes-for-women/articles/suffragettes-violence-and-militancy.

19 Christabel Pankhurst was first arrested in 1905 for disrupting a Liberal Party meeting by shouting her demands for votes for women. She went to prison rather than pay the fine. She was subsequently arrested in 1907 and 1909. Released from prison under the 'Cat and Mouse Act', Christabel fled to France, where she orchestrated a militant campaign for universal suffrage. Upon her return in 1914, at the outbreak of the First World War (which she supported), she was arrested once more and went on hunger strike to (successfully) secure an early release.

20 Christabel Pankhurst, 'What Militancy Means', *The Suffragette*, 2 May 1913, 492.

21 Pankhurst, 'What Militancy Means', 492.

22 Filippo Tommaso Marinetti, 'The Founding and Manifesto of Futurism [1909]', in *Futurism: An Anthology*, ed. Lawrence S. Rainey, Christine Poggi and Laura Wittman (New Haven, CT: Yale University Press, 2009), 51.

23 Pankhurst, 'What Militancy Means', 492.

24 Bishop, *Artificial Hells*, 3.

25 Bishop, *Artificial Hells*, 3.

26 *The Baader Meinhof Complex*, directed by Uli Edel, produced by Wolf-Dietrich Brücker and Bernd Eichinger (Germany: Constantin Film Verleih, 2008).

27 Ulrike Meinhof, *Everybody Talks about the Weather … We Don't: The Writings of Ulrike Meinhof*, ed. Karin Bauer, trans. Luise Von Flotow, POLS (New York: Seven Stories Press, 2008).

28 The Pankhursts and Meinhof were both educated and cultured before choosing to turn to militancy. Christabel Pankhurst and Meinhof both came from respectable backgrounds that have links to art. Christabel's sister, Sylvia, was an artist and Meinhof's father was an art historian. Both of Meinhof's parents held doctorates (her father was a museum director and her mother a teacher). Pankhurst's father was a barrister and her mother was a shop owner who also worked as a registrar.

29 Ulrike Meinhof, 'From Protest to Resistance', in *Everybody Talks about the Weather … We Don't: The Writings of Ulrike Meinhof*, ed. Karin Bauer, trans. Luise Von Flotow, 1st ed. (New York: Seven Stories Press, 2008), 239.

30 Bishop, *Artificial Hells*, 3.

31 Dominic Fox, *Cold World: The Aesthetics of Dejection and the Politics of Militant Dysphoria* (Winchester: 0 Books, 2009).
32 Fox, *Cold World*, 43.
33 Fox, *Cold World*, 67.
34 Samuel Taylor Coleridge, *The Complete Poetical Works of Samuel Taylor Coleridge*, ed. Ernest Hartley Coleridge, vol. 1 (Oxford: Clarendon Press, 1975), 363–4.
35 Bishop, *Artificial Hells*, 276.
36 Claire Bishop, 'The Social Turn: Collaboration and Its Discontents', *Artforum* 44, no. 6 (February 2006): 181.
37 Grant H. Kester, 'Another Turn', *Artforum* 44, no. 9 (May 2006): 22.
38 Jerrold Levinson provides a comprehensive reader for this field of aesthetics. Jerrold Levinson, ed., *Aesthetics and Ethics: Essays at the Intersection*, Cambridge Studies in Philosophy and the Arts (Cambridge: Cambridge University Press, 1998). See also Noël Carroll, 'Art and Ethical Criticism: An Overview of Recent Directions of Research', *Ethics* 110, no. 2 (2000): 350–87.
39 Ella Peek, 'Ethical Criticism of Art', in *Internet Encyclopedia of Philosophy*, accessed 27 November 2018, https://iep.utm.edu/art-eth/.
40 Oliver Conolly, 'Ethicism and Moderate Moralism', *British Journal of Aesthetics* 40, no. 3 (2000): 302, https://doi.org/10.1093/bjaesthetics/40.3.302.
41 Peek, 'Ethical Criticism of Art'.
42 See Leo Tolstoy, *What Is Art?*, trans. Richard Pevear and Larissa Volokhonsky, Penguin Classics (London: Penguin, 1995).
43 Peek, 'Ethical Criticism of Art'. According to Ella Peek, 'the terms "autonomism" and "aestheticism" can be used interchangeably.' While there may be subtle differences, they are not important for this book. I prefer the term 'autonomism' because it refers to art's autonomy from ethics and politics.
44 Oscar Wilde, *The Picture of Dorian Gray*, eBook (Sweden: Wisehouse Classics, 2015), 6.
45 Bishop, *Artificial Hells*, 17.
46 Bishop, 'The Social Turn: Collaboration and Its Discontents', 180 (italics in original).

47 Berys Gaut, 'The Ethical Criticism of Art', in *Aesthetics and Ethics*, ed. Jerrold Levinson (Cambridge: Cambridge University Press, 1998), 195 (italics in original).
48 Theodor Adorno, 'Commitment', trans. Francis McDonagh, *New Left Review* I, nos 87–88 (1974): 88.
49 Adorno, 'Commitment', 89.
50 Adorno, 'Commitment', 89.
51 Adorno, 'Commitment', 88.
52 Adorno, 'Commitment', 84.
53 Adorno, 'Commitment', 84.
54 Adorno, 'Commitment', 78.
55 Theodor W. Adorno, 'Engagement', in *Noten Zur Literatur*, ed. Rolf Tiedemann (Frankfurt am Main: Suhrkamp Verlag AG, 1965), 412.
56 Georg Lukacs, 'Propaganda or Partisanship?' trans. Leonard F. Mins, *Partizan Review* 1, no. 2 (1934): 36–46, http://www.bu.edu/partisanreview/books/PR1934V1N2/HTML/files/assets/basic-html/../../../index.html.
57 Georg Lukacs, '"Tendency" or "Partisanship?"' in *Art in Theory, 1900–2000: An Anthology of Changing Ideas*, ed. Charles Harrison and Paul Wood, trans. David Fernback (Oxford: Blackwell, 2003), 413–17.
58 Charles Harrison and Paul Wood, eds, *Art in Theory, 1900–2000: An Anthology of Changing Ideas*, 2nd edn (Malden, MA: Blackwell Publishing, 2003), 413.
59 Andrew Hemingway, 'John Reed Clubs and Proletarian Art–Part I', *Against the Current*, no. 177 (2015), https://againstthecurrent.org/atc177/p4467/.
60 Theo van Doesburg, 'Anti-Tendenzkunst: An Answer to the Question: "Should the New Art Serve the Masses?"' *De Stijl* 6, no. 2 (April 1923): 18, https://nl.wikisource.org/wiki/De_Stijl/Jaargang_6/Nummer_2/Anti-tendenzkunst.
61 van Doesburg, 'Anti-Tendenzkunst', 19.
62 Léger, *Vanguardia*, 12.
63 Adorno, 'Commitment', 88.
64 Bishop, *Artificial Hells*, 276.
65 Jean-Paul Sartre, *'What Is Literature?' and Other Essays*, trans. Steven Ungar, Paperback edition (repr., Cambridge, MA: Harvard University Press, [1948] 1988), 38.

66 Sartre, *What Is Literature*, 36.
67 Sartre, *What Is Literature*, 68.
68 Sartre, *What Is Literature*, 68.
69 Walter Benjamin, 'The Author as Producer', in *Selected Writings Volume 2, Part 2 1931–1934*, ed. Marcus Bullock and Michael W. Jennings, trans. Rodney Livingstone, Paperback edition, vol. 1, Walter Benjamin Selected Writings (Cambridge, MA: Belknap Press of Harvard University Press, 2005), 768.
70 Benjamin, 'Author as Producer', 768.
71 Benjamin, 'Author as Producer', 769.
72 Benjamin, 'Author as Producer', 769.
73 Benjamin, 'Author as Producer', 769.
74 Benjamin, 'Author as Producer', 770.
75 Benjamin, 'Author as Producer', 777.
76 Sartre, *What Is Literature*, 39.
77 Thomas Hirschhorn, Alison Gingeras, Benjamin. H. D. Buchloh and Carlos Basualdo, *Thomas Hirschhorn* (London: Phaidon, 2004), 31.
78 Thomas Hirschhorn, *Critical Laboratory: The Writings of Thomas Hirschhorn*, ed. Lisa Lee and Hal Foster (Cambridge, MA: MIT Press, 2013), 238.
79 Thomas Hirschhorn, 'Doing Art Politically: What Does This Mean?' in *Critical Laboratory: The Writings of Thomas Hirschhorn*, ed. Lisa Lee and Hal Foster (Cambridge, MA: MIT Press, 2013), 72–7.
80 Adorno, 'Commitment', 78.
81 Oliver Marchart, *Conflictual Aesthetics: Artistic Activism and the Public Sphere* (Berlin: Sternberg Press, 2019), 12–14.
82 Marchart, *Conflictual Aesthetics*, 14.
83 Jacques Rancière, *Aesthetics and Its Discontents*, trans. Steven Corcoran (Cambridge: Polity Press, 2009), 60 (italics in original).
84 Marchart, *Conflictual Aesthetics*, 44.
85 Rancière, *Aesthetics and Its Discontents*, 57.
86 Jacques Rancière, *The Politics of Aesthetics: The Distribution of the Sensible*, trans. Gabriel Rockhill, reprint (London: Continuum, 2011), 63.
87 Bishop, *Artificial Hells*, 29 (italics in original).
88 Rancière, *The Politics of Aesthetics*, 63.

3 Avant-garde militancy

1 Marc James Léger, *Vanguardia: Socially Engaged Art and Theory*, Illustrated edition (Manchester: Manchester University Press, 2019), 2.
2 Léger, *Vanguardia*, 15.
3 Guy Debord, *Society of the Spectacle*, trans. Ken Knabb, New Authorized Translation edition (repr., London: Rebel Press, [1967] 2004), 106 (italics in original).
4 Gene Ray, 'Art Schools Burning & Other Songs of Love and War', *Left Curve*, no. 30 (2006): 92.
5 Ray, 'Art Schools Burning', 93 (italics added).
6 Boris Groys, 'The Topology of Contemporary Art', in *Antinomies of Art and Culture: Modernity, Postmodernity, Contemporaneity*, ed. Terry Smith, Okwui Enwezor and Nancy Condee (Durham, NC: Duke University Press, 2008), 71.
7 Mikhail Aleksandrovich Bakunin, *Bakunin on Anarchy: Selected Works by the Activist-Founder of World Anarchism*, ed. and trans. Sam Dolgoff (New York: Vintage Books, 1972), 57.
8 Groys, 'The Topology of Contemporary Art', 71.
9 Groys, 'The Topology of Contemporary Art', 78.
10 Groys, 'The Topology of Contemporary Art', 72.
11 Friedrich Wilhelm Nietzsche, *The Will to Power*, trans. Walter Arnold Kaufmann, Vintage Books (New York: Random House, 1968).
12 Keith Ansell-Pearson, 'Introduction', in *On the Genealogy of Morality*, Revised Student edition, Cambridge Texts in the History of Political Thought (Cambridge: Cambridge University Press, 2007), xx.
13 Friedrich Wilhelm Nietzsche, *On the Genealogy of Morality*, ed. Keith Ansell-Pearson, trans. Carol Diethe, Revised Student edition, Cambridge Texts in the History of Political Thought (Cambridge: Cambridge University Press, 2007).
14 David Hopkins, *Dada and Surrealism: A Very Short Introduction* (Oxford: Oxford University Press, 2004), 7.
15 Helena Lewis, *Dada Turns Red: The Politics of Surrealism* (Edinburgh: Edinburgh University Press, 1990), 5.
16 Ray, 'Art Schools Burning', 92.

17 Gavin Grindon, 'Surrealism, Dada, and the Refusal of Work: Autonomy, Activism, and Social Participation in the Radical Avant-Garde', *Oxford Art Journal* 34, no. 1 (2011): 91, https://doi.org/10.1093/oxartj/kcr003.
18 Grindon, 'Surrealism, Dada, and the Refusal of Work', 91.
19 Matthew Gale, *Dada & Surrealism* (London: Phaidon, 1997), 135–6.
20 Mehring in Grindon, 'Surrealism, Dada, and the Refusal of Work', 91. In his footnotes, Grindon lists six different sources for his quotation, all of which are written in German. He does not credit the translator for his English version, which I assume he did himself.
21 Gale, *Dada & Surrealism*, 123.
22 Ray, 'Art Schools Burning', 93.
23 Hopkins, *Dada and Surrealism*, 140.
24 Mikkel Bolt Rasmussen, 'The Situationist International(s): The Realization of Art', *International Journal of Aesthetics and Philosophy of Culture* 3, no. 3 (2018): 9, http://www.ijaphc.unibuc.ro/index.php/jurnale/article/view/1.
25 Rasmussen, 'Situationist International(s)', 8.
26 Martin Lang, 'Spectacular Malaise: Art and the End of History', *Art & the Public Sphere* 8, no. 1 (1 July 2019): 64, https://doi.org/10.1386/aps_00006_1.
27 Liam Considine, 'Screen Politics: Pop Art and the Atelier Populaire', *Tate Papers*, no. 24 (Autumn 2015), https://www.tate.org.uk/research/publications/tate-papers/24/screen-politics-pop-art-and-the-atelier-populaire.
28 Mikkel Bolt Rasmussen, 'The Situationist International, Surrealism, and the Difficult Fusion of Art and Politics', *Oxford Art Journal* 27, no. 3 (2004): 384–5.
29 Peter Bürger, *Theory of the Avant-Garde*, trans. Michael Shaw, Theory and History of Literature 4 (Minneapolis: University of Minnesota Press, 1984), 58 (italics in original).
30 David Hopkins, ed., *Neo-Avant-Garde*, Avant-Garde Critical Studies 20 (Amsterdam: Rodopi, 2006), 2.
31 Bürger, *Theory of the Avant-Garde*, 61.
32 Guy Debord, 'The Situationists and the New Forms of Action in Politics and Art', in *Situationist Anthology*, ed. and trans. Ken Knabb,

Revised and Expanded edition (Berkeley, CA: Bureau of Public Secrets, 2006), 414, http://www.bopsecrets.org/SI/newforms.htm.

33 Benjamin H. D. Buchloh, 'Theorizing the Avant-Garde', *Art in America* 72, no. 10 (November 1984): 19–21; Benjamin H. D. Buchloh, *Neo-Avantgarde and Culture Industry: Essays on European and American Art from 1955 to 1975* (Cambridge, MA: MIT Press, 2000); Hal Foster, 'What's Neo about the Neo-Avant-Garde?' *October*, no. 70 (Fall 1994): 5–32.

34 Grindon, 'Surrealism, Dada, and the Refusal of Work', 95.

35 Gavin Grindon, 'Second-Wave Situationism?' *Fifth Estate*, no. 350 (Summer 2009): 11.

36 Grindon, 'Surrealism, Dada, and the Refusal of Work', 95.

37 Ron Hahne and Ben Morea, *Black Mask & Up Against the Wall Motherfucker: The Incomplete Works of Ron Hahne, Ben Morea, and the Black Mask Group* (Oakland, CA: PM Press, 2011), 4.

38 Hopkins, *Dada and Surrealism*, 6.

39 Claire Bishop, *Artificial Hells: Participatory Art and the Politics of Spectatorship* (London: Verso, 2012), 42.

40 Marinetti in Bishop, *Artificial Hells*, 44.

41 Christine Poggi, *Inventing Futurism: The Art and Politics of Artificial Optimism* (Princeton, NJ: Princeton University Press, 2008), 1.

42 Filippo Tommaso Marinetti, Umberto Boccioni, Carlo Carrà and Luigi Russolo, 'Against Passéist Venice (1910)', in *Futurism: An Anthology*, ed. Lawrence S. Rainey, Christine Poggi and Laura Wittman (New Haven, CT: Yale University Press, 2009), 67.

43 Marinetti et al., 'Against Passéist Venice (1910)', 67.

44 Bishop, *Artificial Hells*, 46–7.

45 Hahne and Morea, *Black Mask & Up Against the Wall Motherfucker*, 5–6.

46 Hahne and Morea, *Black Mask & Up Against the Wall Motherfucker*, 6.

47 Christopher Gray, *Black Mask & Up Against the Wall Motherfucker: Burn It All Down: Flower Power Won't Stop Fascist Power: The Story of a Small, Underground 1960s Revolutionary Group in New York City* (Minneapolis, MN: The Daybreak Collective, 2001), 2.

48 Hahne and Morea, *Black Mask & Up Against the Wall Motherfucker*, 157.

49 Hahne and Morea, *Black Mask & Up Against the Wall Motherfucker*, 80 (random capitals in original).
50 Hahne and Morea, *Black Mask & Up Against the Wall Motherfucker*, 82.
51 Gray, *Black Mask & Up Against The Wall Motherfucker*, 8.
52 Hahne and Morea, *Black Mask & Up Against the Wall Motherfucker*, 13.
53 Hari Kunzru, 'The Mob Who Shouldn't Really Be Here', *Tate Etc.*, Summer 2008, http://www.tate.org.uk/context-comment/articles/mob-who-shouldnt-really-be-here.
54 Martin Bright, 'Investigation: The Angry Brigade', *Observer*, 3 February 2002, https://www.theguardian.com/theobserver/2002/feb/03/features.magazine27.
55 Jonathan Green, 'The Urban Guerrillas Britain Forgot', *New Statesman*, 27 August 2001.
56 Gavin Grindon has researched this history and he acknowledges that there are different accounts for the reasons why the English Situationists were expelled. See Gavin Grindon, 'Poetry Written in Gasoline: Black Mask and Up Against the Wall Motherfucker', *Art History* 38, no. 1 (February 2015): 185–7, https://doi.org/10.1111/1467-8365.12129.
57 Kunzru, 'The Mob Who Shouldn't Really Be Here'.
58 Grant H. Kester, 'Another Turn', *Artforum* 44, no. 9 (May 2006): 22.
59 Claire Bishop, 'The Social Turn: Collaboration and Its Discontents', *Artforum* 44, no. 6 (February 2006): 179.
60 Grant H. Kester, *The One and the Many: Contemporary Collaborative Art in a Global Context* (Durham, NC: Duke University Press, 2011), 31.
61 Kester, *The One and the Many*, 11.
62 Park Fiction in Kester, *The One and the Many*, 24.
63 Claire Bishop, 'Antagonism and Relational Aesthetics', *October*, no. 110 (Fall 2004): 79.
64 Bishop, 'Antagonism and Relational Aesthetics', 66.
65 Bishop, 'Antagonism and Relational Aesthetics', 78.
66 Sadie Plant, *The Most Radical Gesture: The Situationist International in a Postmodern Age* (London: Routledge, 2002), 5.

67 Emmett Williams and Ann Noel, eds, *Mr Fluxus: A Collective Portrait of George Maciunas 1931–1978* (London: Thames and Hudson, 1997), 9.
68 Slavoj Žižek, *Trouble in Paradise: From the End of History to the End of Capitalism*, eBook edition (New York: Melville House, 2015), 185.
69 Žižek, *Trouble in Paradise*, 185.
70 Slavoj Žižek, 'How Mao Would Have Evaluated the Yellow Vests', *RT International*, 21 December 2018, https://www.rt.com/op-ed/447155-zizek-yellow-vests-france/.
71 Slavoj Žižek, *Against the Double Blackmail: Refugees, Terror and Other Troubles with the Neighbours* (London: Allen Lane, 2016), 131.
72 Frances Stracey, *Constructed Situations: A New History of the Situationist International*, Marxism & Culture (London: Pluto, 2014), 10.
73 Jon Erickson, 'The Spectacle of the Anti-Spectacle: Happenings and the Situationist International', *Discourse* 14, no. 2 (1992): 37.
74 Stracey, *Constructed Situations*, 2.
75 Stracey, *Constructed Situations*, 9.
76 Stracey, *Constructed Situations*, 10.
77 Erickson, 'The Spectacle of the Anti-Spectacle', 43.
78 Erickson, 'The Spectacle of the Anti-Spectacle', 41.
79 Erickson, 'The Spectacle of the Anti-Spectacle', 50.
80 Raoul Vaneigem, *The Revolution of Everyday Life*, trans. Donald Nicholson-Smith (repr., London: Rebel Press, [1967] 2001), 114.
81 Bishop notes that 'When examining artists' motivations for turning to social participation as a strategy in their work, one repeatedly encounters the same claim: contemporary capitalism produces passive subjects with very little agency or empowerment.' Claire Bishop, 'Participation and Spectacle: Where Are We Now?' in *Living as Form: Socially Engaged Art from 1991–2011*, ed. Nato Thompson (New York: Creative Time Books, 2012), 35.
82 Bishop, *Artificial Hells*, 277.
83 Bishop, *Artificial Hells*, 30.
84 Bishop, *Artificial Hells*, 277.
85 Bishop, *Artificial Hells*, 340 (n. 83).
86 Claire Bishop, ed., *Participation*, Documents of Contemporary Art (London: Whitechapel Gallery, 2006), 11.

87 Bishop, *Artificial Hells*, 12.
88 Thomas Hirschhorn, Alison Gingeras, Benjamin. H. D. Buchloh and Carlos Basualdo, *Thomas Hirschhorn* (London: Phaidon, 2004), 25–6.
89 Hirschhorn et al., *Thomas Hirschhorn*, 27.
90 Hirschhorn et al., *Thomas Hirschhorn*, 28.

4 Tactical confrontations

1 *Mierdazo* can be translated literally from Spanish as 'big shit'. It has been referred to descriptively as 'poop attack' but I feel that 'shit storm' is more appropriate.
2 Brian Holmes, 'The Errorist International: Washed Up on a Beach in Australia', *Transversal*, 29 January 2007, http://transform.eipcp.net/correspondence/1170076372.html.
3 I was the recipient of a Santander Mobility Award.
4 Zukerfeld in Jennifer Ponce de León, *Another Aesthetics Is Possible: Arts of Rebellion in the Fourth World War* (Durham, NC: Duke University Press, 2021), 187.
5 Ponce de León, *Another Aesthetics Is Possible*, 189.
6 Marina Sitrin, 'Horizontalism and the Occupy Movements', *Dissent Magazine*, 2012, https://www.dissentmagazine.org/article/horizontalism-and-the-occupy-movements.
7 Marina A. Sitrin, *Everyday Revolutions: Horizontalism and Autonomy in Argentina* (Zed Books, 2012), 3.
8 Federico Zukerfeld in Santiago García Navarro, 'International Errorista: The Revolution through Affect. Part 2', LatinArt.com, 2 July 2006, https://www.latinart.com/aiview.cfm?start=2&id=358.
9 Loreto Garin in García Navarro, 'International Errorista'.
10 Mark Bray, 'Horizontalism', in *Anarchism: A Conceptual Approach*, ed. Benjamin Franks, Nathan Jun and Leonard Williams, eBook edition (New York: Routledge, 2018), 138.
11 Ana Longoni, 'A Long Way: Argentine Artistic Activism of the Last Decades', in *Collective Situations: Readings in Contemporary Latin American Art, 1995–2010*, ed. Bill Kelley Jr and Grant H. Kester, trans.

Fabian Cereijido, Illustrated edition (Durham, NC: Duke University Press, 2017), 103.

12 Zukerfeld said this at The Politics of the Social in Contemporary Art Conference at Tate Modern (15 February 2013). He was referring to Manzoni's *Merda d'artista* (1961), where the artist canned his excrement for sale as an artwork.

13 Christopher Gray, *Black Mask & Up Against the Wall Motherfucker: Burn It All Down: Flower Power Won't Stop Fascist Power: The Story of a Small, Underground 1960s Revolutionary Group in New York City* (Minneapolis, MN: Reprinted by The Daybreak Collective, 2001), 8.

14 Zukerfeld in García Navarro, 'International Errorista'.

15 Ponce de León, *Another Aesthetics Is Possible*, 191.

16 Ponce de León, *Another Aesthetics Is Possible*, 189.

17 Ernesto Guevara, *Guerrilla Warfare: A Method* (Peking: Foreign Languages Press, 1964).

18 Bray, 'Horizontalism', 138.

19 Andrew Flood, 'An Anarchist Critique of Horizontalism', The Anarchist Library, 24 February 2014, https://theanarchistlibrary.org/library/andrew-flood-an-anarchist-critique-of-horizontalism.

20 Flood, 'An Anarchist Critique of Horizontalism'.

21 Bray, 'Horizontalism', 142.

22 Bray, 'Horizontalism', 142.

23 Bray, 'Horizontalism', 145.

24 Flood, 'An Anarchist Critique of Horizontalism'.

25 'Propaganda of the Deed', The Anarchist Library, accessed 26 August 2022, https://theanarchistlibrary.org/category/topic/propaganda-of-the-deed.

26 Neville Bolt, David Betz and Jaz Azari, 'Propaganda of the Deed: Understanding the Phenomenon', Whitehall Report Series (London: Royal United Services Institute for Defence and Security Studies, 2008).

27 Bolt, Betz and Azari, 'Propaganda of the Deed', 2.

28 Bolt, Betz and Azari, 'Propaganda of the Deed', 2.

29 Ponce de León, *Another Aesthetics Is Possible*, 190.

30 Ponce de León, *Another Aesthetics Is Possible*, 189.

31 Sebastian Loewe, 'When Protest Becomes Art: The Contradictory Transformations of the Occupy Movement at Documenta 13 and Berlin Biennale 7', *FIELD: A Journal of Socially Engaged Art Criticism*, no. 1 (2015): 188–9.

32 John Vidal, 'Reverend Billy Faces Year in Prison for JP Morgan Chase Toad Protest', *Guardian*, 25 November 2013, sec. Environment, https://www.theguardian.com/environment/2013/nov/25/reverend-billy-jpmorgan-chase-toad-protest-talen.

33 'Russian Artist Pyotr Pavlensky Sentenced over Paris Bank Fire', *Artforum* (blog), 15 January 2019, https://www.artforum.com/news/russian-artist-pyotr-pavlensky-sentenced-over-paris-bank-fire-78313.

34 Anastasia Chaguidouline, 'Borders and Forms', *On Curating*, no. 50 (2021): 150, https://www.on-curating.org/issue-50-reader/borders-and-forms.html#.YyoaaXbMLb0.

35 Chaguidouline, 'Borders and Forms', 149.

36 Peter Sloterdijk, *Rage and Time: A Psychopolitical Investigation*, trans. Mario Wenning (New York: Columbia University Press, 2010).

37 John Holloway, 'Afterword: Rage against the Rule of Money', in *What We Are Fighting For*, ed. Federico Campagna and Emanuele Campiglio (London: Pluto Press, 2012), 199–205.

38 Mark Fisher, *Capitalist Realism: Is There No Alternative?* (Winchester: 0 Books, 2009), 78.

39 Sloterdijk, *Rage and Time*, 205.

40 Nato Thompson, ed., *Living as Form: Socially Engaged Art from 1991–2011*, Illustrated edition (New York: Creative Time Books, 2012), 31; de Certeau's terms are complex, and Thompson's interpretation is somewhat reductive, but will suffice for my purposes. For a more complete understanding of the tactical and the strategic, see the 'General Introduction', in de Certeau, *The Practice of Everyday Life*.

41 Thompson, 'Living as Form', 31.

42 Nicolas Bourriaud, *Relational Aesthetics*, trans. Simon Pleasance, Collection Documents sur l'art (Dijon: Presse du réel, 2002), 45.

43 Bourriaud, *Relational Aesthetics*, 31.

44 Bourriaud, *Relational Aesthetics*, 13.

45 Roberta Smith, 'Museum as Romantic Comedy', *New York Times*, 31 October 2008, Online edition, sec. Arts, 32, http://www.nytimes.com/2008/10/31/arts/design/31gugg.html?_r=1&.

46 The term 'flash mob' only became popularly used after 2003, when *Harper's Magazine* editor Bill Wasnik flooded the streets of New York City with strange performances, starting at Macy's department store – the site of Black Mask's action in 1967 that I described in Chapter 3. What distinguished Wasnik's spontaneous street performances from their neo-avant-garde predecessors is that they were organized online or by mobile phone, using the internet or SMS messaging – technologies that scarcely existed just a few years earlier.
47 Rebecca Walker, 'Turning Tricks: Culture Jamming and the Flash Mob', in *Culture Jamming: Activism and the Art of Cultural Resistance*, ed. Marilyn DeLaure and Moritz Fink (New York: New York University Press, 2017), 304.
48 Walker, 'Turning Tricks', 310.
49 Walker, 'Turning Tricks', 301.
50 Situationist International, 'Definitions', in *Situationist International Anthology*, ed. and trans. Ken Knabb, eBook (Berkeley, CA: Bureau of Public Secrets, 2006), 61–2.
51 Walker, 'Turning Tricks', 305.
52 Walker, 'Turning Tricks', 305.
53 Walker, 'Turning Tricks', 306.
54 Gavin Grindon, 'Art and Activism', *Art Monthly*, no. 333 (February 2010): 12.
55 John Jordan, 'On Refusing to Pretend to Do Politics in a Museum', *Art Monthly*, no. 334 (March 2010): 35.
56 Occupy Museums, 'Occupy Museums!' *Occupymuseums.org*, 19 October 2011, https://www.occupymuseums.org/index.php/about.
57 Occupy Museums, 'Occupy Museums!'
58 For more information about Arts against Cuts, see Louis Hartnoll, Lucy Killoran, Robyn Minogue and Sophie Carapetian, eds, *Bad Feelings: Arts against Cuts*, Common Objectives (London: Book Works, 2015). For more information about their action at the Turner Prize ceremony, see Steve Klee, 'Rancière against the Cuts', *Third Text* 27, no. 2 (2013): 177–88, https://doi.org/10.1080/09528822.2013.774189.
59 Matthew Taylor and Jonathan Watts, 'Revealed: The 20 Firms behind a Third of All Carbon Emissions', *The Guardian*, 9 October 2019, sec.

Environment, https://www.theguardian.com/environment/2019/oct/09/revealed-20-firms-third-carbon-emissions.

60 See, for example, Anny Shaw, 'BP Ends 26-Year Sponsorship Deal with Tate', *Art Newspaper – International Art News and Events*, 11 March 2016, https://www.theartnewspaper.com/2016/03/11/bp-ends-26-year-sponsorship-deal-with-tate; Henri Neuendorf, 'BP to End 26-Year Tate Sponsorship in 2017', *Artnet News*, 11 March 2016, https://news.artnet.com/art-world/bp-ends-tate-sponsorship-2017-447041.

61 Liberate Tate, 'Confronting the Institution in Performance: Liberate Tate's Hidden Figures', *Performance Research* 20, no. 4 (4 July 2015): 84, https://doi.org/10.1080/13528165.2015.1071042.

62 John Jordan, 'Clandestine Insurgent Rebel Clown Army', in *Beautiful Trouble: A Toolbox for Revolution*, ed. Andrew Boyd, eBook (London: OR Books, 2012), 306.

63 Christian Scholl, 'Bakunin's Poor Cousins: Engaging Art for Tactical Interventions', in *Cultural Activism: Practices, Dilemmas and Possibilities*, ed. Begüm Özden Firat and Aylin Kuryel (Amsterdam: Rodopi, 2010), 170.

64 Scholl, 'Bakunin's Poor Cousins', 170.

65 Jordan, 'Clandestine Insurgent Rebel Clown Army', 305.

66 Jordan, 'Clandestine Insurgent Rebel Clown Army', 307.

67 Scholl, 'Bakunin's Poor Cousins', 173.

68 Scholl, 'Bakunin's Poor Cousins', 173.

5 The absurd and the dysfunctional

1 Mike Bonanno, Andy Bichlbaum and Bob Spunkmeyer, *The Yes Men: The True Story of the End of the World Trade Organization*, Illustrated edition (New York: Disinformation, 2004), 11.

2 Bonanno, Bichlbaum and Spunkmeyer, *The Yes Men*, 11.

3 Bonanno, Bichlbaum and Spunkmeyer, *The Yes Men*, 11.

4 Bonanno, Bichlbaum and Spunkmeyer, *The Yes Men*, 12.

5 The Yes Men, 'The Yes Men: An Interview', interview by Marilyn DeLaure, in *Culture Jamming: Activism and the Art of Cultural Resistance* (New York: New York University Press, 2017), 419.

6 'The Death Toll', International Campaign for Justice in Bhopal, 2021, https://www.bhopal.net/what-happened/that-night-december-3-1984/the-death-toll/.

7 Suketu Mehta, 'A Cloud Still Hangs over Bhopal', *New York Times*, 3 December 2009, https://www.proquest.com/docview/1030689738/abstract/B9813080DC7348C8PQ/1.

8 The Yes Men, 'Dow Does the Right Thing', The Yes Men, 1 December 2004, https://www.theyesmen.org/project/dow-does-right-thing.

9 The Yes Men, 'Dow "Help" Announcement Is Elaborate Hoax', The Yes Men, 3 December 2004, https://theyesmen.org/project/dowbbc/denial.

10 The Yes Men, 'Dow's Golden Skeleton', The Yes Men, 28 April 2005, https://yeslab.org/project/dows-golden-skeleton.

11 Roy Harris Jr, 'Jury in Ford Pinto Case: "We Wanted Ford to Take Notice"', *Washington Post*, 15 February 1978, A2.

12 Arthur D. Little, 'Public Finance Balance of Smoking in the Czech Republic', web.archive.org, 1 October 2011, https://web.archive.org/web/20111001035336/http://hspm.sph.sc.edu/courses/Econ/Classes/cbacea/czechsmokingcost.html.

13 Brian Whitener, 'Introduction', in *Genocide in the Neighborhood*, ed. Colectivo Situaciones, trans. Brian Whitener, Daniel Borzutzky and Fernando Fuentes (Oakland, CA: Chainlinks, 2009), 20.

14 Jennifer Flores Sternad, 'The Rhythm of Capital and the Aesthetics of Terror: The Errorist International, Etcetera …', in *Art and Activism in the Age of Globalization*, ed. Lieven De Cauter, Runem De Roo and Karl Vanhaesebrouck, Illustrated edition, vol. 8, Reflect (Rotterdam: NAi Publishers, 2011), 218.

15 H.I.J.O.S. – *Hijos por la Indentidad y la Justicia contra el Olvidado y el Silencio* – Sons and daughters for identification and justice for the forgotten and silenced (my translation).

16 Flores Sternad, 'The Rhythm of Capital and the Aesthetics of Terror: The Errorist International, Etcetera …', 218.

17 Ana Longoni, 'A Long Way: Argentine Artistic Activism of the Last Decades', in *Collective Situations: Readings in Contemporary Latin American Art, 1995–2010*, ed. Bill Kelley Jr and Grant H. Kester, trans.

Fabian Cereijido, Illustrated edition (Durham, NC: Duke University Press, 2017), 104.

18 Longoni, 'A Long Way', 102.

19 Longoni, 'A Long Way', 104.

20 Jennifer Ponce de León, *Another Aesthetics Is Possible: Arts of Rebellion in the Fourth World War* (Durham, NC: Duke University Press, 2021), 165.

21 Rodrigo Marti, 'Grupo Etcetera', in *Collective Situations: Readings in Contemporary Latin American Art, 1995–2010*, ed. Bill Kelley Jr and Grant H. Kester, Illustrated edition (Durham, NC: Duke University Press, 2017), 59.

22 Marti, 'Grupo Etcetera', 59.

23 Jacques Rancière, *Aesthetics and Its Discontents*, trans. Steven Corcoran (Cambridge: Polity Press, 2009), 54.

24 The Yes Men have released two films: Dan Ollman, Sarah Price and Chris Smith, *The Yes Men*, Documentary Comedy (USA, MGM; United Artists, 2003); Andy Bichlbaum, Mike Bonanno and Kurt Engfehr, *The Yes Men Fix the World* (USA, HBO, 2009).

25 Loreto Garin in Santiago García Navarro, 'International Errorista: The Revolution through Affect. Part 2', LatinArt.com, 2 July 2006, https://www.latinart.com/aiview.cfm?start=2&id=358.

26 Alain Bieber, 'I Revolt Therefore I Am', in *Art & Agenda: Political Art and Activism*, ed. Robert Klanten, Matthias Hübner, Alain Bieber, Pedro Alonzo, Gregor Jansen and Silke Krohn (Berlin: Gestalten, 2011), 51.

27 Juraj Bednar, 'Moral Reform by Ztohoven: An Ultimate Hack', juraj.bednar.io, 6 January 2013, https://juraj.bednar.io/en/blog-en/2013/01/06/moral-reform-by-ztohoven-an-ultimate-hack/.

28 Ztohoven's account used to appear on their website but is no longer available. It is accessible online on Juraj Bednar's website. From memory, the text appears to be the same.

29 Bieber, 'I Revolt Therefore I Am', 112.

30 Paolo Cirio, 'If We Can't Stop Corporations from Hiding in the Cayman Islands to Avoid Taxes, We All Need to Become Pirates', in *Disrupting Business: Art and Activism in Times of Financial Crisis*, ed. Tatiana Bazzichelli and Geoff Cox (Brooklyn, NY: Autonomedia, 2013), 31–8.

31 Monica Steinberg, 'Financial True Crime: Art, Para-Journalism, and Data-Driven Storytelling', *Art History* 44, no. 2 (2021): 272, https://doi.org/10.1111/1467-8365.12571.
32 Steinberg, 'Financial True Crime', 273.
33 Paolo Cirio, 'Art Interventions and Disruptions in Financial Systems: An Interview with Paolo Cirio', interview by Marisa Lerer; Conor McGarrigle, *Visual Resources: An International Journal of Documentation* 34, nos 1–2 (3 April 2018): 160, https://doi.org/10.1080/01973762.2018.1437971.
34 Steinberg, 'Financial True Crime', 273.
35 Cirio, 'Art Interventions and Disruptions in Financial Systems', 157–8.
36 Cirio, 'Art Interventions and Disruptions in Financial Systems', 159.
37 Steinberg, 'Financial True Crime', 275.
38 Cirio, 'If We Can't Stop Corporations from Hiding in the Cayman Islands to Avoid Taxes, We All Need to Become Pirates', 31.
39 Paolo Cirio, *Flowcharts* (Morrisville, NC: Lulu Press, 2019), no pagination.
40 Cirio, *Flowcharts*, no pagination.
41 Paolo Cirio, 'Takedown Notice: A Conversation with Paolo Cirio', interview by Liz Flyntz, *Afterimage: The Journal of Media Arts and Cultural Criticism* 42, no. 5 (2015): 16.
42 Cirio, 'Takedown Notice', 16.
43 McKenzie Wark, *A Hacker Manifesto* (Cambridge, MA: Harvard University Press, 2004), para. 020.
44 Wark, *A Hacker Manifesto*, para. 020.
45 Karen Kurczynski, 'Expression as Vandalism: Asger Jorn's "Modifications"', *Res: Anthropology and Aesthetics* 53–54 (March 2008): 293–313, https://doi.org/10.1086/RESvn1ms25608823.
46 Sadie Plant, *The Most Radical Gesture: The Situationist International in a Postmodern Age*, eBook Edition (London: Routledge, 2002), 87.
47 Situationist International, 'Definitions', in *Situationist International Anthology*, ed. and trans. Ken Knabb, eBook (Berkeley, CA: Bureau of Public Secrets, 2006), 62.
48 Rancière, *Aesthetics and Its Discontents*, 54 (his square brackets).
49 Guy Debord and J. Gil Wolman, 'A User's Guide to Détournement [1956]', in *Situationist International Anthology*, ed. and trans. Ken

Knabb, Revised and Expanded eBook edition (Berkeley, CA: Bureau of Public Secrets, 2006), 25.

50 Debord and Wolman, 'A User's Guide', 25.

51 Umberto Eco, 'Towards a Semiological Guerrilla Warfare [1967]', in *Travels in Hyperreality: Essays* (San Diego: Harcourt Brace Jovanovich, 1986), 140, http://archive.org/details/travelsinhyperre00ecou.

52 Eco, 'Towards a Semiological Guerrilla Warfare', 35.

53 Guy Debord, *Comments on the Society of the Spectacle*, trans. Malcolm Imrie, Radical Thinkers (London: Verso, 1998).

54 Eco, 'Towards a Semiological Guerrilla Warfare', 142.

55 Eco, 'Towards a Semiological Guerrilla Warfare', 142.

56 Eco, 'Towards a Semiological Guerrilla Warfare', 142.

57 Plant, *The Most Radical Gesture*, 131.

58 Plant, *The Most Radical Gesture*, 147.

59 Eco, 'Towards a Semiological Guerrilla Warfare', 142.

60 Eco, 'Towards a Semiological Guerrilla Warfare', 143.

61 Mark Dery, 'The Merry Pranksters and the Art of the Hoax', *New York Times*, 23 December 1990, Online edition, sec. Arts, https://www.nytimes.com/1990/12/23/arts/the-merry-pranksters-and-the-art-of-the-hoax.html.

62 Marilyn DeLaure and Moritz Fink, eds, *Culture Jamming: Activism and the Art of Cultural Resistance* (New York: New York University Press, 2017).

63 Mark Dery, 'Foreword', in *Culture Jamming: Activism and the Art of Cultural Resistance*, ed. Marilyn DeLaure and Moritz Fink (New York: New York University Press, 2017), xi. Dery puts this description in quotation marks.

64 Mark Dery, 'Culture Jamming: Hacking, Slashing, and Sniping in the Empire of Signs', in *Culture Jamming: Activism and the Art of Cultural Resistance*, ed. Marilyn DeLaure and Moritz Fink (New York: New York University Press, 2017), 47.

65 Marilyn DeLaure and Moritz Fink, 'Introduction', in *Culture Jamming: Activism and the Art of Cultural Resistance*, ed. Marilyn DeLaure and Moritz Fink (New York: New York University Press, 2017), 6.

66 Simon Ford, *The Situationist International: A User's Guide* (London: Black Dog, 2005).

67 DeLaure and Fink, 'Introduction', 8.
68 Gene Ray and Gregory Sholette, 'Introduction: Whither Tactical Media?' *Third Text* 22, no. 5 (September 2008): 524, https://doi.org/10.1080/09528820802439989.
69 Critical Art Ensemble, 'Tactical Media at Dusk?' *Third Text* 22, no. 5 (September 2008): 535, https://doi.org/10.1080/09528820802440078.
70 Critical Art Ensemble, 'Tactical Media at Dusk?' 536.
71 Critical Art Ensemble, 'Tactical Media [1996]', in *Institutional Critique: An Anthology of Artists' Writings*, ed. Alexander Alberro and Blake Stimson (Cambridge, MA: MIT Press, 2009), 432.
72 Ray and Sholette, 'Introduction', 519.
73 Ray and Sholette, 'Introduction', 520.
74 Ray and Sholette, 'Introduction', 521.
75 Critical Art Ensemble, 'Tactical Media at Dusk?' 537.
76 Boris Groys, *In the Flow*, eBook edition (London: Verso, 2016), 44.
77 Groys, *In the Flow*, 45.
78 Gregory Sholette, 'Merciless Aesthetic: Activist Art as the Return of Institutional Critique. a Response to Boris Groys', *FIELD: A Journal of Socially Engaged Art Criticism*, no. 4 (Spring 2016), http://field-journal.com/issue-4/merciless-aesthetic-activist-art-as-the-return-of-institutional-critique-a-response-to-boris-groys.
79 Sholette, 'Merciless Aesthetic'.
80 Sholette, 'Merciless Aesthetic'.
81 Sholette, 'Merciless Aesthetic'.

6 Demonstration

1 Boris Groys, *In the Flow*, eBook edition (London: Verso, 2016), 55.
2 Gavin Grindon and John Jordan, *A User's Guide to (Demanding) the Impossible* (Wivenhoe: Minor Compositions, 2010), 4.
3 Mark Fisher, *Capitalist Realism: Is There No Alternative?* (Winchester: 0 Books, 2009), 17.
4 Rebecca Solnit, *Hope in the Dark: Untold Histories, Wild Possibilities*, 3rd edn (Chicago, IL: Haymarket Books, 2016), xxii.

5 Scholl, 'Bakunin's Poor Cousins: Engaging Art for Tactical Interventions', 165.
6 Scholl, 'Bakunin's Poor Cousins', 166.
7 Oliver Marchart, 'Public Movement: The Art of Pre-enactment', in *Not Just a Mirror: Looking for the Political Theatre of Today*, ed. Florian Malzacher, eBook edition, Performing Urgency (Berlin: Alexander Verlag, 2015), 149.
8 Scholl, 'Bakunin's Poor Cousins', 166.
9 Oliver Marchart, 'Public Movement: The Art of Pre-Enactment', in *Not Just a Mirror: Looking for the Political Theatre of Today*, ed. Florian Malzacher, eBook edition, Performing Urgency (Berlin: Alexander Verlag, 2015), 149.
10 Scholl, 'Bakunin's Poor Cousins', 159.
11 Mark Fisher, *Capitalist Realism: Is There No Alternative?* (Winchester: 0 Books, 2009), 81.
12 The New York Times, 'Tracking the States Where Abortion Is Now Banned', *New York Times*, 24 May 2022, Online edition, sec. US, https://www.nytimes.com/interactive/2022/us/abortion-laws-roe-v-wade.html.
13 The New York Times, 'Tracking the States'.
14 Bishop, *Artificial Hells*, 283.
15 Lucy Ash, 'How Banksy Bailed Out Russian Graffiti Artists Voina', BBC News, 5 March 2011, https://www.bbc.com/news/world-europe-12645902.
16 Jordan, 'Clandestine Insurgent Rebel Clown Army', 307.
17 'Art before the Law', *Frieze* (blog), 24 February 2012, https://www.frieze.com/article/art-law.
18 Alexei Plutser-Sarno, 'The VOINA Art-Group («War»). Actions 2006–2012', *Plucer Live Journal* (blog), 2012, http://plucer.livejournal.com/266853.html.
19 Voina, '7th Berlin Biennale: Statement by Voina', 2012, http://en.free-voina.org/post/22267051835.
20 Yulia Tikhonova, 'Voina and Innovation', *Flash Art* 44, no. 279 (July 2011): 46–8.
21 Tikhonova, 'Voina and Innovation', 47.

22 Kyle Chayka and Alexander Forbes, 'Voina Explains Why Firebombing a Police Tank Is a "Piece of Art"', *Blouin Artinfo*, artinfo.com, 5 January 2012, https://web.archive.org/web/20191124195820/https://www.blouinartinfo.com/news/story/755205/voina-explains-why-firebombing-a-police-tank-is-a-piece-of-art.

23 Forrest Muelrath, 'Art Insurrectionists', *Bomb Magazine*, 10 January 2011, https://bombmagazine.org/articles/art-insurrectionists/.

24 Tom Parfitt, 'Banksy Pledges £80,000 to Russian Radical Art Group Voina', *Guardian*, Sunday, 12 December 2010, Online edition, sec. Culture, http://www.guardian.co.uk/artanddesign/2010/dec/12/banksy-russia-voina-donation?INTCMP=SRCH.

25 Ash, 'How Banksy Bailed Out Russian Graffiti Artists Voina'.

26 Artforum, 'Czech Police Detain Founding Member of Voina Art Collective for Hooliganism in Russia', *Artforum* (blog), 5 October 2016, https://www.artforum.com/news/czech-police-detain-founding-member-of-voina-art-collective-for-hooliganism-in-russia-63925.

27 Oliver Johnson, 'War on the Ru-Net: Voina's Dick Captured by the FSB as a Networked Performance', *Third Text* 27, no. 5 (September 2013): 599, https://doi.org/10.1080/09528822.2013.832075.

28 Johnson, 'War on the Ru-Net', 591.

29 Carrie Lambert-Beatty, 'Twelve Miles: Boundaries of the New Art/Activism', *Signs: Journal of Women in Culture and Society* 33, no. 2 (January 2008): 309–27, https://doi.org/10.1086/521179.

30 Lambert-Beatty, 'Twelve Miles', 321.

31 I conducted a major longitudinal study of artists' educational backgrounds as part of my doctoral research. The study covered thirty years of data. This included all Turner Prize nominees (from its inception in 1984 to 2013, inclusive), all British and American representatives at the Venice Biennale and the winners of several major art prizes including Becks Futures, the Celeste Art Prize, EASTInternational and the Jerwood Painting, Drawing and Sculpture prizes. The study showed that 98 per cent had trained at art school with 95 per cent having studied art at undergraduate level (the rest studying at postgraduate level after having studied a different subject at undergraduate level). Only 2 per cent had no art school education at all, but this figure includes artists who have studied other, sometimes related subjects. For example, Jeremy Deller studied

art history at both undergraduate and postgraduate levels and Tino Sehgal studied dance but subsequently crossed over into performance. These findings, with full datasets, are available in my doctoral thesis: Martin Lang, 'Militant Art' (Doctoral thesis, Canterbury, University of Kent, 2015), https://kar.kent.ac.uk/50237/.

32 Gene Ray, 'Art Schools Burning & Other Songs of Love and War', *Left Curve*, no. 30 (2006): 85.

33 University of the Arts London, 'Art, Ethics and Social Change Online Short Course', arts.ac.uk, accessed 28 August 2022, https://www.arts.ac.uk/subjects/curation-and-culture/short-courses/art-history-and-criticism/art,-ethics-and-social-change-online-short-course-csm.

34 In the United States, these include: MFA in Art and Social Practice Art (Queens College CUNY); MFA in Design for Social Innovation (School of Visual Arts, New York); MA in Arts Politics (Tisch School of the Arts, New York), which explicitly states that it aims to train arts activists. In the UK, we have MA Art and Politics (Goldsmiths); BA Philosophy, Politics, Art (Brighton); MA Social Sculpture (Oxford Brookes); BA Curating with Politics (Essex) and MA Art and Social Practice (University of the Highlands and Islands).

35 Maryland Institute College of Art (MICA), 'Art of Activism Graduate Programs', Art & Education, 2013, https://www.artandeducation.net/announcements/108744/art-of-activism-graduate-programs-call-for-applications.

36 Jordan, 'On Refusing to Pretend to Do Politics in a Museum'.

37 Jordan, 'On Refusing to Pretend', 35.

38 Thompson, *Living as Form: Socially Engaged Art from 1991–2011*, 242.

39 In September 2015, *ArtReview* reported that Leonid Nikolayev (Nikolaev) had died at the age of thirty-one, 'following an accident while cutting timber outside Moscow'. ArtReview, 'Leonid Nikolayev, 1984–2015', *ArtReview*, 29 September 2015, https://artreview.com/news-29-sep-2015-leonid-nikolayev/. 'Leonid Nikolaev' was also the name of the assassin who killed Sergei Kirov, the first secretary of the Leningrad branch of the Communist Party.

40 *Fight Club*, directed by David Fincher (USA, 20th Century Fox, 1999).

41 Ponce de León, *Another Aesthetics Is Possible*, 227.

42 Ponce de León, *Another Aesthetics Is Possible*, 235.

43 Ponce de León, *Another Aesthetics Is Possible*, 230.

44 Internacional Errorista, '"We Are All Errorists" – Errare Humanum Est. First Declaration by the Errorists', Transform, 10 November 2005, http://transform.eipcp.net/correspondence/errorists-cp01en.html.

Select Bibliography

Adorno, Theodor W. ‘Engagement’. In *Noten Zur Literatur*, edited by Rolf Tiedemann, 409–30. Frankfurt am Main: Suhrkamp Verlag AG, 1965.

Adorno, Theodor W. ‘Commitment’. Translated by Francis McDonagh. *New Left Review* 1, nos 87–88 (1974): 75–89.

Alberro, Alexander, and Blake Stimson, eds. *Institutional Critique: An Anthology of Artists’ Writings*. Cambridge, MA: MIT Press, 2009.

Apel, Dora. *War Culture and the Contest of Images*. eBook edition. New Directions in International Studies. New Brunswick, NJ: Rutgers University Press, 2012.

Artforum. ‘Russian Artist Pyotr Pavlensky Sentenced over Paris Bank Fire’. *Artforum* (blog), 15 January 2019. https://www.artforum.com/news/russian-artist-pyotr-pavlensky-sentenced-over-paris-bank-fire-78313.

Badiou, Alain. *Ethics: An Essay on the Understanding of Evil*. Translated by Peter Hallward. Radical Thinkers. Reprint, London: Verso, [1998] 2001.

Badiou, Alain. ‘Does the Notion of Activist Art still Have Meaning?’ Keynote, Miguel Abreu Gallery (New York), 13 October 2010. https://vimeo.com/16453571.

Bakunin, Mikhail Aleksandrovich. *Bakunin on Anarchy: Selected Works by the Activist-Founder of World Anarchism*. Edited and translated by Sam Dolgoff. New York: Vintage Books, 1972.

BAVO, ed. *Cultural Activism Today: The Art of Over-Identification*. 1st edition. Rotterdam: Episode Publishers, 2007.

Bazzichelli, Tatiana, and Geoff Cox, eds. *Disrupting Business: Art and Activism in Times of Financial Crisis*. DATA Browser 05. Brooklyn, NY: Autonomedia, 2013.

Bednar, Juraj. ‘Moral Reform by Ztohoven: An Ultimate Hack’. juraj.bednar.io, 6 January 2013. https://juraj.bednar.io/en/blog-en/2013/01/06/moral-reform-by-ztohoven-an-ultimate-hack/.

Bilal, Wafaa, and Kari Lydersen. *Shoot an Iraqi: Art, Life and Resistance under the Gun*. eBook edition. San Francisco: City Lights Publishers, 2008.

Bishop, Claire. 'Antagonism and Relational Aesthetics'. *October*, no. 110 (Fall 2004): 51–79.

Bishop, Claire, ed. *Participation*. Documents of Contemporary Art. London: Whitechapel Gallery, 2006.

Bishop, Claire. 'The Social Turn: Collaboration and Its Discontents'. *Artforum* 44, no. 6 (February 2006): 178–83.

Bishop, Claire. *Artificial Hells: Participatory Art and the Politics of Spectatorship*. London: Verso, 2012.

Bolt, Neville, David Betz and Jaz Azari. 'Propaganda of the Deed: Understanding the Phenomenon'. Whitehall Report Series. London: Royal United Services Institute for Defence and Security Studies, 2008.

Bonanno, Mike, Andy Bichlbaum and Bob Spunkmeyer. *The Yes Men: The True Story of the End of the World Trade Organization*. Illustrated edition. New York: Disinformation, 2004.

Bookchin, Natalie, Pamela Brown, Suzahn Ebrahimia, Colectivo Enmedio, Alexandra Juhasz, Leónidas Martin, MTL, Nicholas Mirzoef, Andrew Ross, A. Joan Saab and Marina Sitrin. *Militant Research Handbook*. New York: New York University, 2013.

Bourriaud, Nicolas. *Relational Aesthetics*. Translated by Simon Pleasance. Collection Documents sur l'art. Dijon: Presse du réel, 2002.

Boyd, Andrew, ed. *Beautiful Trouble: A Toolbox for Revolution*. eBook. London: OR Books, 2012.

Bresolin, Thomas. 'Daily Hunger Strike Statements'. Blog. *Blind Tom Bresolin* (blog), 2012. http://blindtombresolin.blogspot.co.uk/2012_08_01_archive.html.

Bruguera, Tania. 'Political Art Statement'. taniabruguera.com, 2010. http://www.taniabruguera.com/cms/388-0-Political+Art+Statement.htm.

Buchloh, Benjamin H. D. *Neo-Avantgarde and Culture Industry: Essays on European and American Art from 1955 to 1975*. Cambridge, MA: MIT Press, 2000.

Buchloh, Benjamin H. D. 'Theorizing the Avant-Garde'. *Art in America* 72, no. 10 (November 1984): 19–21.

Buchloh, Benjamin H. D., Rachel Churner, Zainab Bahrani, Judith Barry, Christopher Bedford, Claire Bishop, Susan Buck-Morss, Critical Art Ensemble, T. J. Demos, Rosalyn Deutsche, Okwui Enwezor, Hannah Feldman, Harrell Fletcher, Coco Fusco, Liam

Gillick, Mark Godfrey, Tim Griffin, Hans Haacke, Rachel Haidu, David Joselit, Silvia Kolbowski, Carin Kuoni, Carrie Lambert-Beatty, Pamela M. Lee, Simon Leung, Lucy R. Lippard and Nato Thompson. 'Questionnaire: In What Ways Have Artists, Academics, and Cultural Institutions Responded to the U.S.-Led Invasion and Occupation of Iraq?' *October*, no. 123 (Winter 2008): 3–184.

Bürger, Peter. *Theory of the Avant-Garde*. Translated by Michael Shaw. Theory and History of Literature 4. Minneapolis: University of Minnesota Press, 1984.

Campagna, Federico, and Emanuele Campiglio, eds. *What We Are Fighting for: A Radical Collective Manifesto*. London: Pluto, 2012.

Carroll, Noël. 'Art and Ethical Criticism: An Overview of Recent Directions of Research'. *Ethics* 110, no. 2 (2000): 350–87.

Certeau, Michel de. *The Practice of Everyday Life*. Translated by Steven Rendall. Berkeley: University of California Press, 1988.

Chaguidouline, Anastasia. 'Borders and Forms'. *On Curating*, no. 50 (2021): 139–56.

Chatzichristodoulou, Maria, and Janis Jefferies, eds. *Interfaces of Performance*. London: Routledge, 2016.

Chayka, Kyle, and Alexander Forbes. 'Voina Explains Why Firebombing a Police Tank Is a "Piece of Art"'. *BLOUIN ARTINFO*, artinfo.com, 5 January 2012. https://web.archive.org/web/20191124195820/https://www.blouinartinfo.com/news/story/755205/voina-explains-why-fire bombing-a-police-tank-is-a-piece-of-art.

Cirio, Paolo. 'Takedown Notice: A Conversation with Paolo Cirio'. Interview by Liz Flyntz. *Afterimage: The Journal of Media Arts and Cultural Criticism* 42, no. 5 (2015): 16–20.

Cirio, Paolo. 'Art Interventions and Disruptions in Financial Systems: An Interview with Paolo Cirio'. Interview by Marisa Lerer; Conor McGarrigle. *Visual Resources: An International Journal of Documentation* 34, nos. 1–2 (3 April 2018): 157–67. https://doi.org/10.1080/01973762.2018.1437971.

Cirio, Paolo. *Flowcharts*. Morrisville, NC: Lulu Press, 2019.

Citron, Atay, Sharon Aronson-Lehavi and David Zerbib, eds. *Performance Studies in Motion: International Perspectives and Practices in the Twenty-First Century*. Illustrated edition. London: Bloomsbury Methuen Drama, 2014.

Clarke, Roger A. 'Information Technology and Dataveillance'. *Communications of the ACM* 31, no. 5 (1988): 498–512. https://doi.org/10.1145/42411.42413.

Colectivo Situaciones, ed. *Genocide in the Neighborhood*. Translated by Brian Whitener, Daniel Borzutzky and Fernando Fuentes. Oakland, CA: Chainlinks, 2009.

Coleman, Gabriella. *Hacker, Hoaxer, Whistleblower, Spy: The Many Faces of Anonymous*. eBook edition. London: Verso, 2014.

Coleridge, Samuel Taylor. *The Complete Poetical Works of Samuel Taylor Coleridge*. Edited by Ernest Hartley Coleridge. Vol. 1; 2 vols. Oxford: Clarendon Press, 1975.

Conolly, Oliver. 'Ethicism and Moderate Moralism'. *British Journal of Aesthetics* 40, no. 3 (2000): 302–16. https://doi.org/10.1093/bjaesthetics/40.3.302.

Considine, Liam. 'Screen Politics: Pop Art and the Atelier Populaire'. *Tate Papers*, no. 24 (Autumn 2015). https://www.tate.org.uk/research/publications/tate-papers/24/screen-politics-pop-art-and-the-atelier-populaire.

Critical Art Ensemble. 'Tactical Media at Dusk?' *Third Text* 22, no. 5 (September 2008): 535–48. https://doi.org/10.1080/09528820802440078.

Dafoe, Taylor. 'Russian Performance Artist Pyotr Pavlensky Charged after Setting a Bank on Fire in Paris'. *Artnet News*, 20 October 2017. https://news.artnet.com/art-world/pyotr-pavlensky-charged-fire-1123637.

De Cauter, Lieven, Runem De Roo and Karl Vanhaesebrouck, eds. *Art and Activism in the Age of Globalization*. Illustrated edition. Vol. 8; Reflect. Rotterdam: NAi Publishers, 2011.

Debord, Guy. *Comments on The Society of the Spectacle*. Translated by Malcolm Imrie. Radical Thinkers. London: Verso, 1998.

Debord, Guy. *Society of the Spectacle*. Translated by Ken Knabb. New authorized translation edition. Reprint; London: Rebel Press, [1967] 2004.

DeLaure, Marilyn, and Moritz Fink, eds. *Culture Jamming: Activism and the Art of Cultural Resistance*. New York: New York University Press, 2017.

Doesburg, Theo van. 'Anti-Tendenzkunst: An Answer to the Question: "Should the New Art Serve the Masses?"' *De Stijl* 6, no. 2

(April 1923): 17–19. https://nl.wikisource.org/wiki/De_Stijl/Jaargang_6/Nummer_2/Anti-tendenzkunst.

Dvorák, Michal, director. *Občan K. (Citizen K.)*. Czech Republic: ROMEOfilms, 2012.

Eco, Umberto. 'Towards a Semiological Guerrilla Warfare [1967]'. In *Travels in Hyperreality: Essays*, 135–44. San Diego, CA: Harcourt Brace Jovanovich, 1986. http://archive.org/details/travelsinhyperre00ecou.

Eco, Umberto. *Travels in Hyperreality: Essays*. San Diego: Harcourt Brace Jovanovich, 1986.

Erickson, Jon. 'The Spectacle of the Anti-spectacle: Happenings and the Situationist International'. *Discourse* 14, no. 2 (1992): 36–58.

Feldman, Hannah. 'Sound Tracks: The Art of Jennifer Allora and Guillermo Calzadilla'. *Artforum* 45, no. 9 (May 2007): 336–41; 396.

Firat, Begüm Özden, and Aylin Kuryel, eds. *Cultural Activism: Practices, Dilemmas and Possibilities*. Vol. 21. Thamyris/Intersecting: Place, Sex and Race. Amsterdam: Rodopi, 2010.

Fisher, Mark. *Capitalist Realism: Is There No Alternative?* Winchester: 0 Books, 2009.

Flood, Andrew. 'An Anarchist Critique of Horizontalism'. The Anarchist Library, 24 February 2014. https://theanarchistlibrary.org/library/andrew-flood-an-anarchist-critique-of-horizontalism.

Ford, Simon. *The Situationist International: A User's Guide*. London: Black Dog, 2005.

Foster, Hal. 'What's Neo about the Neo-Avant-Garde?' *October*, no. 70 (Fall 1994): 5–32.

Fox, Dominic. *Cold World: The Aesthetics of Dejection and the Politics of Militant Dysphoria*. Winchester: 0 Books, 2009.

Franks, Benjamin, Nathan Jun and Leonard Williams, eds. *Anarchism: A Conceptual Approach*. 1st edition. London: Routledge, 2018.

Gale, Matthew. *Dada & Surrealism*. London: Phaidon, 1997.

García Navarro, Santiago. 'International Errorista: The Revolution through Affect. Part 2'. LatinArt.com, 2 July 2006. https://www.latinart.com/aiview.cfm?start=2&id=358.

Gkoutziouli, Katerina, Marianna Christofi and Maria Varela, eds. *Heath Bunting: How to Build a New Legal Identity*. Athens: Frown Tails, 2014.

Gould, Robert. 'Roma Rights and Roma Expulsions in France: Official Discourse and EU Responses'. *Critical Social Policy* 35, no. 1 (2015): 24–44. https://doi.org/10.1177/0261018314545595.

Gray, Christopher. *Black Mask & Up Against the Wall Motherfucker: Burn It All Down: Flower Power Won't Stop Fascist Power: The Story of a Small, Underground 1960s Revolutionary Group in New York City*. Minneapolis, MN: The Daybreak Collective, 2001.

Grindon, Gavin. 'Second-Wave Situationism?' *Fifth Estate*, no. 350 (Summer 2009): 11, 50–1.

Grindon, Gavin. 'Art and Activism'. *Art Monthly*, no. 333 (February 2010): 9–12.

Grindon, Gavin. 'Surrealism, Dada, and the Refusal of Work: Autonomy, Activism, and Social Participation in the Radical Avant-Garde'. *The Oxford Art Journal* 34, no. 1 (2011): 79–96. https://doi.org/10.1093/oxartj/kcr003.

Grindon, Gavin. 'Poetry Written in Gasoline: Black Mask and Up Against the Wall Motherfucker'. *Art History* 38, no. 1 (February 2015): 170–209. https://doi.org/10.1111/1467-8365.12129.

Grindon, Gavin, and John Jordan. *A User's Guide to (Demanding) the Impossible*. Wivenhoe: Minor Compositions, 2010.

Groys, Boris. *In the Flow*. eBook edition. London: Verso, 2016.

Guevara, Ernesto. *Guerrilla Warfare: A Method*. Peking: Foreign Languages Press, 1964.

Hahne, Ron, and Ben Morea. *Black Mask & Up Against the Wall Motherfucker: The Incomplete Works of Ron Hahne, Ben Morea, and the Black Mask Group*. Oakland, CA: PM Press, 2011.

Halvorsen, Sam. 'Militant Research against-and-beyond Itself: Critical Perspectives from the University and Occupy London'. *Area* 47, no. 4 (December 2015): 466–72. https://doi.org/10.1111/area.12221.

Harrison, Charles, and Paul Wood, eds. *Art in Theory, 1900–2000: An Anthology of Changing Ideas*. 2nd edn. Malden, MA: Blackwell Publishing, 2003.

Hartnoll, Louis, Lucy Killoran, Robyn Minogue and Sophie Carapetian, eds. *Bad Feelings: Arts against Cuts*. Common Objectives. London: Book Works, 2015.

Hemingway, Andrew. 'John Reed Clubs and Proletarian Art–Part I'. *Against the Current*, no. 177 (2015). https://againstthecurrent.org/atc177/p4467/.

Herrera, Tania. 'Militant Research'. *Krisis Journal for Contemporary Philosophy*, no. 2 (2018): 10–11; 113–14. https://krisis.eu/wp-content/uploads/2018/07/Krisis-2018-2-Tania-Herrera-Militant-research.pdf?.

Hirschhorn, Thomas. *Critical Laboratory: The Writings of Thomas Hirschhorn*. Edited by Lisa Lee and Hal Foster. Cambridge, MA: MIT Press, 2013.

Hirschhorn, Thomas, Alison Gingeras, Benjamin. H. D. Buchloh and Carlos Basualdo. *Thomas Hirschhorn*. London: Phaidon, 2004.

Holmes, Brian. 'The Errorist International: Washed Up on a Beach in Australia'. *Transversal*, 29 January 2007. http://transform.eipcp.net/correspondence/1170076372.html.

Hopkins, David. *Dada and Surrealism. A Very Short Introduction*. Oxford: Oxford University Press, 2004.

Hopkins, David, ed. *Neo-Avant-Garde*. Avant-Garde Critical Studies 20. Amsterdam: Rodopi, 2006.

Ingram, Alan R. 'Making Geopolitics Otherwise: Artistic Interventions in Global Political Space: Making Geopolitics Otherwise'. *The Geographical Journal* 177, no. 3 (September 2011): 218–22. https://doi.org/10.1111/j.1475-4959.2011.00415.x.

Internacional Errorista. '"We Are All Errorists" – Errare Humanum Est. First Declaration by the Errorists'. TRANSFORM, 10 November 2005. http://transform.eipcp.net/correspondence/errorists-cp01en.html.

Jackson, Ken. 'The Great Temptation of "Religion": Why Badiou Has Been so Important to Žižek'. *International Journal of Zizek Studies* 1, no. 2 (2007). https://zizekstudies.org/index.php/IJZS/article/view/32/29.

Johnson, Oliver. 'War on the Ru-Net: Voina's Dick Captured by the FSB as a Networked Performance'. *Third Text* 27, no. 5 (September 2013): 591–606. https://doi.org/10.1080/09528822.2013.832075.

Jordan, John. 'On Refusing to Pretend to Do Politics in a Museum'. *Art Monthly*, no. 334 (March 2010): 35.

Kelley Jr, Bill, and Grant H. Kester, eds. *Collective Situations: Readings in Contemporary Latin American Art, 1995–2010*. Illustrated edition. Durham, NC: Duke University Press, 2017.

Kester, Grant H. 'Another Turn'. *Artforum* 44, no. 9 (May 2006): 22.

Kester, Grant H. *The One and the Many: Contemporary Collaborative Art in a Global Context*. Durham, NC: Duke University Press, 2011.

Klanten, Robert, Matthias Hübner, Alain Bieber, Pedro Alonzo, Gregor Jansen and Silke Krohn, eds. *Art & Agenda: Political Art and Activism*. Berlin: Gestalten, 2011.

Klee, Steve. 'Rancière against the Cuts'. *Third Text* 27, no. 2 (2013): 177–88. https://doi.org/10.1080/09528822.2013.774189.

Knabb, Ken, ed. *Situationist International Anthology*. Translated by Ken Knabb. Revised and Expanded eBook edition. Berkeley, CA: Bureau of Public Secrets, 2006.

Kunzru, Hari. 'The Mob Who Shouldn't Really Be Here'. *Tate Etc.*, Summer 2008. http://www.tate.org.uk/context-comment/articles/mob-who-shouldnt-really-be-here.

Kurczynski, Karen. 'Expression as Vandalism: Asger Jorn's "Modifications"'. *Res: Anthropology and Aesthetics* 53–54 (March 2008): 293–313. https://doi.org/10.1086/RESvn1ms25608823.

Lambert-Beatty, Carrie. 'Twelve Miles: Boundaries of the New Art/Activism'. *Signs: Journal of Women in Culture and Society* 33, no. 2 (January 2008): 309–27. https://doi.org/10.1086/521179.

Lang, Caroline, and John Reeve. *The Responsive Museum: Working with Audiences in the Twenty-First Century*. London: Routledge, 2016.

Lang, Martin. 'Militant Art'. Doctoral thesis, University of Kent, 2015. https://kar.kent.ac.uk/50237/.

Lang, Martin. 'Counter Cultural Production: A Militant Reconfiguration of Peter Bürger's "Neo-Avant-Garde"'. *Re·bus – a Journal of Art History and Theory*, no. 8 (2017): 24–49. https://www1.essex.ac.uk/arthistory/research/pdfs/rebus/rebus_issue_8_vol_1.pdf#page=27.

Lang, Martin. 'Hazlitt on Aesthetic Democracy and Artistic Genius'. *The Hazlitt Review* 14 (2021): 25–36.

Lang, Martin. 'Spectacular Malaise: Art and the End of History'. *Art & the Public Sphere* 8, no. 1 (2019): 63–82. https://doi.org/10.1386/aps_00006_1.

Lang, Martin, and Thomas Bresolin. 'Militant Training Camp: The Debriefing'. *Sanat Dünyamiz*, no. 131 (2012): 30–41.

Lang, Martin, and Tom Grimwood. 'Militant Training Camp and the Aesthetics of Civil Disobedience'. *Krisis Journal for Contemporary Philosophy*, no. 3 (2012): 37–51.

Léger, Marc James. *Vanguardia: Socially Engaged Art and Theory*. Illustrated edition. Manchester: Manchester University Press, 2019.

Levinson, Jerrold, ed. *Aesthetics and Ethics: Essays at the Intersection*. Cambridge Studies in Philosophy and the Arts. Cambridge: Cambridge University Press, 1998.

Lewis, Helena. *Dada Turns Red: The Politics of Surrealism*. Edinburgh: Edinburgh University Press, 1990.

Liberate Tate. 'Confronting the Institution in Performance: Liberate Tate's Hidden Figures'. *Performance Research* 20, no. 4 (July 2015): 78–84. https://doi.org/10.1080/13528165.2015.1071042.

Loewe, Sebastian. 'When Protest Becomes Art: The Contradictory Transformations of the Occupy Movement at Documenta 13 and Berlin Biennale 7'. *FIELD: A Journal of Socially Engaged Art Criticism*, no. 1 (2015): 185–203.

Lukacs, Georg. 'Propaganda or Partisanship?' Translated by Leonard F. Mins. *Partizan Review* 1, no. 2 (1934): 36–46. http://www.bu.edu/partisanreview/books/PR1934V1N2/HTML/files/assets/basic-html/../../../index.html (accessed 4 August 2023).

Lukacs, Georg. '"Tendency" or Partisanship?' In *Art in Theory, 1900–2000: An Anthology of Changing Ideas*, edited by Charles Harrison and Paul Wood, translated by David Fernback, 413–17. Oxford: Blackwell, 2003.

Malzacher, Florian. *Not Just a Mirror: Looking for the Political Theatre of Today*. Performing Urgency 1. Berlin: Alexander Verlag, 2015.

Marchart, Oliver. *Conflictual Aesthetics: Artistic Activism and the Public Sphere*. Berlin: Sternberg Press, 2019.

Marx, Karl, and Friedrich Engels. *Marx and Engels on Literature and Art: A Selection of Writings*. Edited by Lee Baxandall and Stefan Morawski. St Louis, MO: Telos Press, 1973.

McKee, Yates. 'Allora & Calzadilla: The Monstrous Dimension of Art: Interview with Jennifer Allora and Guillermo Calzadilla'. *Flash Art* 38 (January/February 2005): 96–9.

McKee, Yates. 'Wake, Vestige, Survival: Sustainability and the Politics of the Trace in Allora and Calzadilla's Land Mark'. *October*, no. 133 (2010): 20–48.

McKee, Yates. *Strike Art: Contemporary Art and the Post-Occupy Condition*. Paperback edition. London: Verso, 2017.

Meinhof, Ulrike. *Everybody Talks about the Weather … We Don't: The Writings of Ulrike Meinhof*. Edited by Karin Bauer. Translated by Luise Von Flotow. POLS. New York: Seven Stories Press, 2008.

Moren, Lisa. 'Algorithmic Pollution: Artists Working with Dataveillance and Societies of Control'. *Media-N: Journal of the New Media Caucus* 13, no. 1 (20 August 2017): 58–85. http://median.newmediacaucus.org/uncovering-news-reporting-and-forms-of-new-media-art/algorith

mic-pollution-artists-working-with-dataveillance-and-societies-of-control/.
Muelrath, Forrest. 'Art Insurrectionists'. *BOMB Magazine*, 10 January 2011. https://bombmagazine.org/articles/art-insurrectionists/.
Neuendorf, Henri. 'BP to End 26-Year Tate Sponsorship in 2017'. Artnet News, 11 March 2016. https://news.artnet.com/art-world/bp-ends-tate-sponsorship-2017-447041.
Nietzsche, Friedrich Wilhelm. *The Will to Power*. Translated by Walter Arnold Kaufmann. Vintage Books. New York: Random House, 1968.
Nietzsche, Friedrich Wilhelm. *On the Genealogy of Morality*. Edited by Keith Ansell-Pearson. Translated by Carol Diethe. Revised student edition. Cambridge Texts in the History of Political Thought. Cambridge: Cambridge University Press, 2007.
Pankhurst, Christabel. 'What Militancy Means'. *The Suffragette*, 2 May 1913, 492.
Peek, Ella. 'Ethical Criticism of Art'. In *Internet Encyclopedia of Philosophy*. Accessed 27 November 2018. https://iep.utm.edu/art-eth/.
Perry, Colin. 'Heath Bunting'. *Art Monthly*, no. 334 (March 2010): 30.
Plant, Sadie. *The Most Radical Gesture: The Situationist International in a Postmodern Age*. eBook edition. London: Routledge, 2002.
Plutser-Sarno, Alexei. 'The VOINA Art-Group («War»). Actions 2006–2012'. *Plucer Live Journal* (blog), 2012. http://plucer.livejournal.com/266853.html.
Poggi, Christine. *Inventing Futurism: The Art and Politics of Artificial Optimism*. Princeton, NJ: Princeton University Press, 2008.
Ponce de León, Jennifer. *Another Aesthetics Is Possible: Arts of Rebellion in the Fourth World War*. Durham, NC: Duke University Press, 2021.
Pooke, Grant. *Francis Klingender 1907–1955: A Marxist Art Historian Out of Time*. London: Gill Vista Marx Press, 2007.
Princenthal, Nancy. 'Taking Liberties'. *Art in America* 93, no. 11 (December 2005): 70.
Rainey, Lawrence S., Christine Poggi and Laura Wittman, eds. *Futurism: An Anthology*. New Haven, CT: Yale University Press, 2009.
Rancière, Jacques. *Aesthetics and Its Discontents*. Translated by Steven Corcoran. Cambridge: Polity Press, 2009.
Rancière, Jacques. *The Politics of Aesthetics: The Distribution of the Sensible*. Translated by Gabriel Rockhill. Reprint. London: Continuum, 2011.

Rasmussen, Mikkel Bolt. 'The Situationist International, Surrealism, and the Difficult Fusion of Art and Politics'. *Oxford Art Journal* 27, no. 3 (2004): 365–87.

Rasmussen, Mikkel Bolt. 'The Situationist International(s): The Realization of Art'. *International Journal of Aesthetics and Philosophy of Culture* 3, no. 3 (2018): 7–14. http://www.ijaphc.unibuc.ro/index.php/jurnale/article/view/1.

Ray, Gene. 'Art Schools Burning & Other Songs of Love and War'. *Left Curve*, no. 30 (2006): 81–96.

Ray, Gene. 'History, Sublime, Terror: Notes on the Politics of Fear'. In *The Sublime Now*, edited by Luke White and Claire Pajaczkowska, 133–54. Newcastle upon Tyne: Cambridge Scholars Publishing, 2009.

Ray, Gene, and Gregory Sholette. 'Introduction: Whither Tactical Media?' *Third Text* 22, no. 5 (September 2008): 519–24. https://doi.org/10.1080/09528820802439989.

Rokeby, David. 'Algorithmic Pollution'. Lecture presented at the Cyber Insecurities Panel, Pepco Edison Place Gallery (Washington, DC), September 2013.

Rothkopf, Scott. 'Embedded in the Culture: The Art of Paul Chan'. *Artforum* 44, no. 10 (Summer 2006): 305–11.

Ruf, Beatrix, ed. *Allora & Calzadilla*. Zurich: JRP|Ringier, 2009.

Sartre, Jean-Paul. *'What Is Literature?' And Other Essays*. Translated by Steven Ungar. Paperback edition. 1948. Reprint. Cambridge, MA: Harvard University Press, 1988.

Sharpe, Matthew, and Geoff M. Boucher. *Zizek and Politics: A Critical Introduction*. 1st edn. Edinburgh: Edinburgh University Press, 2010.

Sholette, Gregory. 'Critical Art Ensemble'. In *Oxford Art Online*. Oxford University Press, 16 September 2010. https://doi.org/10.1093/gao/9781884446054.article.T2088814.

Sholette, Gregory. *Dark Matter: Art and Politics in the Age of Enterprise Culture*. Marxism & Culture. London: Pluto Press, 2011.

Sholette, Gregory. 'Merciless Aesthetic: Activist Art as the Return of Institutional Critique. A Response to Boris Groys'. *FIELD: A Journal of Socially Engaged Art Criticism*, no. 4 (Spring 2016). http://field-journal.com/issue-4/merciless-aesthetic-activist-art-as-the-return-of-institutional-critique-a-response-to-boris-groys.

Shukaitis, Stevphen, David Graeber and Erika Biddle, eds. *Constituent Imagination: Militant Investigations/Collective Theorization*. Edinburgh: AK Press, 2007.

Sitrin, Marina A. *Everyday Revolutions: Horizontalism and Autonomy in Argentina*. London: Zed Books, 2012.

Sitrin, Marina A. ed. *Horizontalism: Voices of Popular Power in Argentina*. Edinburgh: AK Press, 2006.

Sitrin, Marina A. 'Horizontalism and the Occupy Movements'. *Dissent Magazine*, 2012. https://www.dissentmagazine.org/article/horizontalism-and-the-occupy-movements.

Sloterdijk, Peter. *Rage and Time: A Psychopolitical Investigation*. Translated by Mario Wenning. New York: Columbia University Press, 2010.

Smith, Terry, Okwui Enwezor and Nancy Condee, eds. *Antinomies of Art and Culture: Modernity, Postmodernity, Contemporaneity*. Durham, NC: Duke University Press, 2008.

Solnit, Rebecca. *Hope in the Dark: Untold Histories, Wild Possibilities*. 3rd edn. Chicago, IL: Haymarket Books, 2016.

Steinberg, Monica. 'Financial True Crime: Art, Para-Journalism, and Data-Driven Storytelling'. *Art History* 44, no. 2 (2021): 256–84. https://doi.org/10.1111/1467-8365.12571.

Stracey, Frances. *Constructed Situations: A New History of the Situationist International*. Marxism & Culture. London: Pluto, 2014.

Tarka, Sissu. 'BorderXing: Heath Bunting'. *Afterall: A Journal of Art, Context and Enquiry* (March 2009). https://www.afterall.org/article/borderxing.heath.bunting.sissu.tarka.

Tate. 'Activist Art – Art Term'. Tate. Accessed 9 October 2018. https://www.tate.org.uk/art/art-terms/a/activist-art.

The Yes Men. 'Dow Does the Right Thing'. The Yes Men, 1 December 2004. https://www.theyesmen.org/project/dow-does-right-thing.

The Yes Men. 'Dow's Golden Skeleton'. The Yes Men, 28 April 2005. https://yeslab.org/project/dows-golden-skeleton.

The Yes Men. 'Dow "Help" Announcement Is Elaborate Hoax'. The Yes Men, 3 December 2004. https://theyesmen.org/project/dowbbc/denial.

Thompson, Nato. ed. *Living as Form: Socially Engaged Art from 1991–2011*. Illustrated edition. New York: Creative Time Books; MIT Press, 2012.

Tikhonova, Yulia. 'Voina and Innovation'. *Flash Art* 44, no. 279 (July 2011): 46–8.

Tolstoy, Leo. *What Is Art?* Translated by Richard Pevear and Larissa Volokhonsky. Penguin Classics. London: Penguin, 1995.

Tomkova, Denisa. 'From Dialogical Aesthetics in Eastern European Art to "Falling in Love" with the Other(s): Discourses on Hospitality in Contemporary Europe'. *Third Text* 34, nos 4–5 (September 2020): 481–500. https://doi.org/10.1080/09528822.2020.1836814.

Vaneigem, Raoul. *The Revolution of Everyday Life*. Translated by Donald Nicholson-Smith. Reprint. London: Rebel Press, [1967] 2001.

Voina. '7th Berlin Biennale: Statement by Voina'. *Free Voina*, 2012. http://en.free-voina.org/post/22267051835.

Wark, McKenzie. *A Hacker Manifesto*. Cambridge, MA: Harvard University Press, 2004.

Wilde, Oscar. *The Picture of Dorian Gray*. eBook edition. Sweden: Wisehouse Classics, 2015.

Williams, Emmett, and Ann Noel, eds. *Mr Fluxus: A Collective Portrait of George Maciunas 1931–1978*. London: Thames and Hudson, 1997.

Žižek, Slavoj. *The Universal Exception*. Edited by Rex Butler and Scott Stephens. Expanded edition. London: Continuum, 2007.

Žižek, Slavoj. *The Sublime Object of Ideology*. Paperback edition. Essential Žižek. Reprint. London: Verso, [1989] 2008.

Žižek, Slavoj. *Trouble in Paradise: From the End of History to the End of Capitalism*. eBook edition. New York: Melville House, 2015.

Žižek, Slavoj. *Against the Double Blackmail: Refugees, Terror and Other Troubles with the Neighbours*. London: Allen Lane, 2016.

Ztohoven. 'Citizen K'. Ztohoven.cz. Accessed 18 October 2021. https://www.ztohoven.cz/?page_id=87.

Index

www.ingramcontent.com/pod-product-compliance
Ingram Content Group UK Ltd.
Pitfield, Milton Keynes, MK11 3LW, UK
UKHW021814290725
461334UK00004B/35

9 781350 346789

John Francis Hunter, author of THE GAY INSIDER, says:

"*All Is Well* is, to date, the best work of fiction of the new gay literature. Its theme is liberation, played with deceptive simplicity and not a trace of political bombast. Yet it *is* political, in that it is a paean to a way of life that is counter-culture all the way. Suspenseful and phantasmagoric, swift-moving yet entirely thorough in all its revelation of a metamorphosis that could be Everyman's, *All Is Well* grabs you and keeps you—and if you dig its message will never let you go. The captive gay, or even part-captive, who carefully reads and really understands and actually applies the wisdom of this novel won't need a shrink and can get by without an organization or any formal experiment in consciousness-raising.... What's more, *All Is Well* is a novel of, for and about sex, with some astoundingly erotic scenes that are as profound a manifesto of the right to discover and be one's total self as any rhetoric on the essential subject that I've heard or read. I recommend it wholeheartedly as a must to today's—or tomorrow's—American male homosexual."

NOTE: *All Is Well* is the third of the "All" books, a sequel to the bestselling *All Or Nothing* and *I Want It All.* An expanded and rewritten version of *All Or Nothing* is currently in preparation, and will be published soon by The Other Traveller.

DEDICATION:

This book is for all those who have been there—and for all those who are only beginning to realize that's where they are going—with a special note of gratitude and love to The Stoned Freak Typing Company's Brother Jack.

But most of all, this book is for Herb.

ALL IS WELL

Dirk Vanden

THE OLYMPIA PRESS

First published in Great Britain in 1972 by
The Olympia Press Limited,
20 Rupert Street, London W1

Printed in Great Britain by Oxley Press Ltd

ISBN 700 414 30 4

AUTHOR'S NOTE

In all of my previous books, sex has necessarily been the predominant theme, because whether or not their assumptions were correct, my publishers insisted on "hot sex" and lots of it, the kinkier the better, with a little plot and characterization tossed in here and there for good measure. Olympia has allowed me far more freedom in writing *All Is Well;* the sex is still there (as it must be in gay novels as well as gay lives) but only as one of many aspects of the story. Some readers may find the sex scenes less masturbatory as a result. I've had to make a decision—to write "just another sex book" or to test my convictions that gay people want to understand themselves and one another more than they want to jack off. After all, there are thousands of books which supply masturbatory fantasies for those who want them; there are very few books which advance the idea that being gay isn't as wretched and sinful as we've all been taught to believe it is.

There is a tremendously exciting reformation going on, all over the world, and I feel that gay people are going to wake up and find themselves in the vanguard of that reformation. But in order to "wake up" we must first understand ourselves—and that, more than anything else, is what *All Is Well* is all about.

Dirk Vanden

PART 1

Chapter 1

The note was creased and worn from many openings and refoldings. The printing was childish and the spelling atrocious, but I knew that no child had conceived such a frightening thing:

DERE ROBBER. THIS HERE IS A WARNING. YOU ARE GOING TO DIE. YOR A WIKID AND TERIBEL MAN. YOU HURT PEEPLE. YOR WIFE HATES YOR GUTS AND THE GIRLS AND YOR SUN ALSO. BUT I HATE YOR MORE. YOU DESERV TO DIE AND IF GOD DONT GIT YOU I WIL.

PS. YOR SUN IS A QUEER IF YOU DONT NO THAT ALL READY. IF YOU THING I AM FOOLING ASK JERY ASHBY. SO HA HA. THE JOKE IS ON YOU.

SINED YOU NO WHO

My hands were shaking as I angrily folded the note. I wanted to rip it to shreds, or crumple and burn it—get rid of it, forget it! What a blessed relief it would be just to get it out of my mind, if only for a couple of hours, or even a few minutes! Instead, I opened and read it again. The action had become a new habit—reading it, refolding it, unfolding it to read it again....

Just two weeks ago it had come in the mail—two weeks that were now beginning to seem like two years. It had been lying innocently on my bed (where Kate always put the mail addressed specifically to me—fortunately) along with the telephone bill and a real estate brochure, addressed to *MR ROBBER THORNE.* I'd laughed at first, muttering, "Some idiot doesn't know how to spell Robert." Then I'd opened the evil thing!

PS. YOR SUN IS A QUEER....

I pressed my hands hard against my legs, trying to stop them from trembling.

I needed a drink.

I looked at my watch; my plane wasn't due to start loading for another ten minutes or so. I shuddered at the thought of taking that flight, but it had to be done. And I knew I could face it a lot more easily with a good stiff drink in my stomach.

I put the note and envelope into my briefcase, then stood wearily, glancing toward the huge front windows of the San Francisco airport. With the late afternoon sun slanting across the glass, the windows had become partly opaque, and for a few moments I studied my transparent reflection. At least I didn't look as bad as I felt. The new clothes helped. I nodded to myself, thinking that Virginia, my secretary, would be delighted when I came in Monday morning: "Oh, wow, you did it! Oh, Mr. Thorne, now you really *do* look like him!" She insisted that I looked like her "very most favorite" movie star, Sean Connery, and although I couldn't quite see the resemblance, I'd kept his James Bond image in mind, buying the new jacket and trousers. I still wasn't sure that I liked the snug-fitting bellbottoms, but maybe that was simply because I wasn't used to them. Or maybe it was because I felt foolish for spending almost a hundred dollars just to please my secretary—but, dammit, a man needed to please *somebody* once in a while.

What the hell? Other men my age were wearing

bellbottoms, some of them a lot tighter and gaudier than these; the young man who'd sold them to me had insisted, "Oh, yes, sir, I'd say these were *super*-conservative. I mean, no one's going to think you're a hippie or anything like that."

I was distracted from my thoughts by a growing uneasiness, sensing that someone was watching me. I tried to see who it might be by looking at the other reflections in the window, but the images were too hazy, and the glass kept wavering, each time someone came through the doors from outside.

I sat down again, trying to look casual—but my heart was starting to beat faster and the muscles in my stomach were tensing almost painfully: it wasn't the first time today that I'd felt someone was watching me.

I'd awakened in my hotel room that morning with the vivid impression that someone was there in the room with me; even though that proved untrue, I couldn't get rid of the conviction that someone had been in the room sometime during the night. I'd found nothing actually missing or noticeably out of place, but somehow it had seemed that things were *not quite* as I'd left them. Then later, walking along Van Ness on my way to the American Graphic Designers' Association conference, I'd had the impression that someone was following me. Once more I'd been unable to confirm the suspicion. It had happened again in a coffee shop, just before the last session of the conference. I'd gone through the day with the increasingly uneasy premonition that something was going to happen—something bad, maybe even disastrous.

And now it was happening again!

I turned in the seat. At first there seemed to be no one the slightest bit interested in me, but as I glanced through the busy, noisy crowd, for some reason my eyes kept returning to a man standing at a bookstall about ten feet away. He was seemingly intent on reading a paperback novel, but something about him—I couldn't tell what—gave me the feeling that he wasn't reading the book at all.

He glanced up, and I turned away, but not before his gaze had met mine in a way that convinced me he'd been the one watching me. Moreover, I had a strangely uncomfortable feeling that I recognized him.

I was sure he wasn't anyone I knew well—at least not at the present; something in my mind hinted that I'd known him a long time ago, maybe in college. If that were true, it would explain why he'd been watching me; he could have been trying to remember where he'd known me before—just as I was doing.

I glanced over my shoulder again. For a moment I thought he had gone—or had realized I'd seen him and had ducked behind one of the racks—but then I saw him at the counter, buying the book he'd been looking at. Obviously he was making no attempt to hide. At the moment he was leaning on the counter, looking thoroughly unconcerned, waiting for the cashier to bring back his change, casually watching the crowd moving around him.

He was a large man and rather good-looking—or perhaps "rugged" was a better word. I guessed he would stand an inch or so taller than I—maybe six-two or six-three. Dark hair, broad shoulders, a solid, muscular body. (I decided that women would probably find him very "sexy".) There was something about him that seemed out-of-place, and it took several moments before I could decide what it was. He looked so natural and at ease in his clothing that it wasn't until I'd looked around at several other men that I realized what made him look different. Most of the men I could see were dressed like myself, in sport coats and slacks, or in business suits; he was wearing a plain white T-shirt and the tightest pair of levis I'd seen in a long time. With his faded denim jacket hanging over one muscular arm, he looked like a burly sheepherder just down from the hills, freshly scrubbed, ready for a "night out in the Big City". But a *friendly* sheepherder. He didn't look at all sinister or dangerous. I couldn't quite picture him sneaking into my room, or skulking after me in the street. He looked more like the type who would march up and say, "Hey, don't I know you from somewheres?"

The only thing that really disturbed me about him was the obscene slouch he affected, which tightened his levis even more, displaying a thick and embarrassing bulge in his crotch; even from where I was sitting, the details of his sex organs were obvious. There was no way anyone could have helped noticing.

He stood up from the slouch as the cashier said something behind him, and I looked up to his face—and found his eyes looking directly at mine. He nodded and grinned, then turned to the cashier, and I quickly looked away, embarrassed at having been caught staring.

A tinny voice startled me: "Your attention please. United Airline's flight nine-seventeen, nonstop to Salt Lake City, is now loading at gate twenty-two...."

The voice pushed all thought of the man totally out of my mind. I sat staring out of the window again, feeling numb. Now that the moment had come, I didn't want to get on that plane! I'd planned it all so carefully up to this point, but now that the end of my plan was in sight I didn't want to complete it. I wanted to rush back outside, jump into the nearest cab, and speed back into San Francisco.

But I couldn't do that and I knew it; I had to go through with it; I had to be sure.

Now it was even too late to have that drink!

The announcement came again and I reluctantly stood up and started toward the long corridor to the loading ramps.

"Hey! Hey, you! Wait!"

The voice was like a blast of icy wind. I stopped short, my back muscles tensing like fists along my spine. I wanted to turn, to glance back casually, but for a terrible moment I couldn't move. Wildly in my mind I saw several men coming toward me, guns drawn from secret holsters, handcuffs open, ready to arrest me for some dreadful crime I hadn't committed.

"Hey! Your briefcase."

I looked down at my empty hand. "Oh, God!"

The note was in that briefcase!

I spun around—and almost collided with the man who'd been watching me. He smiled as he held out the briefcase, and I forced myself to smile calmly as I took it. "Thank you," I told him. "Don't want to lose that." I added: "Nothing really valuable in it, but I wouldn't want to just leave it behind."

He nodded and smiled again. "Good thing I noticed."

"Yes. Thank you."

Now that we stood face to face, that feeling that I knew him grew even stronger. I waited before saying anything, hoping he'd ask: "Aren't you Robert Thorne? Remember me? I'm..." But he didn't. I watched his brown eyes for a flicker of recognition, but if there was any he didn't let it show.

I felt foolish asking, but I had to know. "Do I know you from someplace?"

He looked startled. "I don't think so."

"Oh." I looked down uncomfortably. "I...just thought...the way you were....staring...."

"Me?" He chuckled softly. "I thought *you* were staring."

"No," I said quickly. I could feel my face burning again. "At least, I didn't mean to. I'm sorry if... I just had this feeling I knew you. Sorry."

"Hell, that's okay. Don't apologize."

"Well, thanks for finding the briefcase." I hesitated, unsure of what to say next—he looked as if he expected me to say something.

"Are you on nine-seventeen?" he asked.

"What? Oh, yes. Yes, I am."

"Well...." He grinned. "That's a pleasant coincidence. So am I. I guess we'd better hurry." He started down the corridor, then paused to look back at me.

I laughed nervously, feeling like a flustered kid, then hurried to catch up with him. As I fell into step beside him I asked, "Do you live in Salt Lake?"

"Unfortunately."

"Oh? You don't like it?"

"Even less after spending a week here. Oh, it's okay, I guess, if you happen to be a good Mormon—which I'm not." He paused for a moment, then asked: "How about you?"

"Pardon me?"

"Are you a good Mormon?"

"No," I said. "Not a *good* one."

"Well, then, you should know what I mean. Ah, but San Francisco! Now there's a *real* city for you."

"Yes," I agreed. "I've certainly enjoyed it."

"Yeah," he said softly, as though remembering something pleasant, "it's just about the only place I know of where a guy can really find just about anything he's looking for, you know? You here on vacation?"

"No. Business."

"Oh. Did you get out at all?"

"Not too much."

"Well...." He was silent for a moment as we walked, then laughed softly. I turned to him, wondering what he had found amusing. He seemed lost in some memory, unaware I was looking at him. Even though he'd denied it, I couldn't get over the feeling that I recognized him. I guessed he was roughly the same age as I, or a year or so younger—in his early thirties at least; we were both built about the same, although his musculature was better defined than mine; both of us were dark-haired. Maybe that was it! Maybe, somehow, he reminded me of myself. To a casual stranger, seeing us walking together, we might easily have looked like brothers. Of course, I was clean-shaven, while he sported a thick moustache and bushy sideburns; and his hair was somewhat long: neatly trimmed, but definitely longer than I liked to see hair on a man. Still, I had to admit that it didn't look particularly bad. It went with that overall "sheepherder" image; it suited him.

I reminded myself that I had to get over my aversion to long hair on men. It was a lesson I'd had crammed down my throat at the Design Conference, where at least half of the men had worn long hair, moustaches, even full beards. As a matter of fact, a couple of times I'd caught myself staring into a mirror, wondering what I might look like with a nice bushy moustache—but I'd put the idea out of mind very quickly. Virginia would get a big kick out of it, but our customers wouldn't. Not in Salt Lake City, Utah. Not those straitlaced old bastards. With them, my problem was to look *more* mature, not less, and I knew they would equate even a moustache with "hippies", as I had done. At thirty-five I looked more like thirty—which was remarkable considering all I'd been through lately—and sometimes I had trouble convincing a new account that I was mature enough to have my own company, experienced enough to handle their precious advertising campaign, even though *Bogen & Thorne* was one of the better-known agencies in Salt Lake, and had been for several years.

The plane was only about three-quarters full, and we were apparently the last two passengers. There were several pairs of seats still vacant. I glanced around the cabin, about to ask the man whether he'd prefer the front or the back of the plane, when he said, "Well, good. We can both get window seats. Talk to you later."

In spite of the strange way we'd met, I'd assumed we would sit together and talk on the way home. I'd been thinking it would be a relief to talk to somebody, get my mind off my problems. But apparently my "new friend" wasn't all that interested in conversation. I shrugged off my momentary disappointment and said, "Fine. After dinner, maybe."

"Right." He nodded, then slid into a seat in front of the wings. I continued back almost to the rear. With my briefcase in the aisle seat, I strapped myself down by the window. As a stewardess came by, checking seat-belts, the jet shuddered and started away from its berth. For a few minutes I watched the airport buildings recede in the gathering twilight; then, as the plane rumbled and shuddered, waiting for clearance for take-off, I took the note out of my briefcase and slipped it into my inside coat pocket. It wasn't too likely I'd forget it again, but I didn't want to take chances.

Even though I'd resisted the impulse to read the note again, I couldn't keep myself from thinking about it. The threat to my life didn't particularly worry me, mainly because I could not take it seriously. Nor was I shocked by the idea that Kate hated me; I'd been living with that fact for years. No, the thing which disturbed me was that PS—that supposedly tossed-in fill-up about Chuck. To me, that was the core of the message, and the rest merely windowdressing, carefully designed to confuse or frighten me, to distract me from the real threat of the thing: blackmail! Naturally I was hurt and disgusted by the accusation that my son was a homosexual—what father wouldn't be? Although I might have understood and forgiven him even that "youthful indiscretion" (after all, he was only sixteen) if he hadn't been so stupid, or so intentionally spiteful, as to let someone know about it. Because, whoever he was, that someone was obviously determined to put me through whatever hell he could devise—make me feel guilty and miserable because, supposedly, it was a father's fault when a son turned homosexual, etc., etc.—all as a buildup to another note requesting a few thousand dollars in return for his silence.

I wasn't fooled for a minute by the childish printing and spelling. I was certain the writer could spell as well as I. He'd been "mature" enough to know how to address and mail the envelope.

The more I thought about it, the more I was convinced that the clue to the culprit's identity lay in the note itself: "If you think I am fooling, ask Jerry Ashby." No matter what else might be wrong with Chuck's so-called "best friend", he wasn't stupid. He was smart enough to pretend to be stupid—if he saw something in it for him. The whole thing could easily be one of Ashby's wild schemes to make money for one of those underground groups he belonged to, that he'd talked Chuck into joining. With the morals those kids had, he wouldn't be above setting up his best-friend for something like this: getting him drunk—or worse, doped up—then seducing him, with one of his long-haired cronies in the closet taking pictures. But if I could catch him in a compromising situation himself, that would be the end of it right there. Also it would give me a legitimate reason for forbidding Chuck to ever see him again.

The big jet was moving now, faster and faster down the runway. I leaned close to the window, looking down as the ground suddenly dropped away from under us, and a bright thrill coursed through my body. I loved that moment of takeoff; it always reminded me of riding in elevators when I was a child. San Francisco grew smaller and smaller as the jet climbed over the Berkeley hills. The day had been clear and cloudless and now the sun was a flattened fiery red ball sinking into a golden ocean. The early evening sparkle of lights around the shimmering bay slowly faded in a light haze, then vanished beyond the edges of my window.

It was truly a beautiful city, I thought. Throughout both days of the AGDA conference, I'd toyed with ideas of moving there permanently, but the ideas had all been impractical, simply wishful thinking. (I couldn't move anywhere at least until Chuck was old enough to take care of himself; I had a responsibility there which I wasn't about to abandon.) I'd had to decide to be satisfied with an occasional visit whenever some artist or design or advertising group had a conference. Still, it was a pity I'd had to leave early. I could have spent all day tomorrow, Easter Sunday, just wandering around in the bright spring sunshine—through Ghiradelli Square, or in Golden Gate Park, maybe taking one of the boat tours of the bay.

Well, no use torturing myself; I'd have to spend Easter at home. I could only hope that it wouldn't turn into a sordid fight with Chuck.

Low ranges of hills passed under us, fading sunlight illuminating their western sides, darkness gathering behind them. I watched strange unfathomable light-patterns on the ground—cities, towns, freeways, airports—again very tempted to wish I hadn't taken the flight. No one expected me home until late tomorrow night.

But that, of course, was the whole point: nobody expected me. I'd arranged it that way for a definite reason, and now I had to go through with my plans.

Humorlessly I thought: *Oh, what tangled web's we weave....*

But I had to be sure—and this was the only way I could think of to be sure. I had to catch him in the act. It was a rotten thing to do, deliberately tricking my own son, but it had to be done. Any other way, he could simply deny the accusation. I had to surprise him, take him off his guard. If he knew I suspected him, I'd never find out anything.

I was tempted to confront him with the note and tell him, "You've made your bed, now lie in it!" Running around with that hippie crowd, getting involved with that underground newspaper, getting himself kicked out of school for those ridiculous protests. I'd asked him a hundred times to stop seeing that damned Jerry Ashby, but he just wouldn't listen. Constantly giving me that smug silence that said, "What do you know about anything? You're an old man!"

"Good evening...."

My heart lurched against my chest and my head jerked up, half expecting to see that man standing over me, knowing what I'd been thinking. I cursed myself for being so jumpy. I was acting as though *I* had done something wrong.

"...your captain, John Everest. Welcome aboard United's flight nine-seventeen to Salt Lake City. We are slightly behind schedule, but we've got a good tail-wind and should make it up. Our projected arrival time is nine thirty-five. We will be flying at an altitude..."

Nine thirty-five. That would put me home about ten, or a little after. If the note were true, if Chuck were having...an affair...with the Ashby kid, that would be just about the perfect time to catch them. Like Chuck, Ashby lived at home with his parents, and if I'd guessed rightly, he'd be the first to suggest that they spend the evening at our place. With Kate in Ogden–she'd have left early this morning–and me in San Francisco, they'd think they had the whole house to themselves for the night. At least that's how I'd planned it. That's why I'd decided to go to the AGDA Conference in the first place; that's why I'd suggested that Kate take the girls to spend Easter vacation with her parents in Ogden; that's why I'd made such a point of telling Chuck I wouldn't be home until Sunday night. Let Ashby hang himself with his own rope! I'd suspected the kid of being queer from the first moment I'd seen him, and if my suspicions were correct, I was sure he would jump at the bait I'd held out to him.

Of course, Ashby wasn't the only suspect. My partner, Ed Bogen, was right up there, second on the list; but before I risked making a fool of myself, confronting Ed, I had to eliminate Ashby.

"Sir?" I jerked around. A pretty blonde stewardess was leaning over the vacant seat next to mine, smiling brightly. "We'll be serving dinner in about ten minutes," she said sweetly. "Would you care for a cocktail first?"

Even though I'd been thinking about getting a drink, back in the airport, and even though I knew that I needed one to relax me and get my mind out of the rut of stewing over that damned note, still I felt a reluctance to say "yes" immediately. Old habits were hard to break. I'd been a good Mormon teetotaler up until five years ago, except for a brief lapse during high school, and I still couldn't help feeling a kind of smug hostility toward anyone offering me a drink. Even now I made it a practice to never drink liquor in a public place where any of my customers might see me. But this, I reminded myself, was not Salt Lake; there was no one on the plane who might recognize me (with the possible exception of the man who'd been watching me) so, finally, I smiled back up at the stewardess and said, "Yes, I believe I will."

I selected a miniature Smirnoff from her tray.

"Would you like a mix?" she asked. "Seven-Up? Ginger Ale?"

"Seven-Up will be fine."

She poured the beverage into a cocktail glass. "Enjoy your flight, Sir."

"Thank you."

I watched her move on to the next seats, wondering what kind of attitude a girl had to have to seem happy like that all the time? I emptied the little bottle into the glass, then raised a silent toast to the smiling hostess: *Here's to you, pretty thing. May you never get married and have children and problems.*

Kate had looked like that, once, many years ago. Not that pretty, of course, not then—Kate had been a late bloomer, and her beauty, when I'd started going with her, had been more of an inner glow, a spiritual beauty. Now that had reversed itself; now she was a physically attractive woman, with nothing but an ugly void inside.

I leaned back, sipping the cocktail. That had been so long ago. Seventeen years. How she had smiled then! How delightfully she had laughed—the laughter of innocence! How I had loved just being with her, watching her smile, hearing her laugh....

"May I?" The man who had rescued my briefcase stood in the aisle, holding his cocktail glass.

I smiled up at him and moved the briefcase under my seat, grateful that he'd stopped my dark mood before it had really taken hold of me. "Sure thing."

He sat with a loud sigh, adjusted himself (with those tight pants of his, I guessed that sitting down was something of a problem) then turned to me. He lifted his glass. "Here's to San Francisco." He took a quick sip. "God, I really hated to leave. I had one very nice thing going.... But, *c'est la vie,* as they say. 'All things must pass,' as good old George puts it." He grinned. "I'll warn you, I'm already a little bit drunk. One sweet little old lady gave me hers. Very Christian of her, wouldn't you say?"

"Very," I said, grinning back at him. He was the type who could charm little old ladies out of their gold teeth if he took the notion. His appearance was disarming; just to look at him, you'd expect him to swagger and swear like a sailor, but when he came out with something like *c'est la vie,* it took you off your guard. I decided he could be a fantastically successful salesman—or con man.

"By the way," he said, "we didn't introduce ourselves. I'm John Adams."

I reached across to shake hands. "Robert Thorne."

"Okay to call you *Bob?*"

"I'd rather you didn't," I said quickly, then added:

"I'm not being rude; I just don't care for the nickname."

He shrugged. "So what's new and exciting in your life, Robert?"

"Not very much."

"Well, that's too bad. When I'm King, everybody will have at least one new and exciting thing happen at least once a day."

"I hope I'm around when you get to be King."

He looked at me, smiling as though we shared some kind of secret. "I hope so too." He took another sip of his drink. "How many of these things do we get?"

I shrugged. "I really don't know. One, I guess."

He patted my arm. "Not if old John has anything to say about it. When we land in good old New Jerusalem, I fully intend to be as *non compos mentis* as possible."

I laughed. "You really hate Salt Lake, don't you?"

"No, not really." He leaned out into the aisle and called, "Oh, Miss...." then sighed and settled down into the seat. He started to say something, then grimaced. He muttered, "Pardon me," and squeezed his hand under the waistband of his levis, tugged at something, then sighed again. "No," he said, "it's just that a place like San Francisco can spoil you, you know? You want something, just reach out and grab it. In Salt Lake we're still playing all the old games, and man, I'll tell you, I've had Oscar Wilde up to here, you know?"

Before I could say, "No, I don't know. What does Oscar Wilde have to do with it?" the stewardess appeared with her tray. "Yes, sir?"

"Hello again," John Adams said brightly. "My friend and I would certainly appreciate another little drink—if it's not against the rules."

She smiled like a light being turned on. "Of course." As I watched her pour the drinks, I realized why John had adjusted himself; her eyes strayed several times to his prominent crotch. As much as it annoyed—or embarrassed—me, John obviously knew how to get the best mileage out of his "physical attributes". Surprisingly enough, except for a quick glance at her bosom, John seemed not the least bit interested in his admirer. I decided he was probably so used to it, it had ceased to be a novelty to him. When she had gone, he turned to me, lifting his glass. "What shall we drink to, Robert?"

I shrugged. "You choose. I can't think of anything worth toasting."

"My God, is it that bad? Let's see.... How about sex?"

I lifted my glass. "Whatever *that* is." I finished what was left of my first drink and exchanged it for the fresh one. When I glanced up, John was staring at me, frowning dramatically, but with a mischievous sparkle in his eyes.

"Wellllll," he drawled, "if I remember what my Mommy told me... What's the matter, Robert? Aren't you getting your share of the goodies?"

I tried to think of an amusing answer, something to match his bantering tone, but he'd hit on a subject a little too close to home for me to make jokes about it. In fact I began to wonder at that point whether John Adams and I had anything in common that we could talk about. Obviously he was a real cockswain with the ladies, and no matter how I might want to, I knew I couldn't match clever sexual anecdotes with him. "I'm getting along," I said.

"Getting along? Come on. A guy like you, just *getting along?*"

"It's a long sad story, John. I could write a book." I chuckled humorlessly. "But I'm afraid it wouldn't be a very interesting book." I glanced out the window and took another drink.

"Look," he said seriously. "Am I bugging you or something? I tend to be slightly aggressive when I'm drunk."

"No," I said quickly, "of course you're not 'bugging' me. It's just...just a personal problem I've had on my mind. It's hard to shift gears."

"Oh, yeah. Yeah, I know how that is. Maybe I should go grab us another couple of drinks. I'm sure she'd let me have them."

I turned to him, grinning. "I'm sure she would, too. No, that's all right. This one will hit me in a minute or two."

"Fine." He smiled, then his gaze shifted to the window. "Beautiful, isn't it?"

For a moment I didn't turn, but looked at his face. There was something about this man that intrigued me and frightened me, both at the same time. I knew that he wasn't at all what he seemed, with his levis and T-shirt and scruffy boots. His words and the tones of his voice belied the rough, uncultured exterior. I had the feeling that John Adams wasn't like any other man I'd ever met. I had an almost overwhelming desire to touch him.

I turned quickly to the window. Outside, all traces of daylight had gone and the stars were breathtakingly brilliant—but they seemed so remote, so vastly far away. Something inside me seemed to swell and burst open and I shuddered, gritting my teeth to keep from suddenly starting to bawl like a little kid! I felt so unbearably lonely!

What the hell is the matter with me?

All day long those crazy thoughts about being watched and followed, and now... Here this guy had come back to talk to me, to offer his company, maybe even his friendship, and I couldn't even *talk* to him! I felt as though my entire body, including my brain, was trussed up with invisible cords. And that terrible feeling that something disastrous was coming closer and closer and closer!

I closed my eyes tightly, turning so he couldn't see.

Suddenly, vividly, I saw Kate, and she was laughing. I could almost hear the taunting, scathing sound of it.

Damn you, Kate Jensen! Damn the moment I ever laid eyes on you!

"...in a black mood, aren't you?"

At the sound of his voice, Kate's image vanished. I took a deep breath and turned to him. "I'm sorry, John."

"Do you feel like talking about it? I'm a very good listener."

I tried to smile. "I'm afraid it would bore you stiff. Look, I'm sorry. I really do want to talk to you, John, but..."

"I understand. You think maybe you'll feel better after dinner?"

"I'm sure I will. As soon as this damned drink gets going."

"Okay." He nodded, then stood up, tugging at his levis again. "I'll see you then." He started away, then turned and regarded me. "Robert..." He came back and stood pensively looking down at me. "Did you really think I was staring at you, back at the airport?"

The question was completely unexpected and it flustered me; I couldn't help twisting it into some kind of accusation. "Well...yes. I *thought* you were."

"Why? I mean, why did you think I'd be staring at you?"

"I told you, I thought maybe we knew one another."

"And that's all?"

I shook my head helplessly. "I don't understand what you're getting at."

"Nothing really—except a confession of sorts. I didn't think I was staring, but I had noticed you."

"Oh?"

"Should we talk about it after dinner?"

I nodded unsurely. "All right..."

"Don't look so worried, Robert. It's nothing world-shattering. I just thought you looked like somebody I'd like to know." He grinned, then winked, and then walked away, leaving me feeling as though someone had jerked a rug out from under me.

The dinner was soggy, but relatively warm and tasty, and by then the alcohol had relaxed me to where I could almost enjoy it. As I ate, I thought about John Adams' "confession of sorts". In a way, it made me feel better, because it reassured me that I hadn't been imagining things, and that let me hope I hadn't imagined the other times I'd felt I was being watched. I hoped that I hadn't put him off by being so damned gloomy. I really did want to get to know him. If he'd give me another chance, maybe I could tell him about myself. I knew that I desperately needed *someone* to talk to, someone I could confide in. These last two weeks I'd begun to realize how little I'd talked to anyone since that morning I'd walked into Kate's room in the hospital, five years ago, so proud and happy and so anxious to see my twin daughters—only to have my entire world shattered by three words: "They're not yours."

And now I was so bound up, so shut away in my own private miserable world, nothing had been able to get through to me. It seemed I'd been in some kind of emotional deep-freeze for five numb, endless years. I couldn't even remember those years! One day had followed another, and somehow five years had gone by. I could remember that morning in the hospital—and then the evening I'd come home and opened that note—but in between those two times was a vast grey void.

Perhaps, I thought, receiving that note would turn out to be a good thing. Perhaps it had jarred me enough to rouse me out of the deep-freeze. Instead of simply living with the problem, perhaps I could somehow come to terms with it, maybe even settle it. If it turned out that Jerry Ashby wasn't the culprit (and I prayed, for

Chuck's sake, that he wasn't) then I'd be forced to confront Ed Bogen; it would all have to come out then, the whole dreary, ugly mess, and perhaps that would be good.

Ed had once been my closest friend, as well as my business partner, and it was just possible that a shred of our original friendship could still function. It wasn't all that improbable that Ed had written the note to force such a confrontation. I was sure that he knew I was well aware of who the girls' father really was, and it was possible that he was as miserable about it as I was.

Maybe that was the "disastrous" change I'd felt coming.

After dinner I finished what was left of my drink, waiting for Adams to join me again. As the minutes dragged by, I leaned back in the seat and closed my eyes, thinking again about San Francisco...that bright afternoon I'd gone walking down by Ghiradelli Square ...the young, bearded artists, half-naked, in ragged faded levis, their paintings propped up along the sidewalks... bright-eyed long-long-haired girls selling strawflowers... posters of naked boys and girls, running along seashores, over grassy hills...*MAKE LOVE, NOT WAR*...musicians standing on street corners, singing songs about Love and Peace....

"...Sir?"

A hand touched my shoulder.

"Sir?"

I sat up, forcing my eyes open—and looked up at the pretty blonde stewardess. "We're beginning our approach to the Salt Lake Airport," she said. "Would you fasten your seat belt, please?" Sleepily I fumbled to fasten the clasp; she leaned over to help me, then smiled and said, "Thank you, Sir."

I felt the plane tilt into a bank, looked out the window. Salt Lake City looked like a bed of warm embers, heaped up in a dark "firepit" of the mountains.

Other embers trailed north and south, with little glowing beds marking other towns. I wanted to feel warm and happy at the sight of "home", but I couldn't. The hour was approaching when I'd have to confront Chuck, and I felt no comfort at all in that thought.

For a few moments I wondered why John Adams hadn't come back after dinner, but then I decided that, like everything and everyone else in life, he had been merely another "promise" that couldn't be fulfilled. I couldn't allow myself to be upset about it.

The plane finished its turn and the city moved to the opposite side of the plane. My window looked west toward the lake. The night was sharply clear. I could have counted the cars on the freeway.

Lucky devils, I thought. Some of those cars were going to San Francisco. How I wished I could have been in one of them.

To my amazement, John Adams was waiting at the bottom of the ramp. He fell into line beside me, putting his hand on my shoulder. "I came back to talk," he said, "but you were asleep."

"I guess I dozed off after dinner."

"Yeah. With that dinner, I don't blame you. It feels like a big lump of lead in my gut. Where you headed now?"

"Home," I said.

"How about letting me buy you a beer?"

I considered it, then shook my head. "I'd better not, John. It's sort of important that I get right home."

"Someone expecting you?"

"Well...not exactly. It's too complicated to explain, John."

"Oh, well." He shrugged and took his hand away from my shoulder. "Maybe some other time."

"Yes," I said. "Definitely."

"You mean that?"

I glanced at him, wondering why he should sound so

surprised. Had I seemed that standoffish? "Of course I mean it. I'm not always in such a lousy mood."

He smiled brightly. "Well, good." He reached into a pocket and gave me a small piece of paper; it had his name and telephone number carefully hand-printed. "I hoped you'd feel that way. Maybe dinner some night?"

"I'd like that." I put the paper into my coat pocket, next to the envelope. "Maybe some evening this week," I said. "My wife's out of town."

He turned to look at me, and for a fleeting moment there was an expression of confusion on his face. "Your wife?"

"Yes," I said. "She's in Ogden for the week. Took the girls to Grandma's for Easter."

"And what she doesn't know won't hurt her, is that it?"

I laughed. "It wouldn't hurt her even if she did know."

"I see. Well...I'm not married, Robert." He said it as though there were some kind of secret meaning in the words.

"You're lucky."

"You still want to come to dinner?"

"Of course—unless you're a lousy cook."

He laughed and gripped my shoulder again. "How old are they—your kids?"

"The girls are five; they're twins. And my boy is sixteen."

He frowned. "You're kidding. Sixteen?"

"I married young."

"Jesus, I'll say you did. How old were you, twelve?"

"No. We were both eighteen." I smiled, watching him silently adding eighteen and sixteen—plus one for the pregnancy. Most people had trouble believing that I had a sixteen-year-old son. Sometimes I had trouble believing it myself.

As we approached the baggage-return area, I spotted a Men's Room. My bladder had been uncomfortably full when I'd awakened on the plane, and I knew if I didn't go now, I'd be miserable on the drive home. I told John, "Excuse me," and turned aside into the room, assuming that we'd finish the conversation as we waited for our luggage.

I heard someone follow me into the room, but I didn't bother turning to see who it was; I stepped up to a urinal and concentrated on the splash of the stream in the cigarette shreds and filters. I was almost finished when I felt that uncomfortable awareness that someone was watching me. I glanced sideways.

John Adams stood at the next urinal; he was looking directly down at my penis.

And I couldn't help noticing that his own penis was standing out from his fly thick and half-erect. He was milking it lazily.

For a moment I was too stunned to think; all I could do was stand there and stare back at him. And in that moment, he reached out toward me—and touched me.

A chill shot through my body.

"Very nice, Robert," he whispered.

I jerked back, turning quickly away, frantically stuffing myself back into my shorts. It was all beginning to make sense to me now.

"Robert...."

I felt a hand on my shoulder. Blind fury erupted inside me and I spun around to face him, knocking his hand away. "Don't you touch me, you—" I shuddered painfully.

"Hey, now, hold on just a damn minute."

"You go straight to Hell, you filthy...*pervert!*"

Suddenly he started to laugh, and that only heightened my fury. "You sonofabitch! I'll call the police!"

"Oh?"

His pants were still open, his erection slowly drooping downward, jerking as it did.

"I'd think twice about telling anyone, Robert. Just

remember, it's your word against mine. And you really don't know who I am, do you? They might just believe me—and think *you* were the *pervert.*"

We stared at each other for a long moment; then he shook his head sadly and eased his limbering organ into his tight pants, adjusted it, then calmly zipped up. He put his hand on my shoulder and squeezed. "I'm really very sorry, Robert. It would have been fun."

He walked calmly out the door.

I stood as though frozen to the spot, staring after him, a terrible empty feeling deep in my body.

Chapter 2

The door of the Men's Room slowly eased itself closed, and I stared at it, unable to move, unable to slow down my churning mind long enough to decide what to do next. My hands had begun trembling; the muscles of my back were now tensing spasmodically; my legs felt as though they would buckle any moment.

I tried to move forward, aware that I couldn't just stand there, shaking like an idiot; someone would come in and see me! But my body lurched drunkenly sideways and I had to catch one of the pipes on the urinals just to keep from sprawling on my face.

I fumbled in my pocket for a dime and somehow managed to get into one of the toilet stalls, where I sat numbly, holding my head, trying to talk sense to myself, for what seemed like an hour. I heard the door open and close many times, watched shoes shuffle past on the dirty tile, listened to splashing and gurgling noises—until finally I felt I could walk again.

I told myself over and over that nothing disastrous had actually happened; all he had done was touch me; I hadn't asked him to touch me; there was no reason at all to blame myself for anything that had happened. There was no way I could have known why he'd been staring at me, why he'd been so "friendly", why he'd kept touching me, squeezing my shoulder.

The fact that I'd been preoccupied with a problem which concerned homosexuality was nothing but a coincidence—it had to be. Just one of those damnable ironies that Fate seemed to delight in. I was certain I'd neither done nor said anything to make him believe I had even a casual interest in the subject, let alone might be willing to subject myself to his degenerate idea of "fun"!

But then why the hell was it affecting me like this?

I could not understand why *I* was the one feeling so

helplessly wretched. It should have been just the other way around: *I* should have walked out that door, leaving *him* feeling rejected and miserable.

There was only one thing I could blame myself for, and that was for not guessing his real motives in the first place: I should have realized that normal men simply were not that friendly, that eager to get to know strangers. I should have realized he was queer just from the way he ignored that stewardess—it hadn't been for her benefit he'd adjusted his crotch; that had been strictly an attempt to intrigue me.

I felt like a complete fool. How could I have been so damned gullible, thinking we could be friends, thinking I could talk to him, tell him my troubles? Thank God I'd been in a bad mood and hadn't started babbling to him about Chuck and the note!

But I couldn't stop feeling that something beautiful had been spoiled. It seemed that a door of some sort had been opened, just slightly, and beyond that door had been something I'd wanted all my life, something warm, sincere—something beautiful—and then the door had been slammed in my face. I couldn't get his image out of my mind—so damned handsome, so very charming—standing there with his penis sticking out, telling me how sorry he was, how much "fun" it could have been.

Well, I told myself, *you've met your first real live queer.* That was certainly nothing to be ashamed of; it didn't mean there was anything wrong with me, just because I'd attracted a pervert.

When I finally came out of the Men's Room, the baggage return area was deserted; my overnighter was going around and around on the revolving table, all by itself. I picked it up and walked slowly out to the parking lot, feeling as though I'd been kicked in the head. I seemed to be walking in a dream, knowing I was dreaming but unable to wake myself up.

I located the Volkswagen, inspected it all around, then got in and took my bottle of vodka from under the back seat. The stuff burned like fury in my throat, but I forced it down, knowing I had to do something to get out of this terrible lethargy. I had to forget what had happened, put it completely out of my mind. It was only an isolated incident that could have happened to anyone. Just a couple of hours out of my life. Tomorrow, I told myself, it would seem like a dream, so why not start right now treating it as such? Just a nightmare, nothing more. I'd had plenty of nightmares before.

I chuckled, feeling slightly better: most of my life, recently, had seemed like a series of nightmares. There was no reason to let this particular one upset me any more than the others had done.

But there was a lesson to be learned, I decided: I couldn't allow myself to be gullible; I couldn't keep hoping that "beautiful doors" would miraculously open for me. Life wasn't like that. Life *was* a continuing nightmare. Hopes and promises were nothing but fantasies. The best any man could reasonably hope for was just to get by. To want anything more was to open yourself childishly to one disappointment after another—and that, when you considered it logically, was nothing more than self-torture—insanity—it was what the psychologists called "immaturity". A man had to grow up and get over his childish, idealistic notions of "friendship" and "beauty" and "love". Those were Sunday School promises. A man had to face reality and learn how to live with its ugliness, that was all.

And one of life's ugly realities still lay ahead of me. The sooner I got home and faced it, the better we'd all be for it.

I was feeling much more my old self as I drove onto the freeway and headed the car east toward the city. I'd managed to relegate John Adams to the position he richly deserved—to that of a nightmare creature. Instead of feeling threatened by the man, I could now begin to feel sorry for him. What a miserable hell his life must be, courting strange men in airports, propositioning them in restrooms.

Actually, I ought to be glad it had happened, because it gave me even more reason to try to save Chuck from that kind of life. Being forced to think it through the way I had, now maybe I could explain it to Chuck in terms he could understand.

I rolled down the window of my little bug, letting the cold tingle of wind calm me even more. The weather seemed to have changed while I'd been out of town; maybe spring had come at last. We'd had a long and cold winter, but now I could see that many of the trees were leafing out; soon the flowers would start blooming. Hopefully we'd be able to enjoy springtime for a few weeks, before the wretched heat of summer started making things miserable again.

I followed the freeway east to the Sugarhouse exit, drove past *Bogen & Thorne, Advertising* to make sure it hadn't burned down or been broken into in my absence, then followed 9th East to 13th South. I parked a block away from the house, had another quick drink, then locked the car and started the last few hundred feet of the distasteful journey on foot.

In spite of the alcohol my heart was thudding like a drum in my chest. I wanted to rehearse what I would say, but I had no idea what I would find. Would all the lights be blazing away, the stereo tuned to that damnable rock-and-roll station? Fifteen or twenty long-haired hippies doped-up in the front room, or scattered throughout the house? Would the lights all be out, with Chuck and his...whatever...sequestered in his room? This was something I hadn't been able to plan in advance. Just as long as I could get in the front door before anyone heard me, there'd be no way for them to escape without my hearing or seeing them.

What would Chuck do if he was in bed with Ashby? An image came into my mind—of Chuck standing naked at the top of the stairs, blinking down at me...but the image was hazy; what would my son look like, naked? I hadn't seen him undressed, even in a swim suit, since he was nine or ten years old.

I slowed my stride and thought about that: I really didn't know what my son looked like. He'd shot up like a weed since starting through puberty, and now he stood almost as tall as I. According to Kate, he was wearing clothes only one size smaller than mine, which meant he was going to be a very hefty guy. He had my features and coloring, and his body seemed to be large and muscular. At sixteen, he was a very handsome boy. Manly-looking....

I cringed! *Manly-looking!* Was that all it was? An appearance?

I remembered thinking how "manly-looking" John Adams had been—thinking what a cockswain he was with the ladies!

I stopped and stepped under the shadow of a freshly-leafed tree. *I did not want to find out that my son was a queer!* For at least the thousandth time I asked myself: *What will you do if he is? Throw him out? Try to talk sense to him? Quote the law, or the Bible? Plead with him to change?*

I glanced at my watch—just past ten-thirty.

I took a deep breath, squared my shoulders, started walking again. It had to be done. I had to be sure. One way or the other, like it or hate it, I had to be sure.

A dim light was burning inside; I guessed it was coming from the kitchen, or perhaps the upstairs hallway. I didn't know what kind of car Jerry Ashby drove, so I didn't bother checking the cars parked along the street. The driveway was empty. I walked very carefully up the front steps, held the keys tightly to keep them from rattling as I painstakingly opened the front door.

Silence greeted me.

I tiptoed into the kitchen. The stove light was on. The kitchen was spotlessly clean, just as I'd left it. I went up the stairs, holding tightly to the banister, stepping over the ninth tread which squeaked. The upstairs was dark. No hint of light spilled under Chuck's closed bedroom door. At the top of the stairs I closed my eyes and took several deep breaths, trying to calm my heartbeat.

"Anyone home?" I called.

No answer.

"Chuck? Are you home?"

Nothing.

I went to his door, hesitated, feeling a strange, almost sexual excitement deep in my stomach. I shoved the door open and quickly switched on the light.

The bed was empty. It was still very carefully made up, as though he hadn't been home at all since I'd left.

I leaned against the door frame, feeling like a balloon being deflated. All of my planning and sneaking had been for nothing. I could have stayed another full day in San Francisco—and completely avoided that depressing encounter with John Adams.

I stood for a long time staring vacantly into Chuck's room; then I wandered inside and sat on the edge of his bed, despondently glancing around at the walls—at the high school pennants, the blue-bordered Awards for Scholarship, a poster of the Caterpillar from *Alice in Wonderland*, and another of a gloomy-looking man with a black hat and a long beard, with a stained-glass window behind him. By the head of his bed was a tiny cartoon, pinned where the light from the bedlamp would shine on it, of Charlie Brown, leaning his head forlornly against a tree. There was no caption, but it didn't need one; the simple cartoon spoke eloquently of resigned frustration.

The room didn't seem like a teen-ager's bedroom;

there were no model airplanes, no pictures of sports heroes, no football or basketball or track awards. If my son were a reliable example, teen-agers had changed a great deal since I'd gone through that stage.

As I stood up to go out, I noticed two photographs on his dresser. One was of Chuck and me: a snapshot I'd completely forgotten, taken many years ago on one of our vacations before the girls had been born. Chuck had been about eight years old then. We were standing in front of Old Faithful in Yellowstone Park, hand-in-hand, both of us grinning happily at the camera. The other picture was an enlarged color Polaroid of Kate and the girls. I'd seen it a hundred times before, but looking at it now, Kate's smile appeared pathetically forced and there seemed to be a haunting sadness around her green eyes. Even so, she was a beautiful woman; no matter how I felt about her, I had to admit that. And the girls would look just like her eventually; they were both carbon copies of Kate as a child; both had her fair skin and freckles, her red hair which would deepen into auburn as they grew older. Like Kate, they would both be "plain" children and teen-agers, and then blossom in their twenties.

The pictures made me feel extremely uncomfortable, and I quickly moved out of Chuck's room, switching off the lights, closing the door quietly after me.

The house felt suddenly chilled.

I turned up the thermostat, then went into my room and wearily took off my coat and tie. I sat for a long time on my own bed, listening to the silence in the house. I felt I'd reached a dead-end, with no place to turn, no other road to follow. There was no way of knowing when Chuck might be home, or even if he'd be home at all. I cursed myself for ever having planned the stinking deceptive trip in the first place; it had caused nothing but problems, from beginning to end.

Finally I decided there was no point in just sitting. I

might as well go get the car and bring it around; if Chuck came home now, he'd see the lights and know I was home anyway.

I pulled the car into the driveway, then brought my luggage upstairs, intending to unpack and then shower, and maybe go out to a late movie. I was opening my suitcase when a blinding pain suddenly slashed through my head!

It was over and gone before I knew what had hit me, but I must have blacked out for a moment because I found myself sitting on the bed, clutching my head, with the suitcase and my clothes in a heap on the floor.

"What the hell...?"

I sat up slowly, blinking, gently shaking my head. I could still feel a dull throbbing, but no real pain. I hoped I wasn't going to start getting migraines! Monday, I'd have to go see Dr. Carter and tell him about this; maybe I ought to have a full physical. I hadn't been taking very good care of myself these last couple of weeks.

Maybe *that* was the cause of those other strange things that had been happening—those feelings of being watched, the spells of depression, that trembling, the headaches. Maybe I just needed some kind of tonic, or vitamins, or something in my diet. Yes, I'd go to see Sam first thing Monday morning.

I gathered the clothes from the floor, put most of them in the dirty-clothes hamper, hung up the rest, undressed, and was just starting out for the shower when I saw the envelope, propped up against the mirror of my dresser.

I grabbed it, then sat on the edge of the bed, my hands trembling, cold sweat tickling down from my armpits.

The first letter had come in a plain white business envelope, with my name and address printed in ink; this envelope was a 5x7 manilla, and there was just one word on the front of it: *ROBBER.*

When I saw what was inside, my stomach lurched and threatened to spew out the meal I had had on the plane!

"Oh...my God...!"

There were six photographs. Six unbelievably disgusting, evil photographs!

I lowered my head, closing my eyes, clutching the bed, desperately trying to quiet the nausea. Even with my eyes closed I could see the disgusting things! As though each one had been indelibly burned into my brain! I'd heard on the news, and read stories in the *Tribune*, that such filth was being printed and sold, mailed to unsuspecting children, peddled in "smut shops" to those so-called "adults" who were sick enough to enjoy looking at such things—but I had never expected to see such things myself!

I remembered one street in San Francisco—the only part of the city I'd seen that had made me glad I didn't live there—with "adult book shops" and "adult movie houses" block after block after block!

What kind of a sick mind...?

I wanted to crumple the evil things, burn them, destroy them. I half-expected the ceiling to collapse on me just for having them in the house.

But in spite of my revulsion and terror, my eyes kept returning to the pictures. Slowly I spread them out on the bed.

They were all of the same two men (neither was Chuck, thank God!) both muscular and—even then I couldn't stop myself from thinking it—both rather handsome. "Manly-looking". One wore a black leather jacket, a motorcycle cap, and high shiny black boots; otherwise he was completely exposed. The other wore nothing but boots, and his hands were tied behind his back. The first picture showed him kneeling in front of the other—you could see the rope around his wrists looped tightly down to his boots—watching as the standing one played with himself. The second one showed him...*licking* the other one's testicles, his chin up between widespread legs, and a large, slick penis lying on his forehead. In the third and fourth shots the standing one had moved around behind the other—had him bent backward, his body arched so that his own erect penis stood straight out—and was holding his head tilted back at a painful angle, trying to force his hard organ into the man's mouth. The fifth was a closeup, showing lips pressing hard against pubic hair, the entire penis completely engulfed by that mouth!

And the sixth photograph, the most disgusting, and yet somehow the most spellbinding of all, showed the kneeling one's face, his mouth open wide, tongue sticking up—and above it, a slick-shiny hand tight around the thick head of that amazing penis, milking a thick bright gob of semen down onto that upreaching tongue. There were other gobs and shining trails all over the kneeling man's face—on his forehead, down his cheeks, in his hair!

I couldn't stop looking at the filthy thing!

My stomach was churning, my mind roiling with disgust and fear—but I could not take my eyes from that frozen moment of depravity! I kept wondering how anyone could be so desperate for money—or so mentally deranged—or so doped-up—as to pose for such photographs. At first I was sure that the shots had been faked, the two models photographed at different times, but the last shot disproved that idea. It was too clear, too sharp, too obviously real to be faked. That semen was real and that penis was real, and...

I jerked my head up, turning away. I stood quickly, fighting to steady my breathing, to keep my stomach under control.

I heard something—a laugh? Someone moved, just over my left shoulder.

I spun around—and looked at myself in the mirror over the dresser. I stood there stark naked, looking back at myself. I had an erection!

A deep tingling was boiling in the pit of my stomach.

Now the nausea came full force! With my hand tightly clamped on my mouth I ran stumbling into the bathroom and fell over the toilet and heaved! Raw alcohol and bile gushed out of me!

I slammed the seat down and flushed the toilet, then knelt there, my head resting on the cool white enamel, asking myself who it was that hated me so much as to send that letter and those photographs. What kind of desperately sick mind could be that disgustingly evil?

Weakly I sat up, becoming aware of the icy-cold tile under my legs.

This latest turn of events forced me to reconsider my earlier evaluation. The first letter could have been mailed by anyone, but the pictures had not come through the mail. That meant they'd been deliberately planted in my room by someone who had access to the house, and that limited the field of suspects considerably. What I needed to do now was to find out which of Chuck's friends he'd had over in my absence. Jerry Ashby was still number one on my list. But now a new name had added itself: Chuck himself.

Did he hate me so much he could go to such lengths to hurt and embarrass me?

He might.

I remembered the time, just a few months ago, when Kate had been turning the mattress on his bed and had found a small plastic bag filled with marijuana taped to it. I could still see Chuck sitting on his bed looking bored, refusing to meet my eyes as I threatened him, then pleaded with him, then threatened again. I remembered him looking up when I'd finally, in total frustration, run out of words.

"You gonna kick me out?"

I'd slammed my fist down on his dresser, then struggled to control myself, clenching my teeth to keep from hitting him. "Is that...what you think I should do?"

He had shrugged then—so utterly casual and contemptuous: "That's up to you, man."

"Goddammit, Chuck! Stop calling me *man!* I'm your father!"

"You're a man, aren't you?"

"That has nothing to do with it!"

"Oh?" He had studied me, then shrugged again. "Whatever you say...*Pop.*"

In the bathroom I struggled to my feet, rinsed my mouth out, washed my face in the basin. I studied my red-eyed reflection in the mirror. "Why does he hate me so much?" I asked aloud.

No one answered.

It wasn't likely that anyone would answer tonight. I could feel the silence and emptiness of the house pressing in on me. There was no sense looking for Chuck tonight. My plan had failed. If he came home now with one of his friends, he'd see the car in the driveway and leave without even bothering to come inside.

And I was too sick of the cloak-and-dagger routine to want to hide the car again, turn off the lights and sit in the darkness waiting on the offchance that he might bring someone home later.

Perhaps, after all, the best approach would be a direct confrontation tomorrow—or whenever he finally decided to come home. Kate and the girls would be gone for a full week, and Chuck and I would have the house all to ourselves. Maybe, just maybe, I could approach him in a way that would inspire at least honesty, if not respect.

When we'd caught him with that bag of marijuana, I'd started off on the tack that I didn't know what the stuff was (even though it was painfully obvious, with the cigarette papers in the sack with the powdery green stuff). By playing it wide-eyed innocent I'd engendered only contempt in him: "Oh, come off it, Dad! You know damn well what it is. Why don't you come right out and say it? It's *grass!* Pot! Dope!"

Just come right out and say it: "Chuck, I got this letter in the mail...do you know anything about it?"

Yes or no. If I didn't hedge, maybe he wouldn't either.

"Are you, Chuck?"

"Am I what, Dad?"

"What it says in the letter?"

"And what's that, Dad?"

"You know perfectly well! You've just read it!"

"Can't you say it out loud, man? Saying it out loud won't make it more real than it already is. Like that bag of grass. It was grass whether you could say it out loud or not."

"All right, then, Chuck–are you...queer?"

"Do I suck cocks, is that what you mean, Dad?"

I shuddered, shocked by my own imagination! I detested that phrase!

I tried to turn the scene off, but it continued in spite of me. Chuck was entirely capable of being just that blunt about it. I'd seen copies of the underground paper he worked on, and that phrase, along with others, was rather common. If it came to that, I'd have to say: "Yes, Chuck, that's exactly what I mean. Do you... suck...cocks?"

"No, Dad, I don't."

Imaginary or not, a surge of relief poured over me.

"You see, Dad? If you'd just come and asked when you got that note..."

I'd been judging Chuck guilty without benefit of a trial–with no more evidence than an evil, illiterate note. In effect, I'd been as disgusting as the note itself, assuming that it told the truth.

There were dozens of other possibilities beyond the obvious ones: Chuck was a good-looking boy, very popular at school, except with the administration. It was entirely possible that one of his classmates—maybe someone who worked with him on that underground paper, or simply anyone who resented his wide popularity—had sent the note, not to hurt me, but to get back at Chuck for something I knew nothing about. And if that were the case, I'd allowed myself to be taken in by the lie; I'd compounded that lie by believing it—or, just as bad, by being afraid it was true. And by doing that, I'd made the rest of the note true: by believing the accusation, I'd been, truly, "a wicked and terrible man".

I forced a smile at myself in the mirror. For the rest of the night, at least, I promised myself I'd stop being a damned fool!

Relishing the sense of relief my decision brought, I turned on the shower. I stood under the nozzle, letting the water spray on the top of my head, run down over my body. Slowly but surely the helpless frustration seemed to wash away. I closed my eyes and allowed myself to enjoy the tingle of the water pelting my skin. I could feel the relaxation spreading out through my body.

The thing that would feel really good right now, I thought, was one of Antonio's rubdowns.

I turned my back on the spray and applied soap to my front parts, again closing my eyes to relish the feeling of my hands slickly kneading my tense muscles. How great it would feel to relax in a steamroom, take a quick dip in the cold plunge, and then let Antonio pound and stretch me back into feeling like a decent human being again. The only trouble was, the Sugarhouse Businessman's Health Club was closed weekend nights. So, unfortunately, a steam and massage were out of the question. Still, dammit, it seemed like a good idea—there were other steam baths in the city.

And I had to do something!

I knew if I went to bed now, I'd lie awake all

night—if for no other reason, just worrying about Chuck, waiting for him to come home.

At least I could check the yellow pages.

I got out of the shower with a new sense of purpose, feeling better than I had for a week, maybe longer. I towelled dry, then went back into the bedroom. I cringed, seeing the photographs still lying there! What if Chuck had come home when I'd been in the shower and seen the things? I scooped them up, intending to take them downstairs and burn them in the fireplace.

Then suddenly it occurred to me that I might still use these pictures to catch whoever was playing this stinking game. Fingerprints! If I did have to go to the police after all, I could hand over these pictures as Exhibit B. Let them check for fingerprints. There would also be fingerprints on the letter. Find a matched set—besides my own, of course—and we'd have the troublemaker!

I got the letter out of my coat pocket, handling it carefully by the edges, and slipped it into the manilla envelope along with the photographs. I glanced for a last time at the final picture. The sheer depravity of it was overwhelming. I simply could not imagine anyone actually...catching semen in his mouth!

What would it taste like?

I stopped myself from even trying to imagine it, remembering that I'd just heaved my guts up into the toilet.

I tried to think of a good place to hide the envelope. I didn't want Chuck getting hold of it—or Kate, for that matter, although I chuckled at the idea of Kate finding such pictures under my shorts; it was almost worth doing just to see her reaction. I looked around the room. The dresser, of course! But not in a drawer—under the bottom drawers, where the skirt of the thing went all the way down to the floor. You couldn't see under it—and how often did anyone take the drawers all the way out?

I pulled out the bottom drawer and carefully pushed the envelope back into the farthest corner, then stood up, nodding to myself in the mirror. I couldn't help comparing my own image to those of the men in the photographs. They were younger, of course, but not that much younger. I was only thirty-five, and that was a long way from being "old". And I still had a rather good build. There was maybe a little excess fat around the midsection, but not if I stood straight. There weren't many others in the Health Club who had bodies half as good.

It was just a shame that I didn't have someone besides myself to appreciate it. Kate had once taken great delight in my naked body, as I had in hers. It had been a long time ago, but I remembered how it had been then, the lights out, under the covers, her hands exploring my body as though each time were new. Gentle fingers trailing over my chest, down my stomach. That little noise that she made in her throat when she touched my excited penis. I remembered how beautiful it had felt, then, to ease into the warmth of her body, how the feeling had come into me, spreading out....

In the mirror I watched my penis begin to rise. This time the reaction was coming from thoughts of a woman, which was normal and sane and acceptable, and I stared at it with fascination.

I stroked it lightly, watched the tingling gooseflesh spread down over my legs. How long had it been? Five years, at least. I hadn't touched Kate since that terrible day when she'd told me about Cindy and Dorene, when I'd moved forever out of "our" room into "mine"—the guest room. It seemed impossible, thinking about it. Five years!

In all that time I'd had no sexual outlet beyond what my imagination could devise for me, lying in the dark with the covers pushed back, masturbating to fantasies of how it had once been. (Even in my fantasies I'd been "true" to Kate.)

It felt so good, squeezing it.

Five years!

How had I ever got myself into such an impossible mess? I glanced up, eye to eye with myself. How much longer could I endure the situation? Sex was a natural function of the body. That was why the Mormons had rejected the idea of celibate priests: part of man's function was to marry and, through sex, have children.

I leaned back, beginning a slow kneading motion. I had a *good* body! Just tighten it, like this, and it looked every bit as good as either of those guys. Tight, you could see all the little ridges of muscles, that flat shield at the base of my belly, the thick auburn hair trailing up from my crotch, curling over my stomach, spreading out on my chest—and my chest was a good chest! Firm and full. No fat there. My pecs didn't look like sagging breasts, the way Ed's did. But then, Ed was a slob. He hadn't been, in the beginning, when we'd first met in college, but he'd turned into one. I couldn't understand what Kate saw in him. Certainly he was nowhere near as "well-hung" as I was—at least, he didn't seem to be, those times I had seen him in the showers at the Club. (But then, Kinsey has proved that women are not particularly interested in the size of a man's organ, but more in the techniques used to deploy it.) Well, she was welcome to him and to it, and to whatever pleasures either could give her. Over the years I had stopped resenting the fact that she had him to please her while I had no one but myself—*almost* stopped resenting it. There were times, such as now, when the resentment came back, when I wished I could be as careless a whore as she was, times when the need became so overpowering that I couldn't help resenting her.

What would it feel like to have it sucked by another man?

My hand stopped massaging and jerked away. I felt a

coldness grip my body. I turned away from the mirror, thoroughly ashamed of the thought.

I had to stop thinking about sex! There was simply no sense frustrating myself, torturing myself.

And I had to get out of this house. Empty and silent, it seemed to be forcing my mind into areas I did not want it to explore. If possible I wanted to find something to do tonight which would stop me thinking entirely.

I decided another drink wouldn't hurt anything; I'd heaved up all that I'd consumed on the plane and in the car. I dressed quickly, then hurried downstairs to the kitchen, where I mixed a good stiff Screwdriver. Then I went into the hallway to check the Yellow Pages. There were three or four listings for "Baths", but one ad attracted my attention instantly:

Now Under New Management
Uintah Plunge
Natural Hot Springs
Men Only–Expert Masseur
Open til 2 A.M. every nite
Come! Relax! Enjoy life!

That sounded just fine.

I turned off the lights and started out, then paused at the door; if Chuck did come home tonight (with or without a friend) there was no reason for him to worry about where I had gone (it seemed silly to leave him a note saying "Gone for a steam-bath"). I hurried back through the house, making sure everything was put away as though no one had been there. Once again at the front door, I paused to look back–and the house didn't seem nearly as depressing or threatening now. Just another empty house.

I relaxed more and more as I followed the old highway out to the north section of town. I decided that one reason I felt good again—besides the booze—was that I'd passed a certain crisis successfully; I'd made the decision not to spy on Chuck, not to trick him into anything, but to confront him directly and honestly. Now at least I had a goal I wasn't ashamed of. Not a very long-range goal, but a goal nonetheless, and that was something I hadn't had for a very long time.

It was as though there had been a voice in my mind, sitting back in a dark corner whining and complaining and criticizing, and generally forcing my life in a direction I hadn't wanted it to go; and it seemed that by making the decision, I had pushed the voice back into a dark little room and closed and locked the door.

Even the memory of those photographs had lost a lot of its power to disturb me. After all, they were only photographs, not "reality"—and certainly not any part of my reality—and those men were two out of millions of men; why should the images to two unimportant perverted men bother me in the slightest? Quite simply, they shouldn't!

I even turned the radio on, and hummed along with the music as I drove. I was fairly sure I remembered the place I was headed for; as a child, whenever we'd come to Salt Lake, I had wanted to go swimming in those mysterious "Natural Hot Springs" in a place that reminded me of a sultan's palace I had seen in a history book. Then the place had seemed huge, the lawns and the shrubbery like those of an "estate". I seemed to remember the name *Paradise Spa.* But neither of my parents had enjoyed swimming, and they never would trust Bill and me to go out by ourselves. If my guess were correct, tonight I would finally get to see the inside of that once-fascinating place.

At night, and in the few dim lights burning in the parking lot and along the sidewalk in front of the building, my "sultan's palace" didn't seem to have changed much at all, except that it looked a great deal smaller. As I walked up the front steps, I saw broken glass and pieces of plaster and strips of peeled paint lying everywhere in the rank lawn and under the untended shrubbery. No wonder it looked the same as it had fifteen years ago; from all I could see, it seemed fairly likely they hadn't painted or repaired anything in all of those fifteen years! An aura of gloom and decay seemed to hang in the huge foyer; it was like walking into a set for a Tennessee Williams play. There were ugly white plaster holes in the peeling, pea-green painted walls. Tiles were missing from the "mosaic" on the floor. Beyond the entry to the pool there had once been an elegant coffee shop; now the doors had been boarded up, and a crude sign that looked ten years old read *TEMPORARILY CLOSED.*

Behind a once-handsome, now chipped and ragged, long marble-topped counter a young man sat in an ancient swivel chair, his eyes intent on a book. I was surprised to see someone so young; I was used to seeing middle-aged men behind desks at health clubs. This boy couldn't have been much over twenty-one, if he was that. His age probably wouldn't have bothered me if it hadn't been for his condescending, contemptuous attitude, which seemed to have become a trade-mark for the young people recently. The chair squeaked as he reluctantly stood up, but only once did his eyes flick away from his paperback novel, and then they very blatantly started at the top of my head and swept slowly down to my feet, without so much as a flicker of friendliness. He shoved a battered tin box at me and muttered, "Two bucks. Put yer stuff you don't want stolen in there."

I forced a laugh, nervously wanting to get some kind of human response from him. "Two? Is that all?"

"It ain't the Ritz, honey," he growled.

I laughed foolishly. "No, I...guess it isn't."

He put my money in the cash register, put the box

into a cabinet, tossed a towel and the key—attached to an innertube ring—on the counter before me, then sat down again in his swivel chair, without once taking his eyes off the book (which was called *Queens Of The Range*—with a grotesquely amateurish drawing of half-naked cowboys that looked, in my opinion, more like cow*girls* except for the blatantly detailed *bulges* in their crotches).

I turned away from the desk almost in a trance; I couldn't believe it. It was more like a dream than reality. Some distant, sober part of my mind whispered *Get out of here!* and although I realized the sense of the warning, I couldn't shake myself loose from that hypnotized feeling. It was like finding an abandoned mine-shaft in an area where no mine-shaft is supposed to be, and in spite of the crumbling walls and the loose timber you feel compelled to go inside, if for no other reason than a morbid curiosity to see if the thing will collapse once you get in.

I walked down a long hallway where most of the lights in the ceiling were out, through swinging doors, and into a large, cracked, peeling, boiled-egg smelling room. There were perhaps fifty toilet-sized stalls in two back-to-back rows, with narrow corridors between them. The floor of the room was concrete, and once upon a time it had been painted maroon, but the corridors and the floors of the rooms had been worn to the original grey of the cement. Many of the rooms had no doors on them at all, and many more had no locks. My stall, number 17, was in the middle aisle, and it was only a verification of a certainty I'd felt since entering the front door, that this wasn't the place I'd been looking for. The walls of my cubicle were literally covered with grossly crude drawings and childish propositions:

Show hard on for blow job.

Don't bother. Jack off. These queens should take cocksucking lessons.

You didn't find the right queen, honey.

Honey! I suddenly realized the attendant had called me *honey!* It hadn't even registered at the time! I wanted to be outraged, but all I could do was giggle drunkenly. The giggling made me dizzy, and I sat down on a narrow bench to avoid falling. It felt as though a depth charge had suddenly exploded in my stomach, shooting raw alcohol out into my bloodstream. My head was swimming! I couldn't even think.

I put my head down between my knees and took deep breaths, and the dizziness passed. I'd never had such a strange reaction to alcohol before. But I felt much better as I stood up—almost cavalier. I'd seen no one, heard no one moving around or talking; it was quite likely that I was the only one here. In which case, why should I worry about what kind of place it was? If they had a steam room, I'd use it. If they had a masseur (which I very much doubted) I'd use him. I wanted a steam and a massage and I'd paid two good dollars to get in the place, so I'd get my money's worth and then get out. Why not?

I undressed, wrapped the towel around my waist, and ventured in search of the steam room. I found it next to a crumbling shower area where the three old-fashioned nozzles all were dripping with fascinating counter-rhythms: *Splash-splash, drip-splash, plop-drip-plop, splash....* When I saw the door into the steam room itself, I stopped short and laughed out loud: the hinges of the wooden-slab door had been wired together with bailing wire! I pushed the door open and steam billowed out, licking me with warm fingers. It felt great!

The light in the ceiling was so dim I couldn't see two feet in front of me. I moved slowly into the room, my hands sweeping the air in front of me until my knees struck a tiled bench and I almost fell on my face! I sat down, reached around, found a wall, and slid back to lean against it. I sat for a minute, hugging my knees, then tentatively spread myself out until I was lying full-length on the warm bench. The towel around my waist was uncomfortable. I loosened it slightly, then, reminding myself I was alone, removed it entirely and rolled it into a pillow for my head.

It was like lying naked in a huge, warm, wet, dark womb. The steam swirled between my legs, feeling like somebody breathing. I allowed my hands to move down over my slickening body, down to my genitals. The sensations were delicious! The steam and the warmth of my hands and my own perspiration—the darkness, the wetness—safe in a womb, shut away from the world, where no one could see or know what I did. All of my problems seemed so far away! No past, no future, just the present now. The letter, the pictures, Chuck, Jerry Ashby, Kate, the girls, Ed Bogen—all these seemed like insubstantial ghosts left behind in another world, exorcised by the soft-swirling steam.

Masseur or no, the steam had been an excellent idea.

Someone coughed.

I sat up, grabbing my towel to spread it quickly over my crotch. My throat suddenly felt like a hand had grabbed it. The cough came again. I tried to sound casual: "Hello. I thought I was alone."

"Not quite," said a voice. "I'm here."

"Sorry."

"What for?"

I laughed. "I don't know."

The voice was silent for several long minutes, and I peered through the steam trying to see its owner; I could see nothing but a dim void.

"Would you like to trade rubdowns?" the voice suddenly asked.

"Do what?"

"Trade rubdowns?"

"Oh." I laughed again. I knew I ought to be nervous, perhaps even frightened, but in the darkness of the room nothing seemed quite real. For all I knew the stranger was sitting back in some corner holding a knife, ready to slice me into small pieces—but I couldn't get worried about it. His voice was soft, rather gentle. He didn't sound dangerous. Just another guy like myself enjoying the steam. "I'm afraid I don't give very good rubdowns," I told him. "I was hoping they'd have a masseur."

"That's just in the daytime."

"Oh."

He was silent again, and I finally decided the conversation had ended and lay back, adjusting the towel more comfortably over my midsection. Not that I was particularly worried about his seeing me. If I couldn't see him, he shouldn't be able to see me.

"Would you like one?" His voice seemed to be nearer. I sat up again, squinting, trying to see through the steam. I thought I could make out a dark form vaguely in the shape of a man, standing by the bench, down by my feet.

For some crazy reason I remembered the scrawl on the cubicle wall: *Show hard for blow job.* I remembered my imaginary conversation with Chuck: "*Just come right out and say it.*" Feeling giddy and daring, I said, "One what?"

"You know—a rubdown."

"Oh. Sure, I'd love one. Are you a masseur?"

"Me? Goodness, no. But I'm pretty good—or at least some people think so. We do it all the time out here. Trade rubdowns, I mean. It's much less expensive than Joseph. He's the real masseur. And, anyway, he's not very good. He doesn't go all the way—if you know what I mean."

I decided to let that one pass. I had a pretty good idea of what he meant, but I wasn't about to let him know that. Also, I didn't want to get myself into an embarrassing situation by misinterpreting his remark. It was possible I didn't know what he meant.

"I'll get some soap." The dark form moved to the door. Light suddenly billowed into the room. For a moment I saw him almost clearly as he passed through the doorway. He was young-looking, tall, very thin, and completely nude. I couldn't be certain, but it looked as though he had half an erection—his penis arching out and down from his crotch like the trunk of a baby elephant.

As I waited for him to return with the soap, that locked-up, sober part of my mind told me to get up and leave, but my body seemed to have a will of its own, and it didn't want to move. And besides, it was a little like gambling—a vice I had never allowed myself—was he or wasn't he? Would he or wouldn't he?

I remembered those photographs. One by one they presented themselves to me, superimposed on the steam. I thought about John Adams in the Men's Room, reaching out, wanting to fondle my penis, muttering, "Very nice, Robert." Such things did go on in the world; I couldn't stop them by pretending they didn't exist. But surely I had the moral strength of character not to feel threatened by other men's perversity!

The door swung open again and I twisted to look up, but the door had closed before I could get a really good look at him. I felt a hand on my stomach. A wild shudder wrenched through me. "Want to turn over?"

"Sure." I rolled over, trying to keep the towel over my middle, covering my buttocks—but he pulled it away.

"You don't need that in here."

I put the towel under my face.

He started at my shoulders, soaping my back, down to my buttocks. His touch was gentle, but surprisingly professional. Almost as good as Antonio. In a way, he was better; Antonio started pounding the minute you were spread out on the table, but this guy took his time working up to the pounding. He massaged my shoulders, fingers probing into the tense muscles, relaxing them, down my spine.... When he kneaded my buttocks the sensation was fantastic! Then, almost too quickly, he worked down my legs, down to my feet. I felt like a limp bundle of delicious sensations. When he kneaded my feet, my entire body quivered. Slowly he worked his way back up to my shoulders. I felt something brush against my upturned palm on the bench. An uneasy chill spread out through my body as I realized that it was the head of his penis I could feel.

My own penis had grown progressively harder—nothing I had tried to do could keep it down. Lying on my stomach, it hadn't particularly worried me, but I was beginning to wonder what I would do when he asked me to roll onto my back. If he were queer and he found out I did have a hard-on, he'd assume I was responding to him—and if he weren't queer, he'd think that I was.

"Okay, roll over."

"I...uh..."

"Hmm?"

"Nothing. I just..." I sat up, stalling for time, desperately thinking, *Go down! Go down!*

"Is anything wrong?"

"No!" I said quickly. "No...nothing."

"Then lie down. Gee, you're so tense."

"Sorry."

"Come on..." He put a widespread hand on my chest and pushed me back. "Relax...." Reluctantly I lay down. His hand stayed on my chest as his other went searching along the bench for the soap. When he found it, he worked over my chest, down across my stomach. "You certainly have a nice body. Are you an athlete or something?"

"No," I said softly, painfully aware of his fingers on my stomach, just inches away from my penis. I held my breath, waiting for him to touch it.

But he didn't. Instead he went around it, down to

my legs. He soaped the insides of my thighs, absently brushing his fingers against my testicles. "Gee, come on, relax. You're so tense! Why are you so tense?"

"It's been a bad day."

"Gee, that's too bad." He clicked his tongue. "You have nice legs. Strong."

"I walk a lot."

"Um-hmmm. Walking's very good for you. I wish I had thick legs like yours. Mine are so spindly and ugly."

Down to my toes again, then slowly back up. "Relax.....relax...."

It was so strange having another man comment on my body. No other man had ever done that—at least not on the positive side. Usually it was something like: "Hey, Robert, you're getting a pot there," or something equally negative. I wanted very much to relax. I wanted to accept this guy's compliments and feel good about them. Obviously he was being very open and honest in praising my body. Obviously my body pleased him.

But that was perverted, and try as I might, I couldn't accept it. The steam seemed to have sobered me, allowing that locked-up part of my mind to come forward and take over again. I lay there waiting for him to touch me in that forbidden area, just once, just a definite touch. Up to now he'd been giving me an excellent rubdown, better than Antonio's, and I could enjoy that. But just let him step out of line and I'd have to do something about it. I didn't enjoy the idea of embarrassing him, but if he asked for it, that's what I would have to do.

And of course, just as I'd feared, just as I'd known he would, he touched it. Offhandedly, as though completely by accident—but we both knew better. I felt my penis quiver; a sweet tingling shot up through my stomach.

"My goodness," he whispered, "you *are* tense."

"Don't worry about it."

He chuckled. "Who's worried?" His fingers closed lightly around it. "You've got a beautiful cock. You should be proud...."

"I am," I said coldly.

I knew that the moment had come. I knew I had to push him away, get up, dress and leave—but I couldn't! It felt as though a huge hand were pressing down hard on my body, pinning me there on that bench.

His soapy-slick fingers began a slow motion, up and down—and the sensations were almost overwhelming! It had been five years since another human being had touched me there, and the feelings seemed a thousand times more intense than when I masturbated myself.

But it's wrong! It's dirty! It's perverted and evil!

But it feels good!

I don't care what it feels like, it's wrong!

I tried to sit up. "I think that's enough."

"Oh, come on, relax." He tried to push me back down, but I shoved his hand away. He giggled nervously, stepped back. My body felt suddenly cold. "All right," he said sullenly, "have it your way."

"I will."

"Oh, I'm sure you will. I've met your type before."

"Have you? And what's that—my *type?*"

"You know perfectly well. You come in here, knowing exactly what goes on, and when someone tries to do something nice for you..."

"Is that what you call it? Something nice? You know what *I* call it?"

"Oh, I'm sure you have all sort of horrible words. You're the kind who just *loves* to have someone make a fuss over *you*, but when it comes to pleasing *them*, then you start..."

The truth of his words jarred me, but that only made me more angry. "And what could I do for someone like you—to *please* you?"

"Absolutely nothing!"

"Oh, no! No, you wanted something, didn't you?"

"Don't be preposterous! I was only being friendly."

"Like hell you were! Come on, tell me what you wanted."

"I didn't want..."

"*Say it!*" I stood up, facing him, my heart pounding with cold fury. "Say it! Tell me what you want."

"Oh, *really!*" He started toward the door but I stepped quickly in front of him.

In the light filtering in from outside I could see him more clearly. His eyes blinked rapidly. He was frightened. His fear started an excitement churning in my body. He knew we were alone in the place. It wasn't very likely the attendant would hear if he yelled for help as long as I kept him in the steam room. I planted my hand on his chest, pushing him back; his body was slick and hot. "Not so fast," I said softly. "I want to hear you say it."

"No!" He bolted away from me, lurching toward the door. I grabbed his arm, spun around, twisting it. "Don't hurt me!" he cried. "Please! I didn't..."

"Just shut up! Don't start yelling, or I *will* hurt you!"

"Please..."

I twisted harder, forcing him down on his knees, facing away from me. "*Say it!*"

"You're hurting me!"

I leaned over him. "Say it, God damn you! Say it out loud."

"Please...don't...hurt me."

"You wanted it, didn't you? You wanted to suck on it, didn't you? You wanted to suck my cock!"

"Yes!" he sobbed. "Yes-yes-*yes!* Please let me go!"

"Oh, no! You wanted me to *please* you? Well, by God, that's exactly what I'm going to do."

"No! I don't want..."

I grabbed his hair, jerking his head back. I stepped

over him. "Just hold still. Hold perfectly still. I'm going to please you!"

I could tell he was crying. I couldn't see the tears but I heard his sobs clearly. The sounds made me feel powerful! I felt I could do anything I wanted to him.

Like the man in those pictures!

I took his head tightly between both hands, stepped over him, bending so my testicles brushed down the back of his head and my penis lay hard on his forehead. "Open your mouth, you cocksucker! Open it! That's what you wanted, isn't it? You..."

"You're hurting me!" he wailed.

"You miserable sonofabitch!" I pushed my cock painfully down, trying to force it between his clenched lips. He twisted his face sideways but I grabbed his hair with both hands and twisted it upright again.

Suddenly it seemed as though this had all happened before, like a dream I'd had hundreds of times and was doomed to go on reenacting again and again and again. He did it each time, turned his head away, refusing to do what I wanted him to.

"Suck me, Billy, please!"

"I can't, Bob! Don't make me! I just can't!"

I pushed him hard, down onto the floor; he sprawled on his back under me and I fell over him, thrusting my crotch heavily in his face. His legs started thrashing; his arms flailed at me, trying to push me off. I had to get *in* him! That was the only way I could finish the dream! I had to get my cock inside those clenched lips and shoot my jizz into him! I had to! The dream would keep coming back, over and over and over until I did!

I saw his cock—dark, long and hard—only inches away from my face. At that moment all vestiges of sanity left me. I desperately needed to finish that horrible dream! I lunged forward and thrust my mouth over his long cock.

I heard a sharp cry bubble up from between my legs.

Thick heat pelted into my mouth! Tacky spurts of his semen shot into my throat, coursed back over my tongue like a flood.

His body went limp under me.

I suddenly realized I had a man's cock in my mouth! I had a man's semen in my mouth! I could taste it!

My stomach convulsed and I threw up into his crotch.

I stood up, shaking, completely enveloped in sick disgust. I grabbed for my towel and spat into it, then heaved again, but my stomach was empty and only a raw sewer taste filled my mouth. My legs wanted to buckle but I forced myself, staggering, toward the door. I limped weakly to my dressing stall, drying myself as well as I could with my wet, soiled towel. Even though I was still damp, I dressed as fast as I could, praying he wouldn't come out of the steam room, desperately hoping he was frightened enough just to stay where he was. If I had to face him again, knowing what I'd just done, I'd be tempted to kill him.

I heard laughter—the sound shot through me like knives.

As I came out of the stall, I saw two young men standing down at the end of the corridor, both naked, their towels hanging over their shoulders. Their laughter stopped as they saw me, and one said, "Well, my dear, we're not the only ones here." They both looked me up and down. "Don't hurry away on our account."

I shoved past them without answering, pushed through the swinging doors, then almost ran down the dark hallway to the front desk. Behind me I heard laughter again.

It wasn't until I was many blocks away from the place that I allowed myself to relax at all. Then I pulled to the side of the street, under the shadow of a large tree, got my vodka from under the seat, and then sat hunched down, gulping the burning stuff until I had emptied the bottle. Then I sat up and looked around, wondering what to do next. I didn't want to go home, but I couldn't think of any place else to go. It was one o'clock, Sunday morning—Easter Sunday—and there was no place else to go. I started the car and pulled back onto the street, heading home.

Home, I thought bitterly. No, I wasn't going *home*—only to the house that I lived in. I had no home.

I had nothing. Nothing at all. No home, no family, and now no self-respect, no honor, nothing! In one night, a few brief drunken minutes, I'd managed to ruin everything I believed in, to invalidate everything I had worked for my entire life. So now it didn't matter where I went or what I did—and the house on 13th South was the only place I could think of to go.

I remembered the feeling I'd had that morning, in the hotel room (had it actually been such a short time ago? It seemed more like a year!) that something disastrous was going to happen. I tried to work up a sense of relief now that the disaster was over—but, as I drove slowly along the deserted streets, a new uneasiness began to creep into my mind: Suppose my premonition had not yet been completely fulfilled?

Suppose the insane events of the past day and evening were only the *beginnings* of that fulfillment?

Chapter 3

It wasn't until I'd parked the car in the driveway that I realized Chuck must be home: the light in the kitchen was out. For a moment I sat in the car, wondering whether or not I should try to sneak into the house, catch him at whatever he was up to—but at that point, after what I had done, I could hardly work up any anger at Chuck for maybe doing the same thing.

I could hear music as I walked up the front steps; through the narrow glass panels around the door, I could see firelight flickering. As I opened the front door, rock music rushed out to engulf me. Two figures lay on the living room floor in the bright glow from the fireplace. Chuck and Jerry. Both were sprawled comfortably, spread-eagled, arms outstretched, hands *almost* touching. Neither seemed to have heard the car or the door; apparently both were completely engrossed in the music—which, strangely enough, I found rather melodic and soothing. I closed the door and stood there watching them, waiting for one to look up and see me. For a long time neither moved; I wondered how they could both be so happy and contented while I was so miserable.

Then Chuck sat up—slowly, dreamily; he leaned on his elbows as his eyes wandered slowly around the room. He looked so peaceful! When he finally spotted me, for a moment he made no move, nothing in his comfortable expression changed. Then, as though suddenly realizing who I was, he stood up. "Hey, Dad!" he said loudly—and Jerry quickly looked up. "Hey, you're...uh...home early. I...uh..." He hurried to the phonograph and the music died. In the heavy silence both boys regarded me.

"Hello, Mr. Thorne."

"Jerry..."

"You okay, Dad?" Chuck asked—there was something strangely fuzzy about his voice, as though he needed to clear his throat. "We...uh...were just...uh...listening...Hey, are you okay?"

I moved away from the front door, feeling extremely uncomfortable. By all indications both boys seemed drunk—and yet I knew that Chuck avidly deplored alcohol. I had no choice but to conclude that my son and his friend were both "stoned". I knew I ought to be furious; I knew I should chastise them; but I couldn't. I simply could not work up any anger. "Yes," I said quietly. "I'm fine. Turn your music back on. I'm just going up to bed."

"We don't need to listen, Dad. I mean, if you're..."

"It's all right, Chuck," I said firmly, and started for the stairs.

"We didn't expect you."

"I know. I decided to come back early. Go ahead, turn the music back on."

"If you're sure."

I nodded wearily. "Chuck, I'm too tired to let anything bother me." I started up the stairs, then paused to look back. "Let's talk tomorrow, Chuck, can we? Will you be home?"

Chuck glanced at Jerry, then up at me. "Yeah, sure, I guess. We, uh, were sort of planning like a camping trip. You know, in the mountains for a couple of days..."

"I don't want to change your plans," I said. "If you're here, fine."

"Maybe in the morning, okay?"

"In the morning will be fine. Well...goodnight, son. Jerry."

They both told me goodnight, watching me with puzzled expressions. The music came back on as I started up the stairs—a lovely female voice softly singing what sounded like a lullaby: "Everything's all right... everything's fine..." I wondered what it was they were listening to; I'd never heard "rock" music quite so relaxing and beautiful.

I went to the bathroom, then into my room, where I closed the door and undressed in the dark. I got into bed and lay there quietly, hearing the distant music, thinking about Chuck and Jerry and how peaceful they'd seemed. I really should have said something, I thought; as it was, I'd given a tacit approval to their conditions. But then, what right had I to chastise them—or anyone? "He who is without sin, let him cast the first stone." It was curious, I thought—drifting slowly into sleep—that the quotation I'd thought of had contained the word *stone.* And there was another Biblical statement sneaking around in the back of my mind. Isaiah or somebody. "If men lie together, let them be stoned." Strange how words took on totally incompatible meanings.

There was a soft knock at my door, then a dim light filtered in as the door opened. "Dad?" Chuck said softly. "Are you sure nothing's wrong?"

I started to say, "Everything's fine," but changed my mind. I wanted to be finished with the lying and deception. "I don't know," I said frankly.

"Look, I'm, uh, sorry...I mean, I guess you could tell we're kind of, you know, high."

I felt myself smiling. "Well, you're high and I'm drunk, and it's no time to discuss it, is it?"

I heard him chuckle softly. "No, I guess not. Look, I'll put off the camping trip if you want."

"Let's talk about it tomorrow."

"Sure. I'll be here, Dad. Goodnight."

"Goodnight, son."

He started to close the door, then leaned back in: "Dad...thanks. I mean for not...well, you know what I mean. Goodnight."

The door closed and I lay in the darkness, remembering the tone of Chuck's voice. I'd never heard him sound so truly concerned. And it had been years since he'd thanked me for anything. I didn't understand how it could be, but maybe, somehow, everything *was* "all right".

I almost felt good as I drifted...deeper...deeper.... I dreamed I was back home, back in Glen Falls, Idaho, where my brother and I had grown up. I was younger—not a child, but not an adult either: I seemed to be myself, at my present age, but there was a "young" feeling about me. I was back on the farm where I'd spent most of my childhood, before we had moved into town, before my father had bought into a business and got himself involved in Church work. At first I wandered through the house looking at things I'd long-since forgotten: the patchwork quilts on the beds, crocheted doilies on the tables, afghans on the sofa and chairs, oval-framed sepia portraits on the walls, the old stove that my father would crank every morning at daybreak, shifting down the dead coals from the night before to start a new fire for a new day.

But the house was empty, and I began to feel uncomfortable and out of place, so I went outside, looking for someone. It seemed to be midsummer; the neatly trimmed lawns were a velvety green; the huge cottonwood trees around the house were in full leaf, with deep delicious shadows under them. I could smell growing things. I wandered through the garden: tomato vines thick on the fences, row upon row of lettuce and cabbage, radishes, turnips, carrots, Swiss Chard, pole-beans, yellow-ripening cantelopes, green-striped half-grown watermelons peeping up from the tangle of vines at the bright sun. I stood at the fence which surrounded the garden, looking out at the fields—alfalfa and wheat and a tall stand of field corn. The sky and the sun and a gentle breeze waving the corn and the wheat. The sound of birds singing, bees humming, leaves and trees and growing things moving softly.

Then I heard someone calling my name—not *Robert*,

but the name I'd been called as a child, *Bobby.* It came drifting through the cornfield on the breeze like a birdsong: "Bobby...oh, Bobby...Bobby-o."

I'd completely forgotten that my father used to call me that. *Bobby-o.*

And then I was running through the corn, the sharp papery leaves gently slapping my face, pollen-dust falling like rain, clinging to my face and hair, and the smell of loose earth and tassle-silk filling my nostrils. "Bobby-o! Bobby-o!"

The corn ended. I stepped out at the edge of the wheatfield and stopped. He was standing in the middle of the field, watching me, the golden wheat rippling around his knees. He was naked.

I'd never seen my father naked, and it shocked me at first—but then it seemed so totally natural, standing in the wheatfield, with the fields green and golden beyond him.

"Bobby-o! Hello!" It had to be my father; no one else had ever called me *Bobby-o.* And yet it wasn't the bulldog-jowled, scowling, fat, Marine-corps-cropped whitehaired man I knew. He was young, deeply sunburned, firm-jawed, muscular, beautiful as a god. Like the old, faded sepia pictures of grandfathers and great-grandfathers back in the house, my father now wore a beard and his dark hair was long. "Bobby! Come to me! I've got a secret! Come to me!"

I ran through the wheat, felt the sharp spears of the heads prickling my legs. Then I knew I was naked too. I knew that was how it should be. I felt no shame in my own nakedness or in his. He put his arms out as I ran to him. "Hurry, Bobby! Hurry! Run! Run!"

I leaped over the furrows, the golden field seemed to blur with my speed. Then I was before him and he was reaching out to me, smiling—as I never remembered him smiling before—and just as our hands touched, he said, "I love you, Bobby-o."

And then I awakened, feeling tears running over my

cheeks. The memory of his voice seemed to echo around the dark room, calling me back to the beautiful dream. For that moment, awake, I felt I could do anything in the world! Anything man had ever dreamed about doing. I could fly like the birds and swim like the fishes. I could, just by wanting to, take myself from this bed and put myself anywhere I chose, just by willing it. But I didn't want to go anyplace except back into the dream. Those fields no longer existed in reality; now they were tract houses. Now my father was a grumpy old man, too engrossed in loving his church to give love to the people around him. I wanted to know instead that beautiful bearded naked man, arms outstretched, saying: "Bobby, I love you."

I closed my eyes, felt reality slipping away again—but the beautiful dream did not return. Instead I found myself standing deep in the dark heart of some city, with ugly grey-sooty buildings reaching up to a grey sky where the sun was a sickly white day-star and the air all around me was heavy and thick. The man was still there, still reaching out, but he was no longer naked. He wore a heavy black overcoat and a black broadbrimmed hat that shadowed his face. "Follow me!" he commanded, and his voice was like thunder. He turned and hurried away.

I was frightened. I wanted to wake up, to stop this dream and get back to the other, but my feet took me after him. Faster and faster he walked, our footsteps beating out staccato echoes on the walls of the buildings. Then he ran, I followed him, running, my heart pounding as fast as my footsteps. The air grew darker and thicker.

Suddenly he stopped and turned. I stopped short. "Hello, Bobby-o!" his voice boomed.

"Who are you?"

"Who do you think I am?"

"Who are you?"

"You know who I am!"

"Who are you?"

He started to laugh. He threw back his head and the laughter poured out like a river, engulfing me.

"*Who are you?*" I screamed.

The laughter stopped abruptly. He stood tall, looking down at me. "Look." He threw off the hat, ripped the buttons from the overcoat. Once again he stood naked before me. The city disappeared. The white sun became golden. The birds sang and the breeze fingered my body. "I am *you*, you fool!"

He leaped up and for a moment hung suspended above me. Then he raised his arms straight above him and rose into the clear air.

"Wait!" I cried, and jumped after him—and I felt myself rising up, flying! The earth slowly moved away under me, the fields growing smaller and smaller. My body was filled with the most exhilarating excitement I'd ever known. I was free of the earth and of all the miseries and sorrows it represented. I was free! Flying! Following my naked father, diving upward into the sun!

But then I looked down, and I felt the fear gathering. What would happen if I fell?

And the instant I thought it, I felt myself falling—but not to the earth! The earth was no longer there. There were screaming sounds, blackness, emptiness—and then a light, a blinding exploding light, churning, expanding, blossoming all the colors of the spectrum. And I fell into it helplessly.

I heard a voice, soft, but filling everything: "Where is thy brother?"

I heard my own voice, seeming tiny and impertinent: "Am I my brother's keeper?"

"Yes!" the voice cried, and the sound of it crashed through me. "*Yes!*" I screamed at the fury of it. "*YES!*" The sound was like worlds crashing together.

Suddenly the light exploded. I exploded. I screamed...

...and awakened...

...ejaculating!

Someone was pounding on my door. "Dad!"

I was not in my bed! I was standing naked in the middle of the room, both windows wide open and the light from the streetlamp outside reflecting my dim image in the mirror. Bright splotches of semen lay on the floor and the top of the dresser–trailed like thick rain down the mirror.

Chuck was pounding on the door, yelling. My mind was spinning helplessly. I stared at the closed door, waiting for it to open, wondering stupidly what he would do when he saw his father naked with an erection.

"Dad! Answer me! Why's the door locked?"

Relief surged over me, and with it a sense of reality returned. I fumbled along the bed for my robe, stuffed my arms into the sleeves as I called: "It's okay, Chuck. It's okay." My penis was still stiffly erect; I pressed it tight to my stomach and covered it with the robe, strapping it tightly to my body with the belt. I opened the door.

Chuck stared at me, blinking and frowning. A light came from behind him, from his own room, down the hall. He was wearing only his shorts. For a moment I stared back at him. My son was a beautiful young man, broadshouldered, firmly muscled. In that moment I realized that he was truly a part of me; he had come from my body. "You were yelling," he said, and I heard genuine fear in his voice.

"Sorry." I leaned in the doorway; my body wanted to collapse under me. "I guess I had a nightmare."

"Why was your door locked?"

I looked up, into his eyes, then shook my head. "I don't know," I said. "I don't remember."

"You okay, though?"

"Yes, I'm fine."

"You sure?"

I found myself chuckling, reaching out, taking his

forearm in my hand and squeezing it. "Yes, Chuck, I'm sure. Thank you."

He shrugged, then glanced down at my hand as though he couldn't understand why I was touching him. I released the grasp and stuffed my hands into the pockets of my robe, feeling foolish and uncomfortable.

"Dad...?"

We regarded each other, eye to eye. Then he shook his head and turned away.

"What?"

He shrugged, glanced at me, turned away again. "I don't know. You're, uh, okay, though?"

"Yes."

"Well...okay." He started slowly down the hall. At the door to his room he turned briefly and grinned. "You scared me."

"I'm sorry."

"It's cool. See you, okay?"

"Right," I said. "In the morning."

"Right. G'night."

As the door to his room closed, I felt an emptiness creeping up through me. I looked back at my own bed and remembered the dream and the terror. I hurried to the bathroom and took two sleeping pills, went back to my room and cleaned up the mess on the dresser and floor, then collapsed in the bed. Total exhaustion sucked me down into sleep, but in the last fading moments of consciousness I heard an echo of that booming voice: "Where is thy brother? Where is thy brother? Where..."

Chapter 4

The sound of churchbells brought me up from a heavy sleep, and I lay for a long time, listening, staring at the ceiling. "Happy Easter," I told myself softly.

I felt absolutely rotten! My head ached, my body ached, and my stomach felt as though it had been twisted and tied into knots. My legs and back were so painfully stiff I could hardly lift myself out of the bed.

It was just ten o'clock.

I sat on the edge of the bed, remembering other Easter mornings a long time ago, when Chuck was just a small child, before Cindy and Dorene were born. I remembered warm bright sunny days, jonquils and daffodils, my small son clutching my hand, wearing his newest little suit and white shirt and necktie. Singing in Church, speaking of the glorious resurrection of Christ. And afterwards, Chuck and his young innocent friends had scrambled for Easter Eggs hidden in the yard, laughing, yelling, while Kate stood beside me, watching proudly and smiling.

Something incredibly ugly had come into our lives since that happy time. No, not only into our lives, I thought, but into the entire world. Had I still been a religious man, I'd have thought the prophecies of John were indeed coming true. Wars and rumors of wars, pestilence and famine, fathers against sons and sons against fathers, women against men, sickness and degeneracy spreading like a plague across continents. Murders, assassinations, bombings, hijackings, rapes, robberies. What possible happiness could they be celebrating in Church this morning?

I did not want to believe—could not force myself to believe—as so many claimed, that God was dead. Life would make no sense at all if that were true. But something was wrong, obviously. Perhaps God had got thoroughly disgusted with the human race and had gone away to try it all over again, someplace else in the Universe, leaving man to destroy himself, as he seemed so determined to do.

And if that were true—as it certainly seemed to be—what difference could it possibly make that I'd sucked a man's cock last night?

I shuddered, and pain jolted out through my body and head like fire through my nerves. No, I thought. Nothing could justify what I had done. And yet, I *had* done it, and nothing could blot out the memory.

For a long while I sat on the bed, staring at the floor, thinking of nothing except how wretched I felt. When I finally realized I was only wallowing in self-pity, I forced myself up, put on my robe, and headed for the shower. The door to Chuck's room was partially open and I paused to glance in at him. He was sprawled peacefully, half-uncovered, on the bed, one arm under his pillow and his face cradled in the crook of his elbow. *My son*, I thought, *my beautiful son. What kind of heritage have I given you—has the world given you?*

Sixteen years ago it had seemed such a beautiful idea to have a child, especially a son. I'd been so proud, so happy; I'd promised myself I would give him a good life, a better life than I'd had, growing up. But so many things had gone wrong in those sixteen years. Too many things.

But then as I stood there, watching him sleeping, I remembered how concerned he'd been for me last night. I remembered how he'd thanked me for not blowing up when I found out he was "high". And I remembered a phrase of that song they'd been playing: "Everything's all right...everything's fine...."

Perhaps things were not quite as bad as they seemed.

In the bathroom I took a couple of aspirins, then showered and shaved. My body still ached and my head felt as though a steel band had been permanently tightened around it, but I'd relaxed enough to feel halfway human again. I dressed, then went downstairs, intending to fix breakfast.

I stared into the refrigerator. No eggs; no bacon; two stale butt-ends of a loaf of bread. Well, hell, the idea of food hadn't really appealed to me, except that I knew I should get something in my stomach to straighten out those knots. I made toast and a pot of instant coffee, then wandered out, cup in hand, into the back yard. It was a beautiful day. The sky was brilliantly clear, the sun warm. The grass was beginning to lose its winter-dead brownness, bright yellow-green spears reaching up to the sunlight. Kate's tulips were beginning to open, and the deep green shoots of gladiolas and peonies were nudging the dark earth aside. Any other Sunday morning I'd have been happy to sit out and sip my coffee and enjoy the spring sunshine, but this particular day, it all seemed so worthless. I looked around at the greening bushes, the new grass, the budding flowers, at the house and the trees, and I thought: *This is it! This is my life. This is what I've worked ten years to achieve. A few flowers and bushes, an old house, a couple of cars, and what else?*

A son *maybe*—but that was a new maybe and I wasn't yet sure enough of the possibilities to count on it. I was too used to thinking that Chuck hated me; I couldn't overcome the idea just with the encouragement he'd given me last night. Otherwise, nothing. No one to love or be loved by. No one to help or be helped by. No close friends. A wife who hated me; two "daughters" who liked "Uncle Ed" better than their "father". And even if Chuck did like me, was concerned about me, there was little common ground between us. He was part of me, part of my body, but he'd rejected all of my values. He accepted my money but without appreciation, as though it was simply his due, as though I *owed* it to him for having sired him.

And the job? If someone had walked into the yard right then and said, "I want to get into advertising," I'd have said, "Here! Take my half of the business and welcome!" Because the truth was, I hated my job. Once I had loved it, but that, too, had been a long time ago, before I'd found out about my wife and my partner. Now every day was like hell at the office. I still arrived every morning on time, still spent the day working dutifully, but there was absolutely no enjoyment left in it for me. Going to work was simply the better of two evils, *slightly* preferable to staying home.

What does a man do when his life becomes worthless?

One answer quickly presented itself, but I rejected it instantly. I might not be religious any longer, but I could not contemplate an end to my life, especially an end self-inflicted.

Perhaps I could go away somewhere. Thirty-five wasn't old, not really. And I'd have enough money from selling my share of the company to start something. Perhaps I should give Kate the divorce she so desperately wanted. Give her the house and a car, let her marry Ed and give the girls a real father. Ed could buy me out. I assumed he'd be willing to marry Kate.

But what could I do? Where could I go? How could I ever forget what a mess I had made of my life? Could I ever overcome it?

Although the sun was bright, I felt chilled. I went back inside and poured some fresh coffee, then sat at the kitchen table, despondently tracing the green ivy patterns in the table cloth. The house was so silent!

I tried to remember good things about the house, about sitting at the kitchen table, about tracing patterns in tablecloths. If there had been such times they were too far back in the past to remember.

Perhaps I could go back to Idaho, buy a farm, settle down in some remote corner of some remote valley and get a good dog, raise my own food, depend upon no one. And have no one depending on me.

Thinking of Idaho reminded me of the dream. The old house...the garden...the green fields...and my father? No, that was impossible. That beautiful naked man could not possibly have been my own father. Thinking about it now, I doubted that the man had ever been naked in his whole life, at least not since Grandmother's midwife had first diapered him. My father's abhorrence of nudity had been the genesis of my own. At one point in my life I had practically worshiped my father, incorporating all of his ideas about life literally as "gospel". And even though I'd found myself at odds with the man these past six or seven years, I still found so many of his attitudes cropping up in my own thoughts.

Then how, why, had I dreamed about a naked man?

The realization jolted me! I'd *never* dreamed about naked men! At least, not that I remembered.

At first, in the dream, I'd been sure that the man was my father, but later, as I'd followed him through those dark ugly streets, I'd started to realize that it couldn't be. And then when he'd turned, when he'd thrown off the overcoat, saying "Look!" I'd been certain.

I could still hear his taunting laughter as I'd asked, over and over, "Who are you?" And then: "I am you, you fool!"

But that too was impossible. I didn't have a beard or long hair–and I certainly wasn't planning to grow them. The dream didn't make sense. And the longer I thought about it, the less sense it made. I was forced to decide it was only my mind's unfathomable way of working up to a sexual climax–although I'd never had a wet dream quite like it before.

But that flying sensation had been delicious. I hadn't dreamed about flying since....

"Where is thy brother?"

I sat upright in the chair, staring hard straight ahead, but not seeing the kitchen—seeing, rather, a young boy, about the same age as Chuck. A boy dressed in pajamas and an old plaid bathrobe, standing in the doorway....

The image faded, but the idea remained. *Bill!*

Of course! What an idiot I'd been not to think of it sooner!

"Where is thy brother?"

That man had been Bill! Not me, not my father, but my brother, Bill!

I'd completely shut Bill out of my mind—erased him. We'd been so close as children, two years apart in our actual ages, but more like twins than just brothers. And then we'd had some kind of fight.... I remembered the anger, but I couldn't recall what we had fought about. Or had it been Kate that we'd argued about? I remembered he'd hated her. And that would have made it about the right time. I'd been seventeen when I'd started dating her, and that would have made Bill about fifteen.

The last time I'd seen him had been at my wedding. A year or so later, Mom had written that he'd run off and joined the Marines. It had been...Good Lord! Seventeen years since I'd seen my own brother!

But why should I dream about Bill? I still hadn't answered the riddle of the dream: "Where is thy brother?" That was what God had asked Cain, who had killed his brother. I hadn't killed mine.

I stood up to get another cup of coffee, but I never got as far as the stove. The cup slipped from my fingers and shattered on the floor as I glanced into the front room and saw the envelope tucked under the front door!

My hands were shaking as I ripped off one end and extracted the single folded page. I leaned against the door, holding my arms tight to my sides to stop my hands from shaking the paper. This note was printed, but now the printing was not quite so childish, and the contents were not quite so illiterate:

DERE ROBBER. YOU CANT GET AWAY FROM ME NOW. I NO ALL ABOUT YOU. I HOPE YOU HAVE THE DESENSY TO KILL YOUSELF. YOU DESERV TO DIE. YOU ARE TRYING TO RUNE CHUCKS LIFE THE SAME WAY YOU RUNED MINE. IM GOING TO GET YOU ROBBER! LOOK OUT! XXX YOU KNOW WHO

I took a deep breath and leaned back against the door, closing my eyes. Suddenly I saw John Adams as clearly as though he had been there physically—standing up to the urinal, milking his thick half-hard penis as he looked down at mine. I seemed to feel his hand squeezing my shoulder. "Just remember, Robert, it's your word against mine. And you don't know who I am, do you? They might just believe me and think *you* were the *pervert.*"

"Oh, no," I whispered. "No, it couldn't be....."

You don't know who I am, do you?

YOU KNOW WHO

Where is thy brother?

And, last night, in the steambath, I'd heard myself say: "*Suck me, Billy, please!*"

The pieces were suddenly falling into place!

I remembered, on the plane, thinking that John Adams was not what he seemed to be. I'd been right! And his name wasn't John Adams. The pieces fit together too neatly to be a coincidence. Our meeting had not been accidental. Nor had it been a coincidence that I'd been worrying about Chuck and that note. Jerry Ashby hadn't written the note, nor had Ed. Now I knew who had written it, plus the one I'd just read: the man who had called himself John Adams; the man I had dreamed about, only slightly disguised, last night: Bill Thorne! My brother!

Because now a new piece of the puzzle presented itself. Suddenly, clearly, the memory came back—and it hit me with such a shattering impact that I had to sit down on the couch.

I was sixteen and my brother was fourteen. As children we'd been so close, going everywhere together. But then I'd reached puberty first, and Bill had begun to seem like a silly kid, always carping at me: "Don't do this, Bob, you'll get us in trouble. Don't do that, Bob, it isn't right. What will Dad say? What will Mom say? What will people say?" The thing that had galled me was that most of the time he was right. He was always the "sensible" one, I'd been the "crazy" one, just out for a good time. Driving Dad's car, filled with half of the basketball squad, down to Boise to a whorehouse, leaving poor Bill in the car to keep watch for us. What a bastard I'd been then. Cocky, smug, self-satisfied. I'd stopped going to church, started drinking, swearing....

We had moved into town by then....

It was some time late in July.... I'd been out on a date that night. Bill had wanted to come along but I'd told him to get lost. I was planning to get myself laid and I didn't want him messing it up for me. (He'd come into his own, as far as growing up was concerned he'd shot up two or three inches taller than me, and his body was better: bigger, fuller, broader shoulders, thicker chest—and his whang was the talk of the shower rooms—and yet it seemed he couldn't get out of that "goody-good" stage. As far as I knew he'd never even jacked off. So I didn't want him watching over my shoulder as I tried to get some action out of Jenny Lou Fisher.)

The night had been pure frustration. Jenny Lou had insisted on taking Karen Simpson along, and Karen's boy friend, "Whimpy", was the biggest, fattest, dumbest cluck in the Junior Class. All through the movie, and afterwards parked up on Cemetery Hill, I'd tried to make out, but with Karen and Whimpy along, Jenny Lou wouldn't even touch me. Oh, she'd let me put my arm around her and sneak my fingers inside her blouse, but then suddenly she'd push me away and turn around in the seat to gossip and giggle with Karen. To top it all off, Jenny decided to spend the night with Karen, so I couldn't even take Whimpy and Karen home first.

By the time I got home, three o'clock in the morning, my nuts ached so bad I could hardly walk. And of course I was furious. I slammed into the house and turned on the lights, not giving a damn if I woke someone or not. I rummaged around in the kitchen, massaging my aching groin, getting a hard-on, almost wishing my father would come charging down to see me playing with myself. But he didn't. And I managed to get myself so worked up I knew I'd have to do something to get rid of the pressure. I couldn't go up to my room. Bill was sure to wake up and whine, "What are you doing, Bob? You shouldn't do that. It's not good for you." And I didn't need that on top of everything else.

So I went outside, out into the back yard. There had been a moon earlier, but it had gone down and now everything was dark. Our big elm was only a darker shadow against another shadow of the Wilberson's house next door. I'd left the light on in the kitchen, but it had to filter through the screen door and then the screens all around the back porch, so even if someone did see me, they wouldn't be able to see what I was doing.

I unbuttoned my fly and eased my cock out and started slowly working it. I thought about Jenny Lou and let myself imagine what I *should* have done. I should have just raped the dumb bitch. Everybody in town knew she fucked like a mink. One night I'd been one of five guys she'd taken on, out behind the bleachers on the football field, lying on one of the benches the team used, letting one fuck her while she sucked on another one, getting him ready to screw her next. And Karen knew what a whore Jenny was; Karen wasn't any churchgoing virgin herself. They were probably home right now sticking things up each other's cunt. I should have raped both of them! And let Whimpy watch! Let him stand there and play with his teeny dink while I screwed his girl friend.

I wandered around the yard, completely caught up in my fantasy, seeing myself shoving Jenny up against the trunk of the car, ripping her skirt off, jerking her pants down, shoving it in! Like a damn bull! Fuck her like a stallion! Harder and harder until she screamed—but not stopping. If she did scream I could grab her and force her down and shove my cock into her screaming mouth and shoot my jizz into it!

"Bob, is that you?"

The voice came from the back porch behind me! My heart did a wild somersault in my chest as I tried to shove my cock back in my pants, but it wouldn't go! I turned around, hooking my thumbs into my pockets, spreading my hands over my crotch, fully expecting my father to come striding down the back steps, ready to knock me flat on my ass on the lawn.

Bill stood there, outlined by the light from the kitchen, wearing my old plaid bathrobe. I said, "Oh, shit, it's you! Jeez, Bill, you scared me!"

He came down the steps. "I'm sorry. What are you doing out here? I heard something and..."

Watching him step down like a kid scared to death to dive in a swimming pool, hearing his whining voice, all the anger and frustration of the night welled up and went straight out toward him. I wanted to hurt someone, shock someone, get back at someone—and Bill had politely presented himself. I pulled my hands away from my crotch and stepped into the dim spread of light where I knew he could see my hard-on. "Oh, that cunt

Jenny Lou," I said, knowing the word *cunt* would chill him clear through. "One of these days somebody's going to strangle her! Goddamn pricktease!"

"Wouldn't she...*do* anything?"

The goody-good wouldn't say *shit* if he had a mouthful! I'd told him earlier, just to torment him, that I was going to get Jenny Lou to *blow* me, and he'd gone red as a beet!

"Naw, shit," I said. "She just wanted to tease me. Besides, Whimpy and Karen went with us. That dumb Whimpy—he still thinks his pecker is just something to pee through." I turned slightly in the light and started to play with my cock again.

"You shouldn't do that out here, Bob!" Bill whined. "Somebody will see you!"

"Aw, for Christ's sake, Bill! When the hell are you going to stop being a chickenshit? Who's going to see me? Everybody's asleep in this burg!"

"Dad might. You slammed the door. Maybe he heard you. Maybe he'll come down...."

I laughed and bent backward, working my fist even harder on my cock. "Yeah...I wish the old bastard would come down. I'd show him a thing or two. I'd say, 'Hey, Pop, watch me beat my meat! Watch me shoot my hot jizz all over your fuckin' lawn!' "

Even in the dark I could see his face turn bright scarlet. Every swearword I used hit like a fist in his nuts. "Bob!" he whispered. "Be quiet!"

"Aw, shit!" I turned away from him, still pumping away, and stepped out of the light, into the shadow of the elm tree. I stood there, staring into the darkness, praying he wouldn't go back into the house. An idea had started to form in my mind—a sick, but very exciting idea. I kept moving slowly until I reached the thick trunk of the tree, then I turned and leaned back against it, spreading my legs apart. He was right behind me. "Is this better?" I asked him.

He hunched his shoulders. "I guess so."

"C'mere, Bill." He stepped closer. "You know what Conrad Bigelow told me? He said him and his brother do things for each other. You know what I mean?" (I was making it up, but I knew Bill wouldn't have the guts to ask Conrad about it.)

"No," he said softly, shaking his head.

"Conrad says any time they go out with some girls that won't come across, him and Ed *do things* later."

I heard him swallow hard. "What kind of things?"

"Conrad says Ed takes it up his...you-know-what. And then sometimes they both do what crazy Noel Becker does."

He swallowed again, and his voice was tight when he said, "Noel Becker's a queer! Dad says they should shoot him, just like they would a freak animal."

I laughed. I was really enjoying this. Each time I made him cringe, something inside me tingled wilder and wilder. "That's because Dad's never had Noel Becker *blow* him!"

"Bob!" he gasped. He looked back at the house, then at me. "Have *you...?*"

"Oh, boy, you really are dumb, aren't you? Shit, every guy in school has had old Noel suck 'em off!"

That wasn't quite true, but it sounded good. Maybe not all of the guys had let him, but a lot of them had. Noel Becker was a legend in Glen Falls; if you saw him out walking someplace late at night—and you did almost every night—you just stopped and said, "Hey, Noel, I got something for you." I'd done it twice now.

"That's terrible!"

"Like hell it is. Boy you should try it sometime. He loves it. He sucks and sucks and then swallows your jizz. Jenny Lou spits it out." I was watching his face; I was used to the dark now and I could see that his eyes were looking straight down at my cock! I even imagined I could see his, hard, under his robe, and that really excited me. I knew Bill had a big one, but I'd never seen it hard. I decided right then that I would look at it, one way or another. "Jenny Lou thinks she'll get pregnant if she swallows it. But she's lousy anyway. She's not even a good piece of tail." I took my hand away again so he could see my cock clearly. "Billy..." I said softly. "Do you really like me?"

"Well, sure I do."

"If I asked, would you do something?"

He took a step backward. "Not that, Bob!"

"Then you don't like me!" I turned my back on him. "Go back in the house, chickenshit!"

"What are you going to do?"

"I'm gonna *jack off!* What the fuck do you think?"

"Don't be mad, Bob," he whined. "I just couldn't."

I turned to him. He looked so damn pitiful it disgusted me! This big strapping kid scared to death of the least hint of sex. I wanted to kick him right square in the nuts! And then rip off those fucking pajamas and shove my cock right up his ass!

I reached out and grabbed his robe, jerking him toward me. By then I couldn't have stopped myself if I'd wanted to. I wanted to hurt him. I wanted to do something so bad that he'd never forget it. I ripped his robe open. Sure enough, his cock was as hard as a rock, sticking straight out from his gaping pajamas, so damn big it looked like my forearm! Just the sight of it sent chills all the way through my body. Nobody I'd ever seen had one like that! I reached down and grabbed it and knelt down. "Well, *I'm* not a chickenshit!" I opened my mouth and shoved my face forward and took his cock inside my mouth.

Suddenly his hot cum was spurting! I gagged, but I kept my mouth tight around it, pumping my own cock furiously. I jumped up and forced him down to his knees and shoved my cock into his face.

"Please, Bob! Don't!"

I grabbed his hair tight in one fist, pumping my cock with the other one. I was trying to get the damn thing in his mouth before I came, but his lips were clamped tight.

Then everything exploded! I watched my cum splatter all over his face. It gushed into his hair, his eyes, all over his cheeks. The full load I'd been building up all night!

Then I twisted his hair, forcing his head back, his face up toward me—and leaned over—and spat his cum into his face. "That's *yours!*" I stood back and stripped the last gobs from my cock, flipped the stuff from my fingers. "There now!" I said. "Now you're just as rotten as I am!"

He didn't move. He just knelt there in the grass with my cum and his own mixed together, running over his face, dripping down from his chin onto his pajamas, trailing onto his hairy chest. He didn't say anything. He just looked up at me. I couldn't tell if he were crying or it that was our cum streaking down from his eyes.

The last of my anger drained out of me. I wanted to cry, to kneel down beside him and take him into my arms and tell him how sorry I was I had done such a terrible thing. But I couldn't move either. We just looked at each other. Then finally he stood up, his face shining in the dim light. He wiped the stuff off with the sleeve of his robe. He went into the house without saying a word.

I knew as I watched him go back up the steps that he'd never forgive me. And I knew I would never forgive myself. I felt like Cain in the Bible—except I had done something even worse than killing my brother.

At that point the memory became very hazy. I'd had a terrible fever the next day—screaming, cringing in the bed, as hideous Hell-Monsters slobbered in the shadows of my room, waiting for me to die, waiting to eat my soul, suck it out of my body.

I seemed to remember my mother and father having an argument about calling the doctor—and then some men, standing around my bed, leaning over me, putting their cold hands on my head and praying to have this "affliction" taken from me. And then later, my father sitting on my bed, telling me that I'd been following the paths of Satan, and that the sickness was a warning from God to repent of my evil ways. I remembered him praying: "If it be Thy will, Oh Lord, let this cup be taken from him."

Had I told my father the terrible thing I had done to my brother? Had I, in the delirium of fever, terrified of the consequences of my sin, twisted the truth to make Bill the guilty one, implying that my brother had "tempted" me in a moment of extreme weakness? For reasons I'd never clearly understood, my father had always preferred me to Bill, and I'd learned very early in life the fine art of implication—not really *lying*, simply leaving certain things to my father's imagination, letting him make the decision that Bill was the guilty one.

I must have said something, because I remembered Bill, standing by my bed, his eyes red from crying, just looking at me, pure hatred written all over his face.

And that had been the end of our friendship.

Bill had stopped going to church the same Sunday that I started again—and, even before school had started that fall, he'd taken up with the Caldwell brothers, going out night after night, getting in trouble with the police. I could remember how disgusted I'd been when I heard the guys talking about what a big prick he had, and how he was making out with all the Junior and Senior girls, and how they loved it, and how he'd get drunk and show off, making bets that his cock was the biggest in town and that he could shoot further than any other guy.

It was during the winter that followed that I got to know Kate Jensen. She was one of the school's "wallflowers", the complete opposite of Jenny Lou–shy, plain, serious, and a virgin. We didn't even *talk* about sex until just before the wedding, when the Bishop gave us his "little chat" about marriage and the "proper" use of sex as a means of multiplying and replenishing the earth, as God had commanded in the very beginning, and not simply for pleasure, which was Satan's tool for leading us astray.

I studied the note again: *You are trying to ruin Chuck's life the way you ruined mine.* That *had* to be Bill! If that one horrible night had changed my own life so drastically, I was sure it had changed his just as much. His helling around in Glen Falls had seemed normal–in the sense that he messed with girls rather than boys–but I hadn't seen or heard from Bill for seventeen years; it was possible he'd turned queer in the service, or afterwards, and blamed it all on that night, and on me.

And now that I could remember how it had really happened, maybe he was fully justified in blaming me. I could understand why he would want to punish me by sending those notes, those pictures.

As ye give, so shall ye receive.

Obviously, though, he had no idea how much I'd already been punished–by Kate and by Ed and by Chuck, and, perhaps, even by myself. *Well,* I thought, *the time has come to let him know.* My sin had caught up with me and now I had to make reparations. I had to find Bill and apologize. I was sure now that nothing was wrong with Chuck; Bill had simply used him as a means of getting back at me.

It was amazing, now that I thought about it, how simple the true explanation really was. It would have been easy for Bill to have found me: I was listed in the telephone directory. Knowing my address, he'd have known which school Chuck would go to, and a few "casual" inquiries would have given him the name of Chuck's best friend. He'd simply used the same deceit with me that I'd used with our father–*implying* that Jerry and Chuck were homosexual lovers. Or maybe he'd approached Chuck himself, gained his confidence. Maybe...

I cringed at the thought that Bill might have hated me enough to seduce Chuck–but I pushed the idea out of my mind. I'd made the mistake of believing the note once; I didn't want to make the same error again.

At any rate, somehow Bill had found out I was going to San Francisco, and he'd followed me. He'd been the one in my hotel room. He'd been the one following me on Van Ness, watching me in the coffee shop, dogging my every move, waiting for his chance to approach me, get me drunk, then seduce me. He'd tried to get me drunk on the plane; afterwards he'd suggested a beer. It was ironic that my reason for not succumbing to his charms, for not having that beer, was the very note he had sent me. Had it not been for that, I might have gone to a bar with him, might have let myself be duped into going home with him...."Let's go to my place for a nightcap, Robert. Nobody's expecting you. If you want, you can spend the night there. I've got an extra bed."

I could imagine what he would have done then, with me too drunk to fight him off–holding me down, opening my pants.... And then, afterwards, spitting the stuff in my face, saying: "There! That's yours! Now you're just as rotten as I am!"

Obviously the next order of business was to find Bill and talk to him, and to do it before I got into any discussion with Chuck. I could see that my brother had planned all this very very carefully; if I hadn't guessed who "John Adams" really was, I'd have gone through with my plan of confronting Chuck–and that would have been the real disaster I'd felt coming; Chuck might never have forgiven me for accusing him of being homosexual. Yes, one way or the other, Bill would have had his revenge. I could appreciate how diabolically clever my brother had been.

I still wanted to talk to Chuck about his being "high" last night, but now that could wait—until after his camping trip if necessary.

I put the note back into the envelope and went upstairs intending to get the other note and the pictures, then find the slip of paper "John Adams" had given me—and then take them all to confront the man.

But the note and the pictures were not where I'd left them! In a panic I felt all around under the dresser, removing both bottom drawers. Nothing! I searched through each separate drawer, moved the dresser away from the wall and peered behind it. I found a dime and a pen I had lost several months ago, but no envelopes.

I pushed the dresser back and reached under it again. And this time I found something. Not the envelope: it felt like a small plastic bottle. I'd probably dislodged it from its hiding place by moving the dresser. I pulled it out. It was an old prescription bottle of mine with the label still on it: Nembutal. At first there seemed nothing but cotton inside it, but when I extracted the top layer, there were six small white capsules.

They were not sleeping pills!

I had a sickening feeling that I knew what they were—and an even sicker feeling that I knew *whose* they were.

Dope! Pure poison!

I felt miserable.

Wearily I replaced the drawers. Just a few minutes ago everything had seemed so clear and so simple. Now things were all mixed up again. Who had taken the note and those pictures? Chuck? Jerry Ashby? Or had Bill somehow managed to get in the house last night, between the time I'd gone out and the time Chuck got home? It was possible. We kept a spare key hidden under the front steps. Bill could have kept watch until he'd seen somebody use the key. In fact, Bill might have put those pills under the dresser! Not Chuck at all!

At least that slip of paper he'd given me was where I

had left it, in my coat pocket; but all it had was his name and a phone number, no address.

I went into the hall and checked the directory. Just as I'd suspected, there were several John Adams, but none with the number he'd given me. I called the operator and asked her to verify the number. Yes, it was a new one. His address? Thirteen-twenty-five Richards Street.

Chuck was still sleeping peacefully so I left him a note: *Had to go out for an important meeting. Should be back early afternoon. If possible, put off your camping trip until later today.* I signed it *Dad,* read it over, then inserted *love* before *Dad*, and left it on the floor, just inside his door. I took the little bottle of pills downstairs and locked them in one of the drawers of my desk; no one had a key to that lock except me. I decided to have a quick drink, just a small shot to bolster my confidence; then I got in the car and headed for Richards Street.

As I drove, I tried to decide the best way to approach Bill. My original impulse had been to tell him straight out that I knew who he was and what he'd been doing, to apologize honestly for what I had done to him, and ask him to stop writing those notes. But the more I considered it, the more I began to doubt that the direct approach was the best one. I did not want to risk making him even more bitter toward me than he already was; if possible, I wanted to settle the problem and still remain friends with him—after all, he *was* my brother, even if he was queer. And now that I understood why he was queer, I felt that I had an obligation to help him, if he'd let me. Maybe some of his actions last night on the plane hadn't been completely insincere; maybe he really had wanted to get to know me. There was no way of knowing what had truly been going on in his mind; maybe he'd wanted to tell his troubles to me. I had to be very careful about putting him off again.

If I went to him as though I hadn't figured out anything, as though I really believed he was John Adams—as though the fact that he was queer didn't bother me at all—that might take some of the wind out of his sails. If I could make him believe that the idea of sex between men didn't upset me, then the idea of using it as a kind of emotional blackmail would suddenly become pointless. But beyond that, it would imply an acceptance of him, regardless of his...unusual desires, and that might make him feel better about himself. He might even admit to writing the notes without my having to tell him I'd figured it out.

Strangely enough, now that I'd remembered that evening, back in Glen Falls, I didn't feel nearly as self-righteous as I had last night. Some of the wind had been taken out of my sails, too. I even began to wonder whether, given the chance, he'd try to seduce me again. What possible harm could it do now, anyway, after what I had done in the steam bath?

I found his address easily, a fairly large two-story frame house, sitting back from the street behind a low stone wall and a neatly trimmed yard. It looked as though it had been painted just recently. I felt an excitement starting deep in my body, not entirely unpleasant, as I went up the walk to his front door and rang the bell. For a moment the excitement began to fade when it seemed that no one was home; but then I heard: "Just a minute!"

Suddenly my heart began racing. Suppose I'd been wrong about all of those pieces fitting so neatly into the puzzle? Suppose they fit together *too* neatly? I felt dizzy and reached quickly to steady myself on the doorframe. *I shouldn't be here! I shouldn't be doing this!* I didn't want to become friends with a queer, no matter whose brother he was!

The door opened. He frowned angrily, and I thought: *Please! Just say "Go away!" and close the door!*

But he didn't. He stood there regarding me with a kind of half-triumphant smile slowly erasing the frown, wearing paint-splattered levis, so old and tattered they looked as though they might disintegrate any moment, and an equally old faded brown army shirt. There were small flecks of white on his forehead and hands, and I guessed he'd been painting. "Well," he said. "I didn't expect to see you today."

The sound of his voice, so calm and self-confident, made me feel easier in one way, but much more nervous in another. For a moment I couldn't even remember the reason I'd come here—or the reason I'd given myself for coming. Looking at him now, I remembered vividly that feeling I'd had on the plane, of wanting to touch him. With a shock I realized that I still wanted to. It made not one bit of difference whether he was my brother Bill, or John Adams, or someone whose true name I might never know. He radiated an aura of self-assurance and strength that I wanted to share, to feel for myself. How had I ever got it into my mind that he was miserable? *I* was the one who was miserable! By all of the values I prized so highly, he should have been cringing at the sight of me, terrified that I might have the police waiting out on the street to arrest him, and *I* should have been the one looking triumphant.

"Hello...John," I swallowed hard. "I guess I should have called...but...I was afraid you'd hang up on me."

"I probably would have. What's happening?"

"I want to....apologize."

"I see."

"May I come in?"

He studied me carefully, his eyes moving slowly from my face down to my crotch and back up again. He shrugged and stepped back. "Sure. Why not."

I went inside, intensely relieved. It was dim in the front of his house, with all of the drapes drawn over his windows, but I could see he'd been doing some extensive construction: there were saw-horses in one corner; a large part of one wall had been cut away to join a parlor and living room. Paint-splattered drop-cloths lay over most of the furniture. He closed the door, then leaned back against it, folding his arms. "Okay, Robert. Now what?"

I looked up at his face. He was regarding me steadily, unblinking, waiting for me to explain myself. His gaze was so intense that I had to look down—and I couldn't help asking myself if a man guilty of "emotional blackmail" could look his victim in the eye so unwaveringly. Now I remembered the way he had appeared to me *before* that moment at the urinals, before I knew that he was a homosexual; somehow I'd forgotten his original appearance, or had distorted it totally beyond recognition in my imagination. This was not a man who would seduce a sixteen-year-old boy, even if he did hate the boy's father. And there was no hatred in his eyes. There was anger, perhaps.

I wanted to tell him: "I've made a mistake, sorry," and leave. Obviously I was wrong about many things concerning this man, whoever he was, my brother or John Adams—just as I'd been wrong about so many *many* things recently. If I stayed longer I was certain to make even more of a fool of myself than I already had, one way or another. And yet I knew I couldn't leave. I couldn't let the man remain a mystery to me. I shrugged helplessly. "I'm sorry," I said. "I knew what I wanted to say, driving here, but...I don't even know where to begin now."

"May I make a suggestion?" I looked up, meeting his intense eyes again. "How about starting with: 'I'm sorry I called you a filthy pervert'."

I cringed and looked down. "Yes," I said softly. "I am sorry about that."

"You know, Robert, that's really a rotten thing to call a guy. I don't give a damn how upset you were. I mean, as far as I was concerned, you cruised me just as much as I did you. Sure, I'd seen you at the airport, but I hadn't been staring. But, man, you zeroed in on my crotch like you had every intention of doing exactly what I wanted you to. You know? So I tried to be friendly, and you gave me the old fuck-off routine...."

"It wasn't that at all, John," I protested. "I really was upset about something. I did want to talk to you."

"I know. That's what you kept saying. So I thought, 'Okay, the guy's got his mind on a problem, fine, I can appreciate that, but he wants me to come back later.' Well, hell..." He shrugged and moved away from the door. "I should have said something. Instead of being cute and telling you I wasn't married, I should have told you: 'Robert, I'm a cocksucker.' I shouldn't have groped you, especially there in that head. But, man, *filthy pervert*—that's a very bad trip to lay on somebody."

I stared at the floor, feeling like a very small child being sternly reprimanded—but not unjustly. He was right: it was a rotten thing to call a man—especially him. I couldn't help thinking how ridiculous I'd been, imagining that I could "help" him, make him feel "reassured" about himself. He didn't need reassurance from anyone.

"I'm sorry," I said again. "I didn't mean it."

"Are you sure?"

I nodded. "Yes. I wasn't even thinking. I just wasn't expecting..." My voice faltered as he stepped up to me, reached down and brought his hand up under my crotch. Wild tinglings exploded in my stomach, up my spine, on the top of my head. I flinched—then shut my eyes tight, forcing myself to stand absolutely still, to make no move at all that he might misinterpret. His fingers found my penis, now beginning to harden, and closed around it. For a moment it felt as though my body might melt on the spot.

"I still think that's very nice, Robert," he whispered.

I shuddered and swallowed hard. I muttered, "Thank

you," then instantly felt like an utter fool. He squeezed gently, then patted my arm. "Would you like a beer?"

"Uh...yes...I, uh, yes, I would, please."

"Let's go into the kitchen. It's the only room finished down here. I just bought the place a few months ago, and it's still pretty much of a mess."

Weakly, still tingling, and with my hand deep in my pocket, holding my erection firmly so it wouldn't show, I followed him into a large, old-fashioned kitchen. Any other time I might have appreciated all the careful work that had obviously gone into giving it that warm, relaxed feeling–it was very much like our kitchen had been in the farm house, back home–but my mind seemed to have gone almost totally blank. He gestured toward a beautifully-restored old wooden table. "Sit. Make yourself comfortable." He took two cans of beer from the refrigerator, then hesitated. "Would you prefer something harder? Than beer, I mean?"

I shook my head numbly. "No. Beer's fine." He opened the cans and put one on the table before me. I took several deep, cool swallows, then muttered, idiotically, "Mmmm, good."

He chuckled, then leaned against the table, drinking his beer, watching me drink mine. I flinched again as his fingers touched the back of my hand, then traced slowly along the thick vein; the touch was like an electrical current flashing up through my arm and down into my body. "Okay, Robert," he said. "Now tell me the real reason you came here today."

I looked up at his face, feeling like a child again. ("Tell Daddy where it hurts, Bobby.") I shuddered and looked down again. "To apologize...."

"Yes, but you've done that," he said. "If that was all that you'd come for, you'd have said your piece and gone, right?"

I nodded. "I guess so."

"Well?"

My heart was starting to pound again, and my mind

was a helpless jumble of confusion. Did he know why I'd come here, thinking he was my brother? Or did he mean something else by the question? I realized that now was the time to ask him about the notes, about his true identity, but my mind refused to form the questions. Dimly I realized that I didn't want to know the answers—not yet; I wanted something to happen first. "I'm not sure, John," I said.

He went to the refrigerator. "You want another?" I nodded, lifting the can to my lips to finish it. He put the new can on the table, then wandered back to look out of the window above the sink. He stood there silently for several long moments and I found myself looking at him in a way I had never looked at a man before, at the way his levis clung tightly to his muscular legs and his buttocks; his body had become an exciting thing to consider.

"Robert...Clear up something for me, will you? Are you gay?"

I couldn't help laughing; the question seemed ridiculous. "Not particularly."

He looked over his shoulder, frowning; then he grinned. "I wasn't asking if you were happy. But you answered the question anyway, didn't you? Gay means queer, Robert. I was asking if you were a cocksucker."

"Oh." The word jarred me, and my first impulse was to react angrily, to say "No!" emphatically—but I knew if I said it, he might simply shrug and say, "Too bad. Why don't you go home now?" I took a long drink of the beer, feeling my penis starting to rise again. "I've... done it...a couple of times."

"Oh?" He turned to face me, leaning back with one elbow on the top of the sink, standing as he had when I'd first seen him in the airport, leaning on that counter of the bookstand. "Well, that's interesting. I wouldn't have guessed it." He regarded me with a look of challenge in his eyes. "Did you enjoy it?"

Again I wanted to say "No!" but now I could see the firm outline of his genitals under the thin faded denim—and his penis was growing, slowly lengthening, thickening. My mind was churning, but I understood that something completely new was happening to me: one of the most exciting men I had ever seen was getting excited himself—over *me!* Twice I had wanted almost desperately to touch him; it occurred to me suddenly that I *could* touch him! He was a homosexual; he *wanted* me to touch him! It wouldn't be dirty and perverted to him—and if it wasn't to him, how could it be for me? It couldn't be both dirty *and* beautiful; it had to be one or the other. I wanted it to be beautiful.

"I was...drunk," I said. "I don't remember."

"Are you drunk now?" he asked.

"...A little."

He pushed himself away from the sink and walked slowly across the room until he was standing before me. I could not take my eyes from his crotch; the closer he came, the more clearly the outline of his penis stood out; I could even see the ridge around the head of it.

He unbuckled his belt. "This is what you came here for, isn't it, Robert? This is how you wanted to apologize, isn't it. You decided it might not be bad like the others. I'm not like the others, am I, Robert?"

"No...."

"You think maybe with me it would be good..." He tugged his shirt up from his levis. "...Because I'm a man..." He opened the buttons, slowly. "...Because I've got a man's body...and I *act* like a man."

A fantastic vacuum was opening, deep in my body—a need so desperate, I knew I could never control it. I *needed* to touch him! Yes, that's how I wanted to apologize—in the most meaningful, the most personal way possible!

He opened his shirt, pulled it over his arms, and tossed it onto a chair. I reached out and touched his stomach. It was covered with thick black hair—but the hair felt so soft—and the skin of his belly was tight over firm muscles. And warm! The excitement within me became a storm! My penis strained painfully, frantically hard against my pants. He opened the top snaps of his levis, inched the zipper down. I could see just the base of his cock, nestled in a thick tangle of black pubic hair. He reached into the spreading V...closed his fingers around his cock...inched it upward...then pulled it out!

A brilliant thrill lashed through my body!

Slowly I moved my hand down from his belly, down over the white hollow of his leg.... I slipped my hand slowly under his cock, cradled it in my palm, watched it jerk and grow harder, rising upward. It was beautiful! I'd never thought of a man's cock as beautiful, but his was—like a living piece of sculpture—almost like a holy thing.

I leaned forward, closing my eyes; felt the warm tight head of his cock touch my lips. I shuddered—but not with revulsion—now I trembled with hunger. I needed to take him inside me, take his cock into my mouth, to engulf it, *his cock!* The most beautiful, personal part of his body. I opened my mouth and took it in. He moaned softly. His hands touched my shoulders—and the touch felt so good!

"Suck it, Robert," he whispered. "Suck my cock, Robert." In my mind I could both feel and see his warm blood surging into his cock, swelling it thickly inside my mouth. "That feels so good, Robert...."

His hips started a slow easy rhythm, and with each gentle thrust his cock hardened and reached deeper and deeper into my mouth. His hands tightened on my shoulders. I cupped my hand under his balls, felt them tightening upward. Inside me fantastic sensations were swirling and building. "Oh, God!" His body tensed, his fingers dug hard into my shoulders—and then sweetness exploded! I felt his cock surging, felt thickness and heat shooting into my mouth! His semen came gushing out, out from his beautiful body, through his beautiful cock, to flood over my tongue—and I swallowed each starchy torrent like a man dying of thirst!

He moaned and leaned over me, breathing heavily; the warmth of his breath tingled my cheek. "Oh, yes...." He laughed weakly. "Oh, man, I needed that." He squeezed my shoulders. "And I needed *you* to do it, damn you. I was so fucking frustrated last night."

"I'm sorry."

He stood up and took a deep breath, then grinned down at me. "That's okay. You made up for it." He leaned over me again and gripped my shoulder—then his hand moved down my arm, to my leg. He knelt down before me, pushing me gently to lean back in the chair. He unfastened my belt, unzipped my pants, pulled them down. I stared at his face as he concentrated on tugging my shorts down, saw him grin as my cock flipped up. He tugged my hips forward—his touch was like fire on my buttocks. He leaned his head down. I gasped and closed my eyes as a warm flush spread slowly through me: the sweetest, most delicious feeling I could possibly imagine. He took my cock into his mouth slowly, deliberately, as my body flinched and trembled in the chair, inch by inch, until it was in him completely. A hand squeezed my balls and the other gripped one cheek of my ass, and his throat started constricting, milking my cock. I raised up in the chair and his mouth went down even further; my body convulsed, and I came! The sweet storm inside me went cascading out of my cock into him, one incredible explosion after another, until I collapsed in the chair, my arms like limp cloths dangling at my sides, my body feeling like a shapeless lump of flesh.

"You needed that too, didn't you?" The sound of his voice brought reality crashing back into my mind. I sat up in the chair, running my tongue over the slick residue of his semen still clinging to my teeth and the roof of my mouth. I clenched my teeth hard to keep from being sick. A voice whispered in my mind: *"Now you're just as rotten as I am."*

I opened my eyes and saw him, sprawled in a chair, his cock still hanging out of his gaping fly. I looked down at myself, saw my shorts and pants down around my ankles, my cock limp, shining wet, white semen still seeping out from it onto the chair. I stood quickly and turned my back to him, pulling my shorts and pants up.

"Something wrong?"

I shook my head, fighting to keep my voice steady. "No. Everything's just fine."

"Well, good," he drawled. "Cause that's how it should be." He sat up, grinning broadly. "How about another beer?"

All I wanted at that moment was to get out as quickly as possible; but I knew that I had to stay long enough to ask a couple of questions. I sat down again. "Sure."

He stood up and casually tucked his cock back into his levis, then sauntered over to the refrigerator. I watched him, thinking, *He's still beautiful!* But the voice in my head lashed at me: *"He's a pervert! And so are you!"*

He brought back the beer, then sank heavily into the chair. "Jesus, I'm exhausted."

I took a long drink, then set the can down with a thunk on the table. "Who are you?"

He looked up. "What?"

"Who are you?"

"What do you mean, *who am I?* I'm me. I don't..."

"What's your name?"

"Are you playing some kind of game? You know what my name is."

"Please! Just tell me your name."

"John Adams."

"Are you telling me the truth?"

"What is this, Robert? Of course I'm telling..."

"You're not Bill?"

"Bill?" He shook his head. "No, I'm not Bill. Who's Bill?"

"What did you mean...at the airport?"

"What, when I groped you?"

"No. You said I didn't know who you were. You said, 'You really don't know who I am, do you?' Tell me why you said that."

"Oh." He started to laugh, then apparently saw my expression. "Sorry," he said quickly. "This is something serious, isn't it?"

I nodded.

"Well...It can't hurt anything now. I wanted to scare you—that's all. I realized what a dumb thing I'd done and I thought maybe you might actually call the cops. And if you had...quite honestly, they *would* have believed me. You see, Robert, I'm an attorney."

I blinked at him stupidly, feeling cold all over. "An attorney?"

He nodded. "And there I was, doing the very thing I tell all my clients not to do—cruising the head—groping a guy in a public can. You don't believe me, do you?"

I shook my head miserably. "I don't know. Yes, I guess I do."

"Just a minute." He stood up and went into the hallway; when he came back he put a small white card into my hand: *John Christopher Adams: Attorney at Law.* The address was one of the professional buildings downtown. "Did you really think I was someone named Bill?"

I stood up, putting the card on the table. "Yes," I said. "That's why I asked if I knew you."

"And all this time, you thought... I don't know whether to be pleased or insulted."

"Neither," I said quickly. "Well...John. I think I'd better go."

"Do you have to?"

"Yes. My son's waiting."

"Okay." He followed me out to the front door. "Are we still on for dinner this week?"

I turned to look at him—naked to the waist, his body still bright with sweat. I wanted to say yes, but I knew that I couldn't. "I don't think so. But thanks."

He put his hand out and took mine to shake it firmly. "If it makes you feel better," he said, "I really enjoyed that. I'm sorry if you didn't."

"But I did, John. And that's the whole trouble." I hesitated, waiting to say more, but it seemed there was nothing more to be said. I stepped outside, glanced back at him. "Goodbye, John."

"Robert."

I hurried out to my car without looking back.

Chapter 5

Driving home I heard the churchbells again. Easter services letting out. I glanced into the rearview mirror at my own eyes. *Cocksucker!*

What a way to spend Easter!

It had all become too utterly ludicrous to be believed.

And I still had not found out who was sending those notes—who had stolen those pictures. But that no longer mattered. Nothing mattered. I was a robot driving the car, making all the appropriate motions, but not giving a damn what they accomplished. My life as I'd known it was finished. It might start again—or it might not—but it made not one bit of difference to me at that point whether it did or it didn't.

Chuck was gone when I got home. The note I had left him was on my bed, with a new message scrawled under mine: *Jerry came by to pick me up. Back around three. Chuck.*

I was glad he was gone. In the mood I was in there was nothing I could have said to him. I lay down on the bed, listening to the silence in the house, remembering John Adams and what I had done to him; but now there was no emotion whatever attached to the memory. I felt the exhaustion creeping up through my body and abandoned myself to it.

Some time later I heard the front door bell. I sat up, realizing I had been asleep. Drained and exhausted, I got up and went downstairs. This time when I saw the envelope under the door, I felt nothing. I was simply too weary to care any more. I picked it up, ripped it open, and unfolded the single sheet. Something small and white dropped onto the floor, but I ignored it and read the note:

DEAR ROBBER: IV DECIDED TO PUT YOU OUT OF YOR MISEREY. YOU CAN FOOL SOME PEEPLE BUT YOU CANT FOOL ME. BUT THAT DOSNT MATTER. YOUR DYING ANYWAY. YOUR BRAIN IS ROTTING. HA HA. SO HERE IS A LITTLE PRESENT FOR YOU, ROBBER. HA HA.

YOU KNOW WHO

I bent down to pick up the thing that had fallen—a small white capsule. I stared at it for a moment, then put it back into the note, which I carefully folded and reinserted into the envelope. I went back upstairs, put the envelope onto the dresser, then lay down again. As I drifted back into sleep, I thought about John Adams again; in my mind I saw him vividly, standing by the kitchen table. I laughed to myself. *I should have known* I thought. I should have known the minute he unzipped his fly. Bill's cock was much bigger than John Adams'. Much *much* bigger.

So the joke was on me. Ha-ha!

I sat up, wide-eyed, my heart pounding madly. My body was freezing cold, drenched with sweat.

I remembered a voice—laughter—ugly, evil laughter.

"Who's there?" I wanted to shout but my voice came out a strangled whisper. "Is anyone there?"

I told myself I was still in my bedroom—which made sense, because I was lying on top of a bed, and it seemed to be *my* bed—but the room was all hazy; I couldn't see the walls. The room was filled with shadows, evil, menacing shadows. I could hear someone breathing!

"Who is it?" My voice sounded tiny and lost, swallowed up by the shadows. "Answer me, please!"

No one answered.

I blinked hard, trying to focus my eyes. I could make out the edges of the windows—a brilliant light was shining around the edges of the blinds, so bright that I couldn't look into it—but it didn't penetrate the shadows.

And I knew someone was hiding in those shadows.

"Please!" I begged. "Please answer me! Who are you?"

No answer. Only that slow rasping breathing.

I struggled to move, to get up from the bed. If only I could get to the light switch, turn it on—then I could see who it was in the shadows. But I couldn't make my body respond. It felt disconnected, like beads on a string. I couldn't make it move! I'd forgotten how to move!

Was I still dreaming? Why couldn't I move?

Something was wrong with me—desperately wrong!

Why was my heart pounding? Why was I drenched with sweat?

Then I became aware of something in my hand, something crumpled. I managed to look down. One hand was clenched tightly around something. An envelope lay on the bed. I opened my hand. Slowly I brought my other hand over and extracted a wadded paper and shakily unfolded it; it was the latest note: *I've decided to let you kill yourself!*

"Oh my God!" I said aloud. Frantically I grabbed for the envelope, ripped it open. The pill wasn't inside it. I looked all around on the bed, shook the paper. That little white capsule was gone!

Someone laughed.

I looked up. The shadows were thicker—and closer! They were gathering around the bed, moving in on me. They were whispering, *"Robber...Robber...you're going to die!"*

"No!"

"Die, Robber, die!"

"NO!" I screamed. *"Get away from me!"*

"Die! Die!"

"GET AWAY! GET AWAY!"

Madly I scrambled over the bed, tumbled onto the floor. *I'm still asleep! This isn't really happening! Dear God, please! Don't let it be happening!*

But I knew it was too late to pray. I knew I had poisoned myself. I was going to die.

"Our Father....who...who art..."

"Die, Robber, die!"

"Our Father....in Heaven...hallowed..."

I couldn't remember the words!

Something was slipping away. I didn't know what it was, but I could feel it slipping—draining out of me!

Now I could barely make my voice work!

"Somebody....help...me!...*Please!!!*"

Suddenly it seemed I was floating above myself, up near the ceiling, looking down. I could see myself clearly, spotlighted, cringing like a terrified animal, curled up on the floor. I understood, in a very detached way, that my body was dying. For all practical purposes it was already dead. Poisoned. I hovered there, floating peacefully, waiting for my body to finally die. I heard my voice whimpering, "Father...forgive me...."

Silly, pathetic man, I thought. *Doesn't he know that he's already dead?*

Then I heard a strange sound, a wild clattering; the echoes of it crashed through the room, piercing my head like raw bolts of lightning. Through the clattering I heard a voice: "Dad! Dad! Dad! Daddad-daddaddaddad!!!"

I was back in my body again. The voice was getting closer. I knew the voice, remembered it from somewhere. It was a friendly voice, not evil, not threatening. The name *Chuck* came into my mind, but I couldn't remember who Chuck was.

I found I could uncurl myself—my body felt solid again, only slightly disarranged. I could move my arms, uncover my eyes so I could look at the door. In the process I had to look over my own body—and I saw I was naked!

Abruptly the room changed. The walls became black, moved away. There were dim orange aureoles hanging in black space. A policeman was coming up the stairs to arrest me. Any moment now the door would crash open and he'd rush in with his gun in his hand. Someone had told them about me and now they were coming to get me! They would put me away in a room in a dungeon, chain me up to the wall. They would torture me, cut parts away from my body, make me confess to my sins.

The door banged open. Light exploded above me, blinding me. I screamed and covered my eyes as the pain swept like fire into my brain. "Dad!"

I curled myself tightly again, holding my breath, praying that he wouldn't see me, that he'd look around, decide there was no one here, and go away. I didn't want to be tortured! I knew I had sinned, knew I had to be punished, but not that way!

I felt hands on my shoulders—warm and sticky. I went limp. Let him think I was already dead; let him think he was too late to torture me!

"Dad, answer me!" That didn't sound like any policeman's voice! I sneaked my eyes open to look at him, but all I could see were feet and legs. He shook me hard, forced my body to uncurl, but I stayed limp, allowing him to straighten my body on the floor, lay me out on my back. "What's wrong with you? Dad! Goddammit! Answer me!"

Chuck!

It was Chuck! My son!

I was naked and my son was touching me, looking at me! *God forgive me!*

I tried to curl back into a ball, but his hands held me flat. "Please," I begged. "Go...away."

"Dad, what the hell is the matter? *Tell me!*"

His voice was so forceful, so determined, I couldn't help answering. "I...took something."

"What did you take?"

"I don't know. It was...p–p–p–" I tried desperately to say *poison*, but all I could manage was "p–pill... pilllll."

"What kind of pill? Dad, tell me!"

"W-white."

"Oh, Jesus!"

He jumped up and rushed to the dresser. I leaned up and watched him, thoroughly confused. He pulled out a bottom drawer and reached inside. I remembered doing the same thing myself, but I couldn't recall what I had found.

At first he looked frightened, and that frightened me, but when he stood up and turned to look down at me, he was *smiling!* He was shaking his head slowly, back and forth, smiling! "You found my stash, didn't you?"

"What?"

"My stash. My caps. You found them."

"In...a bottle?" I asked–it was so hard to make my voice work. Years seemed to pass between the time that I thought the words and the time that I actually said them.

"About so big. With six caps, right?"

"I...don't remember," I lied–I remembered it clearly. I remembered counting the little white capsules. I remembered the one in the envelope. The conclusion was obvious: Chuck had poisoned me! Chuck had written those notes, left those pictures, and then he had stolen them back from their hiding place and put poison there instead, knowing I would find it.

And as I looked up at my son, he changed. He grew larger and his face lengthened. Deep hollows appeared under his cheeks and around his eyes. His skin became transparent and I could see his naked skull leering down at me. He was Satan!

They had taken my son and put Satan himself in his place! Satan would torture me, cut me apart—not the police!

I screamed and tried to crawl under the bed, but he caught my legs, dragging me out, yelling, "Stop it! *Dad!*"

"Leave me alone! Let me die!"

Suddenly he slapped me, hard! Lights and colors and screaming sounds exploded in the room! "You're not dying!" he yelled. "Don't even *think* it!" I tried to crawl in another direction, but he caught me again. "Do you hear me? Dad—*do you hear me?*"

"*Yes!*" I yelled. "Yes! Yes! *Yesssssssss!*"

"Now stop it or I'll clobber you! So help me!"

I went limp, collapsed. He knelt close beside me, his hands on my shoulders. Warm hands, not cold. Satan's hands would be cold—or burning hot—but these hands were just warm. Human hands. Maybe it really was Chuck after all.

"Listen to me. Are you listening? You're not dying, you're just stoned! Do you understand that?"

If men lie together, let them be stoned! Had Isaiah said that, or had it been Jeremiah?

But it didn't make sense. I'd been poisoned, not stoned.

"You're okay, Dad. Believe me, you're okay."

I couldn't help laughing. "I'm...not...*okay!* I've been...poisoned!"

He slapped me again. "That was *mescaline!* That's all!"

"What?"

"Mescaline! Dope! Now settle down, please! Do you trust me, Dad?"

"Trust you?"

"Yes. Do you trust me?"

"I don't...know."

"You've got to! Please. I know how to handle it, Dad. I know how to help you. But you've got to trust me!"

"I don't... Yes! Oh, God! I...don't...know! I *want* to."

"All right, then, do it! Trust me. I know what I'm doing."

"How?"

"Oh, shit! Because I've *taken* it."

"You've...?"

"Yes, man it's just mescaline."

"*Just???*"

"I know you don't understand it, Dad, but it's true. It won't hurt you."

"It's...terrible!"

"Only if you make it terrible! You're forcing yourself on a bummer. Just relax and you'll be okay. Dad, I promise you, you'll be okay. Believe me."

I nodded. I wanted to believe him. I wanted to trust him.

"Can you sit up?"

I remembered I was naked. "No!"

"Sure you can. Come on."

"No...Chuck, I...I don't want to."

"Why not?"

"I... You'll *see* me!"

"Oh, for... What does that mean? I see you right now! You're not invisible, man."

"I'm naked!"

"Oh, wow! So what else is new?"

"Don't laugh at me!"

"I'm not laughing, but Dad, you're not making sense. I've *seen* you."

"But I'm *naked!*"

His hands gripped my arms. "Dammit! I don't give a

fuck! Now sit *up!*" He jerked me up and leaned me back against the bed. I covered myself with my hands.

But somehow I felt calmer. Partly because I had a new problem to deal with: My son had said "*fuck*". He'd said, "*I don't give a fuck!*"

"You...s-said a bad word." Even as I said it, the old-maidish prudishness of it appalled me!

"*What?*"

"Bad word."

"Dad, come on! Don't get hung up on that."

"But...you... You...said..." Now I couldn't even remember the bad word he had said.

He knelt down again, this time with his face close to mine. I looked into his brown eyes. They were so deep! It seemed that if I wanted, I could dive right into one of them. I'd never seen eyes so rich...or so deep...or so *beautiful!* "Hey," he said quietly. "Will you listen to me, man? I mean, just listen, and don't get hung up with *things*, okay? Just listen a minute."

I nodded unsurely. His voice was so patient and calm that I couldn't maintain any anger with him. His calmness reached out to me, spread over me and seeped into my body and mind.

"Okay, now just listen. All you have done is dropped dope, okay? Now I know how you feel about dope because you've swallowed all the shit they—sorry—all the *stuff* they put out on it. But that's all crap, Dad! I mean, sure, some people O.D., and that's it, but you just took a cap, and it's just pure stuff. No speed or strychnine or anything like that. It's not acid and it's not snow or coke or anything. It's just mescaline. Okay?"

"Chuck..."

"You promised you'd listen."

"I'm listening, but..."

"Please, Dad, just hang in, please. I'm trying to explain it."

I couldn't help laughing again. He looked puzzled, then angry. I reached out and took his arm. "Chuck, I'm sorry."

"Jesus Christ, I'm just trying to *help* you!"

"I...*know that*...son! *I know.* But...I...can't... understand...a w-word you're...saying!"

He grinned. Then he laughed—and I laughed with him. We sat on the floor of my bedroom, me stark naked, with my sixteen-year-old son's arm clutched in my hand, laughing like fools! Every time we would start to compose ourselves, we'd look at each other and laugh again.

And as we laughed, all the darkness passed. The fear withered away and went scuttling out the door and down the stairs and out of the house. I felt a beautiful calmness beginning to settle. My body felt solid again, part of me. And I realized how silly, how utterly foolish I'd been acting. All these years I'd been trying to "protect" Chuck by never letting him see my naked body! Always closing the doors, wearing those ridiculous uncomfortable pajamas, or my bathrobe, or something. Something covering up my terrible, shameful body!

Why?

Why had I ever felt that my body was shameful or terrible? God made man in his own image! *His Own Image!* The idea seemed totally new to me, although I knew I had known it all of my life. I could quote chapter and verse. And yet it had never even occurred to me the true implication of the words: IN THE IMAGE OF GOD CREATED HE HIM!"

I felt that I'd discovered one of the most momentous truths in the history of mankind.

Or if not for all mankind, at least for myself, because it meant that *I, me,* Robert Randolph Thorne, had been created in the image of God.

My own Church had taught me that!

As man is, God once was; as God is, man may become.

Why hadn't I believed it? What possible *right* did I have to be ashamed of my body? That would mean that I was ashamed of God!

And that seemed to me to be a sin far worse than anything else I could think of—short of murder. How utterly petty it suddenly seemed to feel guilty for drinking vodka...or coffee...or for that matter, having sex with John Adams! How cosmically inconsequential such things must seem to a God who created man. A God with such vast understanding that he knew how to *create* a living man could not possibly be ignorant of all the problems a man of flesh was heir to. If my own church's doctrine were true, then God had gone through it Himself!

But how terrible, how loathsome, to be *ashamed* of God! And I had been. Ashamed of myself. And by logical extension, that meant I'd been ashamed of my Creator. Clearly that was the sin that I had to repent of.

Suddenly a memory presented itself, brilliantly clear: One day in the fifth grade—it had been springtime; I remembered a flock of robins were where I could see them, out on the greening lawn—our teacher, Miss Bartlet, had brought a very special book to school. We'd been studying *ART*, and this, she said, was the most beautiful art of all, and she'd brought it from her own special collection of books at home. She'd split us up into groups and had one group come up to the big table to look at the book while the others were working on problems.

I could *see* the classroom and Miss Bartlet so clearly! I hadn't thought about Miss Bartlet for...twenty years! And I could see the book. A beautiful, expensive book, with a red cover, wine-red, with gold leaves and stems twining all around one name: *Michelangelo.*

I could understand now that Miss Bartlet had made a basic error of judgment. A teacher in a small country-town school doesn't show pubescent children "naked pictures". At least, not back in those days she didn't.

There were hundreds of pictures—some in beautiful soft colors—of *naked* people! Oh, of course they were statues, and paintings, and drawings, but to us they were *people*, and they were naked, and we giggled and sniggered, and afterward, out in the play-yard, we'd poked one another in the crotches and giggled all over again. We giggled because the pictures had frightened us and we didn't know what else to do. One in particular had frightened me, shocked me more than I'd ever been shocked about anything: a drawing which said under it: *The Risen Christ.* And it showed a muscular man, stark naked, rising up out of a tomb, with a cloth falling away from him. In Church, all the pictures of Jesus had him clothed. Usually he had on long robes where all you could see were his face and his hands and feet. Even on the cross he was wearing a thick cloth wrapped around him to hide the *offending* parts of his body.

My God! How blasphemous to be ashamed of Christ's body!

Of course, I'd told Bill about the book, and, just goading him because he took it so seriously, I'd told him about *The Risen Christ.* And he had told Dad—good old Dad. Good old holier-than-anyone, wife-hating, children-hating, God-loving Dad. And the next day we'd had a new teacher, the one we called Miss Grump—Miss Gray, wrinkled like a prune, with her high screechy voice saying, "What are you giggling about back there? I will not have giggling in this classroom!" Miss Grump who slapped our hands with our rulers and gave us demerits if we had to go to the bathroom and we couldn't get a good mark on our report cards if we had too many demerits. Miss Grump, who said, "Art is for artists," and refused to be tricked into a question about Michelangelo, *or* what had happened to Miss Bartlet. We never saw Miss Bartlet again.

I remembered my father looking smug for weeks after that. Years later, he'd told me he'd had the woman fired–still smugly, still proud of the fact that he'd rid Glen Falls of an Evil Menace. What kind of man could be proud of his own shame? And what kind of fool had I been to allow that man to teach me that shame, to wrap it up in a bright package and say "Here, son, with my blessings"? He had cursed me with his sin!

And I had been trying to curse Chuck with mine!

I wanted to tell Chuck something of the astounding ideas that had been flying through my mind, but I realized that I'd have to explain the ideas, and amplify them, tell him when and how–and I couldn't.

"You okay?"

"Yes, I'm fine."

A sweet voice sang in my mind: *Everything's all right. Everything's fine.*

"Help me up...will you, son?"

"Sure thing. Feeling better?"

"Much."

"Groovy."

"Yes," I chuckled. "Groovy."

And I did, I felt *groovy.* I felt *good.* I couldn't remember feeling this good–this *aware* of myself, of my body and its senses–for a long, long time. I felt strong, and tall, and supremely healthy!

Chuck helped me to stand, and I saw us in the mirror, with me facing it, Chuck turned away. I studied myself; I *looked* good!

"Okay?" Chuck asked.

I turned to look into his eyes. He was smiling, but his eyes showed concern–and something else, something I'd never really seen before, not in Chuck's eyes, not in anyone's–I saw *love!* I saw it and felt it. My son loved me; his eyes said it beyond doubt. My son was concerned for me. My son wanted to help me! And my son didn't give a *fuck* if I was naked or not!

Tears welled up in my eyes and I started to turn away. All the garbage out of my past bubbled up in me, making me ashamed again, this time of my tears, my emotion. Man must not cry, must not show his emotions, must keep everything hidden, his body, his genitals, his emotions, everything! Everything that makes him the least bit worthwhile to his fellow man.

I had dreamed of a man in a black hat and a black overcoat. He had thrown off the overcoat, thrown off his shame, and had risen, like Michelangelo's *Risen Christ*, up into the sky, naked and free. And the man had said to me: "I am you, you fool!"

And there I stood, naked—and feeling more *free* than I'd ever felt! With tears trailing down over my cheeks I squeezed my son's arm and said, "Thank you, Chuck."

He blinked unsurely and shrugged. "What the hell, right?"

I laughed and wept at the same time. "Right.... What the hell?"

Chuck glanced away, blinking, and I realized I was embarrassing him. And with that I also realized what a shock it must have been to him, to hear me yelling at shadows, to come racing up the stairs thinking someone was killing me, only to find me cringing like an animal on the floor. What an overwhelming responsibility he had automatically assumed, to talk me out of my irrational terrors. What grown man would have done it? Could have done it? Surely none that I knew—and that included most of the good Mormons I knew. They'd have gone screaming for the ambulance. Or, worse, if they'd realized what had actually happened, that I'd swallowed "dope", they'd have gone for the police. And now to see his father weeping, on top of everything else, of course it embarrassed him.

"Well..." I said, concentrating hard on putting the words together, "I think...maybe...I can manage...to get dressed." He glanced up at me, grinning. "I still...feel... foolish...even if you...don't care."

"Hey, man," he said quickly, "you shouldn't. No. I mean, you know...I mean, you look just fine."

The tears started again and I moved quickly to the closet. My body still felt slightly awkward, but I found if I didn't try to concentrate on what I was doing, my arms and my legs would do it themselves, automatically. It seemed to take an hour for me to decide what to wear; then I finally decided to copy Chuck's costume; it seemed somehow appropriate: old levis and faded blue shirt—my gardening outfit.

And to hell with shorts!

I'd suddenly become extremely aware of my body, of the pressures and textures of clothes on it. It felt so fantastically good just slipping my old levis on over my legs. And I decided to just let my penis—my *cock* and my *balls*—hang free. From now on, the less I "bundled up" the better I'd like it! It felt marvelous just to move, just to breathe! I'd never imagined the human body could feel so deliciously sensual.

Now that I'd pulled myself more-or-less together, now that Chuck had talked me out of my "bummer", I was beginning to notice all sorts of wonderful, fascinating things: the way things around me took on whole new dimensions. *Light* became a phenomenal thing; *colors* were breathtaking, spellbinding! Things I had seen every day, such as clothes in the closet, the bedspread, the rugs, suddenly seemed totally new to me. The colors and patterns and shapes presented themselves to me like precious gifts—gifts I had blindly ignored until now. Everything I looked at seemed to assume a brand-new *reality*, a "higher" reality than the one I'd been living in.

I had the feeling that I'd done something particularly special and as a reward, mysteries were being revealed to me; hidden truths about the nature and meaning of sizes and shapes, of patterns and colors and textures, became brilliantly clear to me—not in words that I could have expressed, but in understanding, in true appreciation.

It wasn't as though these truths were "new" in any sense of the word; obviously they had existed within each particular thing for as long as that thing itself had existed—and perhaps much, much longer, since the very beginning of anything. I was only now able to perceive and appreciate what had been here all along. At the same time, it seemed that I'd always known those truths, deep in some subconscious, unconscious well of knowledge. There was even a feeling that I'd seen all these things, thought all these thoughts, some time long ago.

Chuck's voice brought me suddenly back from my flight into colors and lights and new/old memories: "I mean...I've always wondered, you know?"

It seemed to me that thousands of years had passed since I'd last heard Chuck talking, and I hadn't the slightest idea what he was talking about. "Wondered... what?"

"About you."

"What about me?"

"Well, you know—what you, you know, looked like."

"Oh."

"I mean, you know, this house has been so fuck—I'm sorry! I didn't.. "

"Chuck," I said, turning to face him, "if...you use... the word with...your...your friends...use it with me... because I want to be your...friend. Okay?"

"Oh, wow! Hey, don't blow my mind all the way, man!"

"Sorry."

He chuckled. "It's okay. It's kind of wild, having your old man blow your mind. Wow!"

He was silent for a while, as I went to the dresser for socks.

"Oh, yeah," he said softly. "What I started to say was important. Because, like, this house, you know, has been so uptight that I've wanted to just stand up and yell at you, you know? And Mom. Both of you. I mean, what's the big deal? What's the point? You know?"

I leaned on the dresser and waited for him to explain himself; when he didn't I said, "No...I don't...know. What are you...talking about?"

"About you! You know...bare-ass, you know? I mean naked. I mean, what's the mystery? Jeez, I've seen naked people before. But here it's like, well, like some, I don't know, big terrific...*secret* or something. Like you didn't see me when I was born or something, or never had to take me to the toilet. You know?"

"Yes. I know."

"Hey, wow!" He laughed and hugged himself delightedly. "I'm actually *talking* to you! I'm sitting here *talking* to my old man! Oh, Jesus, that's beautiful! That really is beautiful." He lay back on the bed, chuckling and turning from side to side. I laughed, just watching him.

When he sat up he shook his head and said, "Yeah, well, I just wanted to say you looked okay. Like Jerry's old man, I mean he's got a pot out to here and he runs around their house in his shorts, even when kids are there. But you look...groovy. I just wanted to say it, that's all."

"Thank you, Chuck."

He shrugged and looked down again and nodded. "It's cool." He stood up quickly. "Hey, was I right?"

"About what?"

"Feelin' good. You feel good, don't you?"

I nodded. "I feel...*wonderful!*"

"Oh, wow! Yeah, you can tell. Man your eyes are like...like fuckin' stars! Hey, I know! Look, can you move?"

I laughed. "Haven't I...been moving?"

"I mean walk, you know, like outside?"

"Outside?" The idea should have terrified me, but it didn't. I knew I was drugged, but I felt a fantastic sense of self-confidence. If Chuck had asked me, "Do you think you could fly?" I would have seriously considered it. "All right," I said. "I...think I can." I hesitated. "Do *you* think...I can? You know...more about this...than I do."

"It strictly depends. I can do it. But like Jerry just gets bombed. It's wherever your head is. If you think you can, then you can. Don't worry, I'll watch out for, you know...things. Anyways, we won't go far. Just up the block, there's this place where I go when I'm tripping." Suddenly a strange expression came onto his face and he seemed about to step back away from me. "Oh, wow!"

"What?"

He shook his head, started toward the door, hesitated, turned: "You know what I just flashed on? When I said that—about when I go tripping? I expected you to clobber me. And you didn't. And that blew my mind." He sniffed and cleared his throat, keeping his face turned away from me. "I'll, uh, be right back, okay?" He spun around and hurried out. I followed him to the door, watched him duck into the bathroom and close the door. Moments later I heard him blow his nose, and I guessed he'd been on the verge of tears himself.

It hadn't even occurred to me to hit him! And yet, thinking about it, I knew that I would have, if I hadn't been "stoned". I had taught my son to be afraid of telling the truth! I had taught him to lie and to cheat and to hide and to sneak out behind my back. I had taught him that when he did tell the truth to expect to be "clobbered" for his efforts.

We were strangers to each other, Chuck and I. Total strangers. It was deeply disturbing to suddenly realize that Chuck knew no more about me and my life and my private thoughts—those that really mattered—than I knew about his. I had shut him almost totally out of my life, and by doing that, had forced him to shut me out of his—as surely as though I'd deliberately planned it!

What an absolute idiot I had been!

I could not understand, could not truly comprehend, how I had lived for thirty-five years without once having realized what a damned fool I had been! It was so patently, painfully *obvious* now! I saw clearly that all of my life I'd been digging a cave for myself—a private, dark, unhappy, miserable little cave where I could hide from myself and from people, from everything! And I'd *forced* myself to stay locked inside it.

With other people's *garbage* piled up over that cave's door! My father's garbage. My mother's garbage. Kate's. Ed's. And my own. Yes, I couldn't blame others for all of the garbage; a good part of it was my own.

I wasn't sure how to get out of my cave—to crawl out from under the garbage—but I knew that I had to. No wonder I constantly told myself I felt "rotten"! I had every reason to feel that way. Anything else, stuck away, buried like that, would have rotted thirty years ago! Perhaps, I thought, it said something about the human spirit to realize how well mine had survived suffocation and premature burial.

Chuck came out of the bathroom, giggling about something, and my mood instantly shifted up into a brighter level. Seeing Chuck happy was something new and delightful to me. But then, I supposed, seeing me happy was an equally "mind-blowing" experience for him.

"We gotta hurry," he said, "or we'll miss it." He started down the stairs. "I saw it out the window. Wait'll you see."

"What is this...this wonderful thing...we're going to look at?"

He looked up with a frown and said, "The sunset!"—as though I'd been the dunce of the world to ask such a dumb question.

The sunset! Of course!

My son Chuck, looking at sunsets?

Why not? What was so outrageous about that? Yes, of course! My beautiful son looking at beautiful sunsets! How long would it take to get it through my thick head that Chuck could not possibly be the monster I'd made him in my miserable imagination? Perhaps the children had indeed discovered a secret their parents had forgotten, or lost. I hated to think that it might be a drug, but that had to remain a possibility. At least it was better than alcohol.

That thought started another one bounding around in my mind as I carefully went down the stairs: Chuck was sixteen. I had started to drink when I was eleven! Eleven years old. I clearly remembered taking my first shot of *Four Roses* out behind old man Witherspoon's barn. I and five other kids my same age. We'd got falling-down, throwing-up drunk and gone stealing watermelons—after first tipping over Mr. Witherspoon's outhouse. And I'd had my first cigarette that night, too. A Fatima. I, myself, had stolen the pack from the drug store.

And Chuck took a pill that made him feel happy. In the total scheme of things, that no longer seemed so enormously alarming. I'd never got drunk and gone out to look at a sunset! I'd got drunk and gone out to look for trouble.

It was far more alarming to realize that it had taken that drug to make me understand myself—or begin to understand myself.

I followed Chuck out of the house—and into one of the most exquisite experiences of my life! *Trees! Flowers! Green leaves*—every possible shade of green. And coolness. The textures of a sidewalk! A lawn-sprinkler, in fading sunlight, became the most dazzlingly beautiful fountain I'd ever seen; millions of droplets of liquid gold on the deep-deep green grass—spiralling into the air—falling! Chuck had to call to me twice to keep me moving.

Halfway through the block, the street climbed steeply up a sharp rise in the hill, and on top of the rise was a vacant lot, with a huge, ugly *For Sale* sign, with a *Sold* sign tacked over it, and rank weeds overgrowing the burned-out remains of the house that had once stood there. (I remembered the house and the night it had burned down.) Chuck led me into the lot, waist-deep in last summer's weeds. I'd long since forgotten what we'd come out to look for, and I thought it might be something in the ruins. They were fascinating. Water-pipes sticking up, rusted and twisted. Smoke-blackened bricks of the basement where someone had scratched *Fuck You* in the soot. Children, probably. I'd known the word at the age of seven,—long before I'd had the slightest idea of what it meant—and I knew that long before I reached puberty. At Chuck's age I was laying Jenny Lou—or Mildred Robbins—or Grace Schulz—or that waitress, what the hell was her name? Carla Something—at least every other week. And I'd already had at least two blowjobs, courtesy of Noel Becker.

Somehow I'd forgotten all that. Somehow I'd managed to pretend that Chuck was still some kind of infant, blissfully ignorant of all the things I'd known long before I was his age. I'd gone skulking around, taking a totally unnecessary trip to San Francisco, sneaking back a full day ahead of my schedule, in order to trick my son into committing an act that I had performed on his uncle when Bill was fourteen. And if I remembered correctly, at least half of the boys in my scout troop "cornholed" each other on our numerous outings. And at least half of those had been with Noel Becker at least once. But that had been *then*, in the past, in a memory, not real any more, and I'd insanely expected my son to be miraculously different.

If I'd respected myself in the least, I'd have realized that Chuck couldn't possibly turn out any worse than I had for undergoing the same kinds of experience. But perhaps that was part of the problem—perhaps more than just part; perhaps almost all of the problem—the fact that I didn't respect myself. I hadn't even liked myself. How had I expected Chuck—or anyone else—even Kate—to like me if I didn't like myself?

"Hey, Dad, turn around."

I turned to face him. "What?"

"Look." He pointed toward the west.

I turned—and the panorama exploded into my mind! Colors! Lights! I was wrenched out of my private world and scattered all over the city, all over the countryside!

A small rounded paring of the sun was still visible over the black jagged rim of the world, out beyond the Great Salt Lake, blinding, pulsing red; and that color was reflected in a long brilliant trail through the dark lake. Above the horizon were thin clouds, floating like bright golden cobwebs around the sun, shifting and changing their patterns as I watched. The sky all across the horizon was dull white, turning grey, silhouetting the black mountains as though they were pieces of a stage setting, lit from behind. Their long-long shadows stretched out almost to the city, where thousands of houses stood out in stark relief, glowing all around their etched edges with the light on their west sides that I couldn't see. All the way down 13th there were red and green traffic lights, brilliant as bright stars on a summer night, changing colors in strangely meaningful patterns, with bright little explosions of orange as they changed. And the cars on the streets were turning their lights on, and the lights were like fireflies floating toward me.

I looked up, straight above me—and fell helplessly into the color of foggy violet! Helplessly into an incredible vastness of sky! As I watched, darkness deepened, creeping up from the east; the color lost its fogginess and became a fantastically soft purple, and then ultramarine; and then a star, just the tiniest pinpoint, started to sparkle, and then more. I felt the light fade from my face. The stars brightened. The sky deepened. The universe opened above me. I understood why poets had called stars "candles". I could understand why the ancients had believed that God hung out the stars—I could almost see an unseeable hand tossing them out into the heavens as a farmer would toss wheat into his field. And it seemed as though that Cosmic Farmer was sowing His stars just to please me, to delight me—and to remind me of His reality, unseeable though He might be.

The stars became intensely personal and enormously meaningful. They seemed, literally, *my stars,* because I felt I was part of the same thing they were part of—everything! And it seemed we had always been part of that totality. Perhaps we had shifted positions, been born and grown old and died and been born again, but the whole was unchanging, eternal—or if it did change, it did so in a way, at a rate which my limited mind could not grasp—any more than it could grasp the meaning of *eternity.* I felt tiny and huge at the same time. Infinitesimal in one sense, boundless in another. A tiny speck on a tiny speck in a cluster of tiny specks floating in an unimaginably vast universe—and yet each speck was like a particle of an atom, and the atom was part of a molecule, and a molecule was a part of...whatever. *Something.* That I couldn't comprehend what that *something* might be was no more alarming than the idea that an atom in my own body could not comprehend me. I laughed at the idea of atoms feeling so self-important that they had the audacity to "know" the thing they were part of.

Chuck's voice drifted into my thoughts, returning me to earth, to the vacant lot, and the dark, cooling ruins of the burned-out house. "What?" I asked.

"You were laughing."

"Oh." I tried to remember what I'd been laughing about. Parts of it came back, but not the whole thing. I looked up into the sky again and said, "I wonder if God even knows when a speck of Him does something."

I realized what I had said and looked at Chuck, fully expecting him to say, "Oh, shit, religion!" Instead, he looked up and nodded his head. "One trip I had," he said softly, "I felt like I really knew. You know? Like I understood the whole thing, but just couldn't tell anyone. And it was like, well, maybe He didn't know, not the way we do, but He knew just the same. Like He *felt* it."

"Do you honestly believe in God, Chuck?"

He said, "Oh, sure," as though he were saying, "Thank you for passing the salt," as though it had never occurred to him not to believe. "I just don't understand Him, that's all. But man, what does that mean? Like you take the world—or those stars. Now, man, I don't know what a star is! Fuck what they teach you in school, man, *I don't know.* Sure, they're suns—but what the hell is a *sun?* I just know they're stars, and, like I say, 'hey, groovy,' you know? But that doesn't change them, or make them real or not real, just because I say, 'hey, stars, man! Wow!' Like these guys going around telling everybody they know what's coming down. Man, they don't know one damn thing more than I do—and that's *nothing!* Some cat told me the other day I was going to Hell, and I just looked at him, you know? I mean, what can you say to a dumb thing like that?"

I stared at my son for a long time, and then turned away, looking out over the city; it was starting to sparkle.

"Like today," Chuck said, "Jerry's folks made him go to Church, you know, *mass,* because it was Easter, and he's Catholic, and they have some kind of big deal thing, you know, about the resurrection and all that. He laughed. "But you know what that dumb nut did? He sneaked out and blew a joint in the bathroom. He told me it wasn't a bad trip at all if you got stoned—all those robes and candles and that organ. That's when he came by for me, after church." He stood up. "I'm sorry I wasn't here when you got home."

"Well," I said, shrugging my shoulders, "that's how it goes, right?"

"Yeah, right."

"Besides..." I hesitated, not sure that I wanted to say the thing I was thinking—but it needed to be said: "If you'd been there, none of this would have happened, would it? Right now we'd probably be stomping around the house hating each other."

"Dad...I couldn't *hate* you. Get pissed off at you, maybe, but..."

"Well, you know what I mean."

"Yeah, right. Well...things work out right, you know? I mean they really do."

We started back down the hill, walking slowly, side by side. I had an impulse to put my arm around Chuck's shoulder, and for a moment I resisted it—but then, when I couldn't think of a single good reason why I shouldn't, I did. He turned to me and grinned. He was almost as tall as I was, and, God, he was a handsome young man! I felt so proud for having sired such a fantastically beautiful manchild!

Back in the house Chuck suggested that we listen to music. Just "light stuff"—as opposed to the "heavier trip" which he had decreed I was not yet ready for. At first I was very reluctant. I'd heard his music before and didn't even consider it music—just a lot of loud banging and twanging and screeching and wailing. But I'd made up my mind to go along with whatever he decided, to trust him as honestly as he'd honestly asked me to. As it turned out, my reluctance quickly faltered and flew away under the onslaught of the music, and I totally lost myself to a world I had never suspected existed. And this time it was a brand new, virginal experience! I'd seen sunsets before (though never so beautiful) but

I'd never really *listened* to rock music. And after the first album, I found it impossible to reconcile what I was listening to with what I had heard before. The Beatles made sense! And that truly amazed me. Some young men named Crosby, Stills, Nash and Young sang fantastically beautiful songs, some so true and piercing that I wept—and I wept without shame. Because those songs became the most intensely *personal* experiences I'd ever had. The singers sang to *me!* They told me about things I had known all my life, about love and beauty and caring, precious things I had thought gone forever from the world—as they truly had in the world I'd been living in; but in Chuck's world they were alive and well. More than that, they were happy! No—*happy* is an empty word compared to the pure joy that those singers gave to me. "We love you," they said, "we really do." And the sounds I had once thought were banging and twanging soared through my head like rivers of rainbows, augmenting and proving the love that the singers proclaimed. *Love one another. Love us. Love yourself. Love the world.* And, to my utter amazement, they even sang about loving God! I understood what Chuck had meant with his expression "mind-blowing" when a man George Harrison said, "You don't need a church-house..."

As Simon and Garfunkle, unlike their names, built a jeweled silver bridge far out in vast space, Chuck started a fire, turned out all the lights, and then sat cross-legged on the floor, watching me. When the last cut of the last album had played, he got up and turned off the set. For several long minutes a tense silence built up in the room. I could *feel* a reluctance—almost a fear—coming from my son.

Finally he sat down on the floor again, facing me. "Dad...when are you going to get to hell out of here?"

I sat up slowly and leaned back against the couch. "What do you mean, Chuck?"

"Dad...you know what I mean."

I did; I knew precisely what he meant; but I found I was still very reluctant to admit it.

"Look, I don't want to start you on a bummer, but, you know, I...I've just got to say it, Dad. I've been wanting to say it for so damn long...."

I took a deep breath and steadied myself. "Then say it, Chuck."

"Please don't get sore. I don't mean it bad any way. I mean, I...well, I just think...oh, shit!"

"Go ahead, Chuck. You think I should give your mother a divorce."

He nodded, looking very unhappy. "Yeah. I do. I mean, why make everybody miserable just because... well, you know, because the two of you can't get along? That's dumb. I mean..."

"Yes," I said softly. "I guess it is dumb."

He leaned forward. "Do you really?"

I nodded. "I guess I've known it was dumb for a long time, Chuck."

"Well...why didn't you do something about it?"

"I didn't know what to do."

"Dad, you do what you do when *anything* goes bad. You just let it go."

"What about you and the girls?"

"Oh, come on, Dad. I may be a dumb kid, but, man, I'm not stupid! I know where Mom goes in the afternoons."

"Where she goes?" That she went anywhere in particular was news to me.

"Don't you know?" he asked.

"I'm not sure. I don't know what you're going to tell me."

"Oh, wow, you mean...? Dad, she sees *him.*"

"Ed?"

"Right."

"On Thursday afternoons," I said quickly, as a new

piece fitted itself into the puzzle. "When he goes to play golf."

"I don't know what he tells you, but they both go to his place. Dad, they really dig each other—and you don't—so why don't you just let it happen?"

I leaned back and looked up at the ceiling, asking myself why it had never occurred to me that Kate and Ed might love one another? I'd been so tied up in my own misery as the cuckolded husband, the put-upon substitute father for two bastard daughters—*blaming them!* Blaming everyone but myself for my problems. Was it possible that Kate and Ed were actually in love with each other? Did Ed love Cindy and Dorene?

Mentally I slapped myself! What an assinine question! Of course he would love them! He was their father.

And me! Arrogant, garbage-inundated, self-hating *me*, had deliberately stood in the way of his claiming his own. If Kate had sinned in loving another man, I had outdone her a hundred times over by standing in their way. No wonder she hated me! No wonder she couldn't stop herself from teaching the girls to hate me too. She had every reason for hating me. How could I have been so completely blind and stupid?

In this new light of self-revelation, I was forced to reconsider Kate's "sin". All these years I'd been thinking of her as a "wanton" woman; it was far more likely that she'd been a "wanting" woman. Chuck had been born during my first year of college, and even though we'd both been delighted to have a child, still he'd been unplanned, and his birth had required Kate's quitting her secretarial position and my taking on two separate part-time jobs. I'd resented the extra work and had blamed it on her "carelessness". My interest in sex had become almost nil since that night with my brother, and I had easily convinced myself that our sexual indulgence was responsible for all of my hardships. We'd had no intercourse at all during the last few months of her pregnancy, and it had seemed not only easy but necessary to avoid it afterward. By the time of my graduation, having sex once a month, even less, had seemed perfectly natural. And Kate hadn't seemed to mind.

I could understand now that I'd practically driven Kate into an affair with Ed—my best friend, welcome at our house any time, night or day. Perhaps Ed had been the reason Kate hadn't minded my lack of attention. And now that I thought of it, Ed had never shown much interest in other women. Had they been having the affair all these years?

Kate had asked for a divorce just about a year before the twins had been born, but I'd still been a good churchgoing Mormon and, of course, had refused her flatly. It was possible that they had actually planned her second pregnancy in an attempt to force the issue!

Suddenly I could think of Kate in a new way—not the harping, sullen woman who grudgingly cooked my meals and kept my house, but a weary, unhappy prisoner kept here totally against her will. When I thought about her in that light, I was amazed that she hadn't long since tried to poison me. Instead, I'd been poisoning myself—and Chuck—and the girls—and Kate and Ed—with my hatred, my *revenge*. That's exactly what I'd been doing, taking out my revenge on them, making them suffer the way I'd imagined they had made me suffer. Worst of all, I realized I'd made two innocent children suffer for something over which neither had the slightest control. They had not asked to be born—neither of me nor of Ed. I understood clearly how unthinkably cruel I had been.

"Sometimes she goes on Mondays, too."

"What?"

"Mom."

"Oh." I took another deep breath. "Well, I guess...she has every right to go. I guess you're right, Chuck. Maybe I should...just let go."

"I don't mean it to sound like I knew more than you do, Dad, but..."

"That's all right, Chuck. Go ahead and sound like it. I'm beginning to think maybe you do."

"...but I think *you'd* be better off, too. Like, you never go anyplace now. I mean, what kick do you get out of anything? You're always so damn...well, you know."

"I know, Chuck. I know it now." I sighed heavily. "I know it now."

We were silent for a while, watching the firelight, feeling the warmth of it flickering across our faces. I knew Chuck was right, that I had to let go; I had to give Kate the divorce, sell the company to Ed, and go.

But where?

And how soon?

If I left, that would mean leaving Chuck, and I didn't want to do that—not now—not after finally beginning to get acquainted with him. "What would you do, son?"

"Me?" He sounded surprised that I'd even consider him important to my decision. "Dad, I can take care of myself."

I laughed, a little sadly. "Yes, I guess that's obvious."

"But look, I've been thinking, like, if you wanted to push it, legally I mean, you know, adultery and all that shit...you could force them to let you have me."

"I don't want to force anybody to do anything, Chuck. I want to be through with that."

"Well, then, what's the problem? Mom wouldn't mind if I lived with you part of the time, like the summers or something."

"Would you mind it?"

"Why should I mind it? I dig both of you. But, like,

I just can't take much more of you *together.* It's burning me out, Dad."

"Well, then...let's stop burning everyone out."

"Will you do it?"

I nodded. "Yes."

"Oh, man!" He leaned toward me and grasped my hand. "You're...you're just great!" He laughed, squeezed my hand, and leaned back, grinning from ear to ear. "You ought to stay high all the time."

I laughed with him. "I guess that's one possibility, but I'm not so sure I wouldn't get hooked."

"Yeah, well...don't get yourself hooked on *anything,* man. Anything. Like you were hooked on this whole thing. It's not just dope that gets you strung out. Like Jerry's old man—he's all strung out over this whole religion thing, and it's like he's got a monkey on him. I mean, it doesn't mean anything to him, he's just hooked on it. He goes through it like somebody shooting horse. And you talk about a bummer, man, I mean Jesus on the cross *all the time!* But, you know, that whole trip ended two thousand years ago—but they keep right on killing him...over and over and over. Man, if they'd just look around...."

"They wouldn't know what they were seeing, Chuck. I didn't."

He smiled. "I'm not really sure you do yet—but you will. It'll come through to you now."

"What will?"

He shrugged secretively. "You'll see. Just keep watching and listening. You'll see. And man, when you do see, it'll blow your head wide open!"

"All right. I'll take your word for it."

"Hey, you know something? I'm starved."

"Now that you mention it, so am I."

"How long you been up?"

"What?"

"How long ago did you drop?"

"I don't remember, Chuck, honestly. I must have been walking in my sleep."

"What a way to go! But, let's see, it was five, maybe five-thirty when I got home. And it's almost ten now...."

"Is it that late?" I suddenly realized I'd completely lost all consciousness of time. For some reason the idea delighted me.

"That's at least five hours, maybe more. You were pretty close to peaking when I got here. Sure, you should be able to drive. Think you could?"

"I don't know. I guess so."

"Things are back, pretty much, aren't they?"

"Yes," I said, "pretty much." Then it struck me that I was not only understanding Chuck, I was using some of his words. More and more through the evening his jargon had ceased being unintelligible and had taken on almost a private meaning between us. And of course, that's what it was—a jargon, a secret language, the private language of a subculture that only an initiate could understand. With the help of the mescaline I was beginning to understand it. I looked around the room, and it seemed relatively normal; the lights were still more vivid than usual, but otherwise things looked more or less as they'd always looked—with the difference that now I seemed to *understand* them. Rooms and furniture had taken on a new meaning to me, but the meaning itself wasn't new, except to me; it was just that I'd finally understood a meaning that had been there all along. "Yes," I said, "I think I can drive. Where should we go?"

"You want a mindfuck? I mean..."

"Why not?" I said calmly. "I don't know what a *mindfuck* is, but I'm willing to learn."

He grinned. "Nothing bad. It's sort of like the other, only in the head."

"Like the other..." I repeated.

"You know what I mean."

"Oh, yes, I know. And I wasn't...what do you call it?...putting you down. I was just thinking. *Fuck* isn't a bad word to you, is it?"

Chuck stood up, beaming. "Dad, you just took a giant step! Come on. I'll show you what a mindfuck is."

At first I felt very awkward, once again disconnected, as I backed the car onto the street and headed across 13th toward Sugarhouse—toward a new restaurant that Chuck called "The Yoko Ono Place" where the "head-crowd" went—but very quickly my mind adjusted itself to the necessities of driving. I was tempted to be distracted by the kaleidoscopic patterns of lights, coming toward me, but I found it increasingly easy to ignore them—realizing there was nothing at all new in what I was seeing and that I could look at lights any time. I was extremely curious about where we were going. I was briefly concerned that Chuck might feel awkward, taking such a "straight-looking" father in among all his friends, but then I understood that it would be nothing less than a kind of triumph for a boy to bring his father in among his peers. Chuck not only wanted to show me his world and to show me as much as he could in the time we had left on my trip, he wanted to show me off to his world as well. I understood that I'd been given a signal honor, being invited to share his world with him.

The restaurant was called *Mother Earth*—but Chuck explained why he called it "The Yoko Ono Place": on the back wall was a huge photograph, blown up to what looked like at least ten times life-size, of a moonfaced Oriental girl, who, he told me—as though announcing the name of a saint—was Yoko Ono. And as we ate, she smiled down on us at though she alone knew the answer to all riddles. The background music was also Oriental; I didn't know whether it was Japanese or Hindu or what, but I found it extremely relaxing, and it seemed to go perfectly with the strange but delicious macrobiotic food the place served. I found myself dreamily luxuriating in the textures and tastes of not just the food, but the music as well; one went with the other, augmented the other; each added new meaning to the other. But more than the food and the music, the thing which impressed me was the people: clean-scrubbed, long-haired girls, looking farm fresh, brighteyed and constantly smiling; shaggy-haired bearded men, looking like Biblical Prophets, smiling as brightly as the girls they were with. As soon as we'd stepped through the front door, a feeling of beautiful peacefulness had drawn me in. Complete strangers smiled at me for no reason at all—both sexes—and I found myself smiling back! It was indeed a new world I'd discovered. It was like finding Atlantis right under my nose. Or, better still, I decided—loooking around at the long hair and beards—almost like finding the New Jerusalem. Maybe John's prophesies were indeed coming true. Men—apparently normal men—*smiling* at one another!

I wished desperately that I could be Chuck's age once again, could be starting my life in this new world, rather than finding it halfway through. How different it was from the Brite-Spot Cafe where I and my own teen-age peers had gathered in Glen Falls: cheap-hamburger joint where we went nightly to "tip a few" in the cars parked out back, and get into a fight. I could hardly remember a night when there hadn't been trouble of one sort or another, usually one young buck beating the hell out of another to prove who was the most *manly*. It was a genuine relief to know that my son preferred places like Mother Earth to the Brite-Spots. Here the young men seemed perfectly content to be whatever they were, without having to prove anything. The thing that continued to amaze me was how peaceful they looked.

There didn't seem to be an ounce of hostility in anyone, and it didn't detract one bit from their masculinity!

Thinking about Glen Falls got me to thinking about Bill. I'd stopped worrying about the notes and the pictures. Something in my mind told me that I knew who the sender was, and that all I had to do was wait; the clues would come. And, anyway, those notes, along with so much of my former life, had become essentially meaningless; at least they no longer carried any kind of real threat. It was still a remote possibility that the sender was in fact Bill, but I didn't think so. Now that I'd disqualified John Adams—the only candidate—I was reasonably certain that Bill wasn't in Salt Lake after all. I'd been wrong about so many things it was almost a foregone conclusion that I'd been wrong about Bill. He probably wasn't a homosexual at all. He was probably married and settled down somewhere....

When we were kids, before that ridiculous scene in the back yard, if ever I had an insoluable problem, I knew I could take it to Bill, and he'd come up with a solution. Sometimes his solutions were not entirely practical, but he had the kind of mind that seemed to be able to see *into* a problem, to see its relationship with everything else. If I could talk to Bill, take a day, or a week, and relax with him, get to know him again, ask him what he thought I should do (not about Kate and the girls; I'd definitely decided to give her a divorce) about myself, and possibly about Chuck. Being younger, maybe Bill was more in touch with Chuck's generation than I was.

But above all, I just wanted to see him again. And this time, with the real one, I'd apologize honestly.

How to find him? The answer was so ridiculously simple, I wondered why I hadn't thought of it much sooner. Surely he kept in touch with the folks? I checked my watch; it was late, and I knew they'd have gone to bed hours ago, but I wanted to do it now while I still had the courage.

"Would it be okay if I made a phone call right now?" I asked Chuck.

"Sure. I'll rap with somebody."

In the back, near the doors to the rest rooms, was a pay-telephone. I dialed the operator and had her place the call, charging it to my special number at work. I counted seven rings, then mother's anxious voice said, "Yes? Hello?"

"Mom? It's Robert."

"What's wrong?"

"Nothing, Mom. Nothing. Everything's fine. Mom, I'm sorry for calling you this late, but...do you know where Bill is?"

"Couldn't it wait until morning?" she grumbled. "Well, since you're calling, just a minute." I could hear her muttering, and I pictured her leafing through all the clutter of Dad's roll-top pigeon-hole desk. He kept it looking neat, but nothing was ever where it should have been. "It was on his Christmas card," she said absently. "I wonder if Daddy threw it away."

"Don't you have it in your address book?" I asked.

"No, dear. We just heard from him a few *weeks* ago. Five whole years he just disappears, and then he sends us a Christmas card. Yes...here it is. Why are you suddenly interested in your brother? I thought..."

"It's a long story, Mom. Where does he live?"

"San Francisco," she said.

I cursed softly, away from the mouthpiece—*I'd just come from San Francisco!*

"I can't hardly read it, Robert, the post office smudged it. Two-something-something Fourteenth Avenue."

"Thanks, Mom, that's all I need. Sorry to wake you."

"How's Kate and the children?"

"They're fine, Mom. Everything's fine."

"Please don't be angry with me for asking the question. It doesn't mean I...*suspect* you of anything...or even that I'll be angry with you if...well, one way or another."

"Okay," he said seriously.

I took another deep breath. "I've been...worried... well, not exactly *worried*, but...*concerned*...about you and Jerry."

There was a long moment of silence. Then Chuck said, "Oh," very flatly.

"It isn't that I don't think you're old enough to handle your own problems, Chuck. I've realized tonight that you're really a lot older than I was at your age. And when I was your age..."

"Dad..."

"Yes, Chuck?"

"I know what you're going to ask."

"Do you?"

"Sure. Funny thing. I expected it months ago."

I glanced toward him again; he was soberly staring down at his feet. The expression on his face made me feel like someone was getting set to open a trap door directly under me.

He cleared his throat. "Dad..." he said softly—and I was sure I could hear a tremor in his voice—"things... well, aren't the same, like when you were a kid. I mean, sex isn't...you know...such a big deal any more."

The trap door opened.

He did know what I was talking about!

"I mean," he continued, "if two people think they can groove with each other, well, they do. You know? Nobody gets uptight any more."

"I don't think that's completely true, Chuck. It might be true with you...and your friends, but..."

"Well, who else is important?"

"Myself. Your mother. Even your sisters. Chuck, something might seem completely innocent to you, but if someone found out...someone who didn't feel it was quite so innocent..."

"Okay, right. But, I mean, who's going to be hurt? I mean..." He made a helpless sound in his throat. "Dad...it just doesn't *mean* anything. Look, if, like you get upset, okay? About something I'm doing. Well, it's just what you're *thinking*, not what I'm doing! Don't you see that?"

"Chuck, let's get this straight. What are we talking about?"

"Me and Jerry. Aren't we?"

"I'm not certain we're talking about the same thing. What about you and Jerry?"

"Well, Jesus, Dad...I mean...isn't that what you wanted to know? Hey, I don't want to get in a mess. What are *you* talking about?"

"I'm...talking about a...a relationship...between you."

"You're talking about sex, right?"

"Yes."

"Okay. Right. You were right, Dad. I'm just surprised it took you this long to figure it out."

"Chuck, are you telling me that you *do* have a... homosexual relationship? With Jerry?" The words sounded like those of a judge, getting set to pronounce a dreadful punishment.

"Dad...we ball each other, okay?"

"I see."

"But it still doesn't *mean* anything. Not what you think it does."

"And just what do I think? I told you...promised you..."

"Dad, you think it's something terrible. You think it's some horrible *crime*, and I'll ruin my whole life or something."

"It could, Chuck."

"It's just *sex!* Dad, I dig Jer and he digs me. We like each other, the same kind of things. What's the big deal?

I mean, it doesn't mean we don't dig chicks too."

"Just sex." I remembered, earlier, discovering something; I'd said, "Fuck isn't a bad word to you, is it?" And my son had said, "Dad, you just took a giant step!" Apparently neither the word nor its implications were bad to Chuck; it was still "just sex".

"Have you been with a girl, Chuck?" I asked.

"Well, sure."

"Many?"

"Dad..."

"Let's be honest, Chuck. We've gone this far. Let's go on being honest. I promised I wouldn't judge you, and I won't. But I want to know."

"Okay. Sure, I've...been with girls."

"And Jerry?"

"Yes."

"Any other boys?"

"Yes."

"Many?"

"Jeez, Dad, I don't keep score!" He thought for a minute, then said, "Four. Four guys. They were all my friends. And there's another guy I know wants to."

We had reached Jerry's. Reluctantly I pulled into the driveway and sat staring at the bright splash of my headlights across the Ashby's garage. I had asked Chuck the question and he had given me an honest answer—and now I didn't know what else to do or to say. I felt no emotion whatever, neither anger nor relief. I felt empty.

"Dad..." Chuck gripped my arm. I looked down at his hand, his strong young fingers, then up into his eyes; I remembered how brown and deep and beautiful they'd been earlier. "Please don't get strung out about this. Please! Tonight's been so great. Don't spoil it, please."

I swallowed hard and nodded, trying to force a smile—but I couldn't. "All right, Chuck."

"Have you changed your mind?"

"About what?"

"About me going with Jerry. I mean, it's going to happen again, Dad. We'll be all alone in that cabin."

I nodded. I knew it would happen again, no matter what I said or did, if not with Jerry, then with somebody else. The note had been true; my son was homosexual. The bewildering thing to me was that he didn't seem the least bit concerned about it. He was concerned about my being worried, but not about the thing itself.

Maybe he was right and I just wasn't thinking clearly enough to see it; maybe it wasn't as much of a big deal as I wanted to make it.

"No," I said. "You go ahead."

"You're sure."

"Yes."

"Thanks, Dad. Look, don't worry, huh? I mean, really. I'll come out okay."

"Yes, I guess you will–with or without your old man asking you a lot of dumb questions."

"I'm glad you know, though. I wanted to tell you."

"Did you?"

"Well, sure. I mean, if something's a secret, then it always turns into a big deal–and this isn't, believe me. Times have changed, Dad. They're still changing."

"I hope you're right. Well...you'd better go inside."

He sat silently, then muttered, "Okay," and opened the door. "We'll talk more about it when I get home, okay?"

"Okay, Chuck."

But even as I said it, I knew that I wouldn't be there when he got home. I didn't know where I would be, but I wouldn't be there.

I wasn't even sure that I'd ever see Chuck again.

Desperately I reached out and clasped his hand. "I want to tell you just one thing, Chuck, so you'll know, so you won't worry about what I'm thinking." The words poured out before I could stop them: "I'm not angry. I can't be...because...I've...I've done it, too, Chuck. And...well, I just wanted you to know. Because you've been...honest with me."

There was no change in his voice or his attitude, no surprise or hostility; he asked, "Is that why you and Mom don't get along?"

"No. At least, I don't think so. I really don't know, to be honest, Chuck. But, anyway, I'm not angry with you."

He got back into the car, but now he was clutching my hand tightly. Suddenly he leaned forward and kissed me. He said, "I love you, Dad. I don't care what happens." He sniffed hard and extracted his hand from mine to quickly wipe under his eyes. "Look, I better go. See you, okay?"

I could barely make my voice work; my mind was nothing but a foggy daze. "Okay," I said. The door slammed. Chuck walked down the long driveway, paused, standing in the car's headlights, waved, and then disappeared between the garage and the house.

I backed the car onto the street, barely conscious of what I was doing. I could still feel the pressure of his lips on mine. I could not remember ever having kissed my son on the lips.

I couldn't make my mind settle down. Hazy, unintelligible thoughts seemed to be flying in a hundred directions all at once. I tried to remember all that had happened during the evening, to forget what Chuck had just told me, to bring back that delicious happiness, that clear, clean perception that allowed me to understand things—but it all seemed to have happened long ago, to someone else.

For no reason I could think of, I did remember one thing: I remembered, when I'd called Bill, saying, "This is Bob." I hadn't called myself that for at least fifteen years. But somehow I'd felt like *Bob*, talking to Bill. But now I was *Robert* again, right back where I'd started, and all of the problems I'd dismissed through the evening as inconsequential were back haunting me.

I pulled into our driveway and turned off the lights, then sat for a long time staring at the dark windows of the house. We hadn't left a light burning. I did not want to go inside. I kept telling myself that my fear was unreasonable, but I knew something deadly was waiting inside for me.

But I couldn't stay in the car all night. The night had become very cold. And I was so tired, I could hardly keep my eyes open. Finally I got out, and locked the car, and started toward the front steps....

I hesitated, seeing the shadows clustered around the front door.

I heard something behind me and spun around. I couldn't see anyone, but it seemed I could hear heavy breathing—*and I remembered that sound!*

Freezing fear started low in my spine and spread upward; my heart started pounding. I raced to the front steps, leaped up, frantically trying to get the key into the lock. Just as I managed to unlock the door and swing it open, a cold hand grasped my shoulder. And a voice, right behind me, said, "*Robber*—I'm going to kill you!"

I screamed and lunged into the house.

I saw shadows rushing at me, heard them hissing and growling. My foot struck the doorsill...and I felt myself falling....

PART 2

Chapter 1

I felt myself falling and tried to grab for the door, but I fell on my stupid face anyway. "Shit!"

I got up on my elbows and looked around. He was gone. He was always gone!

Damn him! Why was that?

He'd been so damn close this time, right there where I could reach out and grab him. But dumb me, I just had to yell at him and scare him. Why couldn't I stop doing stupid things like that?

This time would be different, though. He was still in the house. I was sure of it. He'd been just inside the door when I grabbed for him, and he hadn't run back out over me. He was too scared of me to do that.

But he might go out through the kitchen door.

I jumped up and turned on the light and then ran into the kitchen. Nope! The door was still bolted from inside. Detectives knew that meant somebody was still inside, because you couldn't lock a door like that from the outside.

So I knew he was still in the house.

But that didn't make it much easier. He knew lots of places to hide from me, places where he hid every time I got out of that room he kept me in. But this time I felt stronger than ever! This time I felt like I wouldn't get scared and pass out like I always did, and then have him really killing him. I just wanted to get out whenever I could and do things for fun. But not any more. No, sir! Once I stopped fucking around and figured things out, I knew that he had to die or I'd never get out of that spell of his. But this time I had to think it out and make plans about how to do it. I couldn't just do things or say things that came into my head, just for the hell of it.

First of all I would find him, and then...skoosh! Right through the fucking heart. And then...then I would cut him up and throw him in the garbage can! Wouldn't that be just funny as hell, to find him out in the garbage can? With his eyes open, just staring at you....

Well, that's where he belonged. In a damn garbage can.

"Hey, Robber!" I yelled. "I'm gonna throw you in the gar–"

Damn me! I clamped my hand over my mouth. Why the hell did I do that? All that would do was just scare him and he'd find a place to hide where I never could find him.

Dumb stupid shit!

Wouldn't it be great if I could get him tied down, like those pictures? Tie him down and make him watch when I cut his cock off! Whack!

My cock started getting hard, just thinking about it. Whack!

Maybe I shouldn't really kill him, just cut his damn cock off! He didn't need the damn thing anyway. The dumb shit never used it. That's why he hated me so much, because I liked to use mine, and he thought that was terrible! Oh, that was wicked and sinful and disgusting. The dumb shit!

Get him gagged and tied up so he couldn't say anything but just sit there and go blink-blink when I cut *his cock off!* Blink-blink! *Cut his balls off too! Do it slow, real slow, so's he'd have to just sit there and watch. Maybe cut the skin off first and play with them hanging there. Maybe suck his old cock like I did Billy's and then just as he started to shoot–snip-snip! No jizz! Just air!*

And then *cut his cock off.*

But I had to go ahead and kill him afterward. He had to die. There was no other way I could ever get rid of him.

I could put his cock over the fireplace, like those things they did with deer's heads. Just his cock and his balls on this wooden shield. And the people from church would come in and be sitting there, talking about sins from the Bible, and they'd look up and see his cock sticking out! They'd just sit there and pee all over theirselves!

First I had to find him.

And then I would have my fun!

Whack! Whack!

Now where would he be?

He might be in the basement–but if I went down there and he wasn't there, he could be sneaking out while I wasn't looking.

For a minute I couldn't think what to do. I hated for things to get complicated so I had to decide *things. Then I got an idea! I grabbed one of the chairs from the table and propped it against the door, under the doorknob. Detectives did that. That way he couldn't get out if he was in the basement and I was upstairs.*

I went up the stairs two at a time. His door and Chuck's were both open, and I didn't think he would hide in the room with the door open–but he might! He was tricky that way. He just might be in one of those rooms, with the door left open, just to make me think *he wasn't there.*

I went to the door of his room and reached in and

turned on the light. From all I could see, he wasn't in there.

I left the light on and went to Chuck's room and reached in and turned on the light, but Chuck's room looked empty too. I listened to see if I could hear him breathing, but I couldn't.

I went to his wife's room—and then the girls' room—and then to the bathroom—and he wasn't in any of them! Of course I didn't go inside. I had to decide which one he was probably in before I went inside one myself.

I was confused and I hated to be confused! I liked things that were easy.

It was funny. The lights were all blazing away like we were having a party.

Well, I'd have me a party, by damn! When Robber was dead, I would have me a party! I'd take all my clothes off and run around and jack off on everything. All over his fucking house!

But I still had to find him. I kept getting distracted.

I could do all the things that I wanted to do when old Robber was dead!

Well, I had to pick a room. I couldn't just stand here all night. He might really be in the basement after all, and here I was wasting my time making dumb decisions.

Then an idea came to me. "Hey, Robber," I called. "I'm gonna stay right here until you come out. You hear? I'm gonna stay...right...here—in the hall!"

Then, holding the knife so I could stab him the minute I found him, I went tiptoe into his room. Quiet as a mouse I looked in his closet—felt way back to the back, even down on the floor, but he wasn't there. Then I went to the bed and looked under it. It was dark underneath, but I figured out lifting the covers so some light could get under—and he wasn't there either.

But on top of the bed was the last note I'd left for him. That showed what a fool he was, just leaving it lying there. I picked it up and smoothed out where he'd crumpled it, then I folded it and put it in my pocket. After I'd killed him I could hide it with the other things so they never would find any clue about who done it.

When I stood up and turned to go out, I saw him! He was standing behind the dresser.

Dumb, stupid shit! I had figured that all out the last time! When I poisoned him! He hid in the mirrors!

We stood there, just looking at each other. And then I began to feel funny. Damn him! He was working that spell on me again!

Damn him! Damn him!

Had to kill him!

Had to!

I raised my knife—but he had one too!

I felt dizzy!

What if he killed me too? I didn't want to die!

I had to do *something! I was getting scared again.*

I closed my eyes and yelled, "Die!!!" *and jumped at him, aiming my knife just as hard as I could at his heart!*

Glass splintered and I collapsed.

"Die!" The echo slowly faded: "Die...die.....die......"

My heart was pounding insanely! I was covered with cold sweat!

I sat up, clutching my chest, taking deep breaths to calm myself down.

Someone had just tried to kill me! A madman!

But he'd splintered...and vanished!

It wasn't until I stood up and saw the shattered mirror that I began to realize what had happened. I looked at my fragmented image and started to remember:

I'd felt hands on my shoulder, and I'd stumbled over the doorstep—and then I'd awakened, sitting on the floor of my room, in a cold sweat, terrified! The memory of coming through the front door, and then awakening in my room, were both vivid, normal memories. The rest of it seemed like a dream—but a dream I remembered.

I'd been a child again.

A child in a grown man's body.

I'd been looking for a man, intending to kill him.

The knife I had dreamed about lay on the top of the dresser. The man I now looked at in the mirror was the man I'd been trying to find in my dream—the one I'd intended to kill.

Myself.

"Oh, my God!"

I sent those notes to myself!

I could dimly remember—using "his" desk, "his own" paper and envelopes, thinking what a funny joke it would be on him. I remembered how hard it had been to write at first; I hadn't been sure how to spell the words or punctuate the sentences. But the second time had been easier, and the third even easier.

But those hadn't been dreams!

Nor had this been a dream! I remembered turning all the lights on, looking for "him"—and I'd thought about having a party and running naked....

I ran into the hallway. All the lights were on and the doors were all open. I ran downstairs and found the chair propped under the basement doorknob. I jerked the chair away from the door and replaced it by the table, then sat down, shaking all over.

A voice wailed, "*Robberrrrrr....*"

I leaped up, expecting to see him right behind me!

"Stay calm!" I told myself. "Think it through."

It felt as though something were *sucking* at my mind—something terrible!

"*Stay calm! Damn it!* Stay calm! Stay calm! Think it through! Don't panic, don't panic, don't panic!"

The sound of my own voice comforted me—but I knew that that sucking *madness* was still clawing to get into my mind.

"Coffee!" I raced around the room, repeating, "Coffee...coffee...coffee..." as I got a cup and a spoon and the instant coffee, my hands shaking almost uncontrollably. "Coffee...coffee...coffee..." I turned on the hot water faucet. "Coffee...coffee...coffee...coffee!" I couldn't wait for the water to get hot! It was only lukewarm but I stirred it viciously and gulped it down, then made another cup.

Slowly the trembling stopped. Slowly my mind seemed to cover itself with a barrier, forcing that madness away.

"Sit down," I said aloud. "Calm down and think it through." I sat down. "Okay, maybe if you keep talking...."

Why did this have to happen when I was alone!?

I didn't know what to do.

I was going insane and I didn't have the slightest idea of what to do!

"Please, God, help me!" I whispered. "I know I don't deserve it, but please! I don't want to go crazy! Please! Help me...."

I'd asked Chuck if he believed in God, and he'd said, "Oh, sure."

"I love him!" I said to the empty room. "I love him! He's my son and I love him! I don't care what he does! *I don't care!* I *love* him, God! Please...help me!"

I could feel my heartbeat slowly calming down....

That madness slunk back further...and further....

I deliberately forced my mind to think of unimportant things—like the tablecloth. I had sat there this morning, tracing the ivy. I thought about the table in my mother's kitchen, with the oilcloth covering it.

I couldn't just sit there, thinking of things! I had to *do* something—*take* something! But what? All I had were sleeping pills—and I was utterly terrified of going to sleep. That's when *he* got loose!

"What can I *do?*"

Kate's pills!

"Oh, God! Please let there be some!"

I raced up the stairs to the bathroom. For years Kate had been taking Dexamyl. She told everyone she was keeping her weight down, but I knew Sam had prescribed them as an *anti-depressant!* Just last week, I'd picked up a new bottle for her. If only she hadn't taken them to Ogden with her....

But she had!

I was almost ready to break down and start sobbing, curling myself up in a corner somewhere, when I saw her old bottle, still there. I grabbed it and opened it, holding my breath. There were four halves of those little triangular green ones, the old ones—she'd taken the spansules with her.

I took two halves, gulping the water from the palm of my hand. I put the other two in my pocket. These things were *supposed* to work for six hours or more, but I'd keep the other halves with me, just in case.

Back in the kitchen I had two more cups of coffee. And finally I felt settled enough to try to think through what had happened.

I'd stood here in the kitchen, playing with the knife, thinking hideous thoughts of mutilating "him"....

I couldn't keep thinking of myself as "him"—and yet there were obviously two...parts of me, two individuals, and each had to be "him" to the other.

I wondered if he had a name. The name *Bobby* came into my mind, but I rejected it angrily. That demented would-be murderer wasn't Bobby! Impulsively I decided to call him *Rob*—which was one of the nicknames for Robert that I particularly disliked. After all, he had called me *Robber.*

Idiotically I thought, *What's sauce for the goose is sauce for the gander.*

I chuckled at the incongruity of the thought. It was strangely comforting to know that I could giggle at something as frightening as this. Either it meant I had flipped out, or Kate's pill was beginning to take effect.

I did feel better! Wider awake...stronger.

Rob had thought about being strong. He'd been very sure that when I became tired, was when he became strong. But his strength had been growing recently, obviously! Other times I'd been asleep; but this time he'd come out before I'd got inside the house. Next time...

I hadn't taken that pill of Chuck's while "sleep-walking"! Rob had come out and taken it *for* me. That's when he discovered that I "hid" in the mirrors.

But how could he think about killing me? Didn't he realize he'd be killing himself? Apparently he wasn't bright enough to realize that.

"Idiot!" I said aloud. "You'd be committing suicide."

It seemed that a voice in my head answered, *Liar! Liar!*

"*Suicide!*" I repeated. "Do you hear me."

No!

Was I simply jibbering to myself, I wondered, or was I really in touch with him?

I thought, *This is insane!*

Then nodded my head in amused agreement; it was indeed!

But was *I* insane? I, Robert? Yes, that strange, childish...*thing* inside me was crazy, obviously....

But then I wondered: *Was he?* Remembering his thoughts, they seemed more like those of someone retarded—like Jeff Potter, my college roommate's brother. Jeff acted like a twelve-year-old, but he hadn't been "crazy"; he simply had never grown up; his reasoning powers had remained at the mental level of a child. And judging from those letters Rob had written, the way the spelling and punctuation had improved from one letter to the next, I wondered if that might not mean he was "growing up"—getting brighter each time he got out.

Now that I knew who he was, was it possible he had also guessed who I was? Maybe we could communicate with one another, work this thing out....

What the hell was I doing, thinking about *communicating* with an insanity?

It was crazy to sit here and think about being crazy!

I was tempted to call Chuck and beg him to come home. But what good would that do? This wasn't a mescaline trip; this was real; the person inside me wasn't just a phantom in the shadows, a "bummer". Calling Chuck would just frighten him, and he'd have to wake somebody up to bring him home—I was still far too shaky to drive over and get him.

If only Bill had been more responsive. God! I needed him more than ever now. I'd feel so safe, knowing Bill was around. I'd missed him so much all these years. I'd missed that safe feeling.

Maybe I'd misjudged Bill. Maybe he actually had had an honest reason for not talking tonight. At least I could give him the benefit of the doubt—even if I were clutching at straws. There was no one else I could think of. Mom and Dad surely couldn't help. And Kate wouldn't. Who else was there but Bill?

I ran to the telephone and called the airport. The next flight for San Francisco left at ten o'clock in the morning! I did not dare stay in this house alone all night! Even if I didn't go to sleep, I'd drive myself crazy by sitting and thinking. And if I did go to sleep, I might never wake up.

The clock over the refrigerator read 12:15. I'd have to wait ten hours for the flight. I could almost *drive* to San Francisco by that time!

I started back into the kitchen, then stopped short. *Why not drive?*

Driving would keep me awake, keep my mind occupied. It would take longer than ten hours, of course, but not much. If I drove straight through, I ought to be able to make it in no more than fifteen hours. That would get me there—with the time-difference—around three o'clock!

I didn't have much cash, but I had credit cards. Plenty of identification to cash checks on the way if I needed to.

I wouldn't be needed at the office. Tomorrow, I could call from someplace in Nevada—just tell them I'd changed my plans and wouldn't be home for a week or two. Let Ed run the business; he was going to get it anyway.

I ran upstairs and got out my suitcase and packed again, remembering unpacking it just last night. *Last night?* It seemed like months ago.

The clothes I had on were fine for traveling. I made sure I had my checkbook and credit cards, my driver's license, and as much cash as I could find—eleven dollars in paper and a few cents in change; well, it would have to do.

Downstairs I took several minutes, writing a note to Chuck, telling him where I was going and asking him to tell Kate I would call on the weekend. I signed the note *All my love, Dad,* and left it on the kitchen table.

I made sure all the doors and windows were locked. Outside, as I started toward the car, I found my attention being drawn to the garage. Something hovered on the verge of consciousness, a memory that the garage was *important.* I tried to resist the feeling, but it persisted. I turned on the VW's lights and opened the garage door. My black shadow scuttled quickly over garden supplies, trunks, boxes.... There was something inside the garage that I knew I could not leave behind.

Then, abruptly, I knew what it was I was looking for: Rob's "hiding place". The baby crib. I cringed as I stepped into the garage, sensing the deep shadows above me and back in the corners, but I reminded myself that Rob was *inside* me, and the shadows were just shadows, hiding nothing but the clutter of fifteen years' junk. I found the crib easily, folded, hanging on the back wall, with cardboard tied around it. I reached into an opening of the cardboard and withdrew the brown envelope.

The barrier between his memory and mine was growing thinner all the time. It was even possible that he had been trying to *tell* me not to leave his treasures behind.

In the car, I opened the envelope to make sure everything was there. I found both notes and the pictures, plus a small note-pad that had come up missing several months ago. The first dozen or so pages were covered with strange, grotesque doodlings, naked bodies of menchildren, parts and pieces of bodies—hands and heads, with blood dripping from them—and cocks: long fat cocks, wildly spurting, dripping....

I shuddered and put everything back into the envelope, and put that in the glove compartment. I wasn't at all sure that I wanted that barrier between his mind and mine to come down.

The lights of Salt Lake gathered together, tighter and tighter behind me; the black roadway zipped under me; dark unfathomable shapes on the sides of the freeway became grey blurs whizzing past, caught briefly in the fan of the headlights.

I could definitely feel Kate's pill taking effect. It was almost like being back on the mescaline trip; my mind seemed to be galloping at full speed. The only problem was, I was sweating profusely, and, in the cold air coming in through the wind-wings, my body was tingling, continually on the edge of a delicious shiver; it had a sexual quality to it, like being on the verge of an ejaculation. I'd forgotten how good that could feel!

The road angled south, now moving away from the lakeshore, and a black arm of the mountain began blocking the sparkle of lights in the Salt Lake Valley. If I looked slightly away from them, it seemed they were being snuffed out by a gigantic finger.

I wondered if I'd ever see those lights again. I had a growing sense of *completion*—and the vanishing lights seemed to substantiate that feeling. My life as I knew it—as I'd known it for thirty-five years—was ending. Or perhaps it had already ended. And ahead was my future, like the countryside, hidden in darkness.

Suddenly I understood something else: I'd awakened in my hotel room yesterday morning with a premonition of impending disaster. Now I could see that the notes and the premonition and the feeling of being watched and followed all were parts of the same thing: I'd been trying to tell myself that my life *had* to change, that, in effect, I had to "die". Well, the "disaster" had happened, but in a way no one could have foreseen. And Rob had accomplished his mission: "Robber" Thorne was indeed "dead"; we were leaving his remains scattered all over Salt Lake City—almost as Rob had intended—one part at each place where an aspect of him had died: in that sulphurous steam room, in John Adams' kitchen, in the Mother Earth. Bits and pieces of him lay in that vacant lot, among the weeds and the twisted pipes and the soot-covered bricks with *Fuck* written on them. More pieces were scattered along 13th East, where Chuck had insisted on one last exchange of honesty. What was left of him rested, like the fragments of the mirror, all over the dresser top and the floor of his bedroom.

"That ought to make you happy," I said aloud.

I imagined I felt something like a chuckle in response.

I laughed softly to myself. This was one Easter Sunday I wasn't likely to forget. In a way, the date and the circumstances seemed very appropriate.

Of course, if the old Robert were dead, who did that make me? I truly felt I had definitely changed, but I wasn't sure how, and in how many ways. I was neither Robber nor Rob, but who was I? What would I become?

It was fascinating to think about becoming someone

new. Earlier, on the mescaline, I'd imagined that the change had been instantaneous and complete; but I realized now that such wasn't the case. Now it seemed that the "trip" had been a kind of "visionary" experience—and, after all, that's what the Indians used it for. It had not brought about actual changes, but had given me a foretaste of what I *could* become. Unhappily I found I'd forgotten a good part of that fantastic clarity I'd had earlier. I could remember specific events, such as sitting in those ruins, looking up at the sky, being overwhelmed by the beauty and the idea of the heavens—and yet I couldn't bring back that pure intense pleasure I'd felt, nor even a small fraction of the ideas that had flowed through my mind. The Dexamyl had brought me "up"—out of the terror of lurking madness—but nowhere near as high as I'd been earlier.

Considering it, the events of the evening seemed almost unbelievable. Even more unbelievable was the way I was taking it. By all rights, I should have been jibbering in some corner—like a rat in one of those psychology experiments, where they deliberately drive the poor creature insane by giving him all sorts of stimuli all at once. Of course the Dexamyl was responsible for some of my calmness, but for the most part I felt that the mescaline had prepared me for any number of strange events. I had had my mind grabbed and shaken—the way a dog shakes a rabbit—and my little world had been opened wide enough that I was able to contemplate insanity with a fair amount of equanimity.

But then, from what I could remember of articles I'd read, "split personality" wasn't considered one of the more disastrous insanities. The two personalities might have completely different sets of values, different ways of thinking of themselves, but each could be sane and healthy in its own way.

Also I seemed to remember that the first step toward

a cure for the disease was the recognition of one personality by the other. I had already taken that step. I knew about Rob, and it was seeming more and more probable that he knew about me. Maybe he wouldn't come out again. Maybe now that "Robber" was dead, he'd be content to be absorbed into "the new me"—whatever that might be.

Probably the best thing would be to stop thinking about him. I didn't know that much about psychology, and I didn't want to give myself any false hopes or illusions—or to frighten myself with unreal worries. I'd wait until I could talk it all out with Bill; then together we could decide what to do about Rob.

I turned on the radio and found KSL. They were playing a classical piece that I recognized vaguely; a lovely melodic thing that went very well with the night and the little VW scooting through the darkness.

I stopped for gas at Wendover, the little half-Mormon, half-casino town on the Utah-Nevada border. I set my watch back an hour to 1:30; I'd made excellent time, averaging sixty miles an hour. If I could keep the rate up, I'd be in San Francisco well before three in the afternoon.

And I was feeling great! Not even a hint of a letdown. Even so I picked up two coffees to go at the little cafe next to the gas station, just to play it safe.

I made even better time once inside Nevada, with its wide new freeway and no speed limit. The highway was practically empty—just me and a few trucks. It was 2:45 when I got to the tiny town of Wells, where I stopped again, this time taking a few minutes to sit in the bright cafe (the only thing open in town) and relax from the driving. I chatted and laughed with the waitress about the "nuts" who came in this time of the morning (wondering if she could guess how well I fitted into the category). I decided I didn't need another cup to go; I'd be in Elko in less than an hour. The way I felt, I was sure I could make it.

I caught myself yawning about half an hour later, but that didn't worry me. I didn't feel tired; I just felt like yawning. Now the road was almost totally empty; I passed only one lumbering truck. With nothing besides driving to distract my thoughts, I allowed them to wander back over the events of the last few weeks—back to the time I'd received the first note in the mail. More and more I could remember Rob's secretive activities. I could remember "dreams" I had had, long before the notes started arriving—terrifying erotic dreams, dreams of mutilation, degradation—all of them (I realized now) grossly homosexual in content. After seeing those drawings and doodlings of Rob's, I could begin to understand where the dreams had originated. They were like fantasies of fantasies, dreams twice-removed. I doubted that Rob had ever *done* anything, had ever put his fantasies into practice, otherwise I'd have "awakened" on somebody's doorstep, or out in the car.

There was one dream that seemed more vivid than the others—a night in San Francisco. That one had surely come on the night I'd arrived for the AGDA conference, when I'd gone to bed early, anticipating a long session the next day: I remembered "dreaming" I was out on the streets, bewildered and excited by the cars and the lights and the strange people, frightened and yet fascinated by the "worldly" people wandering around, allowing my imagination to construct elaborate sexual fantasies about them. I remembered a store with a sign that read *Adults Only, Books, Films, Novelties.* Men were continually going into and coming out of the place, and I'd decided I wanted to know what was so interesting inside. The windows had been blocked off with a pegboard display of paperback books that had titles like *Queer Passions* and *Queens on Parade, Boy Watchers, Leather Lovers—Queer* this and *Queer* that, *Gay* this and *Gay* that—all with photographs and drawings of naked men on the covers, their private parts covered with paste-on stars. I'd gone past the store several times, strolling "casually" until I got up the courage to go inside. I remembered the terror and excitement I'd felt as the door closed behind me and I'd looked around, seeing my fantasies explode into life on the walls in huge pictures, high up, above row upon row of magazines and paperbacks–of naked men, with huge cocks half-erect, slick-looking. There were hundreds and hundreds of magazines andd paperback books–*cocks everywhere!*

I'd been amazed to see all those men standing around, so casually leafing through books and magazines, some with obvious erections.

And then I had seen the rack of photographs! Thousands of photographs–naked bodies, hard cocks, men masturbating, men fucking each other, men sucking other men's cocks. Those pictures had seemed almost real to me then. Actual pictures of men doing the things I had only dreamed about.

I remembered thinking how it would upset "old Robber" to see such "sinful" things, and I'd bought a set of them, and then sneaked back into the hotel–up the back stairs like a criminal–with a brown envelope clutched under my coat. The same envelope that was now in my glove compartment.

Remembering those photographs, a sweet tingling began in my groin, and my cock struggled to inch down my pantleg. I squeezed it and delicious shivers spread out through my body. I unbuttoned my fly, reached inside to feel the firm warmth.

In a way it was too bad I wasn't still in Salt Lake. I could go to that steamroom now, knowing what to expect. Lie back and let somebody soap me down and massage me–and this time let him go ahead and suck my cock! God! It would feel so *good* to have it sucked right now!

I started to be shocked by the idea, but quickly

reminded myself that was part of my past; I couldn't allow myself to be shocked by such things—that would be like resurrecting old Robber. I had to keep an open mind, adjust myself to the changes in the world. Chuck had assured me that the world was indeed changing and that sex was "no big deal".

I eased my cock out, tugged my balls to hang out through my fly. What harm would it do to take out those pictures and look at them? I could study them now with a new perspective.

I started to look for a place to turn off, but there were signs that said *Emergency Parking Only.* I didn't want a Highway Patrolman to come by and catch me looking at dirty pictures. But then again, wouldn't he be surprised to come over to the car and shine his light in and see me jacking off? I could show him the pictures and watch him get a hard-on, and then...

I brought myself up short, abruptly dismissing the fantasy. That was something Rob would think about!

A sign came into view: *Rest Stop—2 miles.*

Perfect! All that coffee had worked its way down to my bladder, and I needed to pee anyway. *Piss*, I corrected myself. Only kids said *pee*—kids and self-righteous adults. Old Robber wouldd have said *pee*— or worse: *urinate!* The word seemed ridiculous: *urinate! Piss* was a much better word; you could almost feel the relief.

I saw the lights ahead, lonely and dim, shining down on a building with bright yellow windows. The place looked completely deserted. It seemed so strange, all those lights blazing away, here in the middle of nowhere.

I followed the side road off and parked in front of the rest rooms. My cock had gone limber, and I started to tuck it away—but then on a crazy impulse I opened the door with it still hanging out. I felt brash and daring, even though I knew there was no one within miles to see me.

I walked casually up the sidewalk, my cock and my balls flopping around in the cool tingling air. It was crazy, but very exciting.

The small room was empty. I stepped to the urinal and stood there shuddering deliciously as the hot stream gushed out and went gurgling down the drain. Then I noticed some writing on the wall of the toilet stall:

Hi there, truckdriver! You missed a great blowjob. I stayed here an hour and two drivers stopped. Both of them had big dirty cocks and I sucked them off right here. They said I was better than fucking a cunt. If you have a big cock and a hot load of cum, stop at the next place like this. I'll be waiting for you with my hot mouth.

My cock started getting hard instantly! I could picture the guy, kneeling on the floor of this strange little room, sucking some big burly truckdriver's cock. I remembered John Adams groping me in that rest room—then kneeling before me on his kitchen floor, his face buried hard in my pubic hair, swallowing, clutching my ass.... I put the two memories together and imagined him kneeling here now, reaching out for me, pulling me closer, sucking my cock into his warm foggy mouth....

I leaned back against the toilet wall, closing my eyes, massaging my cock with one hand, my stomach and chest with the other, whispering aloud: "Suck me, John Adams! Suck my cock!" Sweet flushing sensations began swirling in my belly; I spat into my hand, slickly milking my cock, imagining it inside John Adams' throat—until I shuddered and arched my hips forward and shot thick white gobs onto the dusty tile floor.

I fell back against the wall, gasping, suddenly realizing what an idiotic thing I had done! I should have known that a sexual climax would sap my energy!

I staggered to the washbasin, feeling as limp as my cock. I splashed icy water over my face, taking deep gulps of air into my lungs. That revived me a little, but I felt certain that even if I could make it to the car, I'd collapse there and fall asleep instantly. I *had* to take another half of that dexamyl!

I knew it would take twenty or thirty minutes to get into my bloodstream, but I had to stay awake! I couldn't let Rob come out! Not here in the desert! God knew what kind of crazy thing he might try to do.

I swallowed the pill, then wiped off my dripping cock with a paper towel, stuffed it away—then staggered out to the car. For a long time I stood looking inside at the empty front seat, groggily wondering where the other person had gone. Then I realized there had been no other person—only me. The other one was *inside* my head—and I had to keep him there for as long as possible.

I got the car onto the freeway, with the windows wide open, cold wind swirling through the car. There were signs now along the road, announcing *ELKO—15 miles...12 miles*, but I wasn't sure I could hold out that long. If I could get coffee in Elko, that might make the pill work faster....

I yawned.

A voice whispered: "*Relax, Robert. Let go.*"

No!

"*Come on, relax. You're so tense. Why are you so tense?*"

"Shut up!" I yelled.

The voice chuckled. "*You'll never get rid of me that way. Be nice. I like you. You're not like him.*"

"Please," I begged. "Please be quiet, Rob."

"*Relax....relax....relax....*"

"Rob, I'm frightened!"

"*No! Don't do that! That's a bad thing. Mustn't get frightened. Just let me take over, man. I'll take care of you!*"

"You can't drive."

"*Sure I can. I been watching how you do it. It's easy. I drove before, anyway, remember, before old Robber put me away in that room?*"

Suddenly I was out, sitting there at the steering wheel, listening to him tell me: "Got to get gas....in Elko....use credit card....so sleepy...."

"Just go to sleep, man," I told him.

....sleepy....

"Go to sleep, Robert."

I felt good. I felt strong. I felt free!

Robber *was dead! In the morning they'd find him scattered all over Salt Lake City. And now I was getting stronger and stronger. I was growing up! I could feel it!*

I didn't really understand everything that was going on, how two guys like Robert and me could have the same body–but it seemed to make sense. At least, Robert believed it, and, for the time being, Robert was smarter than me. He'd said, "That ought to make you happy"–about old Robber being dead–and it sure did!

Robert had figured it out. I was glad that he did, because I still didn't like to think much. We could get along good, Robert and me.

But he'd made one mistake that kind of made me mad. He kept calling me Rob *and that wasn't my name. I was* Bobby!

I decided to leave him a note when I woke him up. It would say, My name is Bobby, stupid!

There were a few other things that I had to change too. Robert still didn't like me, not really. He still wanted to keep me locked up. But that was because he was scared of me. Maybe I could do things to let him know that he didn't need to be scared of me, like being careful of the car.

Anyway, it wasn't as bad as those terrible names old Robber kept calling me.

But Robber was dead! Dead-dead-dead!

And now I could do all the things that I wanted!

I just had to be careful, like Robert said. I couldn't do anything really bad–even if I could slip back to my room and let him take the blame–because somebody might hurt him, and that would hurt me.

Yes, sir, I was getting smarter and smarter all the time. And it was getting easier and easier to know what was going on, even when I was stuck away in that dark room.

But lately that room hadn't been so damn dark. It was getting to where I could see things and feel things. Not clearly. Not yet. Things were still kind of hazy. But some of the time I could listen in to what Robert was thinking. And I always could hear him whenever he talked to me, either out loud or in his head.

I saw lights ahead, and at first I thought it was another one of those Rest Stops, but it turned out to be much bigger than it looked, and I guessed it was that town Robert wanted me to stop at–Elko. (I couldn't remember where we were going.) Maybe I ought to wake him up and let him do all the things, then take over again when we got out of town.

But not yet. I wanted to have some fun! I wanted to do something wild and exciting.

It scared me a little, thinking about driving through a town–but I figured maybe if I went real easy and slowed down to what it said on the signs, maybe no one would bother me.

It surprised me to see so many lights blazing away. It was four o'clock in the morning. Back home in the morning everybody was sound asleep. But then, I was awake, so it sort of made sense for a few others to be awake too. Maybe they were all going where we were–wherever that was. Maybe we were all going to have a party and all run around the house naked and suck each other's cocks.

I started to look for a place I could park Robert's car without banging it. I drove all the way through the town–real slow, and keeping my eye on the mirror in case somebody started to chase me, ready to wake Robert up the minute anything happened–but nothing at all happened, and I got all the way through town without having to wake him up. Finally I saw a place with its own little parking lot, just off the road. It was called Fred's, and its lights were all on, with a sign that said Cocktails in blue in the window, but without any cars in the lot, so I pulled in. The car jumped and made funny noises when I put on the brakes, but I managed to get it stopped. That ought to make Robert proud of me! It sure made me proud of myself. It made me feel even stronger, knowing I could drive a car all the way through a town, and then stop it and park it without banging it or anyone chasing me! I even remembered to take the keys out and put them in my pocket.

I really was growing up fast!

There was one guy inside the place, sitting down at the end of this little bar. (For the first time in my life I was inside a real bar! Just the idea made me tingle all over.) He looked up and smiled, like he was real glad to see me. "Hi there," he said, and stood up to watch where I'd sit down. "What'll it be?"

For a minute I almost panicked. I couldn't remember what Robert drank. Old Robber drank vodka, and I wasn't about to have that! I saw a sign back behind the bar that said Hamms, so I said, "I'll have a Hamms, please."

"Right!"

It made me feel so good, the way he seemed happy to see me. I wondered if maybe I'd seen him before, but I didn't think so. That damn Robber had never let me have any friends.

He brought me a glass and a bottle and poured the glass full and put it down in front of me. The first sip of the stuff tasted awful, but the second was better.

I looked up and noticed the bartender was standing there watching me, and I wondered if maybe I'd done something wrong. I said, "Thank you very much."

"That'll be fifty cents."

"Oh! Oh, sure!" I stood up and searched through my

pockets and found Robert's money, a wad of paper bills, and some small change. I gave him two quarters and watched him as he took it to put in the cash register. He had on real tight pants and it looked almost like he was naked with that color just painted on him. That got me excited, thinking about him being naked there behind the bar. I could feel my cock getting hard.

When he turned around to come back, I looked hard to see if his cock would show in those tight pants–and it sure did! It looked big! Maybe it would be as big as Billy's.

I wondered how I could get him to take it out and show me. Would he get mad if I just came out and asked him? Probably. You just didn't go up to someone and ask to look at his cock. It would be great if you could, though!

"Something wrong?"

"What?"

"You were staring at me like I had something on me."

"Oh no, I was just..." I looked up at him and he was watching me funny, with his head sort of tipped.

"I wasn't looking at anything."

He stood for a minute looking at me. Then it looked like he made up his mind about something. He got a beer out of the case and opened it for himself and took a long swallow. Then he leaned back on the cabinet, with his legs apart, and scratched himself.

"Oh, man," he said, "this place is so fucking dead tonight. You're my first fucking customer since like two o'clock." He leaned toward me, on his elbow against the bar. "Been uptown?"

"I drove through."

"Yeah, well, I guess things are hurtin' all over, with this fucking inflation, but shit, I get sick of just sitting here, you know? Shit, I could fuck some broad right there...." He pointed to the top of the bar, and then

laughed. "Come to think of it, that's a great idea. Right? Right there on the fucking bar! Now all I need is some chick to walk in."

"Yeah...." I could imagine him taking his clothes off, with this girl laying spread out on the bar. He would look good with his clothes off, I though, with his cock sticking up, hard as a rock. I wished he would go on talking, saying fucking *all the time, talking about fucking a broad on the counter.*

"You had any action tonight?" he asked.

"Any what?"

"Any ass, you know?"

"Oh–no, we've been driving all night."

"Oh, yeah, well, me neither. It's a fucking drag, you know? Who's we?"

"What?"

"You said we *been driving. Your old lady with you?"*

"Oh, no, me and Robert. He let me drive some of the way."

He tilted his head and looked at me funny. "Did he? Well, that was nice of him, wasn't it? Where's he?"

"Oh, he's asleep. Don't worry, he won't wake up."

"Why should I worry? Is he dangerous?"

"Him? Hell no! I just couldn't stay if he woke up, that's all."

He laughed again–and he reached deep in his pocket. I could see his fingers moving as he played with himself.

"He don't like you out fucking around by yourself, huh? You, uh...looking for something specific?"

"Something what?"

"Besides pussy, man! A little of the straight *stuff, maybe."*

It was easy enough to figure out what he meant, the way he was playing with himself–playing with his "straight stuff"! "Maybe," I said.

"Yeah...I kinda figured." He grinned and took his hand out of his pocket. I could see that his cock was

hard. "Don't get me wrong, it don't bother me. What the fuck? Right?"

I laughed. "Right. What the fuck!"

He started playing with himself again, this time on the outside, sort of squeezing it, pulling it up where it showed better. My stomach got to feeling very funny—the way it did when I started to jack off.

"I mean, everybody's entitled to play his own game, right?"

"Right."

"So...what's your game?"

I shrugged my shoulders. I still wasn't completely sure what he wanted to hear. I knew he was interested in getting his cock sucked, just like I was. But it didn't seem like he was offering to suck mine—not by showing me his, he wasn't.

For a minute it scared me, thinking about actually doing *it—but then I thought what the hell? I wanted some excitement, didn't I?*

It might be kind of fun to suck his cock.

"Well?" he said.

"What?"

"Aw, come on, buddy. Are you interested or ain't you?"

"Maybe," I said. "Are you?"

"Well, shit, mac, I wouldn't be standin' here with a fuckin' hard-on if I wasn't."

"Let me see it."

"How much is it worth, buddy?"

I tried to remember how much money Robert had brought. I hadn't expected to have to pay anything, but what the hell? "It can't be too much," I told him. "We didn't bring much cash." I took Robert's money out and counted it. Eleven dollars...and seven cents. I spread it out on the counter. "Is that enough?"

He scooped it up. "Well," he said. "If that's all you got, that's all I get." He put it into his pocket. Then he came around the bar. "Hang on." He went to the door and looked out, then he propped the door partly open with a chair. "It's okay," he said. "This way I can hear if somebody drives up. That's one good thing about this dump, can't nobody sneak up on you. What about your buddy? Will he wake up, you think?"

I smiled and shook my head. "No. He won't wake up till I want him to."

"Okay," he said. "Let's go back by the cans."

I got off the stool and followed him. Near the back of the room, where the bar curved around and there was a little trap door for him to go through, he leaned back on the bar and unzipped his pants and pulled his cock out. It wasn't stiff now, just sort of half-hard, drooping down. It excited me, just seeing it out. I felt I wanted to touch it. It seemed so strange to be reaching out for another guy's cock, but then I remembered that night with Billy and I told myself, Just do what you done then. So I touched it. It jerked up and got harder. The guy was just leaning there, his elbows on the bar, watching what I was doing. I closed my hand around it and squeezed, and he hunched it toward me. "Suck it, baby," he whispered. "C'mon, suck ol' Jessie's cock. Make it feel good."

I got down on my knees and leaned my head forward, watching it get closer and closer. I felt dizzy and funny all over. My own cock felt like it would go off any minute!

Suddenly he reached down and grabbed hold of my head and jammed his cock into my lips. It scraped my teeth and he jerked back. "Don't you bite me, you sonofabitch!"

"I'm sorry! But you...I wasn't ready."

"Well, you get yourself ready, cause I'm gonna fuck your face! And don't bite!"

"I prommfff!" He shoved it into my mouth again. It tasted funny, sort of salty and bitter, but it felt good. It *felt warm and thick and tight and it filled my whole mouth! I clamped my lips over my teeth, so they wouldn't scrape, and then just let him go ahead and fuck, while I reached down and fumbled to get my cock out.*

"Oh, yeah," he was saying. "Oh, yeah, baby, suck it! Oh, man, am I glad you came in here, oh suck it!"

I was pumping my own cock, tingling all over, as he put his hands over my ears and held my head tight and fucked harder and harder....

"Gonna give you my cum, baby! Hot sticky cum! Shoot my load in your fuckin' throat! Fuckin' mouth! Oh, Jee-zuss! Oh, mannnn! Oh...my...God!"

Suddenly he held my head tight and shoved! And the head of his cock went right down my throat, and I felt his hot stuff shooting into me. My own cock went off like a geyser, and I tried to pull back, but he held my head tight, with his cock down my throat, still shooting, and I couldn't breathe! Then I knew what he was going to do to me! He was going to choke me to death with his cock! He was just going to leave his cock down there and just keep shooting and shooting until I was dead!

I didn't want to die!

I was kneeling–with something warm and hard in my mouth, blocking my throat–and my cock was shooting wildly! Hands clasped the back of my head and my face was buried in thick scratchy hair.

"Ohhhhh....*Shit!* Mannnnnnn!"

The thing started softening, inching out of my throat. The hands on my head relaxed, then fell away. I jerked backward and looked up.

A man stood over me, his head tilted backward, his mouth open. His cock was still dripping, white semen oozing out, dropping onto the floor. My own cock was in my hand and my own semen was sticky through my fingers.

I stumbled to my feet, terrified, dizzy, totally disoriented, my body still churning.

A few seconds ago I'd been driving the car on the highway—and then suddenly I was in a strange room with a strange man—with his semen in my mouth! I felt I was going to be sick. I looked for a place to spit, but there wasn't any. I closed my eyes and swallowed. I had to get out of there! But my body was still uncontrollable.

"Oh, man!"

The sound of his voice jolted me into action. I saw what I thought was the door, and stumbled toward it, stuffing my cock in my pants as I went.

"Hey!"

There was a chair propping the door open. I jerked at the door and kicked the chair aside.

"What the fuck? Hey!"

Outside the cold air chilled me, helped wake me up. I looked for the car, spotted it, then ran to it. I heard him laughing behind me. I fumbled to get the key into the lock, and saw that the door wasn't even completely closed! As I backed in a circle, gravel clattering, I saw the man leaning in the doorway. It looked as though his cock was still hanging out. He was laughing and waving to me.

I could only guess which direction to go in. In the "dream" it seemed I'd already driven through town. I turned left, away from the center of lights, then shoved the gas all the way down to the floor. The Volks bucked and then shot away.

I was furious with Rob! The idiot could have got me killed! Or arrested! It was insane, taking chances like that! Right there in the bar! With the door propped open!

"*Imbecile!*" I yelled. "Grow up! You do that again and you'll get us both strangled, and what the hell good will I be to you dead? Or arrested? You get us inside a jail, and I can't get us out!"

I felt a slight "cringing"–like a dog being scolded–but nothing else; no retort.

I tried to calm myself down–but damn him! It was so fucking frustrating, being angry with someone you couldn't see! Couldn't touch! Someone you only *dreamed* about! Not someone sitting here where I could see him, get hold of him, shake hell out of him! I had to *feel* it. I had to *guess* what he was thinking. I didn't even know when he was listening and when he wasn't! I was sick and tired of him!

I felt a kind of whimpering fear–a fear that I might do something–feel for something....

I slapped my hand on my pocket, reached inside....

There wasn't a penny!

I was trying to think of something else to yell at him, when I suddenly noticed the gas gauge: the needle was hovering about a hair's breadth *below* the empty mark! And this car didn't have a reserve tank.

I couldn't get angrier.

Now each new stupidity that piled on the others seemed simply pathetically humorous. It was cruel to yell at him. I could imagine him curled inside his "dark room" frightened and confused and ashamed.

Realistically, I couldn't be angry with Rob. It wasn't his fault he was still a child–it was Robber's. And Robber would never be completely dead until Rob was grown up. They were both parts of each other. One counterbalanced the other–and I was a strange kind of offspring of the two of them. Ultimately I had to take the responsibilities for Robber's mistakes until they were corrected.

And for Rob's.

Even if we ran out of gas, I couldn't blame him. He had only wanted a little excitement. He was still just a child. Well, he'd had his excitement, and I hoped it had taught him a lesson. The sooner he learned, the better off we'd both be.

"But please," I said softly. "Please don't get us into trouble. I'm not blaming you. It's not your fault. But, *please*, let *me* do the thinking. We'll have our fun."

The engine started bucking just as I passed a sign reading *Carlin–1 mile*, and I managed to coast to within half a mile of the little town. By then I was definitely feeling the pill taking over again, restoring my energy and my good humor. And the sky was beginning to go grey; I could see the desert landscape now, and it was beautifully empty. I almost felt good, walking into town. There was only one tiny gas station open, and it wasn't one that would take any of my credit cards. It took fifteen minutes to talk the attendant into taking a check, but he finally agreed, and took down my driver's licence number and the number of every single one of my credit cards; even then he would only go ten dollars. By the time I walked back to my car, the eastern sky was bright, getting ready for sunrise. The air was pleasantly cool, and it felt good.

It was six o'clock when I finally drove out of that gas station, and the sun was a blinding glare in my outside mirror. But it was too late to worry about being late; I'd just have to call Bill from Sacramento or someplace and tell him I'd be late. The important thing was that nothing really bad had happened; I was still in one piece, still alive and reasonably well in spite of everything.

I stopped in Winnemucka and bought a thermos bottle, and for the rest of the trip I kept it beside me, constantly ready to uncork it and gulp down more coffee the minute I felt the slightest indication that Rob might be trying to get out again.

I reached Reno at ten-forty-five. I'd been making good time, but I knew there was no way possible for me to get to San Francisco before three. I wasn't at all hungry, but I decided I ought to have something to eat, and from the cafe I called the office.

Virginia told me that Ed had called just a few minutes before, saying he wouldn't be in either. He was in Ogden. I started to get angry, knowing we had no accounts in Ogden, knowing that Ed's only possible reason for being there was to be with Kate—but then I asked myself *why not?* What right had I to be angry with Ed for wanting to be with the woman he loved—and their children?

"When he gets back, Virginia," I told her, "if you will, tell Ed I want Gary to go over the books. Oh, no—no problem. I just want to know what we're worth. Tell Ed I'll call him later in the week, okay?"

And that—as I hung up the phone—seemed to be one of the last remaining doors to be closed. I felt much better about everything as I started up over Donner Summit. At one point I looked back and saw the stark, empty black hills and desert stretching behind me—like my life; and just after one o'clock, I passed over the summit and started down into the lush green valleys of California. It seemed to me to be beautifully symbolic: I was leaving a dead vacant past, moving into something fresh and new—a rebirth, a coming alive after a long-long empty winter.

I had stopped for gas at a station just west of Sacramento, and was wandering around, feeling on top of the world, filled with a beautiful new optimism—the fields and the trees were so green, and the sky was so bright and blue—when I glanced into the station's office and saw the clock. It was 3:09!

I had completely forgotten about calling Bill!

I raced to the phone booth, but by the time I'd got Bill's number from Information, then change from the station attendant, ten more minutes had passed. I placed the call, angrily castigating myself for not calling earlier as I'd promised. I was assuming he'd asked me to call before three because that was when he went to work.

Three-thirty or four would be about the right time for a second shift someplace. Now I would probably have to wait another eight hours to talk to him.

To my surprise, a deep voice answered the call on the second ring. "Hello?"

For a moment my bright spirits revived: "Bill?"

"No, this is Warren."

I hesitated unsurely; it had never occurred to me that Bill might have a roommate. A woman answering the the phone wouldn't have surprised me, but a man?

"Is Bill there?" I asked.

"No, he left about, oh, twenty minutes ago."

"I see. Is there any way I can call him at work? It's sort of important."

"He won't be at work. It's his day off. Hang on just a minute." Faintly I heard him call, "Hey, do you know where Bill went?" There was a pause. "Will he be at the bar later?" Then: "Still there?"

"Yes?"

"I'm sorry, but we don't have any idea where he might be. You could try calling the bar later on—around ten or so—usually he comes in, but you never can tell."

"What bar is that?"

"The Phoenix," he said, sounding puzzled, as though he'd expected me to know which bar he was talking about. "If he does come in, should I give him a message?"

"Yes," I said despondently. "Tell him his brother called. Thanks."

I was starting to hang up when I heard him say, "Bob?"

"Yes?"

For a moment there was silence, and I thought maybe he'd hung up, but then I heard something that sounded like, "Oh, shit!" and a long sigh. "Bob, I'm sorry. You should have told me who you were. Listen, Bill was expecting your call earlier."

"I know," I said. "I...didn't get a chance."

"Listen, Bob, don't bother about calling that bar I mentioned. I mean, there's no guarantee he'd be there. I'm sure he'll be home by midnight, though. Why don't you call then—or tomorrow."

"All right."

"I'll tell him you called if I see him. He'll be sorry he missed you."

"Yes," I said flatly. "I'm sure he will be. Well, thanks."

I hung up the receiver, then stared at it. I knew I had no right to be angry with Bill; he'd asked me to call before three, and I hadn't. Maybe he'd had an appointment, or maybe a date—although that seemed unlikely at this time of day—but, damn him, if it was his day off, why the hell hadn't he waited just another twenty minutes?

I knew I was being irrational, that missing him had been entirely my own fault, but I couldn't help myself: I remembered the disappointment last night when he hadn't been willing to talk to me, and I couldn't stop thinking that the same thing had happened again. It was the way Robber would have thought and I knew it, but knowing it didn't stop the dark ideas from forming. I shoved the door open and left the booth, feeling weary and disgusted. What the hell was I doing in California anyway? How had I convinced myself that Bill would be happy to see me?

Now the fields were just ordinary fields, the sky was just sky; the filling station was ugly and cluttered—and the attendant was glaring at me, waiting for me to pay him for the gas. I'd been a romantic fool, dreaming about a happy reunion with my brother. The Prodigal Son had returned, filled with Sunday School fantasies about parties and fatted calves, only to discover that no one really gave a damn whether he came back or not.

I was very tempted to turn the car around and go back the way I had come—go back to living in the nightmare. But I knew that I couldn't. I'd been so foolishly confident that the answer to all of my problems would be finding Bill, I'd burned most of my bridges behind me. Even if I got back in time to destroy the note I'd left for Chuck, I'd still be stuck with the promise I'd made him: to give Kate the divorce. I'd already failed in one promise today; I couldn't let myself go back on another one.

There was nothing to do but keep going. On the plane I had wished that I hadn't left San Francisco; well, now I was on my way back and I might just as well finish the trip—although what I would do when I got there was anyone's guess.

I finished the drive in a mood of sullen emptiness. The pill I had taken in Elko was still functioning to keep me awake, but that bright optimism had left me completely. Several times I tried to convince myself that Bill's roommate had been telling the truth, that Bill had waited all day for my call, and would indeed be sorry he'd missed it—but the effort was too much. Old Robber had risen up from his grave and was reestablishing himself, and I didn't have enough confidence left to resist him.

The weather and traffic seemed determined to aid and abet my mood. About thirty miles out of Sacramento, a strong wind began blowing from the west, wintery cold, and just about that same time all four lanes of the freeway began filling. Leaving the Sacramento valley, going down into Vallejo, I left the bright springtime behind me. Foggy clouds scuttled over the sun and finally obscured it completely. The chilling wind blew stronger and stronger from the dark bay. And the traffic grew thicker and thicker. The speedometer needle dropped from sixty to fifty to forty to thirty.... By the time I started across the Bay Bridge, and entered the fogbank, the car was barely creeping along.

And once in the city itself, the traffic was hopelessly

snarled, backed up for blocks behind every entrance and exit to the freeway. It took half an hour just to get from the Fifth Street exit across town to Van Ness, and by then I was thoroughly miserable and exhausted, asking myself why I had ever wanted to come back to such a cold, dreary, grossly overpopulated, inhospitable city? After five or ten minutes creeping up to an intersection, drivers behind me would start honking the instant the light changed, then dart into other lanes to go racing past, glowering out of their streaked, steamy windows; pedestrians would walk calmly against the light, or dart out in the middle of a block, yelling and shaking their fists at me if I didn't see them and stop instantly.

Trembling from fatigue and frustration, I finally managed to find the hotel I'd stayed at before. I parked in the lot and took my suitcase inside, not giving a damn that I looked (and felt) like a tramp in my levis and workshirt, with a two-day black stubble of beard.

Once inside a room, I collapsed on the bed without bothering to unpack or clean up. I was tired and disgusted and I couldn't have cared less what happened if I went to sleep. Let Rob come out; let him get me into any kind of mess he wanted to. What possible difference could it make at this point anyway?

Chapter 2

"You sonofabitch!"

I jumped up off the bed, shaking and mad as hell! That damn Robert had lied to me! He'd promised that Robber was dead. Cut up and scattered all over Salt Lake. And then he'd just sat there and let him wake up and take over again.

That sonofabitch fucking bastard!

So he expected me to get him in a mess, did he? Well, damn him, I'd show him what a mess really was! I didn't even have to think what to do: I'd take off my fucking clothes and just march right out of here and down in that elevator and out through that fucking lobby and on to the street. Right out in the middle of fucking San Francisco!

And he'd wake up stark naked in jail!

The lying, rotten sonofabitch!

I sat on the bed and took off my shoes and socks. Then I stood up and took off my shirt and my pants. I'd fix them both! I'd teach them both lessons they'd never forget.

I could picture some fat lady starting to get on the elevator, then seeing me there without one fucking stitch on, and her running down the hall, and me yelling, "Fuck you, Fat Lady!" and her calling the manager to call the police. "There's a naked man in your elevator!" But by the time the cops got there, I'd be out on the street, dancing and yelling, with my cock and balls flopping around, and everyone stopping and staring.

And then I'd wake up Robert!

Let him try to get out of that kind of a mess!

My body was tingling and my heart pounding like hell, just thinking about it. I went to the door, opened it and stepped out into the hallway. The hall was empty, and that made me feel disappointed, but I thought what the hell, there'll be people to see me downstairs.

I started to close the door, but for some reason it just wouldn't close all the way. It was like I had suddenly got weak and couldn't even close a goddamn stupid door. Fuck it! Leave it open. Let Robert sit there naked in jail and worry about whether some crook had got in and stolen his clothes.

My damn heart was pounding like a fucking drum as I started down the hall. I knew I was getting scared, but this time I wasn't going to let that stop me. Once I got on that elevator, that's all it would take. Once an elevator started down, you couldn't make it stop. It had to go all the way to where you had punched it, and even if I passed out and Robert woke up, he'd have to go all the way down to the lobby, and someone would see him and call the cops!

But damn it, I felt like I was walking through soup! He was fighting me! I could feel him. He was trying to wake up.

But then I saw somebody coming. Way down at the end of the hall.

Too late now, Robert! Too fucking late now!

It was a man, coming toward me. I stopped for a minute, waiting for him to spot me and go yelling back down the hall for the cops. He stopped too, but he didn't yell. He just stared at me.

Then I saw that he was undressed too!

What the hell was he doing? If someone else did it, that spoiled it!

I felt dizzy. My head felt all fuzzy inside. I seemed to remember the man. Did he recognize me? Was that why he had stopped? Maybe he knew me. Maybe he wanted to suck my cock. He seemed like a damn good-looking bastard from all I could see. He was older than me—old enough to be my old man, almost—but *what the fuck? That would make it all the more interesting.*

That would be even better than going downstairs. We'd do it right here in the hallway! Let that fat lady see him just kneeling there sucking away at my cock!

I started toward him—and he started toward me—but the closer I got, the more dizzy I felt. The way he was watching me was the same way someone else used to watch me....

And then suddenly I knew who he was!

"Good God!" I whispered.

I whirled away from the mirror and raced back down the hall and into my room. I slammed the door, bolted it, then leaned back against it, so frightened and furious I couldn't even think. My mind was a maelstrom of savage abuse and recriminations, enraged even more by the utter futility of self-castigation. Vividly I began to see fragments of stories and movies about madmen going berserk, howling and breaking things, tearing at everything including themselves—and I knew I was not very far from that point. How easy it would have been at that moment to start crashing my head into the wall, to scream at the top of my lungs and start pulling my hair out, to rip down those goddamned insipid drapes, throw over the bed, rip the sheets into tatters, hurl chairs out the windows. Just give up and go insane!

That would fix Rob! That would stop him. If I went insane, then he probably wouldn't even exist any longer!

One thing stopped me: an almost comically mundane realization that someone would have to pay for it. And not simply money for damages. They might lock me away in a padded cell, and I might never again remember my real name—let alone Rob's or Robber's—but someone would suffer for what I had done, and I knew that most likely it would be Chuck. ("Hey, Chuck, I hear your old man's in the looney-bin. Like father, like son, right Chuck?")

It would have been such a fantastic release just to let

go—to break everything in sight, and then, in one grand final gesture of triumphant failure, to rip myself open with the shreds and the pieces of the havoc. But I couldn't. And finally I slipped down until I was sitting on the floor, and put my head into my hands and wept—at first with frustration, and then with self-pity, but at last with a purely instinctive need for purgation.

And when it was over, I got up and went into the bathroom and washed my face. Then I went out and sat on the bed, feeling totally empty, but cleansed. I sat for a long time just staring ahead, seeing nothing, thinking nothing, allowing my body to gather its strength mindlessly.

Out beyond my windows, the grey daylight faded; lights came on in unseen buildings, waxing and waning in eddies of fog. In the hallway people came and went, chattering, laughing, sometimes quarreling, sometimes with no more than a soft swish of footsteps on carpeting. And slowly my mind started functioning again. One of my first clear thoughts was that life would go on, with or without me; my suicide or insanity might cause a momentary excitement among the hotel guests, or the people on the street as they hauled me away in a police car or ambulance, but the people would quickly go back to their ordinary lives and I would become nothing more to them than "that nut in the hotel", or "that loony who killed himself", an anecdote to tell the folks back home, then forget. I did not want to become an event in someone else's vacation—not at that price.

I knew that my life had contributed very little to the world as a whole; only a small handful of people even knew I existed; my death or insanity would take away no more than the little I'd put in. Still, that "little" was important to me and I couldn't allow myself to negate it. I had a son—and I had my own life. And, when I considered it, not many people could honestly claim more: a few major prophets, perhaps, and a few Nobel Prizewinners. But not many more.

So why should I be so unforgiving of myself because of my failures? I had tried to live the way I'd been taught to live. I had refused to give Kate a divorce because I'd been taught that divorce was a sin. I had tried to fit myself into a pattern, and it hadn't worked—but how could I be sure which was at fault, myself or the pattern? Maybe I was "different", maybe I had been born "queer"—and not necessarily in the homosexual sense of that word: maybe I'd never be able to make the rules work for me, no matter how hard I tried. But that didn't set me apart from the entire world. There were thousands of people, maybe millions, who were screaming and yelling that the rules didn't work for them either—but they blamed the rules, not themselves. Maybe I wasn't so different after all.

Was I any worse off than my own father? Bishop Matthew T. Thorne, the epitome of American middle-class Godfearing normalcy—a man so respected in Glen Falls by people who would never really know him that his name had become almost holy: *Bishop Thorne!* He had two sons who hated him and a wife who had stopped loving him long ago. He and Mom lived together simply out of habit now, sleeping in different rooms, living separate lives, paying as little attention to each other as possible, simply putting up a "good front" for the relatives and neighbors.

Had Kate and I done worse? Chuck had been no more neglected than Bill and I had been—nor for that matter had Cindy and Dorene. Our lives had become habit too; but by breaking the habit—even though it had involved having my nose rubbed in it—I was giving us all a fresh chance at some kind of happiness, or success, or, if nothing more, at least a more comfortable failure. I'd also regained something I'd thought lost forever: the beginnings of love and respect from my son. I could not throw that away—not by killing myself, nor by running naked through hotel lobbies.

I might not have contributed much to the world, but

by killing myself or going insane I'd ruin any even remote chance I might have of someday doing something that might make a ripple in history. If I did no more than prevent Chuck's being ashamed of me, I'd be doing something worthwhile. There was no sense at all in continuing to punish myself, either through Robber's gloom and self-deprecation or through Rob's childish temper-tantrums.

But I couldn't, in good conscience, blame Rob for his anger with me: I had indeed allowed myself to backslide into becoming Robber again. But the mistake had not been in letting Robber come back from the grave and take over—it had been in believing he was dead in the first place. I hadn't lied to Rob; I'd believed he was dead myself. But Robber was no more dead than Rob was, than I was; as violently dissimilar as we were, still we all had to live in the same body together. I understood now that I couldn't get rid of either of them by ignoring them, pretending they were dead, or by pushing them back into a "dark room" in my mind.

I knew what that felt like now.

I hadn't been "asleep" one second of the time during Rob's angry undressing and stomping out into the hallway. In a way it had been like dreaming: dreaming about being sucked back into a cage in my mind, becoming a prisoner within my own body, screaming without voice, pounding without fists, helplessly hearing my own thoughts turning against me. It had been the most desperate and exhausting effort of my life just to keep him from closing that door—with no hope at all that I'd ever be able to get back to it. Only circumstance had saved me—the lucky fact that some unknown decorator had decided to put mirrors at the ends of the hallways.

For a while I was baffled by Rob's non-recognition of his own mirror-image. Surely he'd looked into mirrors before. But then I remembered his thinking that Robber "hid in mirrors". That too had bewildered me at the time, but now, when I put the two together, I began to understand: Rob had been "put away" into his dark room during those few feverish days back in Glen Falls. I hadn't "changed places" with Bill, then; in effect, I had truly become a new person, almost without memory, because I'd shut out all of my memories of Bill. By suppressing and denying and negating myself, I'd rid myself of the guilt, but I'd also rid myself of the person I'd been—both good and bad. I'd even gone to the extent of suddenly refusing to answer to *Bobby*, insisting on being called *Robert.* Only *Robert* was proper enough for the good, clean, righteous boy I'd suddenly become. But Bobby had not been destroyed by the conversion; he had only been put out of mind, out of consciousness—and there he had lain, a perpetual child, sulking about being locked up by a robber—until Robert had grown unwary enough, or weary enough, for Bobby to come out again. No wonder he behaved like a petulant child. And no wonder he didn't recognize himself. He probably expected to see himself as a sixteen-year-old kid, not a thirty-five-year-old man.

Somehow I had to find a way to make him understand that he wasn't a child any more, that he *was* a thirty-five-year-old man. I could see now that he looked upon me with the same kind of unquestioning acceptance as a child would an adult. It had never occurred to him that *he* would be in jail, right along with me. Somehow we had to make a pact not to endanger our communal body—not to hurt it or get it arrested or have it wrapped up in a strait-jacket. The problem was, how could I convince him? How could I even make contact with him?

On an impulse, I stood up from the bed. In an alcove between bedroom and bathroom was a combination dressing-room/closet with an old-fashioned ladies' vanity and a huge oval mirror. I switched on the overhead light and stood there regarding myself. "That's *you*, Bobby," I said softly. "That's *your* body. You're that damn good-looking bastard you saw in the hallway. You're me, buddy. And you're Robber too. We're all three the same guy, and we've got to face it and live with it. If one of us goes to jail, or kills himself, or goes crazy, that's it for all three of us!"

I began to feel foolish, standing there naked talking to myself. I almost gave in to the impulse to laugh derisively, turn off the light, and try to forget the whole crazy business. *Treat it as an unpleasant nightmare—like everything else!* But that was the old Robber talking.

I told myself: *Yes, it is crazy. That's precisely what it is—it's insane. But that doesn't make it unreal. It won't go away by pretending it doesn't exist or by treating it all as a bad dream. It is not a bad dream; it is real.*

Trying to make it unreal was like constantly closing the doors that I wanted to be opened. I had to deliberately open those doors and then leave them that way. I had to start learning to live with both Robber and Rob, learn to cope with them as parts of my personality, not as two evil spirits who took control of my body. And *I* had to realize that we were the same thing, before either of them could. I had to prove to *myself*, not just them, that it wasn't so bad being me. *All* of me.

I chuckled, thinking about the old song "Why not take all of me?" Another song popped into my mind, from one of those albums Chuck had played for me: "Come together...right now....over me!"

Yes, I thought, it had to be done *right now*. I couldn't put it off till tomorrow, or until after I'd talked to Bill. I had been very childlike myself, thinking I could run back to Bill with my problems, wanting him to say some magic word to make all the bad things go away. I had created the problems myself, however childish or ill-advised I had been, and now I had to solve those problems myself.

I was trembling with apprehension as I let my eyes close, then whispered, "Come out, Rob."

Nothing happened.

"Rob?..."

Bobby! The name snapped into my thoughts like a sharp rebuke. *Bobby, Bobby, BOBBY!*

I nodded. *I'm sorry. I meant Bobby.*

I felt a sullen smugness which quickly became a kind of curious expectancy.

Slowly I opened my eyes.

I looked at myself in the mirror, seeing myself as I had just a moment ago, but now with a new sense of awe and excitement. That was *me* in the mirror! *Me!* The excitement brought out gooseflesh all over my body—and I touched it, feeling the delicious tingle—watched myself touching myself.

I felt sad! Something very precious had suddenly gone from my life. As worrisome and frightening as it had been, still it had been an escape to be able to think of myself as a child again, without all the restraints and restrictions an adult has to live with—without that maddening sense of *responsibility.*

But the sadness passed as I thought about all the nice new things I could do with my adult body. I let my hand run down over my stomach, watching it, feeling it, and down to my cock. At first it felt numb, almost cold, withered in my hand like a little dead animal. That's the way Robber liked to keep it, all of the time—but it didn't feel good that way! I wanted it to feel good. It was my cock, and it was special, and it was beautiful!

It started to get warm, and to grow, and a soft, sweet fluttering began in my stomach.

I wanted to go out and find someone to touch me the way I was touching myself! Someone I could touch the same way. Someone who would touch my cock, and let me touch his, and then suck it! I wanted to find out what this "new" body of mine could feel like when I wasn't all bottled up—when I had all my doors wide open! Right now!

I laughed at my own impatience. *No, not yet.*

I gasped and staggered back as a sudden stunning pain erupted in my head.

Stop it!

The pain seemed to falter.

Bobby! Stop it!

Reluctantly the pain went away. I hadn't realized what a frightening power this childish part of me had developed; I should have known—remembering the headaches and the dizziness and trembling. I took a deep breath, then looked into my eyes in the mirror. "Bobby...don't *you* feel that, when you hurt me? Don't you feel the pain too? I can't let you stay out if you keep hurting me."

For a moment it seemed that the pain would flare again, but then, with a sullen acceptance, it faded—and with it, that feeling of newness. Bobby had gone back into his room to sulk and consider things.

"We'll go out," I promised my reflection. "As soon as we shower and shave and get dressed."

Not just out, I thought, but out to find someone—someone I could touch, someone who would touch me. I wanted that as much as *he* did.

Another thought came into my mind like a dark voice of doom: *You're a queer.*

I cringed, almost turned away; then I looked at myself, from my head to my toes, half-expecting to see myself as a monster, twisted and ugly—but my body hadn't changed in the slightest. I smiled. "All right," I said aloud. "I'm a queer. I'm a cocksucking homosexual and probably have been my entire life, only I just didn't have the good sense to know it. Is your way any better?

Making other people miserable. Is that what you want? To hate yourself for the rest of your life?"

The dark voice grumbled like thunder clouds roiling in my mind, but eventually it too subsided as Robber went back to his room, to ponder my questions.

But I had to stop calling him *Robber.* That wasn't his true name any more than *Rob* had been Bobby's. He was *Robert* the "clean-living", "clean-thinking", "morally-straight", uptight Robert.

Robert and Bobby. The "new" names made them seem much more a part of me—and I'd already discovered that knowing their true names was like having a kind of power over them.

Feeling an almost giddy sense of triumph, I turned from the mirror and went into the front room to get my shaving supplies.

Robert and Bobby...and Bob.

Last night, at the end of my mescaline trip, I'd announced to Bill: "This is Bob." That's who I wanted to be—the collective me, when I managed to pull myself together—that man who had called himself Bob, with all of his fantastic self-confidence and insight and self-assurance, with that wonderful feeling of "everything's all right". That's who I wanted to become.

And I couldn't help feeling that I'd just taken a giant step toward finally becoming him.

I shaved and showered quickly, feeling as impatient as Bobby to get out and start to discover what this new life of mine had in store for me. At the same time, like Robert, I couldn't help being concerned about that new life's being "queer". I knew very little about homosexuals, but for the most part, I didn't like what I knew. The image I had in my mind was of what Ed called "fags"—slim, giggling girl-boys, sashaying around like prepubescent girls pretending to be Ladies, lisping, calling each other "my dear" like a bunch of Edwardian fops transplanted into the twentieth century.

But John Adams had not been like that.

Nor had Chuck.

Chuck had said, "Dad, the world's changing."

Maybe it was. Maybe I could find a place to go where I could meet someone like John Adams. I remembered him telling me what a fine time he'd had in the city, how he'd hated to leave. "Anything you want, just reach out and grab it."

I started to put on my new jacket and bellbottoms, then stopped myself. John Adams had been wearing levis and a T-shirt; I felt I could be reasonably sure that he hadn't dressed that way especially for the flight home. My levis were lying right there by the bed—and my old blue workshirt didn't smell too badly.

As I watched myself dressing in the old-fashioned mirror, it seemed I had made a complete circle these last three days. This room was enough like the one I'd had then as to be practically identical; it would have been very easy to believe that only a few moments had passed—that I'd started to put on the new clothes and thought: *Wait! What's going to happen to me if I do?* And I'd been absorbed by a fantasy, about going home, dying, being reborn, and returning to decide: *No, I'll skip the new clothes and put on some old ones.*

I felt something in my shirt pocket and fished it out: the last half-tablet of Dexamyl. I decided to take it. Right now I was running on pure nervous energy, and that might fail me at any time. I didn't want to depend on a drug, but at the same time I didn't want Bobby or Robert taking over if my energy failed me.

And I still wanted to call Bill later. That had been Robert reacting when I'd ignored what his roommate had told me, deciding instead that he didn't want to talk to me. I might even try calling that bar the roommate had mentioned.

The Phoenix.

I might even enjoy going there personally to look for him; the name sounded very apropos of all that had been happening to me.

Chapter 3

Surprisingly, most of the fog had lifted by the time I came out of the hotel; now it hung like a dark but glimmering blanket over the city, obscuring only the tops of the highest buildings, leaving the streets looking freshly washed and shining. I hurried away from the hotel feeling much the same way, with a new sense of direction and purpose. The last three days had been like a passage through Purgatory, a cleansing, a baptism-by-fire; but this was the real beginning.

Trying to decide where to go, I began to remember the night Bobby had sneaked out to buy those pictures. I seemed to remember the name *Polk Street.* If nothing else, I could go to that store and ask someone where to go. I hated the idea of approaching a stranger to ask, "Where's a queer bar I can go to?" but I couldn't think of any other alternative.

Polk Street was only two blocks up the hill from the hotel. I stood on a corner, trying to remember which way I had turned to go to the bookstore, but I couldn't concentrate on the decision; the atmosphere along the street was almost one of carnival, with costumes ranging from ragged-hippie to tailored suits with ruffled shirts. I began to realize that there was an extremely high percentage of men wandering around, and very few women (and looking more closely at those "women" made me begin to wonder about the true nature of the sexual equipment under their dresses). There seemed to be a feeling of expectancy in everyone I saw—and the way some of them looked at me as they passed, I began to feel that they would like to make me the thing they'd been expecting.

It was not an altogether unpleasant feeling.

One young man hitched his trousers around so that his cock made an even more obvious bulge in the tight fabric, smiling brightly as he walked past. He wasn't a John Adams, but then he wasn't unattractive, and his actions had clearly shown that he wouldn't reject me if I knew how to approach him.

I turned, slowly and casually, to look after him as he walked up the street—then paused to look back before going into a doorway. I looked up at the sign above the door: *The Primrose Path.*

I hesitated only a few moments before going into the bar (pausing as I listened to a conversation in my head: *Turn around, you fool, before it's too late. Keep going. It's a gay bar. They'll all be gay inside. That's what you've decided you are, isn't it? You step inside that door and you're declaring yourself. You'll be telling everyone "Look at me! I'm a queer!" Fuck off! Who cares? Who really gives a fuck if I'm queer or not? Chuck. He's queer too! He'd approve of my going in. "You've just taken your first giant step, Dad." Go ahead. You've got to do it sometime.)* Then I pushed the door open and went in.

For a moment—just as I stepped through the door, as the music and the conversation seemed to pause, as faces turned to look at me—I might have believed I had stepped into an average American semi-high-class neighborhood cocktail lounge, where, for some reason—such as a PTA meeting or a grade-school recital—the young men of the neighborhood had gathered for a drink without their wives. But only for a moment: the atmosphere of carnival I'd felt on the street here became a feeling almost of frenzy. The music was so loud that it rattled my eardrums, but the din of voices was even louder, and there was a stridency in some of those voices which was painful to listen to. The room was not particularly crowded, but it seemed like an anthill—constant movement. In and out the front door, from one booth to another, back and forth to the rest rooms—and I stared, unbelieving, when I saw that the far end of the room was a dance floor, and that the couples there dancing were all males.

I saw the young man who had smiled at me sitting on the second stool down at the bar; the last stool was empty. I tried to look very nonchalant as I wandered to the bar. He turned as I sat down, and I thought he would start a conversation, but then he turned quickly away as though suddenly remembering that he was "shy".

I knew that I couldn't stay here very long; I'd never be able to relax and enjoy myself in this constant racket. There was a feeling of desperation in the room that made me want to hunch my shoulders against it.

The bartender, an otherwise very normal-looking blond young man, was moving around behind the bar in a way that reminded me of an old Fred Astaire movie. When he finally noticed me and came dancing over, he smiled like a toothpaste ad and said, "Hi there, Sweetie, what'll it be?"

I cringed and ordered a beer, deciding not to have any hard liquor until I had found a place much less frenetic than this—and preferably one where the bartender wouldn't call me Sweetie.

I was beginning to wonder if my bright optimism back at the hotel might have been shortsighted: I wasn't even sure that I wanted to talk to the young man I'd followed in—not if he turned out anything like Twinkletoes behind the bar.

"Hi there," said a husky voice behind me. "Do you mind if I scrunch in here?"

I turned to see a man, in his thirties, I guessed, standing with his hands on his hips, his head tipped slightly to the side, smiling at me. He was not unattractive physically; he had on a sweater, but I could see that he wasn't fat, and his tight pants revealed fairly muscular legs—plus an obviously small cock. "Were you talking to me?" I asked.

"Yes, I was. I asked if I could scrunch in beside you, but what I really wanted was to say hello. My name's Tony, but my *friends* call me Sophia. What's your name?"

"Robert," I said automatically. I started to correct myself and tell him "Bob", but decided against it.

"Robert," he said dreamily. "I had a lover named Robert once. Of course, we called her 'Bobette' because she wasn't quite as butch as you are, poor dear. What are you doing way down here by yourself?"

He put his hand on my arm, and I twisted away, pretending I had something in my eye. "It just seemed like a good place to sit," I muttered.

"The smoke in this place is just awful. I keep telling Dennice that she ought to keep Murine on the bar—or gas masks."

The young man on the next stool had been glaring at "Sophia", and now turned away in disgust; he took his drink and went back toward the dance floor. "Sophia" called, "Thank you, darling! You'll be rewarded in heaven." He sat down, leaning to the man on the third stool, grasping his arm. "Hello, Love, listen, I've got something to tell you you just won't believe, so don't go away." Then he turned to me and crossed his legs like a chorus girl. "Well, Robert, may I buy you another beer—or something?"

"No, thank you. I'm only going to have this one."

"What a pity! The girls are just dying to meet you, and I'm supposed to lure you back to the booth and introduce you—but fuck them! Let them suffer. They're evil cunts anyway. They haven't got the courage to come up and talk to you, but once *I* got you back there, my dear, they'd be raping you right on the table! *Some* people are *so* tacky! Where were you planning to go when you leave here?"

"I hadn't decided."

"Are you new in the neighborhood or just slumming tonight?"

"Neither. I'm from out of town."

"Oh! What do you do?" he demanded. "For a living, I mean."

I felt like telling him it was none of his fucking business—but I was so annoyed with him that I was getting intrigued: I wanted to see just how obnoxious he would get before I told him I wasn't the least bit interested in him. "Nothing at the moment," I said.

"Are you an actor or something? I keep getting these flashes that I know you from somewhere. Do you know Kenny Peterson in Hollywood?"

I laughed. "No, I'm afraid not."

"*Are* you an actor?"

"No."

"Well, you certainly should be, my dear. If you ever go to Hollywood, let me know and I'll give you Kenny's smart address. She knows every queen in the industry, and, honey, with your looks, you could fuck your way right up there to become the new Cary Grant or somebody. I see you as a detective, you know? One of those two-fisted he-men that gets the shit kicked out of him, but always wins in the end. My dear, those movie theatres would be *dripping* with cum! *Do* you fuck?"

I almost started to laugh. "When I feel like it," I said, trying to keep my voice from cracking.

"Well, what does it take to get you feeling like it? If you'll pardon my French, I would just *love* to get my asshole stretched to a fare-thee-well tonight. Jesus, I'll bet you're built like a Mack truck! Listen, fuck this shit, let's go home and make babies!"

"I'm sorry," I said quickly, "but I'd rather not."

That stopped him, but only for a moment. "What does that mean? 'I'd rather not.' I'm not good enough for you?"

"You're...not exactly my type."

"Type, shmipe, what's the difference in the dark? An asshole's an asshole, baby, and mine is one of the most educated in town."

"Sorry."

He almost started to glare at me; then he shrugged carelessly and said, "Cheat yourself," and twisted around on the seat to face away from me. "Hello, darling, listen, I'm sorry I ignored you, but I was trying to make time with this supposedly butch number behind me. Listen, you'll never believe what happened to Edwina and I. Well...we got our smart asses kicked out of the Ganymede last night. I am so *sick* of those fucking hippie-queens, I can't tell you. This one really obnoxious fairy with his T-shirt and muscles actually stood there while I got dressed, and then *pushed* me to the office. I was so furious I couldn't even talk! And you *know* how upset I have to get before *that* happens."

I turned away, shuddering, trying to shut his voice out of my mind; but I couldn't get away from it. Even the earsplitting music didn't drown it out:

"We didn't do *anything!*" He giggled. "Well...that's not exactly true. You know Edwina and me when we get together. That poor girl. She's not exactly a charmer in her birthday suit. But she tries. Well, we were both stoned to the tits when we decided to go, and both of us got on a laughing jag, and we just couldn't stop. I mean, we'd go into that steamroom, and there would be all these *intense* fairies just *looking* at each other, and if you even *thought* about groping somebody, she'd jerk away like it was some kind of, I don't know, stevedore convention instead of the nelliest whorehouse this side of the Bronx. Well, to us, it was hysterical! All those big butch numbers who looked like they'd shit if you so much as spoke to them—sucking each other's dicks like it was going out of style. Mary, it was like watching the gay Last Supper—even with You-Know-Who up there on the top shelf, blessing everyone with his big peter! All we had to do was just look at each other, and bust up. Well, you can take that shit seriously just so long, my dear. It was just as well they threw us out, because I was almost ready to puke, it was so *masculine!* At least we got our money back."

I couldn't resist it. I leaned toward him and touched his shoulder. "Excuse me."

He turned slowly to look at me, as though he had never seen me before in his life. "Yes?"

"I couldn't help overhearing your conversation...."

"How unfortunate for you. Perhaps you should see a doctor."

"This place you were talking about—what's it called?"

"Surely you're not planning to take up your sword and go charging off to defend a girl's honor?"

"Not exactly," I said. "I just thought that if you disliked it so much, maybe I'd like it."

Rather than looking insulted, he smiled with an expression of intense relief. "Well, of course! How *gauche* of me not to have known it! I *am* sorry, my dear, but I simply did not realize who you were—with your clothes on and so...*hairless.* But you're one of the *perfect* ones, aren't you? One of the Archangels! Well, darling, the Temple is known as the Ganymede Baths, and it's right at the bottom of Broadway, you can't possibly miss it. I'm sure you'll fit in like a pea in a pod. They can worship you and you can worship them, and I'm sure you'll all be just divinely happy. I don't know the address, but I'm sure you can find it in the Yellow Pages...under *S* for *Shithouse.* Tell them Sophia sent you, won't you? Ta!"

He slipped off the barstool and turned to his friend: "Pardon me, darling, but I must tell my hungry sisters that their Handsome Prince just turned into a Frog."

The Ganymede was indeed listed in the Yellow Pages (under *B*—for *Baths).* I hurried back to the hotel and got my car, hearing "Sophia's" hostile voice in my head like a yippy little dog chasing me, nipping at my heels. I couldn't feel put down by his tirade because I couldn't relate it to myself; I was sure he'd have done the same thing with anyone he'd chosen to pounce on. His very first words to me had been like a challenge: "Like me in spite of my rudeness", as though his ultimate victory would be to submit himself sexually to someone who despised him. I could understand how such a conquest would be food for a downtrodden ego—but I could not understand why someone would go to such lengths to insure that hatred. The whole psychology of victory through submission baffled me, convincing me more than ever that if I couldn't find more homosexuals like John Adams, I'd be much better off going back to Idaho and buying that little farm, miles away from anyplace, getting a dog, and, as well as I could, ignoring completely the rest of the world. After all the trouble I'd been through, making the changes I had so far, I didn't want to go through even more to become someone like Sophia—and start calling myself "Roberta"!

Still, I was pleased with myself for having gone into the bar and stayed long enough to find out the name of an alternative place, without letting the atmosphere, or "Sophia's" glib put-down depress me, as it certainly would have a few hours ago.

I found the address easily—a dimly-lit recessed doorway in a large, apparently deserted office building down near the waterfront. There was no sign on the building, no name on the door, only a small insignia—a line-drawing of an eagle with outstretched wings, with a naked male body clutched in its talons: Zeus carrying Ganymede up to Olympus. A stranger in town would have to know a little classical mythology to be sure he had found the right place.

A few minutes later I found myself walking down a low-ceilinged, softly lighted corridor, carrying a key to room 111 ("To your left and upstairs. Have a nice evening."). Earlier I'd wondered if it would be like the Uintah Plunge, with its peeling plaster and burned-out lights, but once through that second door from the street, I'd realized that this was not going to be anything like that place; both called themselves "steam-baths", but there the similarity ended. Here the atmosphere was thoroughly relaxing. Soft pleasant music seemed to be all around me. Here there were dozens of men wandering around, most of them young, and many of them very attractive, manly-looking, well-muscled, with white towels narrowly wrapped around trim tanned waists. One or two I saw were clean-shaven and short-haired, but most of them had long hair, moustaches, sideburns, many with full luxuriant beards.

I went up a wide stairway, then turned down another long hall, passing open rooms where men lay on their small beds, some on their stomachs, with firmly-rounded white asses contrasting with the tans on their legs and backs; others were propped up on pillows against the back wall, legs spread, casually fondling themselves. Men were wandering along in the hallway, moving in and out of soft pools of light, pausing to look into open doors. There could be no doubt whatever that everyone there was looking for sex—but their complete openness, plus their young virile bodies, gave me more of a feeling of wholesomeness than degeneration. It didn't make sense according to all I had once believed about homosexuals, but I couldn't deny the very healthy atmosphere I felt. That frenetic desperation I'd felt in the bar was totally lacking here. Here there was no posturing, no scurrying, no loud strident voices—in fact for a long time I heard no voices at all, only music.

My room was small, but not like those wretched little toilet-stalls at the other place, with their half-walls and narrow bench; this was completely enclosed, painted a deep restful blue. Near the door, at the end of a bunk-sized bed, was a framed mirror, tilted toward the bed, and above that was a light fixture controlled by a dimmer. On the wall alongside the bed was a colored-charcoal mural depicting two large winged cocks, flying bodiless, each wildly ejaculating into the dark blue, their opalescent semen merging between them to cascade downward toward the bed, becoming beautifully intricate paisley designs which surrounded a legend: *To Fuck Is Human, but a Good Cocksucker Is Divine!*

I sat several minutes on the edge of the bed, staring at myself in the mirror, listening to an argument between Robert and Bobby. I realized that I could sit here all night, and the argument would go on and on endlessly with no hope of finding a realistic answer—the answer lay *out there.* So finally I stood up and undressed (here, they even had clothes-hangers, and a notched rod to hang them on).

Back in the hallway, with my towel wrapped around my waist, the elasticized band of the keys around my arm, I searched for the steam room, following signs that led downstairs and into a long narrow room where two men were towelling themselves. Both of them looked up as I came in. They studied me openly, making no attempt to disguise the fact that they were appraising me sexually.

I had the feeling that I was moving into, becoming part of, some kind of almost-real fantasy. A part of Reality existed here—I was real and my body was real, the men watching me were real—and yet there was a dreamlike quality about everything; a dream just on the verge of awakening.

But for the first time in my life, I began to enjoy being looked at.

There were several long railings attached to the walls, with towels wrapped around them. I hesitated, unsure that I wanted to take off my final defense, my last vestige of "modesty", but I guessed that no one wore their towels into the steam room, and I knew I'd stand out like a sore thumb if I did, so I wrapped it around one of the railings and went around a corner and into a circular shower. I hesitated again in the doorway, seeing three men under the showers, one of them with an erection. I had never before seen, nor imagined I ever would see, grown men nonchalantly exposing their hard cocks to each other—or to anyone else who happened to walk by. But no one seemed the least bit concerned about it, so I decided I shouldn't be either, telling myself it was simply a part of this strange new reality I was experiencing.

I showered, then went into what I guessed was the steam room—except there wasn't any steam. In the middle of four knee-high tiled tiers was the wildest gleaming jumble of naked bodies I could possibly imagine. Six or seven men, sucking each other, masturbating each other, caressing each other. Slightly apart from the jumble, two long-haired men twisted into an embrace, kissing passionately, apparently oblivious to the two others who knelt before them, both faces buried in their crotches, heads bobbing in unison.

My first impulse was to be shocked and outraged—to spin around and race back upstairs—but I thrust that completely out of my mind and stood there, leaning back on a warm slick wall, watching them, feeling my own cock beginning to rise. The drama was beautiful—there was no other word to describe it. It had a freedom and openness that transcended anything I had ever imagined.

The door to the showers opened and I glanced sideways—and felt my heart suddenly pause, and then crash into my throat. The man who stood in the doorway, staring back at me, was tall, broadshouldered, darkly tanned, with wet-curled black hair matted over his muscular belly and chest. His long black hair almost brushed his shoulders, and he wore a thick, shining black beard.

A voice in my head boomed: "Hello, Bobby-o!"

For a moment, the room disappeared, and the two of us stood in a green field, naked, smiling at each other.

Then, without a word or warning gesture, the man stepped into the room and grasped my hand to lead me through still another door, where steam billowed out around us as we entered. The room seemed not to be a room at all, but a boundless space of swirling darkness. I could make out more tiled steps, and more bodies—these dim, dark and ghostly, wavering as the steam curled around them—but I had neither the time nor inclination to study them, to react to them in any way; clutching my hand, the man led me up the steps, higher and higher into hotter and darker and thicker steam. And it felt as though a sweet surging energy was rushing into me through his hand.

My heart was pounding insanely as the man tugged me into a dark corner, then turned to face me. By then I could feel the hot steam collecting all over my body, my pores opening, sweat seeping out, merging with the hot droplets of steam, beginning to inch downward in trickling rivulets. His hands took my arms and pulled me toward him, our bodies pressed together, slick and warm. He reached for my face, held it cupped in his hands as he brought his lips down to mine, pressing his tongue gently between them. I shuddered deliciously, feeling that fantastic energy flushing through my entire body. I opened my mouth, clasped him to me, meeting his tongue with my own.

I could not see them, but I sensed people slowly gathering around us—touching us, watching us. I felt hands on my leg, creeping upward like little animals; fingers found my balls; other fingers wrapped themselves around my cock, tugging it, stretching it, kneading it. I could feel the man's cock hard against my stomach—and it felt huge! A mouth took the head of my cock in, sucked itself upward, swallowing, tugging my cock into sweet flushing heat! Hands worked over my stomach and back, down my spine, gripped the cheeks of my ass. My body became pure sensation—no longer merely a body, but a mass of exquisite tinglings and shimmerings.

Hands on my shoulders were urging me downward—and I lowered myself slowly, twisting as I did, so the mouth on my cock could stay all the way down; I pressed my face against the man's wet muscular body, slipping down his slick hairy chest, and his stomach, until I could feel the thick head of his cock touching my cheek. Somewhere, distantly, I heard music throbbing, as I grasped his tight buttocks and turned my head slowly until the head of his cock rested warmly against my lips. His cock seemed incredibly long! As I took it into my mouth, it seemed to relax suddenly, to become firm without being totally hard—just limber enough to bend and accommodate itself to each curve of my lips and mouth and tongue. Drums pounded in my veins! His cock became more than a cock; it became the most personal extension of his fantastic body, the instrument for an ultimate communion between us—and I wanted to make love to him, through it, in a way I had never made love to anyone, ever. I wanted to make him feel the same dizzying rapture I was feeling. I wanted to take him into me, to make that part of his body also a part of my own. I urged my head closer and closer toward his groin, and his supple cock inched over the back of my throat—and went down! Wild explosions of color and sound and sensation engulfed me. He was moaning above me, his hands clutching my shoulders, his hips starting a gentle tentative thrusting.

With each slow drive that sweet churning within me surged higher and higher, until it seemed that my body could not hope to contain it—and still it grew! He lifted me up and kissed me again, pressing his tongue into my mouth where his cock had been. His hands slipped down my back to my ass. One slick finger sneaked down into the crack and touched the tight opening there. He twisted me slowly, running his tongue down my neck, over my shoulder, and then down my spine. A shaggy head rose up in front of my crotch, and I watched my cock disappear under a thick moustache...just as I felt fingers spreading the cheeks of my ass...and a face pressing between them...and a hot tongue slickly bathing my asshole!

With his hands clutching my hips, he eased upward again; I could feel his hard cock creeping up the inside of my leg, lifting my balls. As the head of it touched the hole, I tensed fearfully; but suddenly the one kneeling before me took my cock all the way down, and his throat started constricting around it, and my body seemed to melt! In that moment I felt a sharp pain—and then an incredible *rush* up inside my guts! And suddenly his body was pressed hard to mine, and I was filled with him! I had never felt anything like it! My body dissolved then and there! I felt nothing except an astonishing fever to have every inch, every particle, of his stunning cock inside me! His hairy arms tightened around my chest as I sank down, felt his cock go in deeper. He eased back, then urged it in harder, even deeper! And the throat on my own cock was milking it, swallowing it!

I felt his body tighten, his arms tense: "Come," he whispered. "Now!"

I felt him explode into me—and the heat of his orgasm surged through my own body and exploded again to go gushing out through my own cock—and into a throat that kept swallowing and swallowing....

Both of us slipped down until we were leaning against the back wall. With one of his hairy arms draped wearily over my shoulder, we leaned against one another, gasping and chuckling, watching the cluster of bodies around us still writhing.

A few minutes later we helped one another to stand, then made our way down and out the door.

There were only two in the outer room now, up on the top shelf, one on his stomach, the other fucking him, oblivious to us or the rest of the world.

We watched one another as we showered, smiling whenever our eyes met, then went out to dry off. My mind was a jumble of things that I wanted to say to the man, but words seemed so foolish at this point. I wasn't sure why, but I sensed that he knew what I wanted to tell him: how good I felt; how deliciously empty and clean; how fantastically *sane* it seemed to stand there face to face with a man I'd just had sex with, and feel no guilt, no shame, no need to withdraw into myself! It was something I'd been waiting for all my life. And it had happened—with him! With a man I had dreamed about—throwing off his black overcoat, standing naked in the sun, calling "Follow me!"

I felt a momentary disappointment when the man tossed his towel over his shoulder, gripped my arm and said, "See you later," and walked out—but it quickly passed. There was no need to run after him and find out his name and address. Either I'd see him again or I wouldn't. I couldn't let myself worry that the "love-of-my-life" might be walking away from me. For the time being my dream-man had performed his function, and I was much more excited about all that had happened to me as a result:

I wasn't hearing voices in my head any more!

No chattering, no scolding, no arguing. Something had happened to Robert and Bobby. They weren't there any more.

I tossed the towel over my shoulder and walked out into the hallway, feeling almost radiant. I didn't even flinch when a man came around the corner and stopped short, staring at my nakedness. He grinned brightly and muttered, "Right on"—but it wouldn't have bothered me even if he'd glowered at me. I wouldn't have cared. I had found something and it didn't really matter who approved or disapproved. The thing I had found was vastly more important to me than a stranger's disapproval; I had found myself—and fuck the world! I was happy.

Chapter 4

For a few minutes I lay on my bunk upstairs, watching the men who went by. I could well understand why "Sophia" had been so uncomfortable here. Among these men, in this atmosphere, naked, there would be no way for such a person to call attention to himself—to make such a desperate *point* of the fact that he was different-by-god-GAY! His sort of posturing and "cleverness" would be totally invalid here, not only unnecessary, but undesirable. An alien from another world would have been no more out of place. All the formalities and socializations had been stripped away; "personalities" had to be hung up with the clothes, left behind in a locked room. He'd been lost, maskless, stripped of his identification. Getting himself kicked out would have been his only means of reassuring himself that he was still as obnoxious as ever. I was sure he'd be telling the story to everyone he knew for as long as they'd listen.

I'd undoubtedly done him a favor by turning him down; he probably thrived on rejection. In a way, "Sophia" was the gay equivalent of Robert, who became disoriented and helpless when something good happened to him, and no matter how much he thought he wanted something good, he had to twist it and torture it until it became bad. Such people were miserable, because misery was their only identification.

What would have happened, I wondered, if, instead of shutting it out of my mind, I'd allowed that night with Bill to make me believe I was homosexual? It was beginning to seem very likely that my desire for him that night had not been merely the result of my frustration with Jenny Lou. I could remember other nights now, nights when I'd lain awake, thinking about Bill just across the room, unable to get the image of his beautiful young naked body out of my mind—feeling my cock getting hard as I thought about his cock—and hating myself for such "dirty" thoughts.

It was possible, even probable that I'd started whoring around with girls like Jenny Lou because of my sexual fantasies about Bill—because homosexuality was to Mormons "an abomination in the sight of God". It was better to spill your seed in the belly of a whore than to jack off, and as sinful as that was, jacking off was infinitely preferable to being an abomination.

"Sophia" had probably made it his life work living up to being an abomination. However wretched and misspent my own life had been, at least I'd been spared that fate.

"Want some company?"

I glanced up to see a man standing in my doorway.

He wasn't at all unattractive, and I certainly did not mean to reject him when I groaned and said, "Not right now," but he pulled himself back from the door, glaring furiously.

"If you're just resting, you should close your fucking door!" he snapped, then marched away angrily.

I stared at the empty doorway, shaking my head. Apparently there were others besides "Sophia" who thrived on rejection—even if it wasn't real—and apparently not all of them were stereotype "fags".

But I supposed he was right, in a way. In this place, an open door would amount to an open invitation. I didn't want to close the door and just lie there in my booth, but I certainly didn't feel up to having sex again. I was reluctant to leave, knowing that once outside the Ganymede doors, I'd be back in "Reality", but I also knew I'd have to face it sooner or later.

Now might be a very good time to go to that bar and try to find Bill. Feeling as good as I did, it wouldn't hurt all that much if it turned out he didn't want to see me. But the more I considered it, the more likely it seemed that, like the man who had just marched so angrily away, I had blindly assumed a rejection where none had been intended. Instead of believing Bill when he'd insisted he did want to talk to me—or his roommate when he'd said Bill *had* waited for my call—I'd allowed Robert's habit of feeling rejected to start operating again.

I dressed quickly and took the key downstairs, where they gave me my own keys and wallet. I asked the attendant if they had a telephone book where I could check for an address. "Sure thing," he said pleasantly, and hauled out a massive volume and pushed it across the counter to me.

I found the address and copied it onto the back of a Ganymede business card. As he put the directory away, I asked, "How do I get to Folsom Street from here?"

"Miracle Mile?" He grinned, as though we shared a clever secret. "It's easy. You just follow Broadway to where it connects with The Embarcadero, then make a right, and go along under the freeway for about eight, maybe nine blocks."

"Thanks."

He nodded and smiled, then buzzed the lock on the door. As I went out, he called, "Have fun. Come back soon."

"Thank you," I called back. "I will."

I felt great as I drove along Folsom. I felt I'd accomplished something tremendous in the last few hours. Looking back, with the benefit of hindsight, I could see that, however slowly, however painfully, I'd been climbing up out of that pit I had dug for myself, bit by bit removing the "garbage" of my life—and now I felt cleansed and free! I couldn't help remembering how I'd raced away from the Uintah Plunge, feeling so wretched and dirty. Now I felt like I'd passed some kind of mysterious test—and had just graduated with honors!

I had no trouble at all finding the bar, but locating a

place to park was another matter; I drove around the block three times before someone pulled out of a space just a few doors away from a large blue sign whereon a golden Phoenix rose out of curling red flames.

As I got out and locked the car, I noticed another car parking across the street. The driver hopped out, looked both ways along the street, then trotted across—and I had a dizzying impression of *deja vu:* I could have sworn it was John Adams! He was dressed almost exactly the way Adams had been in the airport—faded blue denims, low-waisted, flared at the bottoms, a T-shirt and a levi jacket. Then I saw that his hair was much longer than John's had been, and he had a full beard; still I could not shake the feeling that I knew the man.

He was headed for The Phoenix. My heart started beating a bit faster as he paused in the doorway and glanced back at me, as though he shared the feeling that we knew one another. For a moment I thought that it might be Bill, but dismissed the idea as preposterous. My brother with long hair? Impossible!

Or was it? I had dreamed of a man with long hair and a full black beard, and a voice saying: "Where is thy brother?" At first I'd decided that the man had been Bill—but because of the notes and my encounter with John Adams, I'd jumped to the conclusion that Adams was Bill. And when that had proved incorrect, I'd forgotten about the dream—until a black-bearded man had come into that room at the baths to lead me into the steam room. But maybe the dream had been about Bill after all, not John Adams—nor the man at the baths. Considering all that had happened to me in the last few days, why should I find it so difficult to believe that my dream had been prophetic? Such a notion fell into the catagory of "occult nonsense" or pure science fiction—but what difference did it make what sort of "unreal" classification it fitted into? In the last three days my world had been turned upside-down; I'd been discovering that most of what I knew about the world—or *believed* that I knew—was wrong in one way or another. At the same time I'd discovered that many of the things I had previously called "nonsense" or "superstition" had very real germs of truth in them. My "premonition of disaster" had come true—why not my beautiful dream?

But before I could think of something to say to him, the man turned and went into the bar. Music and voices rushed out into the street, then faded as the double blue doors swung closed behind him. I recognized the song that was playing—it was one I remembered from one of Chuck's albums: "All you need is love...."

I hesitated, taking a deep breath, and then pushed the doors open.

In spite of the loud music, just stepping inside the bar gave me a "hushed" almost "reverent" feeling. It was like stepping from a busy, bustling city into an unworldly rustic retreat somewhere deep in the woods. The walls of the long room were covered with weathered wood slabs, lit by dozens of flickering candles; candles were everywhere—big thick ones with several wicks, tall skinny ones, votive candles in sparkling ruby and blue holders.

Back in one corner were ivy-planters, hanging from the ceiling, with candles flickering behind them. Looking at the ivy and the dancing shadows the trailing vines cast on the ceilings and walls gave me the feeling that I'd been here before—a long-ago feeling. I suddenly remembered my Grandmother, a beautiful, gentle, little white-haired lady whose entire life had been one of love. I could almost smell sugar-cookies baking. I could almost see twilit banks of yellow roses growing along Grandfather's front fence. I could almost see hollyhocks and nasturtiums and lilacs and dewy blue morning-glories—and that dark mysterious arbor, covered with ivy, where Bill and I had played "cars" long ago.

The bar itself—the long counter and the cabinet behind it—looked as though it had come straight out of an Old West saloon. High on the wall above the bar, lit by candles in what looked like a church altarpiece, was a large golden design on a blue background; it looked like an *A* and an *O* fused together. Although I was fairly certain I'd never seen the design before, I had an uneasy feeling that I ought to know precisely what it represented—but before I could reason it out, another uneasiness started, deep in my stomach, and I looked around the long room again: every single person in the place was a male.

Forty or fifty long-haired, bearded, mustachioed men stood around casually, laughing, talking—some with their arms around other men's shoulders or waists. Others stood quietly, their eyes closed, swaying and moving with the music. Still others were leaning along the wall, seeming totally lost in contemplation, their faces almost saintly in the flickering candlelight.

Either The Phoenix was a retreat for a very unorthodox monastic order—or it was a gay bar. These men could have been the same ones I had seen at the baths, now dressed in the strangest assortment of costumes I'd ever seen: faded, patched, tattered levis, overalls, underwear tops, worn denim jackets—rawhide vests with no shirts under them—buckskin pants—moccasins—sandals—beaded headbands; one man wore an Indian blanket over his shoulders; another had on a blue workshirt like mine, with a huge red and gold butterfly embroidered on the back. It was a gay bar; it had to be—even though it was the complete antithesis of The Primrose Path.

I began to understand why Bill's roommate—his male roommate!—had sounded so nervous when he'd told me not to bother calling "that bar" he had mentioned. A part of my mind wanted to be shocked or revolted by the possibility that Bill might be gay, too—but all I could do was smile at the idea. I wasn't shocked at all; I was delighted!

I saw the black-bearded man now, leaning against the bar, talking to a blond, long-haired bartender. On the wall directly behind them was a framed oval mirror; written on it were the words: *Love Is An Organic High!*

The man stepped away from the bar and started toward the back of the room, and I started after him.

As I moved through the crowd, another impression of *deja vu* flooded over me. Again it seemed I had been here before—but not in this lifetime; in some other, the memory of which seemed to hover just out of the reach of my consciousness. It was like *coming home*—back to a forgotten beginning—returning from a thousand-year pilgrimage into strange and unwelcoming lands.

It was like being on another mescaline trip! I truly felt *high!* Men smiled at me and I found myself smiling back almost radiantly. There was a buoyant energy in this room that I could feel as surely as though I had touched an electrical wire—the same energy I'd felt at the baths, between myself and the man who had led me into the steam room. Only here it seemed amplified a hundred times!

The music seemed to twist and curl around me, as a husky voice chanted, "Here comes the sun...here comes the sun..."

I followed the man through an archway at the end of the bar, into another long room—then stopped short, suddenly overwhelmed by a painting that took up the full length of one wall: against a panorama of vast blue sky, with just the tops of mountain peaks showing at the base, stood a naked man, larger than life, fantastically beautiful, spreading his arms just for me, smiling with profound welcome.

It was an effort to tear my attention away from the

mural and look around this second room. Apparently others felt equally overwhelmed by the painting; a dozen men were sitting along a low bench against the wall, gazing raptly at the beautiful figure.

There was a small bar in the corner, and the man I wanted to talk to was sitting near the end of it, facing slightly away from me, listening intently to another long-haired bartender—this one with bushy red sideburns and a walrus moustache.

"...Didn't know who the hell it was...." the bartender was saying. "I just assumed it was one of your tricks."

I remembered that voice. ("Bob? You should have told me who you were. Bill was expecting your call earlier.")

"...Got to worrying, so I called Scotty, at the Phone Company, and asked if he could check. Well, he called back just before we left. The call had come from a phone booth in West Sacramento. He's probably in the city right now. I'm sorry, Bill, but I didn't know who it was."

"Dammit! I knew I should have waited. Well...I guess he has to know sometime. Don't worry about it."

I stepped up behind him and put my hand on his shoulder. "Bill?"

He turned to look up at me—then grinned brightly. "Well, hello again. I thought that was you, coming in, but I wasn't sure." He chuckled and patted my ass. "Didn't recognize you with your clothes on—as the saying goes."

I stared at him, my mouth gaping open. "Oh, Lord!" I leaned weakly against the bar and started to laugh—not loudly; it sounded more like a whimpering chuckle. I felt as though I'd just heard the punch line of an incredibly long and involved shaggy dog story!

"What's so funny?" Bill asked.

I took a deep breath, then let it out slowly. "You didn't even recognize me with them off."

He frowned. "Should I have?"

I laughed again. Suddenly I had become the teller of the shaggy dog story; I was still the only one who knew the outrageous punch line. "Not really," I said. "I didn't recognize you either."

"Do I know you?"

I nodded. "Once upon a time," I said. "Long, long ago."

He smiled unsurely, studying me. I could almost *feel* the first piece of the puzzle slip into place: *Click!* His smile slowly faded: *Click...click...click!*

"Bob?"

"Yes."

He closed his eyes and whispered, "No...no...I don't believe it...." He shook his head slowly back and forth, repeating, "No...no...it's just too damned impossible!" He looked up at me. "*You?*" For a moment I thought I saw a flicker of fear in his eyes, but then he started to laugh. He stood up and grabbed me, jerking me to him, and both of us stood there hugging each other, laughing like fools. He stepped back, holding tightly to my arms. "Well...I knew something was going to happen...but I sure as hell didn't expect to meet you...." He turned, grinning, to the bartender. "You can stop worrying, Warren," he said. "He's here." He looked at me again. "Is this what you wanted to tell me last night?"

I shrugged. "More or less. It's a long, crazy story."

"You don't know the half of it! God, it's good to see you, Bob! Hey! What do you think of my bar?"

"Your bar?"

"Well...a third of it." He jerked his thumb toward Warren. "That blabbermouth there is one of my partners. The other one's out on the other bar."

Warren was leaning over the bar, looking thoroughly confused. I put my hand out. "I think we've already met–on the phone."

He shook my hand, muttering, "Will someone please tell me what's going on?"

Bill laughed. "What is it you keep telling me? 'It will all be revealed in due time.' I'll tell you when I find out." He took my arm. "Come on and meet Brad—and then let's go out to the house, where we can really get to know one another."

"What exactly does that mean?" I asked, grinning.

He squeezed my arm tightly. "You know damn well what that means, Bobby-o. We've got a lot of lost time to make up for. Only this time we'll each know who the other one is!"

Chapter 5

It was still fairly early, around ten o'clock, when we left the bar, arranging for Warren to drive Bill's car home after closing time so that Bill could go with me and direct me out to their house on Fourteenth. On the way, as briefly as possible, I told him what had happened; by the time I had finished, it was almost one o'clock, and we were sitting on the floor in the front room of his house, watching the dying flames in the fireplace.

"...But it wasn't until you dragged me into that steam room that things finally started coming together."

He chuckled. "In more ways than one, I would say." He turned from the fireplace to study me. "Well...all I can say is...I'm proud of you, Bob. A lot of guys would have freaked out completely. I'd say you had the makings of a very good head."

I laughed. "I'm glad I have the makings of something."

"Don't sell yourself short. That's Robert talking."

"Sorry," I said. "It's a habit that's hard to break."

"Just stick around for a while. We'll help you break it."

"We?"

"Brad and Warren and me—and a few others. The Family. We've all been through it, one way or another, Bob. Maybe not as dramatically, but we've been through it."

"What was it like for you?" I asked.

He shook his head. "Don't get me started on that or we'll be here all night. Tomorrow maybe." He turned to stare into the fire. "But there is something....Do you feel up to hearing the other half of your story?"

"The other half?"

He nodded. "You only know part of it."

"Oh?"

"Don't look so worried. It's not bad. Scoot over here where I can lie on you."

I moved closer leaning back against the front of the sofa and Bill sprawled out on the floor, resting his head on my thigh. "You know what you said about coming together? Well, that's exactly what's happening, Bob. All sorts of things are coming together. Sometimes it scares me, how fast things are happening—and then other times it seems it's taking forever.

"Bob..." he said softly. "I don't mean to belittle what you've been through. I know guys who would give their left nut to have a mescaline trip like the one you went on. But it isn't unique. I've been there. So have Warren and Brad. So have most of those guys you saw in the bar tonight. And the baths. That's why we opened The Phoenix. That's not a gay bar, Bob. I don't know what to call it, but it sure as hell isn't a gay bar. I keep wanting to call it religious, but that's not what it is. That's a sick word, and this thing that's happening isn't sick at all. It's *more* than a religion. It's *living*, you know? And it's something that's happening right now all over the world. I don't mean it's *going* to happen. It's already happened. And the people who know that it's happened are the ones who are going to be part of it. The others will just sit back and wonder what the hell is going on—like that queen in The Primrose Path you told me about. Dylan says it: 'You don't know what's happening, do you, Mr. Jones?' There are hundreds of rock songs, Bob, maybe thousands.... Sometimes in the bar, I'll be tripping on the music...something I've heard maybe a hundred times, and suddenly I hear something I've never heard before...."

"Messages..." I said softly.

"Exactly! I don't know, Bob. I know what it *seems*

like but I'm afraid to let myself believe it. But it's happening, no matter what you call it. And it's something poor old Bishop Thorne won't understand in a thousand years, because he's waiting for the heavens to open and white doves to fly down—and that's not going to happen. No, you've got to go *inside* for this—inside yourself and inside other people. You've got to get past all the shit on the outside. It may sound corny as hell, Bob, but you know that sign on the mirror in the bar: 'Love is an organic high'? That's not just a clever saying by somebody like Timothy Leary. It's the God's honest truth. The drugs are just a substitute—they grease the way, maybe—they open our heads so we can start to understand what the real high is. I can't knock them, but they're not the real thing, as the Coke people say."

I smiled. "I suppose that's what Chuck was talking about."

"Probably," Bill said. "The kids knew what was happening long before the rest of us ever dreamed of it. Because they had less shit to scrape off than we do." He reached up to take my hand. "Well, anyway...something happened to me yesterday, too. You see, when you called last night, the reason I couldn't talk to you was...I was tripping...just like you were. I *wanted* to talk, but the things in my head were too insane. You see, Warren and Brad and I are buying this piece of property, up above Santa Rosa, and Saturday night after the bar closed, about a dozen of us got together and drove up there. It's really a beautiful place, Bob...twenty acres up at the end of this fantastic green valley...just a couple of farms besides us...foothills and big trees, and this wild little stream going through. We took sleeping bags..." He chuckled. "Nobody got much sleep, but we had them to sit on. Anyway, just before sunrise, about half of us dropped psilocybin—which is pretty much like mescaline and acid. And, Bob, don't laugh—we had the most beautiful Easter Services you can possibly imagine.

"You know what you were telling me...about watching the sunset, and the stars, with your boy? Well, there's a kind of...*multiplying* effect with dope when more than one of you takes the stuff. It was like what you went through, only a dozen times stronger. And we've discovered that we don't all need to drop; if we're really in tune, everybody trips. So, anyway, the point is—when you called last night, I was still so fucking high that I couldn't talk straight. Also, I was scared. Because...call it ESP, call it occult, call it crazy...but I think you were *with* us, yesterday. I thought about you all day long. It was like...like you were there but I couldn't see you. But I knew you were on my trip with me. And then when the telephone rang...I swear to you, Bob, I knew it was you. I knew it, but I wouldn't believe it, you know? Even when you said, 'This is Bob,' and that's exactly what I expected you to say, I still wouldn't believe it. I thought, hell, I've been talking about him all day, and this is just one of the guys pulling my leg. Only it wasn't. It was you. And today...I knew you were coming. I really did. I sat by that fucking telephone all day, just waiting for you to say 'I'm here!' "

"I'm sorry...."

"Hell, don't be. As you see, it all worked out just fine in the end."

"Things have a way of working out..."

"Yes, they do. Do you see, Bob? It all fits together. Something happened to both of us yesterday. Like your dream about somebody calling you Bobby-o. Don't you remember? It wasn't Dad who started calling you that. It was me. That was our 'secret call' when we played hide-and-seek and stuff. Remember?"

"Yes..." I remembered it clearly now.

"Well," he continued, "you had that dream when you got back from that god-awful steam bath, right? Okay, I'll bet we could check the time and it would end up the same damn time we were all sitting around on our sleeping bags, passing joints before we dropped. Because I can remember going off on a whole trip, remembering the farm and the fields and the whole thing, just like you described it. We were all bare-ass naked, sitting around the fire like a bunch of Indians passing the peace-pipe—and that's the same time you dreamed about a naked man with a beard calling you *Bobby-o.* Coincidence my fine ass! And this whole business of 'Where is thy brother?'—and you thinking that lawyer was me—and figuring out I was gay. Coincidence? Sure."

"All right," I said. "It wasn't coincidence. But what was it, Bill? What did we...tune in on?"

"Who knows? He sat up and turned to look at me. "I don't know. When you try to explain it, you end up using all the old words—and they don't work. No," he said, "this is either something brand new, or something very very old. But a whole lot of people are feeling it. Read the magazines. Listen to the rock songs...." He stood up. "Speaking of which...Hang on just a minute, I'm going to punch a button."

A moment later, music poured out through speakers hung high in the corners of the fireplace wall:

"We were born before the wind...."

Bill came back into the room, now pulling his T-shirt over his head. "This is our 'mystical' bar-tape," he said, "for 'high-holidays'—if you'll pardon the expression."

He tossed his shirt onto the sofa, then leaned over me, gripping my shoulders. "It is also very good music for getting up the courage to say something important." His hands slipped down my arms as he knelt beside me; he gripped my hands tightly. "A long time ago, Bob, there was something very special between us. I'm sure now that we both knew it, we just didn't know how to handle it. Bob, I wanted so much not be afraid that night. I wanted so much to do what you asked me to.

Well...it looks as though we've both learned a few things since then—and I'm not afraid now. I love you, Bob. I've loved you all of my life. And, by God, I'm not the least little bit ashamed of it!"

I looked into his eyes, feeling a wonderful, breathless emotion beginning to rise, pushing tears into my eyes. "That's what it's all about, isn't it?"

He nodded. "That's it."

"I love you too," I said softly. "And I'm not ashamed of it either."

Slowly we undressed each other, watching each movement, relishing each touch. There was no rush, no frantic fumbling, no words. I was filled with the most exquisite peacefulness I'd ever known—and words would have demeaned it. Bill and I touched each other, and kissed, and held one another close, our bodies pressed together, our hearts beating like one in a single body. And then he twisted around and we lay side by side on the soft carpet, easing each other's cock into our mouths—and the feelings were vastly beyond anything "sexual". His long supple cock slipped easily into my throat, as though it had always been meant to fit there—and my cock felt exactly the same inside him. We fitted perfectly. And that beautiful energy cascaded between us, until finally it seemed that our bodies and minds had become one thing—incredibly beautiful and open and free. The moment for climax came and went many times, each time lifting us higher and higher into an exquisite luxury—and then, slowly, sweetly, we came at the same time, and his life seemed to pour into me as mine spilled into him. And then we lay quietly, still joined both physically and mentally, long after that last luxurious tremor had faded...just drifting together in the music:

"...Here comes the sun...here comes the sun...it's all right...."

PART 3

Dear Son:

It seems so strange, writing a letter to you. What a shock it is for a father to realize he has never exchanged letters with his own son. But always before, when you were away at camp, etc., it was your mother's job to write the letters. And whenever I was away, it was less trouble to call and say, "Tell Chuck Hello."

But this change goes along with everything else I've been going through (and we'll have to get used to corresponding if we're to know anything about one another from summer to summer). So much has been happening–so many changes, Chuck. But I think you would understand them. I'm sure you would. And I'm beginning to understand your reference to "something" that, when I saw it clearly, would "blow my head wide open". Lately I've got into the habit of listening–are you ready?–to a certain FM "Rock" station, and the songs I've been hearing have a way of making me stop whatever I'm doing and stare at the radio, wondering where I have been all my life! I've been finding a whole new world, Chuck. The one you introduced me to, that night.

I hope you appreciate, even a little, how difficult it is for a man of my generation to admit mistakes to anyone, let alone to his own child. I was raised to believe implicitly in the "rightness" of adults–and I did believe it; I had no choice, because the only alternative available to me was to believe I was "wrong". I was constantly reminded that my father knew more than I did, and since he was in control of almost everything that happened to me, I took it for granted that he knew what he was talking about. I tried to raise you the same way—without even thinking about it—just as my own father never thought about it. That isn't an apology or cop-out, simply an explanation. It's frightening when I think about how much we accept as "gospel" when we are children—and afterward never think to question it.

But there's something that gives me a great deal of hope: Recently I've been meeting people of my own age who are going through the same sort of mind-blowing discoveries I've been making. And we're all involved in a process of sorting through our lives, separating the good stuff from the garbage. The thing which sustains me, keeps me from feeling that I've totally wasted thirty-five years of my life, is the fact that there is good, and quite a lot of it—once you start getting rid of the garbage.

As you know (I assume your mother has discussed some of this with you) I've been living here with my brother, Bill. You know very little about him because I rarely mentioned him—and the reasons for that are too complicated to go into now. But he's really a great guy, Chuck. You can imagine my surprise when I discovered that he is very deeply involved in all of the things we discussed that night—particularly the thing we talked about as I drove you over to Jerry's—if you remember that conversation. (How could either of us forget it?) And he has taken the same kind of approach you have taken. (We'll talk much more about that when I come home to sign all the papers, etc., etc., probably in a couple of weeks. Bill will be with me, incidentally, so you'll have a chance to get acquainted with your "long-lost" uncle. I have an idea you'll like him.) At any rate, through Bill, I've begun meeting some really fascinating and "beautiful" people—my own age. That night in Mother Earth, I felt so sorry that I couldn't be your age, discovering the "New World" through more innocent eyes. Now I understand that that wouldn't be right; I don't need to be a dewy-eyed Innocent to appreciate what's happening. My life-experiences, both good and bad, lend a solidity, provide a foundation, to the discoveries I'm making, which wouldn't be there were I sixteen or twenty-one.

One hears and reads so much about how the young people have matured so much faster than their parents—because of mass-communication, etc. But no one seems to have realized that those same parents have been affected by the same forces. At my age, now, I know more about the world—about "Life" as it is actually lived, than my own parents do, even now—and I'm only beginning to learn! No doubt you are very rapidly catching up with us, but meanwhile, we of my generation, who are waking up to all that is happening, make up what Bill calls "The ELDERS of the Tribe." (All Tribes need Elders!)

*I don't really know what the point of this letter is—I just felt like writing, I guess. Yesterday, Saturday, some of us went up to this property Bill and his friends (*my *friends also, now) are buying—and all day I felt so close to you—as I again renewed my acquaintance with mountains and trees and water and fresh air. I kept remembering what you said about "things having a way of working out right."*

I'm beginning to hope—to believe—that the world is indeed changing for the better. In fact I've had a very strange feeling that we're slowly moving backward *into a better time, as though we'd reached some sort of critical point, and are now very slowly and very carefully backing away from destruction. The changes won't happen overnight, nor without a lot of hard work—but it no longer seems as impossible as it did just a few short weeks ago. Now I can see it happening–and hear it happening–and now I feel I can be part of it. I feel I'll find a way to help build it, make it grow. And how great it is, Chuck, to feel part of something again–especially* this *something. Sometimes when I go out shopping, or whatever, I look around and see the difference between the "New People" and the Old, and I wonder why things can be so obvious to some and so totally unmeaningful to others. But then I remind myself of how deaf, dumb, and blind I was. It takes one hell of a jolt to get yourself out of the habit of believing you know what is going on.*

I'm tremendously excited about the whole thing! And that's a beautiful feeling!

By the way, you probably won't recognize me when I arrive. There are a few additions to my face. I'm afraid your mother will be outraged–even more when she sees your uncle's long hair–but you should appreciate it.

Well, I'd better finish this and get it into the mail. I'm supposed to be helping Bill cut a new "trip-tape" for the place he works at. Every Sunday evening we have a kind of "Celebration" and listen to a new tape of the "Be-Happy" rock songs. Right now he's recording the one I heard for the first time, the night I came home and found you and Jerry so "peacefully" listening in the living room. (Which reminds me: Please give my best regards to Jerry. I'm hoping I'll have time to get to know him better–along with some of your other friends.) Strangely enough–or is it strange at all?–the lyrics to that song provide a very appropriate end to this first letter to you:

"Everything's all right–everything's fine."
Perhaps we can make it come true.
I'll be seeing you soon.

All My Love–
Dad